Insider's Guide to Personal Computing and Networking

Insider's Guide to Personal Computing and Networking

Rick Segal, Series Editor

SAMS
PUBLISHING

A Division of Prentice Hall Computer Publishing
11711 North College, Carmel, Indiana 46032 USA

Trademarks

Screen reproductions in this book were created by means of the program Collage Plus from Inner Media, Inc., Hollis, NH.

Composed in Goudy and MCPdigital by Prentice Hall Computer Publishing.

Printed in the United States of America.

Publisher
Richard K. Swadley

Managing Editor
Neweleen Trebnik

Acquisitions Manager
Jordan Gold

Acquisitions Editor
Gregg Bushyeager

Development Editor
Wayne Blankenbeckler

Production Editors
Keith Davenport
Cheri Clark

Copy Editors
Melba Hopper
Michael Cunningham
Sandy Doell

Editorial Coordinators
Becky Freeman
Bill Whitmer

Editorial Assistants
Rosemarie Graham
Lori Kelley

Formatter
Pat Whitmer

Cover Art
Tim Amrhein

**Director of Production
and Manufacturing**
Jeff Valler

Production Manager
Corinne Walls

Imprint Manager
Matthew Morrill

Book Designer
Michele Laseau

Production Analyst
Mary Beth Wakefield

Graphics Image Specialists
Dennis Sheehan
Jerry Ellis
Sue VandeWalle

**Proofreading/Indexing
Coordinator**
Joelynn Gifford

Production
Christine Cook, Lisa Daugherty,
Terri Edwards, Dennis Hager,
Carla Hall-Batton,
John Kane, Tom Loveman,
R.Sean Medlock, Juli Pavey,
Susan M. Shepard,
Greg Simsic, Angie Trzepacz,
Suzanne Tully, Alyssa Yesh

Indexers
John Sleeva, Loren Malloy

Author Overview

1. Artisoft, Inc. *Peer-to-Peer Networking and Interoperability* 1
2. Beach, Gary J. *Workgroup Computing: It's IT and That's That for Computing in the '90s* 7
3. Berglund, Elizabeth G. *Making the Right Connections... By Wisely Choosing and Successfully Working with a Networking Partner* 15
4. Bickmann, Lee and Bond, Elaine *Better Multivendor Computing Is OURS* 27
5. Bushnell, Nolan *Communicating Naturally in the Digitized World* 37
6. Cheyenne Software, Inc. *Server-Based: To Be or Not to Be? That is the Question!* 45
7. Chumbley, Jeff *Redefining Adapter Performance* 53
8. Corrigan, Patrick H. *The Evolution of the Global Data Network* 61
9. Dell, Michael S. *Remote Maintenance and Support of Networks* 67
10. Edwards, James *The Age of the Enterprise Server* 73
11. Erwin, Jeff *The Hazards of Today's Expert System Technology in Network Analysis Systems* 79
12. Foster, Gail M. *Expert Systems Increase Help Desk Effectiveness* 85
13. Fryer, Bruce *Integrated Connectivity: The Role of Computer Manufacturers* 97
14. Garrett, Kelly and Pastman, Stuart *The New Corporate Development LANscape* 105
15. Gates, Bill *Microsoft Windows NT Operating System* 117
16. Gates, Dirk I. *Portables on LANs—Now and Tomorrow* 135
17. Gianforte, Greg *The Data Center Takes Control of LANs* 145
18. Gill, Robert *The Once and Future NOS* 153
19. Glagow, Steve *Enterprise Messaging—Implementing the Company Post Office* 161
20. Hayes, Dennis C. *The Hayes Philosophy of How a Network Should Work* 167
21. Henderson, Tom *The Mensch of Networking* 179
22. Hollingsworth, Robert *The Evolution of a LAN: ARCNETPLUS* 189
23. Hutchinson, Scott H. *Network Management Today, Tomorrow, and Yesterday* 207
24. Joseph, Michael *The Growing Role of Removable Storage in Networks* 215

25. Kahn, Philippe *Online Complex Processing: A Powerful Alternative to OLTP* 223

26. Lee, King R. *Network Management Tools: Complex to Simple* 231

27. Lubert, Howard E. *The Myths and Realities of Network Management* 241

28. Lytton, Nina *The Open Systems Approach to Enterprise Computing* 249

29. Mailman, Josh *Images in the '90s: Fax and Network Technology Come Together* 265

30. Manzi, Jim *Regarding Groupware* 271

31. Marks, Howard *Windows on NetWare: Tips for Making It Work* 285

32. McCann, John T. *Life Without File Servers: The Great Experiment* 297

33. Microsoft Corporation *Solving Our Customers' Challenges* 303

34. Microcomputer Managers Association *Network Software Licensing* White Paper Committee 315

35. Mulholland, James J. *The Telecomputing Office Environment* 331

36. Myers, Therese E. *Open Systems Are Now Open To DOS Users* 337

37. Olbert, Art *Distributed Computing from the Desktop* 341

38. Rabins, Richard *Networked Databases: A Key to Computing Vitality* 353

39. Randall, Alexander *Recycle Computers: Pass it on!* 359

40. Rogers, Lawrence D. *Is Your Data Really Safe? Will It Be Next Year?* 365

41. Rohal, John P. *Communications Technology Overview* 377

42. Saal, Harry J. *Upping the Rate of Return on Your Most Important Corporate Asset* 389

43. Schatt, Stan *A LAN in Every Pocket: Wireless LANs Today and Tomorrow* 395

44. Schmidt, Ron *The Expanding Role of Intelligent Hubs in the Enterprise Network* 403

45. Sandifer, Chip *In Search of the Ultimate Network Manager* 409

46. Strom, David *Which OS Is for You? It Depends* 421

47. Thomas, Chris *A Brief Overview of Network Management* 429

48. Torresi, Enzo *Serious Network Computing: Why Superservers?* 441

49. Walkenhorst, Sherri H. *Market Research Shows Windows Will Dominate the Desktop* 445

50. Warnock, John E. *Working Towards Standards of Communication* 451

51. Warthen, Brett *Expanding the Reach of LAN-Based Electronic Mail* 457

52. Watson, Danie *Protecting Your Network from Virus Infection* 471

viii

CONTENTS

1 Peer-to-Peer Networking and Interoperability   **1**

Author Bio 1

Executive Summary 2

2 Workgroup Computing: It's IT and That's That for Computing in the '90s   **7**

Author Bio 7

Executive Summary 8

Defining the Technology 9

Key Features of a Successful Workgroup 10

     Ease of Use 10

     Scalability 10

     Security 10

     Heterogeneous Support 11

     Open Access to Other Data and Information 11

     Customization 11

Some of the Pioneers 12

A Word to the Wise 12

3 Making the Right Connections...By Wisely Choosing and Successfully Working with a Networking Partner   **15**

Author Bio 15

Executive Summary 16

Start at the Beginning 18

Making the Right Partnering Choice 19

Some Selection Criteria 20

     Systems Integrator/VAR/Reseller Stability 20

Reference Checks 21
Working Relationships 21
Equipment Knowledge and Vendor Medallions 21
Support Questions 21
Level of Rapport 22
Resources 22
Outside Help 23
Industry Commitment 23
Price versus Value 23
Other Factors 23
Network Management 24
Wrapping it up... 24

4 Better Multivendor Computing Is OURS   27

Author Bios 27
Executive Summary 28
OURS Members 29
Trends and Troubles 30
Available Remedies 31
Key Issues 32
Concerted Approach 33
How OURS Got Started 33
Information Technology Summit 35
More About OURS 35

5 Communicating Naturally in the Digitized World   37

Author Bio 37
Executive Summary 38
The Convergence of Network Technologies 38
Ease of Use Drives Acceptance 39
The Fundamental Issue of Communication 41
The Challenge 42

6 Server-Based: To Be or Not to Be? That is the Question!   **45**

Author Bio...45
Executive Summary...46
Backup 47
Security 48
Management 50

7 Redefining Adapter Performance   **53**

Author Bio...53
Executive Summary...53
Bus Mastering 55
Drivers 55
Packet Burst NCP...56
Frame Sizes and Adapter RAM.................................57
Increased Data Rates 57
Reliability 59
Conclusion 59

8 The Evolution of the Global Data Network   **61**

Author Bio...61
Executive Summary...62

9 Remote Maintenance and Support of Networks   **67**

Author Bio...67
Executive Summary...68

10 The Age of the Enterprise Server   **73**

Author Bio...73
Executive Summary...74
Industry Forces Setting the Stage for a New Market 74

Customer Demand 74

Market Drivers 75

Product Vacuum 76

Rx: The Enterprise Server 76

Anatomy of an Enterprise Server 76

Power 76

Scalability 77

Reliability 77

Openness 78

The Age of the Enterprise Server 78

11 The Hazards of Today's Expert System Technology in Network Analysis Systems   79

Author Bio 79

Executive Summary 80

12 Expert Systems Increase Help Desk Effectiveness   85

Author Bio 85

Executive Summary 86

Major Functions of the Help Desk 87

Managing the Customer Contact 87

Service Provision 88

Problem Tracking and Management
(Problem Control) 88

Where Can Knowledge-Based Systems
Net the Most Advantage? 89

Intelligent Text Retrieval 90

Case-Based Reasoning 90

Rule-Based Expert Systems 91

Neural Networks 91

Checklist for Evaluating Knowledge-Based Systems 92

Applications 92

User Interface 93

Knowledge Base Maintenance 93

Integration with Other Applications 94
Vendor Experience 95
Help Desks Can Realize Substantial Benefits 95

**13 Integrated Connectivity: The Role
of Computer Manufacturers   97**

Author Bio..97
Executive Summary 97
Networking is Not Just a Niche 99
The Early Years...99
The Last Five Years 100
LAN Implementation Today 101
Integrated Connectivity 102
Summary 104

**14 The New Corporate
Development LANscape   105**

Author Bios 105
Executive Summary 107
How Things Used to Be 108
The Personal Computer "Revolution" 108
The Advent of the LAN 109
New Development Challenges—PC/LAN
    Centric Development..110
New Development Challenges—
    the Enterprise Computing Platform 113
Meeting the Challenge..115

15 Microsoft Windows NT Operating System 117

Author Bio..117
Executive Summary 118
Introduction 118
An Evolutionary Path 119
    Mainstream Windows Releases...................................119

A High-End Implementation of Windows 119
Building on the Strength of Windows 120
Productivity and Ease of Use 120
Application Availability 121
Compatibility with MS-DOS 121
The Power of a High-End System 121
The Genesis of Window NT 122
Performance 122
Robustness 123
Responsiveness 123
High Capacity 125
Hardware Support 125
Portability and Scalability 125
Portable Design 126
Symmetric Multiprocessing 127
Security 127
Privileges and Users 127
Process Security 128
Certifiable for C2-Level Security 128
Built-in Networking 128
Built-in Secure File-Sharing and Print-Sharing 128
Platform for Distributed Applications 129
Open Network Interface 129
Access to Non-PC Resources 130
Platform for Advanced Network Computing:
  LAN Manager for Windows NT 130
The Benefits of Windows
in a High-End Operating System 131
System Requirements 133

16 Portables on LANs—Now and Tomorrow 135

Author Bio 135
Executive Summary 136
Docking Stations—Not for Everyone 137
External LAN Adapters—A Universal Solution 139
What's on the Horizon? 142
Getting Rid of the Wires 143

17   The Data Center Takes Control of LANs   145

Author Bio 145
Executive Summary 146
Software Diversity and Freedom 146
    What to Do 147
Vendors, Vendors, Vendors 147
    What to Do 148
One Person per Hundred Users 148
    What to Do 149
Participatory Support 149
Moves and Changes 150
    Suggestions for Taking Control 150

18   The Once and Future NOS   153

Author Bio 153
Executive Summary 154
What is NOS's Role Today? 154
Will Today's NOS Technology
   Be Driven to Commodity? 155
What Exactly is NOS's Future Role
   in Network Computing? 158
What's Next? 159
Is There No Room for Innovation
   in Traditional NOS Servers? 160
Bottom Line 160

19   Enterprise Messaging—Implementing the Company Post Office   161

Author Bio 161
Executive Summary 162
What Is Happening in 1992? 163
How Did We Get to 1992? 164
How Do You Get to the Year 2000? 165

20 The Hayes Philosophy of How a Network Should Work 167

Author Bio 167
Executive Summary 168
The Network Perspective 169
User Needs 170
The Underlying Technology 173
Local Versus Remote 174
The Planetary Network 175
Hayes LANstep 176
Conclusion 177

21 The Mensch of Networking 179

Author Bio 179
Executive Summary 180
A New Services Proposal 181
Favorite Failure Modes 184

22 The Evolution of a LAN: ARCNETPLUS
A statement on Datapoint's advanced local
area networking technology 189

Author Bio 189
Executive Summary 190
Integration and Cost Investment 190
Performance Investment 191
Another Approach to Multispeed Technology 191
ARCNETPLUS 192
   ARCnet's Success in the Marketplace 193
LAN Alternatives: Functional
and Economic Implications 194
   EtherNet 194
   16 Mbps Token Ring Network 196
   Partial Additions of TRN or EtherNet 196

ARCNETPLUS: A Better Solution 197
Standardization 200
Environmental and Physical Considerations 204
Making the Decision for ARCNETPLUS 205
ARCNETPLUS 205

23 Network Management Today, Tomorrow, and Yesterday 207

Author Bio 207
Executive Summary 208
Down on the Wire Five Years Ago 209
Applications Five Years Ago 210
Bridging the Gap 211
Down on the Wire Today 211
Moving from the Wire toward the Applications 212
High-Level Administration Today 213
Where Do We Go from Here? 214

24 The Growing Role of Removable Storage in Networks 215

Author Bio 215
Executive Summary 216
The Satellite User 217
Sensitive Data 219
Multiuser/Single Computer 219
Growing Storage Demand 220
Disaster Recovery 220

25 Online Complex Processing: A Powerful Alternative to OLTP 223

Author Bio 223
Executive Summary 224
OLTP: A Solution for Traditional
   Data Processing Problems 225

Desktop Database's Next Generation 226
OLCP: High-Performance Database Servers
  for Complex Transactions 228
Summary 230

26 Network Management Tools: Complex to Simple 231

Author Bio 231
Executive Summary 232
Which Tools to Choose? 233
  Does It Fit? 234
  Moving Parts 234
  Help? 234
  Prevent Defense 234
Development of the Future 235
  "It's Not Our Fault, Call..." 236
  "Standards, Huh?" 236
  Lots of Parts 236
The Enterprise 236
  Big Picture 237
  Drill Down 237
  Stay In Your Seat 238
  Advice 238
Summary 240

27 The Myths and Realities of Network Management 241

Author Bio 241
Executive Summary 242

28 The Open Systems Approach to Enterprise Computing 249

Author Bio 249
Executive Summary 250

Much Ado About Definitions 251
Open Systems Benefits 253
   Benefits: A Matter of Degree 254
Open Systems Standards 255
   Consensus: The New Approach
   to Setting *De Facto* Standards......................................256
   Multiple Standards Are Inevitable 260
Open Systems Vendors..260
Getting There from Here 263

29   Images in the '90s: Fax and Network Technology Come Together   265

Author Bio...265
Executive Summary 265
Background 266
Computers and Faxes 267
Network Faxing 268
One Goal, Two Paths..269

30   Regarding Groupware   271

Author Bio...271
Executive Summary 272

31   Windows on NetWare: Tips for Making It Work   285

Author Bio...285
Executive Summary 286
   Tip #1—Create an Automated Setup Script
   for Your Users 287
   Tip #2—Update Your User's Shell and IPX
   in the System Login Script 288
   Tip #3—Create a Shared Program Group to Add
   an Application to Many Users' Desktops at Once 288

Tip #4—Restrict Users' Customization
of Program Manager 289
Tip #5—Enable the Screen Savers for Security 292
Tip #6—Create a Permanent Swap File If You Can 293
Tip #7—Turn on FastDisk 294
Tip #8—Use Persistent Connections
for Drive Mappings and Printer Assignments 294
Tip #9—Keep Windows and the .INI Files
on the File Server...295
Tip #10—Automate .INI File Maintenance 295
Tip #11—Remove the DOS Prompt
and File Manager Icons From Users' Desktops 296

32 Life Without File Servers: The Great Experiment 297

Author Bio...297
Executive Summary 297
Life Without File Servers: The Great Experiment 298

33 Solving Our Customers' Challenges 303

Author Bio...303
Executive Summary 303
Customer Challenges 304
Strategic E-Mail Issues 305
E-mail User Growth 305
PC Local Area Networks (LANs) 305
Workgroup Applications 306
An Electronic Messaging Strategy 306
What Is a Messaging Infrastructure? 307
Microsoft's LAN-Based Messaging Infrastructure 308
Workgroup Applications Commitment 310
Open and Customizable Systems 311
Superior Vendor Support 312
Conclusion 313

34 Network Software Licensing   **315**

Author Bio 315
The Microcomputer Managers Association
   White Paper Committee 316
Executive Summary 316
The MMA 317
Licensing Methodologies 318
Problems with the Current Environment 319
    Problems with Licensing Methodologies 319
    Case Study Concerns 322
Survey Data 325
Conclusions 326
Recommendations 327
Summary 328

35 The Telecomputing Office Environment   **331**

Author Bio 331
Executive Summary 332

**36 Open Systems Are Now Open
To DOS Users**   **337**

Author Bio 337
Executive Summary 338

37 Distributed Computing from the Desktop   **341**

Author Bio 341
Executive Summary 342
Bottoms-Up Requirements 343
Traditional Tops-Down Requirements 344
A New Generation of Hardware 344
The Software Platform Comes of Age 346
Delivering Open Systems 347
The Need for APIs 349
The Next Frontier 350
A Paradigm Shift 350

**38 Networked Databases: A Key to
     Computing Vitality   353**

   Author Bio 353
   Executive Summary 354
   Ease-of-Learning 354
   Ease-of-Use 355
   Empowering the End User 356
   Information Handling 356
   Data Entry 356
   File Access 357
   Record Updating 357
   Conclusion 358

39 Recycle Computers: Pass It On!   359

   Author Bio 359
   Executive Summary 360

**40 Is Your Data Really Safe? Will It
     Be Next Year?   365**

   Author Bio 365
   Executive Summary 366
   Backup Test 366
   Test Cases 367
      Scenario 1: Corporation A, Los Angeles, California 368
      Scenario 2: Corporation B, San Francisco, California ...368
   What Is the Problem? 369
      Backup and Archive Planning Profile 371
   PC LAN Evolution 372
      Crisis in Storage Management 373
   Next-Generation Solutions 373
      User Needs 374
   What to Do Today 375

41 Communications Technology Overview 377

Author Bio 377
Executive Summary 378
Industry Trends 379
    Globalism 379
    Deregulation, Privatization, Alternative Providers,
      and Duopolies 379
    Technology 379
    Standards 380
    Online Enterprise 380
Industry Characteristics 381
Industry Framework 382
    Quadrant I 384
    Quadrant II 384
    Quadrant III 385
    Quadrant IV 385

**42 Upping the Rate of Return
on Your Most Important Corporate Asset 389**

Author Bio 389
Executive Summary 390
Facts and Figures 391
Getting a Handle on the Problem 392
It's All in Your Attitude 393

**43 A LAN in Every Pocket:
Wireless LANs Today and Tomorrow 395**

Author Bio 395
Executive Summary 396
Today's Wireless Environment 397
Wireless Awaits the Right Application 399
The Wireless World of the Future 400

44 The Expanding Role of Intelligent Hubs in the Enterprise Network　**403**

Author Bio 403
Executive Summary 404

45 In Search of the Ultimate Network Manager　**409**

Author Bio 409
Executive Summary 410
The Need for Network Management 411
The Problems with SNMP 412
The Goal 414
Standards 417
Summary 417
Checklist of Features 419

46 Which OS Is for You? It Depends　**421**

Author Bio 421
Executive Summary 422

47 A Brief Overview of Network Management　**429**

Author Bio 429
Executive Summary 430
Local Area Networks Change the Face
　of Network Management 431
The Emergence of Local Network
　Management Solutions 432
State of the Industry 433
Intel's Network Management Strategy 434
Intel: Bringing Network Management to the Desktop 434
　Providing Solutions to Manage Desktop Computers 435
　Consolidating Management Functions
　　Into a Unified and Centralized Environment
　　Where all Intel Products Reside 436

Utilizing Single Agent Technology 436
Integrating with Existing and Future
    Management Consoles and Strategies 437
Cooperating with Industry and Standards Efforts
    to Solve Systems-level Management Problems 437
Summarizing Intel's Network Management Strategy 439
Conclusion 439

**48 Serious Network Computing:
     Why Superservers?**   **441**
Author Bio 441
Executive Summary 442

**49 Market Research Shows Windows Will
     Dominate the Desktop**   **445**
Author Bio 445
Executive Summary 445
Market Factors 446
Technology Advancements 447
Market Niche 448
Migration 448
Company Policy 449
Conclusions 450

**50 Working Towards Standards
     of Communication**   **451**
Author Bio 451
Executive Summary 452

**51 Expanding the Reach of LAN-Based
     Electronic Mail**   **457**
Author Bio 457
Executive Summary 458

LAN-Based Messaging: Defining the Players 459

LAN-Based Messaging: The Battleground 461

The Novell MHS Environment 463

What to Choose? 467

How to Contact Vendors Mentioned in This Paper 468

52 Protecting Your Network from Virus Infection — 471

Author Bio 471

Executive Summary 472

How Viruses Threaten Networks 472

The Network Breeding Ground 473

The Changing LANscape of Virus Technology 473

Practicing Safe Network Computing 475

Measuring Your Risk 475

Developing a Protection Strategy 476

What to Do If You Suspect a Virus 477

Identify the Virus and Its Source 477

Organize a Cleanup 478

Preventing Reinfection 479

Putting Viruses in Perspective 479

Index — 481

Foreword

The United States is experiencing a crisis in adult education.

One of every five adults—some 27 million Americans—are illiterate. These people have extreme difficulty dealing with printed materials. An additional 43 percent are only marginally literate. They can use printed materials, but only if simply and clearly presented and not about complex tasks. These people generally avoid situations requiring reading. Here are some relevant statistics:

- The United States ranks 49th in adult literacy among the 156 United Nations member countries.

- Sixty million adults have less than a ninth grade education.

- Our work force lacks the basic literacy skills required to do the jobs assigned to it. Twenty-three million workers have attained at best an eighth grade competency, while 75 percent of new jobs require at least a high school education. Immediate action must be taken if workers are to be sufficiently literate to meet the future demands of an increasingly competitive world economy.

Since 1955, Laubach Literacy has been at the forefront of efforts to provide quality literacy instruction to undereducated adults throughout the United States and around the world.

In more than 1,000 communities in the United States, Laubach programs utilize trained volunteers to tutor functionally illiterate adults in one-on-one and small group settings.

In 1991, more than 154,000 adult learners were taught by more than 100,000 trained Laubach volunteers.

In addition, Laubach's U.S. publishing division provides thousands of schools, prisons, libraries, adult education centers, and literacy programs nationwide with high-quality instructional materials specifically geared to the needs of undereducated adults and those who help them learn.

Thank you Prentice Hall Computer Publishing, Bruno Blenheim, Inc., and the authors who collaborated to publish *Insider's Guide to Personal Computing and Networking*. The support provided from sales of this book will enable adults throughout our country to overcome their illiteracy and live richer, more meaningful lives and will help create a better society for all.

Robert F. Caswell
President & CEO
Laubach Literacy International

Introduction

The computer industry is like the weather in East Texas. Don't like it? Stick around a bit, it will change. For many of us, this type of environment is home. Whether you are a Developer, IS Professional, or simply an end (power) user, the computer industry is at the center of your job, hobby, and many of your waking moments. Change has become the norm, almost expected.

Instead of grumbling about change, we have to deal with it. Our challenge is to seek out information, to understand what is changing and what it means for our particular situation. This is the premise behind this book. Our goal is to provide you—the Industry—with a medium by which a message can be delivered from the right people to the right people.

Where We Have Been

For many of us, the personal computer meant that Heathkit project, a Radio Shack adventure, or an Apple. The introduction of the IBM personal computer changed forever how computers were used and thought of in our society. Until that point, the PC was a game machine, home budget machine, the homework project machine, and a tool to dial the local electronic bulletin board. During my Air Force days, I used a Kaypro "portable" to set up databases for all kinds of projects like balancing flight schedules, training class rosters, and other simple tasks. There were no "real" computers that were available to everyone. My Apple II+ was fun, and programming for the 6502 CPU was a hobby. Getting software on the market was an easy task. Dot Matrix printer for documentation. Ziplock bag for packaging. Marketing was simple. There were only a few magazines, cheap ads, and everybody wanted everything for their computer.

The Tube

For Networking, we first had the model of a mainframe computer with terminals. These terminal connections each got a slice of time and everyone was linked to the home machine. We slid into the minicomputer revolution with help from Digital Equipment Corporation and IBM. These mini machines could be linked to the mainframe systems. We had sharing of printers, disk drives, computing time, and system resources. The early PC days saw "networking" software get its start with terminal emulation software. Sharing printers and resources meant having the PC act like a dumb terminal. Not really a cost-effective use of the device. Prices were still sky high and computing for the masses remained a bit out of reach.

One Step Forward

Next in the technological evolution was the advent of business systems linked using a bus technology. This "S-100" bus era was filled with things like Digital Research's MP/M, the multi-user version of the popular CP/M operating system. The basic premise around this was a box (card cage) with different computer boards performing different functions. You would find, for example, a disk drive controller board that would link up storage devices. There also were workstation or terminal boards. Essentially, these boards had multiple central processing units (CPUs) onboard with a connection for each user. So each user had, in effect, their own computer. This was still limited to the dumb tube, although the tubes were getting much more functional and now had color. This whole segment of the computer industry spawned great companies like Compupro, Konnan, ADS, and STB. Many companies did not survive. Others, however, made the change and continue to be in the computer business having joined the PC/LAN "revolution."

Computing of Today

Today, businesses have choices in computer technology that were not possible ten years ago. PC vendors have taken the opportunity that IBM helped define and are providing PCs that are many times more powerful that the "big iron" of yesterday. Think about what that means to business. Today, for under $2,000, you can create a technology center that is capable of running a small business. CompuServe, one of the largest and most successful electronic information services in the world, brings millions of pages of business research data to anyone with a modem (okay, and a major credit card!). The proverbial "level playing field" can be realized when you look at the technology that is available. It is possible to play like the big boys, compute like the big boys, do research like the big boys, and reap the rewards like the big boys.

What's Inside

Leading companies, such as Adobe, Borland, IBM, Lotus, Microsoft, Quarterdeck, XTree, and others, continue to provide technology that makes today more exciting than yesterday. Within these pages are the thoughts from the best minds and companies in the business. From practical advice on computing peripherals to the evolving world of workgroup computing. The best have come together to provide insightful, timely, and relevant information that you must know. Let's take a look at some of the categories and a small sample of the works contained within.

Operating Systems Today and Tomorrow.

The operating system is the heart of any computer or network. Several papers will aid in your understanding of operating system futures. Robert Gill, one of Gartner Group's best and brightest, contributed an excellent paper entitled *The Once and Future NOS*. This, along with David Strom's *Which OS is Best For You?* paper, will give you some appreciation for the choices and decisions you will be making now and in the future.

The future is presented by two industry veterans: Theresa Myers, CEO of Quarterdeck, and Bill Gates, one of the industry's most successful players and CEO of Microsoft. Bill talks about the world of Windows NT and Theresa shares her thoughts regarding open systems for DOS users. Sherri Walkenhorst of Network Associates will provide you with some interesting OS market share information, and Phillippe Kahn, CEO of Borland, will share his ideas on the complex data processing issues surrounding the operating systems of today.

Network Management and Support

Today, the typical LAN Management team is faced with the daunting tasks of managing the user base, controlling costs, justifying expansion, forecasting growth, and answering software support calls. All of this before morning coffee. Take heart, many top gun talents have put their thoughts down on paper for you. Michael Dell, CEO and Founder of Dell Computer, talks about remote support and maintenance of personal computers. Jeff Erwin, of Protools fame, shares his thoughts on the troubleshooting systems based on expert technology. Gail Foster of Northeast Consulting Resources will tell you how this same expert technology can improve your help desk efficiency.

Scott Hutchinson of Saber Software, King Lee of XTree Company, and Greg Gianforte of Brightwork Development all share ideas on network management. They discuss the tools you need, why you need them, and how to exploit them. Howard Lubert—one of the industry's top network management consultants and sought after network designer—contributed an important paper regarding the *Myths & Realities of Network Management*. It is a must read. The same can be said for the paper from Howard "Networks Are My Life" Marks. Howard Marks is almost a household word when it comes to making the Microsoft Windows operating system work on a network. Sharing his ideas, tips, tricks, and traps; this paper is a classic.

Network Components and Peripherals—Parts-Is-Parts

A network is made up of many components and peripherals. There are a group of papers that help you get the most out of these network parts. Jeff Chumbley—an icon within Novell's electronic support forum, NetWire—offers some expert advice within the pages of his paper entitled *Redefining Adapter Performance*. IOMEGA Corp's Michael Joseph contributed a paper entitled *The Growing Role of Removable Storage*. This paper gives you practical information about this important technology, and it comes from one of the world's leading storage vendors.

You will also find an excellent paper on *Wireless LANs—Today and Tomorrow* by Stan Schatt. Dirk Gates (White & Cromer) gives you some of his thoughts regarding portable computers in his paper entitled *Portables on LANs—Now and Tomorrow*. Josh Mailman (JetFax) covers the fax and in networked environments.

Workgroup Computing

In California, workgroup computing is a programming team sitting in the hot tub with a voice-activated laptop on a bench just to the left of the freshly squeezed guava juice. They know how to do it in CA. Seriously, workgroup computing represents one of the next "giant leaps" in hardware and software technology. I am pleased to tell you about some of the papers you will be treated to.

From the makers of the best selling peer-to-peer NOS—LANtastic—Artisoft provides you with valuable information regarding interoperability of peer-to-peer networks. Gary Beach, noted industry expert and publisher of *ComputerWorld* magazine, has put together some illuminating thoughts in his paper entitled *Workgroup Computing—It's IT and That's That*. Also not to be missed is the paper entitled *Regarding Groupware* from longtime industry veteran, visionary, and CEO of Lotus Development Corporation, Jim Manzi. Lotus Notes is the leading groupware software application and Jim has some important thoughts for everyone interested in groupware and the workgroup computing concept. Finally, John McCann—best-selling author, wizard of NetWare, and top industry consultant—offers an interesting perspective in his paper called *Life Without File Servers: the Great Experiment*.

Electronic Mail and Messaging

The power of computing becomes obvious when you look at the explosion in the use of electronic mail systems and the proliferation of messaging enabled applications. There are a group of papers which will give you important information on how to take advantage of this technology now and how to prepare to go even further in the future. Microsoft Corporation provides a description of their vision in laying out the company's messaging strategy. One of the industry's leading experts on networks and messaging systems—Brett Warthen of Infinite Technologies—provides a paper entitled *Expanding the Reach of LAN-Based E-Mail*. John Warnock (CEO of Adobe Systems) talks about *Working Towards Standards of Communications* and Steve Glagow will round out the insights on messaging with a paper entitled *Enterprise Messaging—Implementing a Corporate Post Office*.

Philosophy and Trends in the Industry

Industry leaders from all segments offer information worth reading if you are planning for the future—you are, right? The father of Pong, author, software designer, pizza lover, and longtime industry visionary, Nolan Bushnell gives you insights into *Communicating Naturally in the Digitized World.* Top industry trainer, consultant, and author, Patrick Corrigan contributes a paper entitled *The Evolution of the Global Data Network* in which he talks about where we are headed as a global computing community. Stuart Pastman addresses *The New Corporate Development LANscape.* Dennis Hayes, the modem community's virtuoso and CEO of Hayes Microcomputing shares his philosophy of network computing in the nineties. Harry Saal of Network General offers provocative and insightful commentary in his paper entitled *Upping the Rate of Return of Your Corporate Network.* You will surely enjoy Tom Henderson's *The Mensch of Networking* in which Tom, with tongue planted firmly in cheek, takes on the industry as only he can. Finally, leading industry organizations such as the Microcomputer Managers Association (MMA) and Open Systems Recommended Solutions (OURS) offer their collective thoughts on such topics as software licensing and open systems.

There is much more that awaits you inside these pages. I've tried to just highlight some of the great work and great people that have taken time out to offer you important thoughts, council, warnings, and friendly chats.

Thanks To All

Besides the authors of these great papers, special acknowledgment and thanks needs to go out to some important behind the scenes people.

Gregg Bushyeager of Prentice Hall Computer Publishing led the charge inside the book publishing world. Without his belief in my idea and determination to ride shotgun over the giant task of coordinating the publishing effort, this book would never have become reality. If you gain even one morsel of knowledge, thank Gregg for getting it to you.

Steve Gross of Bruno Blenhiem Trade Show Management is one of those rare individuals who puts quality above all else. From the seminar programs at shows such as PC-Expo and NetWorld, to the tutorial series at events around the world, Steve never settles for anything less than top-quality. He and Adam Torres were the key players that made sure the Prentice Hall & Bruno Blenheim joint efforts resulted in a nice donation to an important charity: Laubach Literary International.

As you can see, this is a win-win proposition for all involved. The industry gets the opportunity to share important information with its user-base and Laubach Literacy gets some much-needed capital to aid them in their efforts to stamp out adult illiteracy.

Onward

So, fellow professionals, read on. I am pleased that you are with us, hope you enjoy the results of a large literary effort, and would love to hear your feedback. Please contact me in care of the publisher or at any of the addresses below. All of us involved in this project wish you continued success.

Rick Segal, Redmond WA, Aug. 1992

CIS: 76276,2706
Prodigy: FTNP48A
Internet: 76276.2706@COMPUSERVE.COM

About this Book

This book is a small wonder comprised of a range of learned research, probing, and discourse in the disciplines of networking. In our fabulous world of superb and highly-polished technology where achieving men and women astound themselves and each other almost daily and where information is the basis of wealth, the thought of compiling and presenting this kind of material is like Macy's telling Gimbel's.

In a sense, however, that is exactly the basis of networking. It is a sharing of the best resources from the best intelligence to make it possible for humankind to take the next step into tomorrow confident that our shoe is on firm ground.

This compendium will not last forever as a state-of-the-art technology. Even as you read these words, invention and discovery are leaving milestones behind, and this book is passing into history. But it will not die. This book will become a valuable reference tool and will help many students earn advanced degrees in their specialized EDP fields.

Here, then, are the private white papers, the behind-the-scenes developments of the best thinking. These are the jewels of networking spread out for you, representing the very best of current technology and, perhaps, a few hints of what is to come.

Ralph J. Ianuzzi
Bruno Blenheim, Inc.
Show Director
NetWorld

Peer-to-Peer Networking and Interoperability

by Artisoft, Inc.

Author Bio

⧗ ARTISOFT
Revolutionizing Connectivity

Artisoft, Inc., founded by C. John (Jack) Schoof II in 1982, designs and manufactures a full product line of low-cost, award-winning software, hardware, and systems for local area networking.

Artisoft's LANtastic Local Area Network (LAN) is the leading DOS-based, peer-to-peer LAN because it addresses the needs of small- to medium-sized businesses wanting to network anywhere from 2 to 300 computers. Since the introduction of the LANtastic network in 1987, Artisoft's sales have increased from $2.1 million in fiscal 1988 to $73.2 million in fiscal 1992. In just five years, Artisoft has installed over 200,000 LANtastic Local Area Networks, with nearly one million users worldwide. In 1989, 1990, and 1991, Artisoft was ranked by *Inc.* magazine as one of the country's top 500 fastest-growing, privately-held companies.

Based in Tucson, Arizona, Artisoft now employs over 500 personnel. Artisoft has also established 27,000 authorized resellers throughout the

United States, distributors in nearly 70 foreign countries, and international offices in the United Kingdom, Japan, Australia, and Mexico, as well as representatives in France, Germany, Italy, and Spain.

Executive Summary

Peer-to-peer networking has entered mainstream computing with its wealth of features, enhanced performance and security—all the while maintaining its ease of use, low cost, inexpensive support and maintenance. Now the growing challenge for peer-to-peer developers is to help users connect the many diverse, often incompatible, platforms that exist in today's computing environments.

The leading peer-to-peer manufacturers have begun to offer solutions in this very important area. Development is well under way to address the interoperability of different computing platforms. This paper presents an overview of how the peer-to-peer environment is evolving into a viable option for larger-scale corporate networking.

The computer industry has developed more rapidly than any industry in recent memory. We have seen the evolution of computers from mainframes and minicomputers to personal desktop computers, and have witnessed the revolution that each new generation of computers has catalyzed. The technology behind desktop computers and the rapid advancement in their capabilities now rivals the minicomputer and mainframe predecessors in performance and features. A multitude of operating systems and environments have been introduced—DOS, UNIX, OS/2, Windows and the Apple Macintosh—and still others are beginning to appear on the horizon.

The personal computer has played an integral role in the evolution of the local area network from solely client-server systems to include peer-to-peer systems. Although peer-to-peer architecture was first noted for its ease of use, ease of administration, and flexibility, millions of users and many third-party developers now accept it because it has maintained its original qualities while maturing to include new features and increased performance. Peer-to-peer developers must now help users connect the many diverse, often incompatible, platforms that exist in today's computing environments. This is a vision well beyond many of our initial expectations for the peer-to-peer market.

Initially designed for small- to medium-sized businesses, peer-to-peer networks allow users within the same operating environment, such as DOS, to share files and printers. The early versions of DOS-based LANs offered users an inexpensive, easy to use, flexible alternative to client-server networks. There were, however, limitations to the initial technology. Specifically, there were concerns about performance, proprietary hardware, and limited third-party support. Often the peer-to-peer LANs included proprietary network interface cards which didn't allow common network peripheral items, such as repeaters and hubs, to be included in the network. Also, many peer-to-peer LANs supported the NetBIOS protocol, for which few third-party software companies wrote compatible networking applications. As a result, peer-to-peer networking became synonymous with small, entry-level networks.

Today, peer-to-peer networks encompass the performance, features, flexibility, ease of use and administration which make them a viable alternative for not only small- and medium-sized businesses, but also corporate workgroups and corporations themselves. Areas once considered peer-to-peer weaknesses now compare favorably to those of the more expensive client-server networks. Security, once considered minimal in the peer-to-peer environment, has been refined to include user name and password, and DOS file- and record- locking. Multiple levels of access control lists permit an administrator to assign various user privileges, even the day of the week and time of the day that a user can access these privileges.

Many leading peer-to-peer LANs now boast a wealth of features—UPS support to automatically protect valuable data, electronic mail to increase office productivity, disk-caching to enhance the speed of the network, and improved printing capabilities such as immediate printer de-spooling and notification when print jobs are completed. System administration has been enhanced and streamlined to allow administrators to assign group accounts, copy user information from one server to another, log users out of a particular server, and deny access to that server if the administrator needs to perform a backup. In addition, third-party software manufacturers have developed products to add such features as fault-tolerance, connectivity to gateway products, and fax-sharing capabilities.

With the advent of EtherNet technology, peer-to-peer network developers overcame another obstacle in their bid for acceptance. Because EtherNet technology created a standard for network hardware, IEEE 802.3, peer-to-peer operating systems could be developed to run over EtherNet adapters in addition to, or instead of, their proprietary hardware. This standardization also allowed peer-to-peer networks to take advantage of numerous third-party hardware devices, such as repeaters, to extend their cabling segments to much greater distances.

EtherNet technology also improved the performance of the peer-to-peer products. The EtherNet adapters' 10Mbps (megabits per second) speed was a noticeable increase in the performance over many of the proprietary adapters. These technological improvements—the 10Mbps EtherNet standard, disk-caching, the advancement of microprocessors and increased hard disk speed—have all contributed to today's high-performance peer-to-peer products and have helped overcome the low-performance stigma of the earlier products.

Whether connecting 2 computers or 200 computers, flexibility is key when discussing peer-to-peer systems. Users have the choice of setting up multiple servers on the network, allowing users to share a company's resources—files, dot matrix and laser printers, CD-ROM drives, and a variety of other devices—instead of buying additional ones, or running floppy disks from computer to computer. With peer-to-peer technology, the customer maintains the initial key advantages of low cost, ease of use, low memory overhead, and resource-sharing, but now with performance and power comparable to the client-server systems.

With the maturing of the peer-to-peer market and the greater acceptance by customers, software developers now make stronger efforts to ensure compatibility with peer-to-peer technology. Thousands of off-the-shelf software packages now support the NetBIOS protocol and numerous peer-to-peer LANs. In general, off-the-shelf software is less expensive than software packages developed solely for the proprietary operating systems found in many client-server systems.

The number of users supported by a peer-to-peer network also has increased over the past several years. Though the installation of the past hovered around five nodes, today it is not uncommon for customers to be running peer-to-peer networks ranging anywhere from 50 to hundreds of nodes. The Artisoft corporate network at its international headquarters in Tucson is a prime example of the power and flexibility of a peer-to-peer network. With more than 400 nodes and growing, Artisoft's peer-to-peer network boasts a T-1 link to warehouse and manufacturing facilities eight miles away, plus an infrared beam connecting another building.

Now that peer-to-peer operating technology has matured and has been accepted by millions of customers worldwide, more corporate workgroups utilize these systems. With peer-to-peer technology, these users have the freedom to determine and manage their own localized network within the framework of a larger installation. But with corporate America's blessing comes the next challenge for the peer-to-peer industry: interoperability.

Many larger companies have incorporated both yesterday's and today's technology. A large majority of the Fortune 2000-type companies currently utilize mainframe, DOS, Windows and Apple systems for their computing needs. Now, the task at hand is to provide a solution for these customers to allow them to share information between their different computing platforms. In order to continue to increase the peer-to-peer market presence, this need must be addressed.

Once again, the leading peer-to-peer manufacturers have begun to offer solutions in this important area. Because of the large presence Microsoft Windows has within the computer industry, manufacturers focus on products that take advantage of Window's new graphical user interface.

Development is well under way to address the interoperability of different computing platforms. The first introductions to meet the demand of connecting different operating systems focused on the NetWare platform, and today the leading peer-to-peer manufacturers are developing products for the Macintosh and UNIX environments. Early versions of Macintosh connectivity solutions will allow the transparent integration of the Apple Macintosh computers into a DOS-based network. TCP/IP products are now either on the market or just around the corner to address the increasing number of requests for a UNIX connectivity solution.

Interoperability is upon us and remains the next challenge, but there are several other markets just beyond this hurdle. Multimedia, seemingly the next large vertical market, poses another challenge with a wide array of new technology for peer-to-peer developers to utilize. More and more companies have climbed onto the Multimedia bandwagon with voice and video applications.

Long a proponent of voice and multimedia, Artisoft is leading the way for peer-to-peer manufacturers. The Artisoft Sounding Board, introduced in 1990, allows LANtastic Local Area Network users to add voice mail and chat capabilities to their operations. But with our recent introduction of the ArtiSound recorder software, users of any application that supports the Microsoft Windows object linking and embedding protocol can now add voice annotation to that document.

Peer-to-peer networking has entered mainstream computing with its wealth of features, enhanced performance and security, while still maintaining its ease of use, low cost, inexpensive support and maintenance. Without abandoning our core users in small- and medium-sized businesses, peer-to-peer technology is now widely accepted by corporate America. From its modest beginnings of providing file and printer sharing, peer-to-peer networking has evolved into a comprehensive computing solution.

Workgroup Computing:
It's IT and That's That
for Computing in the '90s

by Gary J. Beach
President and CEO of CW Publishing, Inc.,
and publisher of COMPUTERWORLD

Author Bio

President and CEO of CW Publishing, Inc., Framingham, Massachusetts, and publisher of *COMPUTERWORLD*, Gary J. Beach joined the International Data Group family of newspapers and magazines as publisher of *Network World* in 1978. In 1991, he was named publisher of *COMPUTERWORLD*, the industry's newspaper of record for information systems management.

A publishing veteran with more than two decades of experience, Mr. Beach began his career at Haley Communication, later going to Macmillan Publishing. In 1978, he joined McGraw Hill as director of research and was subsequently promoted to district sales manager, then ad sales manager of McGraw Hill's *Data Communications* magazine.

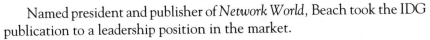

Named president and publisher of *Network World*, Beach took the IDG publication to a leadership position in the market.

In 1991, IDG chairman Patrick J. McGovern appointed Beach to the top post at *COMPUTERWORLD*, the flagship publication of IDG, the leading global provider of information services on information technology, with annual revenues of $770 million and 4,600 employees. Its publishing subsidiary, IDG Communications, publishes 181 newspapers and magazines in 58 countries.

A native of Jersey City, New Jersey, Mr. Beach holds a bachelor's degree in Urban Affairs from Manhattan College. He did graduate work later at Montclair State College.

As publisher of a weekly newspaper that reaches more than 600,000 key IS decision makers, he is active in promoting efforts that raise the information technology industry's awareness of social responsibility, including advocacy of computer literacy among the general public.

Executive Summary

When it comes to information technology, the 1990s will probably be known as the decade of workgroup computing. Hardware, software, networking and human interaction are coming together to become a powerful computing/business platform.

This paper looks at the key features of successful workgroup computing, and gives some examples of how some companies have successfully put workgroup computing to work.

Information Technology (IT) tends to mark its progress in evolutionary developments per decade. Centralized computing flowing out of the mainframe dominated the '60s. The '70s ushered in the minicomputer, and the '80s were remarkable for bringing in personal computing. Ten years from now, as the pundits of IT look back and make their observations on what evolutionary development marked the '90s, I think most will say it was the delivery of hardware, software, networking, and human interaction into a powerful computing/business platform called *workgroup computing*.

Several factors have led to this development. Putting computing power on the desktop in the early 1980s and linking these islands of computing power in a networked fashion in the late 1980s began the workgroup computing era. But Corporate America wants more. With information technology a firmly recognized and cherished corporate resource, corporate management is demanding to know exactly what that raw computing power is doing on the desk and what's transpiring daily in the network. If you're going to put the chips, the bits, the bytes, and the boxes in the hands of workers, give them a truly interactive, humanized computing platform. But more important, accomplish real return on investment. How? Not only by harnessing this computing platform to daily business functions, but by changing and, in some cases, dramatically reengineering those functions. And this is how the evolution of workgroup computing is occurring in thousands of companies today. (See Figure 2.1.)

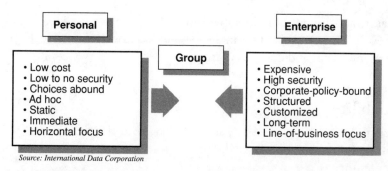

Figure 2.1. Workgroup systems: filling the computing vacuum.

Defining the Technology

What exactly is workgroup computing? A simple definition would be the linking of personal productivity and enterprise-wide business functions. Take it one step further by identifying two basic components in workgroup computing as outlined by International Data Corporation (IDC). One component is the Local Area Network Integrated Office System (LAN IOS) that provides the engine. The second is personal productivity tools such as application software, which includes word processing and spreadsheets and E-mail, bundled with emerging systems and application code software (known as "groupware") that provide the working parts for this engine. And who starts this engine? A particular group of workers who must transact business by interacting with each other fairly frequently.

Key Features of a Successful Workgroup

In a 1992 IDC White Paper on Workgroup Technology, author Ann Palermo identifies several features that make up a well-constructed workgroup:

Ease of Use

Access to and use of the functions within the workgroup must be easy enough that everyone will use it. This includes shielding the user from such things as host interfaces and computer languages.

Scalability

Workgroups can transcend physical locality; thus the degree to which a database of information can be distributed and updated in a timely manner is important.

Security

The users within the workgroup generally define the security. This includes creating view-only, editing rights, create rights, approval/denial rights, access to all or only a portion of the document, and management reporting information access.

Heterogeneous Support

Various individual user requirements preclude the use of only one desktop device or operating environment. Each user in the workgroup will have different levels of use and access to the workgroup applications. A heterogeneous environment is also critical because several types of LAN systems may be in place.

Open Access to Other Data and Information

To serve enterprise-wide business objectives, which is the ultimate goal of the workgroup, access to internal and external databases with full import and export facilities is a critical component in a successful workgroup.

Customization

Lest you think workgroup computing is a total end-user phenomenon, you should understand that workgroup systems achieve customization through the partnership of end users and application programmers. This ensures that the people who know the IT business—information systems management— can best effect successful applications. Thus the application programmer can design the engine, and the end user can decide what parts go in it.

These six key features are what the users in the individual business unit and their information systems management need to pay particular attention to when creating and maintaining a workgroup. What end users, information systems management, and corporate management need to focus on is developing the blueprint for success—that is, defining both the tactical and strategic business objective a workgroup can achieve. A quick example would be using workgroup computing for improving the productivity of sales support personnel. That's the tactical objective. What's the strategic end result? Better customer satisfaction, leading to increased sales.

Some of the Pioneers

Who's out there putting workgroup computing to the test? At Pacific Gas & Electric, the San Francisco-based utility, they moved 20,000 PCs to a GUI-based groupware environment. The result is that 90 percent of the company's raw computing power resides on the desk in a suite of applications which function as a primary "information-enabling tool set" that supports the company's primary objective of information access: "anytime, any-place, in any form, by any employee." The litmus test over time will be if this employee benefit will transcend to a customer benefit.

Another example is that of Bendix Automative Systems, a division of Allied Signal, Inc. In July of 1992 Bendix initiated a multimillion-dollar, multiyear downsizing process from a midrange environment to a multi-LAN platform that will be enhanced by a 5,000-node license for a groupware package. Bendix believes the addition of this groupware is crucial to meeting a strategic quality initiative goal and improved communications by enabling workers in this multinational division to work from the same repository of images, graphics, voice, documents, and spreadsheets across different time zones. The bottom-line objective is reduced response time, critical for this manufacturing-based organization.

A Word to the Wise

Mention productivity and information technology in the same breath, and most people's eyes light up. However, I think it's important to offer a few words of caution on the subject of workgroup computing. This is the first computing platform in which we are not dependent on technology's whims, but in which technology is dependent on our whims. Interpersonal commu-nication skills and the soundness of underlying organizational structures, on a departmental, divisional, and enterprise-wide basis, weigh heavily in just how successful workgroup computing is going to be for the corporation. If your users can't interact successfully in a meeting or on the phone, or if management is not clear on short- and long-term objectives, workgroup computing may not help. And remember, the goal is not to adapt to the technology but to adapt that technology to the business need.

Our current view of the link between technology and the business process is a strong factor in this amazing development of the 1990s. On the technology side, workgroup computing is notable for its thoughtful use of nonproprietary, mostly existing technology and for creating a new type of worker—a worker who is not only computer literate, but competitively computer literate with improved access to enterprise-wide information. On the business side, the platform is helping Corporate America achieve what it must do to stay competitive in the global economy: respond more quickly to market changes and better serve its customer base by transcending geographic and time barriers faster, easier, and more cost-effectively. Bottom-line success has never been more attainable.

Making the Right Connections... By Wisely Choosing and Successfully Working with a Networking Partner

by Elizabeth G. Berglund,
Editor-in-Chief, The Network Report

Author Bio

Mrs. Berglund has been in the business field—in trade magazines, public relations and association management—for over a decade. Currently, she is marketing communications director for LANDA, the trade association for the network industry.

A pioneer in the computer and network publishing arena, she helped found *Electronic Publishing & Printing,* the only magazine intended exclusively for electronic publishing and printing professionals, and was named editorial director/publishing manager in 1986. Previously, Berglund was editorial director of two publications serving the graphic communications industries, *American Printer* monthly magazine and *Graphic*

Arts Products News (a 10-times-a-year product tabloid). As editorial director from 1978 through 1985, she was well known for in-depth reports on particular segments of the printing and publishing industries, particularly those related to computerization and information systems integration.

Among her credits, Mrs. Berglund and her staff took first place in the Maclean Hunter Publishing Co. Editorial Excellence Competition in 1990. Further, she is a past winner of the Jesse H. Neal Award, (the "Pulitzer Prize" of business publications) presented by the American Business Publishers.

In addition, Berglund has been the recipient of several of the American Society of Business Press Editors First Place Design and Editorial Excellence Awards. During her tenure as editor, *American Printer* magazine was named Magazine of the Year in 1985 by the International Association of Printing House Craftsmen, a prestigious graphic arts and printing industry trade association.

Berglund has a B.S. in Economics and Journalism from the University of Illinois.

Executive Summary

While most LANs (local area networks) are installed by systems integrators, VARs (value added resellers), resellers and the like, it is the corporate computing end-user who has to support, administer and maintain that network. Because the LAN is probably part of a mission-critical application, corporate end-users have to understand both the underlying technology and its day-to-day implications. These users need the information to select and work with compatible LAN implementors, and to plan and deliver long-term support.

As a corporate computing end-user, your challenge today is to design and build the right LAN to meet current needs while providing a base for future expansion. You have to be aware of what services your LAN has to deliver, and the costs and trade-offs that need to be made. You must also know how to estimate your platform's performance requirements specifically in terms of your business needs.

You must have a compelling reason for tying all those stand-alone PCs together to create a LAN, and that means having a high payback business need. It is crucial to have a plan for spotting opportunities, evaluating their potential costs and benefits, and selecting the best one(s) for your environment.

Getting the LAN up and running is only the first step—keeping it available to your users determines its real value. The key to success is balancing the needs of the network with your daily responsibilities so that both your boss and the network are happy and healthy.

After making the decision to implement, update or expand a LAN-based business system, corporate computing professionals are faced with the critical decision of finding a technical partner. It is important to remember that this is a long-term relationship. To ensure that both you and your networking partner win, you must place equal importance on the structure of your RFP (request for proposal) as well as the responses it generates.

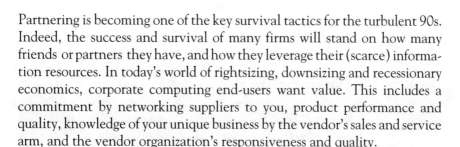

Partnering is becoming one of the key survival tactics for the turbulent 90s. Indeed, the success and survival of many firms will stand on how many friends or partners they have, and how they leverage their (scarce) information resources. In today's world of rightsizing, downsizing and recessionary economics, corporate computing end-users want value. This includes a commitment by networking suppliers to you, product performance and quality, knowledge of your unique business by the vendor's sales and service arm, and the vendor organization's responsiveness and quality.

The rise of PC networks and workstations with processing, storage, voice and imaging capabilities has come in directions and at a speed that are mind-boggling. The accelerating movement away from reliance on a few vendors to reliance on a growing number of large and small vendors for hardware, software, telecommunications, and services only adds to the confusion. Dealing with all of these elements has forced corporate end-user customers to become systems designers and integrators, a complex and costly task.

Yet, having choices—a myriad of offerings from multiple vendors—is good for end-users. Along with this up-side, however, comes the distinctly down-side of dealing with these choices and their complexity. This costs buyers and users time, money, and critical skills, and these costs are on the rise. Savvy end-user organizations are not just interested in trading off one set of costs for another. Ultimately, valuable information integration, or networking, permits working applications to implement business processes and assist workers. In this regard, systems integration issues can be seen as necessary evils for corporate computing end-users. Carefully choosing a networking partner—whether it is an SI (systems integrator), VAR, Consultant, or Reseller—can help you leverage your information resources.

Certainly, the days are past when single vendor solutions could address all of the issues. Today's corporate climate requires multivendor computing solutions that focus on interoperability. However, standards groups, because of their nature and long-term focus, are not the answer. They do not solve today's problems, but rather tomorrow's. For corporate end-users to be more valuable to their companies, they should focus on useful applications and information—not on coping with systems integration and interoperability issues. The right SI or VAR can make a big difference in this context.

Start at the Beginning

Before looking at specific criteria for selecting a network SI/VAR (or re-evaluating your current one), it is necessary to review some basics. For instance, have you been burned by buying a computer system(s) that solved yesterday's problems, but then became ineffective for today—or never did what it was supposed to in the first place? No matter what the price or how elegant the technology, such systems could never have been considered a good deal.

When a network is first planned, there usually are compelling reasons for its existence and specific goals. Often those reasons include: file sharing, database sharing, printer sharing, program sharing, E-mail, data transfer, and telecommunications. As with any other corporate project, the network must periodically be measured against those goals. For example, does the network fulfill the reason for its existence? Is the functionality that existed prior to the network maintained? Are there any additional benefits that were gained? The on-going maintenance and the potential future expansion of the network are other important issues. Furthermore, there is the development of a training plan and preparation for support (inside and out). In addition, corporate information needs that moved toward LANs are now going beyond to wide area networks (WANs) and Internetworks—thereby raising the interoperability issue to an even higher level of significance.

When selecting and working with a compatible network integrator/ VAR, it is helpful to remember the basic steps necessary to successfully implement a network. These include: identifying the current situation; determining the requirements and goals of the network; identifying the hardware and software alternatives, and choosing the best solution for your company; planning the installation; and carrying out the plan. Once the network is in place, successful corporate computing end-users are constantly reviewing and modifying it as necessary. The users also must compare the network with the pre-defined goals—making any necessary adjustments. They must also be concerned with maintaining and expanding the network.

Making the Right Partnering Choice

When selecting and working with your networking partner, remember that you get what you pay for. Conversely, you don't get what you don't pay for. Depending on how far up or down the networking reseller channel "food chain" you go, the kinds of services and support you will get varies greatly, explains Susan Spiner, a well-known LAN industry consultant. Spiner is president of New York City-based Set Marketing On.

For instance, SIs provide the highest level of integration support and service. They understand what technical assessments, requirement analysis, and data modeling mean, and have the fire-power to integrate applications across multi-platform environments. They generally do not resell hardware.

Network System Integrators (NSIs) usually provide hardware integration products and services—frequently across multiple platforms, without applications support. Network Consulting Organizations fit in between SIs and NSIs. They generally do not resell products, but provide consulting services such as network design, product testing, and system requirements analysis. These kinds of companies usually do not get involved with applications development, but can provide a high level of impartial information.

VARs offer a value-added service in addition to the reselling of products at competitive prices. Usually VARs provide a large volume of products and a certain level of support to customers. VARs provide vertical application integration services within a specific business subset such as hospitals, real estate, banks, and law offices.

VADs (value added dealers) resell hardware, software or peripherals and also provide a minimum level of telephone or on-site support.

Retailers are store front organizations that sell products. And, of course, Mail Order lets your fingers do the walking.

Some Selection Criteria

After carefully reviewing the type of networking partner that will potentially have the best fit with your company and its information needs, corporate computing end-users should disseminate RFPs (request for proposals) for the job. Only by communicating openly and clearly with your potential partners will you have the information you need to effectively evaluate all of the proposals—and select a compatible networking partner.

In addition to the details contained in a Proposal for Network Services, there are other factors to take into consideration in your selection of a networking partner, according to Tom Henderson, an outspoken LANDA member, industry veteran, and president of Corporate Networks in Indianapolis, IN. Some criteria for wisely choosing and working with a capable, compatible networking partner follow.

Systems Integrator/VAR/Reseller Stability

How long has the company been in business? Can they provide a list of satisfied customer references?

Reference Checks

Do the firm's stated marketing mottos match the services they actually provide? Matching the SI/VAR's specialties to your corporate needs is crucial to a good working relationship. All companies specializing in LAN-related services are not created equal. Do you require a lot of hand holding or a little? Look for pre-sales support (consulting), implementation (installation) support, and after-sales support. Note: There are box movers and there are service providers. Beware of the differences and the consequences.

Working Relationships

Has the SI/VAR demonstrated a working relationship with the vendors of the equipment that they are proposing to you?

Equipment Knowledge and Vendor Medallions

Has the SI/VAR installed and/or does it use the specific kinds of equipment that are being proposed to you? Does the VAR/SI have specific vendor medallions [i.e.: certifications or designations such as NCE (NETWERC Certified Engineer from LANDA) or CNE (Certified NetWare Engineer from Novell) or authorizations such as IBM Remarketer, or Novel Gold/Platinum reseller, or ACR (Apple Consultant Relations), etc.]? Does the SI/VAR have training on the equipment being proposed? Remember that certifications and/or authorizations are merely one of many indicators of capability when selecting networking VAR/SIs to meet your needs.

Support Questions

How much of the system being configured do you want the reseller to support? Can they support this platform with in-house personnel or by outsourcing? If outsourcing, what is the VAR/Reseller's relationship to the outside source? What is your recourse if there is a problem with the part of the network being outsourced?

With single-vendor networks, it was (is) easy to know exactly who to call for support...not so with the current multivendor state in most companies today. When questions arise in multivendor networks, there is usually enough finger pointing and blame-placing to turn any network manager's hair gray. That's why the correct fit with your SI/VAR is so important.

In the area of technical support, it's probably wise to remember that there is no such thing as "free" tech support. There is pre-paid tech support and there is pay-as-required tech support—but it is never free, notes Paul Donohoe, LANDA chairman and president of PC Technical Services of Elmsford, NY. Systems Integrators, VARs, services firms and even manufacturers spend considerable money on tech support resources. It would be economic suicide not to have revenues to support these expenses.

Certainly, the current trend is for support services to be unbundled. This trend is expected to continue as hardware/software profit margins continue to decrease, which in turn lowers the pre-paid support revenues that can pay for the so-called free tech support. Sophisticated corporate purchasers were instrumental in "prodding" hardware providers to be efficient and provide inexpensive distribution services. It is also expected that they can and will do the same for support providers to offer the best value support for the least cost. The only way that a buyer can evaluate the value of the service is if the cost is known. Once support is unbundled, then service providers can compete to give the best quality service at the lowest cost.

Level of Rapport

What is the rapport level between the Reseller/Systems Integrator's support personnel and the people in your organization who will be dealing with each other? An adversarial posture can wreak havoc within your company. What kind of operator training will be available for your people, and at what cost?

Resources

Can the VAR/Reseller commit the resources necessary to bring about the proposed solution in the time frame agreed upon?

Outside Help

Can the reseller bring in vendor resources if necessary to complete the projects in the same timely fashion?

Industry Commitment

Is the VAR/Reseller a good "industry citizen"? Is the firm a member of, and does it participate in, various societies or associations, such as LANDA, IEEE, NOMDA (National Office Machine Dealers Association), ABCD (The Microcomputer Industry Association)? Do they demonstrate a desire to live in and be a part of the network community at large?

Are you curious how the "above average" network services vendor companies almost always have time to also be good industry citizens by belonging to various associations to promote the betterment of their industry...as well as time for training their employees and also providing training for customers?

Price versus Value

Balance the lowest bid against what you will actually get. Because your network will almost certainly grow in the future, a long-term vision—rather than short-term focus on costs—is a must. Service and support have value; expect to pay for them. In addition, carefully consider the pros and cons of a fixed fee basis arrangement with your network partner versus an hourly rate basis, and consider what each could mean to your project. How did the VAR/SI respond to your RFP? Are there any indications of how sensitive the firm will be to your needs or if the company is service-oriented?

Other Factors

What about the availability of remote dial-in support (which can save time and money) and online diagnostics and troubleshooting?

Experienced VARs/SIs will do a site survey for their protection and yours. This can ensure that the VAR/SI knows, understands, and accepts the environment that they will be working in. Computer systems are important only as a delivery vehicle for a particular solution. Hardware merely supports the functionality and reliability of the system. Understand the difference between a one-time purchase and the need for ongoing support.

Other issues to plan for include:

- security/virus protection
- backup/archiving
- disaster recovery
- inheritance plans (e.g.: who gets the "old" 386s when the newer 486s come in).

Network Management

One of the biggest areas of concern today is that of network management. Since there is no one clear cut definition, you must therefore decide what it means for your organization and its value. Certainly network planning must involve not only technology, but a way to accommodate new corporate demands. This includes the purchase of new hardware/software and whether to let new users on the network. In all cases, the consequences to the network must be analyzed before changes are made. Proper network management procedures for one company may be unacceptable to another.

Wrapping it up...

Overall, corporate computing end-users need to choose a network partner who will help make their organization strong, flexible, and ready to meet the business challenges of the 1990s.

It is especially important to know how your network operates when it's healthy so that you can tell when it's sick and diagnose problems more easily when they occur. Plan carefully, whether you're starting a new network or upgrading an existing one. Keep track of which users are accessing which file servers, e-mail servers, and printers. Measure network traffic periodically, at different times of the day, to get a feel for your network.

When selecting or re-evaluating a networking partner, remember the differences in:

- service levels and quality

- technical expertise in advanced technology

- superior knowledge of application or NOS (network operation system) software

- depth of after-sale support

Looking for help to solve your LAN/WAN/internetworking problems can be expensive—both in time and dollars. Organizations such as LANDA are an excellent way to hook up with those technically competent and savvy networking professionals who can provide solutions to your specific information integration problems.

LANDA currently has over 1,300 reseller, distributor and manufacturer member organizations. It is dedicated to promoting technical competence, professionalism and excellence in the networking arena.

Better Multivendor Computing Is OURS*

by the OURS Group
Written by:
Elaine Bond, President
Lee Bickmann, Consultant

Author Bios

Elaine R. Bond is a Chase Manhattan Fellow and a senior technology consultant for the Chase Manhattan Bank, N.A. Mrs. Bond served as senior vice president, corporate systems executive for 11 years before assuming her current responsibilities.

Active in her industry, she is a member of several N.Y. state and city advisory panels and a frequent speaker. Most recently she was instrumental in founding and has become chairman of an industry group named OURS, a worldwide not-for-profit group of industry users, vendors and service providers that addresses user needs in a multivendor environment.

Before joining Chase in 1981, Mrs. Bond was employed over a 24 year period by International Business Machines Corporation.

She is a director of the board of a publicly held insurance company, Washington National Corp., and is also secretary/treasurer of the Board of Trustees of the Circle Repertory Company, a not-for-profit theater company.

*Open User Recommended Solutions

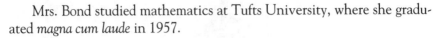

Mrs. Bond studied mathematics at Tufts University, where she graduated *magna cum laude* in 1957.

Mrs. Bond and her husband live in New York City.

Lee Bickmann worked on a number of senior technical staffs at IBM during a 25 year career, including tours of duty with development, manufacturing, marketing and service, both domestic and international. He is assisting the OURS group with membership recruiting, external relations, media communications, and OURS organizational practices and procedures.

Executive Summary

OURS will improve multivendor computing in several ways. It will help to focus the attention of user corporations and vendors on the right tactical issues. It will provide a forum for facilitating solutions, sometimes acting as a catalyst for the synergy that's waiting to happen, sometimes sponsoring projects and workshops. It will ensure that user recommendations take into full account the perspectives of both user and vendor members, and that vendor responses to the recommendations have plans for implementation built in. It will ensure through selective membership that the major perspectives on multivendor computing issues are fully represented and it will promote through the influential voice of its membership the steady, reliable progress of technology to address the needs of multivendor computing.

For information about OURS membership and a calendar of coming OURS events, please contact:

Lee Bickmann
PO Box 536
Stamford CT 06904-0536
203-325-4528

OURS Members

Avon Products, Incorporated
Brigham Young University
Business Systems Group
Centers for Disease Control
Chase Manhattan Bank
Chemical Waste Management, Incorporated
Church of Jesus Christ of Latter Day Saints
Digital Equipment Corporation
IBM Corporation
Intel Corporation
Levi Strauss & Company
Lotus Development Corporation
Lufthansa Airlines
Microsoft Corporation
Ministry of Trade and Industry of Mexico
Morgan, Lewis & Bockius
Motorola Corporation
Novell, Incorporated
Oracle Corporation
Pacific Gas & Electric Company
Rogers Cable Systems, Limited
Shell International Petroleum
Software AG of North America, Incorporated
Standard Microsystems Corporation
Tandem Computers, Incorporated
Telecom Australia
Texaco Chemical Company
US West Communications, Incorporated
Utah Information Technologies Association
Wells Fargo Bank
Ziff-Davis Laboratories

Better computing can be many things. Sometimes it's computing that's faster, or more secure, or more controlled, or more flexible, or anything else you can think of, depending on what the user expects from it.

For the purposes of this article, better computing is assumed to be the kind that takes maximum advantage of those technologies and products which can best meet the requirements of the user. Moreover, better computing is the kind that provides for innovation and for growth.

Better computing is often multivendor computing, because multivendor computing permits the user the widest latitude in the choice of technologies and products. Yet, in order for multivendor computing to be better computing, the question of interoperability must be resolved to ensure that products from different vendors can easily be integrated, managed, and maintained.

To bring about better multivendor computing takes deliberate and concerted effort on the part of users and vendors, which should come as no surprise. What may come as a surprise is that such a consortium of users and vendors has indeed been formed called OURS.

Trends and Troubles

It's not any secret that computing is steadily being dispersed from its original, centralized, mainframe-based blockhouses to networks of smaller processors which are, for the most part, in the hands of end users.

Accompanying the trend toward dispersal are several other related trends, including the emergence of the multivendor environment as a viable option for user corporations; an increasing complexity associated with the use of computers; and a declining opportunity for users to learn what they need to know about their computing environment, whether it be the one they wish to create, or the one that's already installed. As the hardware, software, and telecommunications components of computing have been growing more powerful and sophisticated, the ability to apply them to business problems has not kept pace. In some cases it has actually decreased.

Despite the best unilateral efforts of the most conscientious and diligent vendors, solutions are often hard for users to choose, hard to install, hard to interoperate, hard to learn, and hard to manage. Even after these solutions are in operation, they are often hard to exploit fully, both in terms of function and performance. It's not only the cost-effectiveness of the computing facilities themselves that is compromised, but also the productivity of the end users and the profits of the user corporations.

When there is a single vendor serving the needs of a user corporation, the usability of that vendor's products, and their ability to interoperate with other products (if so designed) are somewhat ensured. Two vendors can often work together fairly successfully. Three vendors might run into some problems. Generally speaking, the complexity of vendor cooperation can be proportional to the number of possible combinations of vendors, taking two at a time. This means, for example, that 5 vendors cooperating on a computing platform can have 10 times as much difficulty as would 2 vendors. What can be done about this nasty aspect of the open systems goal?

Available Remedies

If an important vendor objective is the assurance of open systems capabilities across multivendor products, the most appropriate route is most likely the standards route. In that case, vendors seeking to have their products interoperate with others can decide to implement the necessary standards as an integral part of design, and thereby ensure compatibility. Of course, the compatibility sometimes comes a little harder than that because standards often include optional as well as mandatory definitions.

Standards typically address a strategic rather than a tactical problem, which means that they don't offer much help in the near term. Also, they tend to deal with protocols and interfaces affecting the design and implementation of future products, rather than the operation of current ones.

The nearer term is often appropriately addressed by negotiations between user corporations and vendors, so that current or imminent product solutions can be made to work together in harmony. This is how operability problems have usually been addressed and often resolved: users of a vendor's products form a user group and leverage their common interests through unified action. Unfortunately, when inconsistencies among multiple vendors' products lie at the heart of the problem, single-vendor user groups do not have a forum for presenting their grievances all at once. They must carry their grievances from vendor to vendor, often hearing from each vendor that "it must be the other vendor's product." This is not necessarily an irresponsible vendor reaction, because from a unilateral vendor perspective its own product may well appear to be an "open" one.

Clearly, a multivendor user forum is needed. Indeed, such forums do exist, but they typically focus on very specific issues and the forums are usually *ad hoc* in nature. Furthermore, they generally operate in the same manner as single-vendor user groups, relying entirely on the synergy of users to provide the leverage for negotiating vendor cooperation.

All the above approaches are effective for their individual purposes, but a significant gap remains. A new kind of forum is needed where vendors and user corporations cooperate as equal members. In this situation users and vendors can jointly address near-term, tactical issues of interoperability, and apply the benefits of their unique perspectives toward the multilateral identification and resolution of important multivendor computing problems. OURS is just such a forum.

Key Issues

Three issues are crucial to better multivendor computing. One is a need for *information exchange:* an effective means for user corporations and vendors to share their respective knowledge about multivendor computing environments. Another is a need for *multivendor education:* formal education curricula designed cooperatively by vendors and user corporations. Users contribute requirements and vendors supply course material. The curriculum should provide the comprehensive education and training necessary to install and operate multivendor computing environments effectively. This is not a trivial exercise, as pointed out by Craig Goldman, chief information and technology officer of Chase Manhattan Bank, at the first OURS conference: "We need evaluations, plans and methodologies; and we need a product-to-product matrix of what works and what's been tested. We need performance and capacity information, and reliability statistics, and migration plans. We need standardized virus-testing criteria and certification. We need honest, open, and confidential interchange of information for any partnership to work." The third issue is *software licensing:* a need to develop a rationalized and standardized solution to the problems that arise from the varied terms and conditions of software licenses, especially in multivendor environments.

Concerted Approach

Tactical issues arising from multivendor computing need to be approached in a coordinated way. Of course, users have much to contribute about the problems they experience when they try to make essentially alien products interoperate. But these experiences have to be orchestrated with those of other users to produce the greatest influence on vendors. The vendors then have to work together to develop the appropriate responses to the problems. The close involvement of service providers, including resellers, consultants and system integrators, and other parties who support the implementation of multivendor computing, is necessary to ensure that recommended solutions are viable ones that can be successfully installed and operated. Most importantly, the concerted efforts of users, vendors, and service providers have to be non-competitive, non-argumentive, and synergistic.

OURS has implemented precisely this approach, and is in effect the answer to the questions raised by Peter Lewis, editor, reporter and columnist of *The New York Times*, at the OURS conference last March: "Why can't users and vendors get together to openly and honestly share information that will make it easier for me to buy and use computers, and easier for them to sell them? Why can't vendors cooperate with other vendors, and users with other users, all working together for the common good?" This is what OURS is all about.

How OURS Got Started

OURS was inspired by Ray Noorda, the founder and CEO of Novell, who by the time of PC Expo '91 had long been sounding out user communities on the need for a multivendor user group. The users were always favorable to the idea, but they took no action to make it happen. When Ray was invited to deliver the keynote address at PC Expo '91, he thought it would be a good opportunity to move things along.

Elaine Bond, then senior vice president, corporate systems, at Chase Manhattan Bank, received a call from Ray who asked her to join him in announcing the creation of OURS at PC Expo '91. Once she made that commitment, she went on to lead the effort that created OURS. She recruited and chaired an organizing committee of seven, which labored over the summer of 1991 and laid the groundwork for OURS.

In October, 1991, coincident with the NetWorld conference in Dallas, OURS was born. The basic organizational structure was agreed upon: OURS was to be a non-profit user group, with vendor and service-provider members having representation on the board of directors. Elaine Bond was elected chairman of the board and president of OURS. Issues were to be addressed by *ad hoc* committees, co-chaired by vendor and user members. Maximum use of volunteerism was to be relied upon to conduct the affairs of the group. The official mission of OURS was spelled out, emphasizing the importance of the user:

To promote interoperability of vendor products so that they may be easily integrated, managed and maintained in user computing environments in support of their organizations' objectives.

User members of OURS are committed to working with all other members in identifying tactical needs and recommending solutions. Vendor and service-provider members of OURS are committed to working with all other members in providing information, education, and workable responses to interoperability requirements. Thus, working together, OURS members achieve a perspective on interoperability issues that can't be gained unilaterally. As a result, solutions will have successful implementation built in.

The newly formed OURS group adopted as its first order of business an immediate focus on the three issues mentioned earlier: information exchange, multivendor education, and software licensing.

Information Technology Summit

In March, 1992, the members of OURS produced its first major event at Salt Lake City—the Information Technology Summit (ITS). The conference brought together executives from vendor and user corporations to work out cooperative approaches to multivendor computing issues. The conference was attended by OURS members, along with over 100 other executives and senior members of the information systems management community.

Keynote speakers at the conference included the aforementioned Craig Goldman, Peter Lewis, and Ray Noorda.

Three workshops at the conference addressed the issues of information exchange, multivendor education, and software licensing, and this work resulted in the creation and chartering of three task forces to continue the efforts under the auspices of OURS.

A survey conducted at the ITS conference produced high marks for OURS, with over 70% of the participants reporting that the workshops were effective and met their expectations. Over 80% indicated that they would be interested in participating in future conferences and workshops.

More About OURS

As of summer 1992, OURS had more than 30 members and was rapidly growing (see the recent membership roster earlier in this paper). In line with the objectives of OURS, most of the members are user corporations, but by September about a dozen major vendor corporations and several key service providers were on board to give the growing organization a healthy mix of viewpoints. OURS growth will be managed carefully to preserve this mix, and in accordance with the belief that it can help to effect significant solutions through the actions of a relatively small but highly influential consortium.

The task forces on information exchange, multivendor education, and software licensing are preparing to conduct new workshops at the OURS Fall Conference in October, as a continuation of the work they have been doing since March. Already, OURS members are becoming privileged subscribers to an electronic mail network that will be the online vehicle for information exchange among all members. Similarly, the multivendor education task force is defining a core curriculum addressing key multivendor education requirements.

And, if there needed to be proof that synergy really works, some of the vendor and user members of OURS have begun a dialog intended to produce some type of a "what works with what" deliverable.

Communicating Naturally in the Digitized World

by Nolan Bushnell
Chairman, OCTuS

Author Bio

Nolan Bushnell is one of Silicon Valley's early computer pioneers. He founded Atari in 1972 with the invention of PONG and thus started the video game industry. In 1977 he opened the first Chuck E. Cheese restaurant, which combined fast food, electronic games, and musical entertainment by computer-animated robot characters. Bushnell founded Catalyst Technologies in 1981 as an "incubator" to mass-produce small businesses. A partial list of the companies founded by Catalyst includes ACTV, Axion, Androbot, ByVideo, Compower, Etak, and Magnum Microwave. Bushnell is currently chairman of OCTuS, a San Diego-based company that is developing a user interface to unify all forms of communication on computer and telephone networks.

Executive Summary

We humans have always divided our time between two primary activities: work and play. Work values and play values have always defined and characterized cultures. For the past 25 years, technology has been bringing those two activities—those two environments—together in ways never before possible. I've been intimately involved in this development in both the work and play environments. I believe an acceleration of the merging of these two environments through the merging of the communication, computer, and entertainment industries is going to happen in the next decade. To get there, the physical layers of networks, including the telephone network, will become irrelevant. The user interface layer will reflect humans' natural communications tendencies. This means that ease of use will become an absolute requirement, and the technology behind this front end will become sophisticated and flexible enough to reflect peoples' virtual realities. The real challenges ahead in creating these ideal systems will be dealing with diverse network and communication standards as well as creating an interface that is responsive to individuals' sensory preferences. This development will cause a great deal of chaos and a great deal of opportunity in our public and private lives, at work and at home. The results will benefit all consumers. This development will also reorganize and reconstruct our communities. It will ultimately reinforce and redefine values both locally and globally.

The Convergence of Network Technologies

In the computer industry, there is a great deal of attention being paid to networks and networking; everyone is talking about LANs and WANs and enterprise networks. Discussions about the benefits and inevitability of networks eventually turn to discussions of the hardware and software components of networks. Usually, in all this talk about networks, the most powerful and ubiquitous worldwide network is rarely mentioned—the telephone network.

As the telephone business becomes more and more digital, and as modems become faster and faster, the distinctions between computer local area networks, wide area networks, telephone networks, and even cable TV networks and cellular networks will decrease. The communication distinctions will blur first of all at the physical layer. After all, bits are bits, and how we move them and in what form, whether over fiber, copper, or airwaves, and with what protocol become less important, particularly as bandwidths increase.

As the physical layer becomes irrelevant and invisible to communication, design challenges of the future will focus on making the operating system and application level equally irrelevant and invisible. One of the foremost design criteria will be ease of use.

Ease of Use Drives Acceptance

We use several devices to communicate both locally and globally. At work we place and receive phone calls and try to remember how to forward a voice-mail message with the same device. We use a different device, the PC, to access the company's database and to send and receive mail messages. In most cases, we also generate a document on that device, print it on a printer, and then send that document through another device, the fax machine.

Technology is now reaching a point where we will soon be able to unify all of these different messaging devices under what is being commonly referred to as computer-telephone integration (CTI). Simply put, hardware and software will be available that will enable us to use the desktop PC and phone for voice, voice mail, e-mail, data, fax, graphics, and video transactions. For example, we will be able to set up a conference call from a phone list on our PC screen and share a document with the conference participants. We will be able to immediately fax someone a document while we are on the phone with them. We will be able to create a document and simultaneously fax, print, and e-mail it. We will be able to have real-time groupware and screen sharing.

But the unification of computer and telephone technology that will make this all possible has many requirements. There is necessary hardware, from integrated chip sets to boards and interconnects between the phone, PC, and PBX. There also needs to be software applications that are powerful and cost-effective. As spreadsheets and word processing drove the market for PCs, I believe multimedia business applications will drive the CTI market. Government regulations, issues of standardizing interfaces and APIs, and the requirement for cross-platform communication will create the chaos I mentioned earlier.

There is also the issue of a common user interface. CTI will add powerful features and functions at the desktop, but without a standard interface that provides easy and unified access to those features and functions, they will go unused or underused. We see an example of this underuse happening today with fax, e-mail, and printing. Many companies are offering partial solutions to all of these functions, both as stand-alone and on PC LANs. However, there is no unification. One must jump from one application to another in order to fax, e-mail, and print.

Take fax as a specific example. Currently, less than 5 percent of the installed base of LANs are equipped with fax services. In addition to the interface issue, I believe that there are two other reasons for underuse:

- Most users don't understand the benefits and applications of network communication services.

- Most vendors view communications as a network application, rather than a network service. We are seeing the same kind of stand-alone product implementation for voice and telephony from most vendors. The same thing is true with powerful telephone features made inaccessible because of obscure codes and protocols. They are all being unused or underused because of their user "unfriendliness."

We need to take the point of view that fax, voice, and telephony should be available as services, not applications, on the network. This needs to be extended so that stand-alone home, mobile, and small office communications products will be inherently "network aware" so that users have the ability to locally or remotely plug into network services. The telephone and cable TV companies are uniquely positioned to provide this remote link. I envision consumer demand soon driving fiber-optics wiring installations into homes.

Indeed, fax, voice, and telephony should be as transparently available to all applications as are network printers. The market for products that can provide this and the applications and services associated with them is in the hundreds of billions of dollars.

The Fundamental Issue of Communication

Until now I really have been talking around some fundamental issues. What do I mean by "communication," "network," and "information"?

I believe that when we read a book, watch television, work at a computer, or play a video game, we are in an "information environment." Networking is fundamentally about communications and the importance of communications in the way people actually create, organize, exchange, and use information. When it comes to communication, we humans are primarily parallel in and serial out. We can take intellectual input both visually and aurally simultaneously. However, our primary means of intellectual output, such as speech, writing, and drawing, are serial.

So what we really want is to have our electronic communication systems reflect our natural communication tendencies. A successful system will have a high degree of virtuality. People should be able to work (and play) with information naturally, manipulate data comfortably, and share information easily. We need to create systems that enable a person to utilize the tremendous bandwidth of input we have and process and exchange our information on the output wave as quickly and efficiently as possible. When we're in the output mode, we want to maximize the continuity process of the way we think or express that thought. Some people like to type, some people like to dictate, others prefer masses of legal pads or large white boards. Whatever a person's preferred method, we must create an electronic system which outputs in a message form that can be as easily created and sent as possible.

In my own case, I would rather view something than listen, but I would rather dictate a memo or letter than type it. I also like to illustrate what I am discussing on a white board. I need a system that invisibly, easily, and flexibly accommodates my preferred methods of input and output, which, by the way, may change depending on the content of my current task.

I believe also that the message type is less important than the message content, but what is most important is the message source. We don't want to scan our messages based on whether the message is a fax, a piece of mail, a voice mail, or an e-mail. What we really want to do is find out what are all the messages that have come from a certain person or group of people, people with whom we are working on high-priority projects. The system we want has to allow messages of any form to be sorted by predetermined criteria and then presented to us in the method easiest to view and respond to.

All messages should be readable; even voice mail should be readable. Most people who have had to deal with even small volumes of voice mail will agree that there are few things in life more tedious than the serial process of listening to voice mail messages. The system now has the additional requirement of message form conversion—in this case, voice mail to text.

So I'll put my personal system together. On my computer screen (and this can be my screen at home, at work, or on my portable in a hotel room) I have an in-box with messages from various people whom I have prioritized. I can activate the computer through screen touch, keyboard, mouse, or voice. I can read voice mail messages, or I can both read and listen to a message if, for instance, it is a voice annotated document. I can scan my e-mail messages and respond to them with a voice message. I can dictate a document and read it as I am speaking. The communication and resultant productivity possibilities go on and on. The features of this system are based on the technology advancements possible with the integration of the computer and telephone addressed earlier.

The Challenge

Designers of these new systems will have to deal with some subtleties that have not been dealt with before. The interface to a world of information can't merely be about representing information, it must be about doing things with the information, from experiencing it to more subtle goals, such as identifying the author's point of view. We need to create systems that can generate multiple representations of information, that are responsive to an individual's sensory characteristics, skills, and needs.

What this means is that communications and computer designers must broaden their focus from machines that merely generate information to the virtual worlds people experience. In most instances, the entertainment industry is farther ahead in this development phase than the communications or computer industries. Consumer electronics is really on the leading edge of interface issues. For years, entertainment and consumer electronics have been successfully modifying computer and communications technology for their consumers. The computer and communications industries need to begin taking a look at what entertainment and consumer electronics have found out about users. Entertainment is really the economic justification for the merging technologies; after all, there are more consumers than there are businesses.

It gets back to one of my strong beliefs: information technologies, whether at work or play, have a personal and social context. Information technologies have been coevolving with human organizations since our ancestors drew pictures on rocks. Evolving information environments have always brought with them wholesale community reconstruction. The merging of the telecommunications, computer, and entertainment industries over the next decade is going to have a greater impact on our lives than the combined individual impacts of these three industries over the past 25 years. At the very least, the information age will finally become fully participatory.

Server-Based: To Be or Not to Be? That is the Question!

by Cheyenne Software, Inc.

Author Bio

 Cheyenne Software, Inc.

Cheyenne Software, founded in 1983 and publicly held since 1985, is a leader in the development of sophisticated local area networking (LAN) management software products.

Cheyenne Software was founded with a mission to develop problem-solving software and create the tools needed to ease the day-to-day pressures associated with managing and controlling a growing network: security, backup, and management. The unique architecture of Cheyenne's products centralizes the "service" component on the network to operate from a strategic location, the file server. As a result, the traditional file server is transformed into a platform on which a variety of integrated services, such as backup and restore, network management, facsimile and security services, can be built.

Cheyenne was one of the first software development companies to pursue the vision of server-based solutions. The company has engineered its products with an architecture based on the client/server model, enabling Cheyenne to maximize the strength, performance, and integration capabilities available in the file server. ARCserve, Cheyenne's backup and restore solution, remains the industry's only true server-based backup and restore product.

Cheyenne's assistance in developing Novell's backup device interface for NetWare 3.11 is well known in the industry. The company's products, ARCserve, ARCserve/Solo, Monitrix, InocuLAN, FAXserve, and Cheyenne Utilities, are marketed on an international basis through strategic OEM partnerships as well as an extensive distribution network.

Executive Summary

How do you develop problem solving software and create the tools needed to ease the day-to-day pressures associated with managing and controlling a growing network? The following paper discusses the advantages and benefits associated with using server-based software applications in three primary areas of concern: network backup, security, and management.

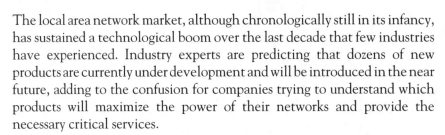

The local area network market, although chronologically still in its infancy, has sustained a technological boom over the last decade that few industries have experienced. Industry experts are predicting that dozens of new products are currently under development and will be introduced in the near future, adding to the confusion for companies trying to understand which products will maximize the power of their networks and provide the necessary critical services.

How do you develop problem solving software and create the tools needed to ease the day-to-day pressures associated with managing and controlling a growing network: security, backup, and management? In the "good old days" these types of services were only available in a mainframe environment. By centralizing the "service" component on the network to operate from a strategic location, however, the traditional file server is transformed into a platform on which a variety of integrated services, such as data and network management, facsimile, and security services, can be built. This eliminates frustration and the need for additional hardware.

In addition, the network speed and flexibility once considered negligible have become the competitive stage on which many hardware vendors perform. The right software application, specifically server-based applications, can provide vendors with the differential they need to shine in the light of such intense competition.

The following are brief discussions of the advantages and benefits associated with using server-based software applications in the three primary areas of concern: network backup, security, and management.

Backup

Traditionally, tape backup devices have required a dedicated backup workstation reserved solely for backups at designated times. This workstation needed to be logged into the network on supervisor status to access attached workstations and servers to perform backups. This approach significantly limited performance as network data traveled from a server (or workstation) across the network (typically EtherNet or ARCnet) to the backup workstation. Wire speeds were typically in the 8–10 megabyte per minute range, rendering it impossible to backup large networks encompassing a substantial level of data in the traditional backup window of opportunity (after business hours). In addition to the limited speed and performance capabilities, security issues were prevalent while the workstation remained logged in throughout the backup process, providing an easy point of entry for any user regardless of their rights on the network. This security loophole is unavoidable with a workstation-based solution.

In 1989 the introduction of a Novell NetWare server-based backup application revolutionized network data management and tape backup. This application, ARCserve, developed by Cheyenne Software, required the tape drive to be connected to the file server. The connection allows data to pass directly from the server hard disk drive across the bus to the tape drive. This configuration eliminated the need for critical network data (located on the file server) to travel across the network wire to a backup device. Performance is unaffected by wire speeds, therefore backup speeds in excess of 55 megabytes per minute can be achieved.

An increasing number of backup applications within the Novell NetWare operating environment are being developed as server-based applications. Not all server-based backup applications maintain true "client-server" architecture. Client-server backup applications are those applications whose client "front-end" (user interface) is located on a workstation rather than accessing the application via the NetWare server console. When a user submits a job for data movement, such as backup, restore, and archive, the server portion of the software actually performs the work. The user in turn becomes the client of their server, submitting jobs or requests for data transfer. There are many distinct advantages associated with client-server architecture, including: increased flexibility in operating applications from anywhere within the network, increased performance through the elimination of traffic on the LAN, and enhanced security of the file server resulting from the inability of unauthorized users to access the server.

Security

Network security can be defined on several different levels, but the most serious and potentially damaging security threat to "hit" LANs in recent years has been the computer virus. Computer viruses are a growing problem that can only be effectively dealt with by practicing safe computing and by purchasing an antivirus product.

Perhaps more important than buying an antivirus product is having it resident and up-to-date on your PC at all times. In a recent study commissioned by members of the National Computer Securities Association and conducted by Dataquest, the average company owned 2.3 antivirus products. However, the study also concluded that only 15 percent of all PCs actually had protective software loaded and running. With so few PCs protected, it is not surprising that more companies are reporting virus attacks. The question is, why are so few users protected?

There are five main reasons why users do not have adequate protection installed on their PCs/Networks.

1. Workstation-based only antivirus products require a high degree of intervention by generally uneducated users.

2. Many workstation-based products require frequent manual updating.

3. Traditional workstation-based antivirus products require a large amount of RAM.

4. Scanners produce a great many false alarms or fail to detect even the most common viruses.

5. Users often remove antivirus software from their autoexec.bat files because of reasons stated in 3 or 4.

Server-based applications, that is, those that run as NetWare Loadable Modules (NLMs) or Value Added Programs (VAPs), offer several distinct advantages over workstation applications. Client-server architecture allows the LAN Administrator to centralize applications on the file server, thus enabling the administrator to control access to the LAN and ensure that all users have the necessary applications installed on their workstations. An antivirus product which resides on the server not only protects all server volumes, directories, and files against infection, but could protect the workstations as well. A server component coupled with a workstation TSR (Terminate-and-Stay-Resident) program effectively eliminates all entry points for viruses.

Many workstation-based antivirus products scan server volumes on demand. However, this type of scanning often requires a dedicated PC and causes extensive network traffic. Applications running as a VAP/NLM operate completely in the background, requiring minimal interaction. In addition, they can guarantee notification of virus activity to selected users and LAN Administrators. Further, server scanning by a VAP/NLM minimizes performance degradation and traffic problems on the LAN.

Server-based applications can continuously monitor workstations to ensure that they have workstation TSRs loaded. The most prevalent problem with workstation antivirus software is that most users don't have it loaded; using a VAP/NLM will ensure that an unprotected workstation never gains access to the LAN. Even a sophisticated hacker would have extreme difficulty bypassing this check by the VAP/NLM.

Workstation antivirus protection generally provides real-time virus protection through a TSR on that workstation only. Workstations can be configured to scan server volumes, but only at prescheduled intervals or on demand. Real-time protection at the server provides continuous monitoring of all files as they enter or exit the server. Since LAN infections double every six minutes (according to a Brightwork Study), scanning at intervals is simply not enough. Real-time protection at the server is the only way to ensure that the network remains virus free.

Finally, server-based antivirus software eliminates the time-consuming task of updating workstations with new virus signatures. NLMs provide a convenient vehicle to deliver new signatures to workstations as users log in. A simple update program is installed in the systems login script which will compare the signature file on the server with that of the workstation. If a workstation is found to be running an old version of the application, it is automatically updated.

Server-based antivirus software represents a new generation in security applications. Providing complete control to the LAN administrator, these applications substantially reduce the risk of an unsuspecting user infecting the LAN. They eliminate the tedious task of manually updating individual workstations and protect the most vital information resource on the network: the file server.

Management

One of the key aspects of managing a sophisticated LAN is to maximize the use of the available hardware components, reduce expenditures for additional hardware, provide more automated services to users, and increase productivity. The introduction of server-based facsimile services caters to each of these objectives. Providing network users with access to facsimile services from their workstations enables a LAN administrator to more fully use the existing power of the file server without purchasing a dedicated workstation, fax server, or fax machine. It also automates a service which traditionally has been time consuming and inefficient: waiting in line for the fax machine.

Computer facsimile was first introduced in late 1984. It wasn't until four years later that users started "en masse" to install fax cards in their PCs. Users instantly realized the benefits of computer-based fax, including reduced costs, ease-of-use, and quality of transmission. LAN fax solutions began to experience a similar growth one year later. As other users witnessed their colleagues utilizing this powerful application, they wanted it, too. Rather than installing a fax card in every PC, LAN fax solutions were pursued which allowed the configuration of a centralized "fax server." This fax server was a dedicated PC where all the fax cards resided. Jobs were queued on either the file server or the fax server for eventual transmission through the fax server. This solution allowed all network users to enjoy the benefits of computer-based fax without the additional costs of purchasing their own fax boards and installing telephone lines.

Dedicated network fax servers require the cost of purchasing/maintaining an additional node on the network. In addition, these centralized fax servers often provide security loopholes and traffic bottlenecks. Both the industry file server hardware and the NetWare 3.x network operating system have become so robust and powerful that it is now more efficient to provide LAN fax as a service within the network file server.

Server-based facsimile software should allow the user to prepare documents in their DOS, Windows, or even e-Mail application, and define when, where, and to whom the document will be sent. Users save on hardware because no dedicated workstation is required as a fax server, and save on maintenance because one less node is required on the LAN. With an NLM, security risks are reduced because phone books, logs, and faxes are protected under the NetWare security. Also, server-based technology eliminates unnecessary LAN traffic because files are sent directly between the client to the server.

Time and time again, we see the advantages of server-based applications in all areas of network management and service. Efficient, effective, automated procedures—the list goes on and on. So, *Server-Based: To Be or Not to Be? Is there really a question?*

Redefining Adapter Performance

by Jeff Chumbley
Director of Product Marketing, Thomas-Conrad Corporation

Author Bio

Jeff Chumbley is the director of product marketing for Thomas-Conrad Corporation, an Austin, Texas, manufacturer of token ring, EthernNet, ARCnet and 100Mbps (megabits per second) TCNS hardware, and Sectra network management software. Chumbley has served as network administrator for large corporate networks, assisted users as a NetWire SysOp for several years, written several articles on networking, and recently published the *LAN Desktop Guide to Printing*, NetWare Edition (Sams, 1992).

Executive Summary

Networking software recently began to take advantage of the available high performance hardware platforms. While hardware or software

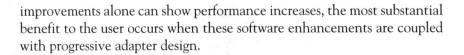

improvements alone can show performance increases, the most substantial benefit to the user occurs when these software enhancements are coupled with progressive adapter design.

Finding (and eliminating) performance bottlenecks is a goal of every network manager. Whether you have a three node NetWare Lite system or a 3,000 node campus wide or company wide network, performance is always a top consideration. Recent changes in software enable network managers to squeeze more and more throughput from their nets, but software alone can't provide all the performance improvements that are available. The hardware must be able to support the new software designs and features before the enhancements can really be noticed.

The first question that always enters a discussion about performance is which network protocol is best. The ARCnet versus EtherNet versus token ring question has consumed hundreds of hours, countless magazine pages, and megabytes of CompuServe message space. The problem with most of these discussions is they never seem to focus on the real bottlenecks or the real solutions. Often, the implementation needs improvement, not the protocol.

As anyone familiar with performance testing of networking hardware and software can tell you, the adapter interface, driver quality, operating system, network configuration, machine capabilities, and test suites have as much (or more) effect on the test results as the protocol. With properly designed networks, capable machines, and fair test suites, three variables can be removed from the performance equation. Now the differences lie primarily in the hardware, the supporting drivers, and the capabilities of the operating systems used.

Bus Mastering

Adapter hardware for token ring and EtherNet is available in a wide range of price and performance models, from simple 8-bit adapters with relatively slow shared memory or programmed I/O interfaces to 16- or 32-bit bus master adapters. With nonbus master adapters, the CPU must suspend processing and move data packets to and from the adapter whenever the adapter requests. With slow adapters and busy networks, this demand can put a real strain on system resources. The CPU spends significant time just getting packets on and off the adapter. Bus master adapters, especially when combined with machines having processor cache, offer significant performance improvements. The improvements come by moving data from the adapter to system memory without CPU intervention, thereby leaving the CPU free to continue processing data rather than servicing adapters.

Machines that run multitasking operating systems, such as NetWare 386, OS/2, the upcoming Windows NT, and even applications such as Windows, benefit more from enhanced adapter design than do straight DOS machines. With DOS, when a packet is requested the CPU would not be doing much anyway. The last request was "get this data," and so the CPU waits for the data. When the data arrives, the CPU services it and presents it for the application. Freeing the CPU for other tasks is not particularly useful, because the "other task" is to wait for the packet. Multitasking operating systems are another story. In almost every case, the CPU could continue processing other application time slices while one application waits on a data packet.

Drivers

Adapter drivers are an important part of the performance equation. Small changes within a driver can result in huge performance differences. Poorly written adapter drivers require the adapter to do more actual work, and the CPU must spend much more time moving data to and from the adapter. Bus master adapters' drivers are especially critical. If the driver doesn't transfer data directly from the adapter into the proper memory location, the data must be moved twice (called a double copy)—which can be a real performance hit.

Drivers need to be flexible and reliable. Handling bad packets and other errors in an appropriate manner is normally the responsibility of the driver. Efficiency in design allows drivers to load into the smallest memory space possible and to use Virtual DMA Services when appropriate memory managers are available.

Packet Burst NCP

In addition to software enhancements such as multitasking, NOS protocol changes are occurring that enable bigger performance improvements from adapter hardware. Novell's packet burst NCP protocol improves network performance by reducing the number of requests necessary to move data. Without packet burst, NetWare requests are limited to 4K in size. The workstation makes 16 requests to read in a 64K file from the server. The server must process the 16 requests and initiate 16 response packets to the workstation. With packet burst, up to 64K of data can be requested at one time, reducing the number of request packets sent by the workstation and processed by the file server to just one. The actual data packets currently are limited to 4K, so you still have 16 responses to move the data back to the workstation.

These 16 responses are where adapter design again comes into play. Packet burst is a self-pacing protocol, which allows it to work as efficiently as possible without overrunning the workstation. Slow adapters take too much time moving data off the adapter and don't have sufficient throughput to enable the file server to send the 16 responses quickly. Overall, the workstation doesn't get the data any faster than if it had simply requested the 16 packets one at a time, as it did without packet burst.

Packet burst is most beneficial for workstations when used in conjunction with bus mastering adapters. Because the server sends several responses to the workstation in each burst, the workstation's CPU can start processing the first of the packets while the adapter continues to receive the remaining ones. This parallel processing decreases the total elapsed time between reception of the first packet and final processing of the last packet in the burst.

Frame Sizes and Adapter RAM

Another way of increasing efficiency on the network is to increase the size of the data frames being transferred over the network. The bigger the data frames, the fewer needed to move the same amount of data. Token ring (running at 16Mbps) operates with frame sizes of 18K. Operating systems and LAN drivers taking advantage of the larger packet sizes demand more from the adapter hardware. The adapters must be able to buffer larger packets and to move an increased amount of data (larger packets) each time.

Unfortunately, adapter memory already limits some token ring adapters to smaller frame sizes when operating in certain modes, such as when loading part of the driver into adapter memory. The memory constraints will hinder these adapters more and more as the frame size continues to grow. Even without taking away part of adapter memory for the driver, token ring adapters limited to 128K of memory are likely to receive congestion errors as the frame sizes grow towards 18K.

Adapters with upgradable memory will provide better performance and increased reliability. Memory sizes of 512K or even 1M or more may be required to operate in busy networks with 18K frames. Offloading drivers to the adapter to reduce workstation memory certainly will make the increased memory a requirement—if the adapter is to maintain an acceptable level of performance.

Increased Data Rates

One obvious way to improve performance is to increase the data rate of the protocol. Given equally high-quality, properly designed adapters, 2.5Mbps ARCnet will be slower than 4Mbps token ring, which will be slower than 10Mbps EtherNet, which will be slower than 16Mbps token ring. As mentioned earlier, sufficiently poor designs are available in any of these protocols to change the ordering manner any way desired. All things being equal, however, the data rates of the protocols will determine the performance ordering.

With each increase in data rates, new thresholds are crossed. No threshold is more significant than the cabling. Not long ago, the industry was working on a way to get EtherNet to work on UTP, 4Mbps token ring was questionable on UTP, and 16Mbps token ring mandated STP cabling. With improvements in adapter designs and cable quality, UTP is an accepted standard for all these protocols and data rates.

If your performance needs are beyond what the standard protocols can deliver, the next step is a 100Mbps product like TCNS or FDDI. The goal of TCNS is to deliver 100Mbps performance to the desktop at a low cost. For less than the price of a token ring adapter, the bottlenecks of the network are virtually eliminated. Single station performance goes well beyond what is capable on even a fully utilized token ring or EtherNet network.

Should you need to continue utilizing "standards" accepted protocols, FDDI remains the only high speed alternative at this time. FDDI and the copper-based implementations have been a long time in ramping up to the reputation that has preceded them. Even now as more and more product comes to the market, performance of the adapters is lackluster. Most FDDI adapters available deliver performance similar to EtherNet or 16Mbps token ring.

But don't blame FDDI. The potential is there to deliver FDDI adapter products that outperform other protocols significantly. There appears to have been more of a focus on standards compliance and copper-based implementations than on actually making the adapters perform. That's unfortunate, because one of the main reasons for choosing FDDI in the first place is to achieve performance levels that are (or should be) unattainable with EtherNet or token ring.

Beyond 100Mbps live the gigabit networks. Although they are still in the lab stage, gigabit LANs have the potential to displace FDDI before FDDI even gets started—and at 10 times the data rate. If a standards approved product is into the market before FDDI has a strong hold, it has the opportunity to do quickly what FDDI has been promising—offer high reliability and blistering speed.

Reliability

Reliability is one of the often neglected aspects of the performance equation. The speed of a network doesn't really matter if it isn't available. As mission-critical applications migrate to the network, the importance of network availability, ease of troubleshooting, and need for fault recovery increases. Remember, the adapter must handle every byte of data that moves across the network without corrupting a single bit.

Conclusion

Putting together a fast, reliable network doesn't just happen. Choosing adapter hardware that has features and capabilities that can grow with your needs is critical if you want to be able to use tomorrow's software when it becomes available. Progressive adapter design doesn't just solve yesterday's problems today; it also provides a base for solving tomorrow's problems.

The Evolution of the Global Data Network

by Patrick H. Corrigan
Managing Director, The Corrigan Group

Author Bio

Patrick H. Corrigan is the Managing Director of The Corrigan Group, a consulting and training firm based in Sausalito, California. He is a nationally recognized authority on local area networks and is the coauthor of *Building Local Area Networks with Novell's NetWare* (M&T Books). Mr. Corrigan lectures and teaches extensively in the areas of LAN management, planning, and design and has written numerous articles on LAN-related topics. His consulting work focuses on LAN system planning, management, disaster prevention and recovery, and LAN product marketing. Mr. Corrigan is a member of the NetWorld Dallas Advisory Board and is a frequent speaker at industry events such as NetWorld, PC Expo, UNIX Expo, Netcom, NETUCON, and LANDEX. Mr. Corrigan can be reached through CompuServe at 75170,146.

Executive Summary

The desktop computer revolution spawned the local area network revolution. Now, the need to share information is creating the wide area network revolution and a global data network. The process will not be easy, with roadblocks, problems, pitfalls, and cultural and economic changes along the way.

Eight or nine short years ago, anyone who suggested that networks of PCs could someday replace mainframes would probably have been considered a fool at best and a dangerous lunatic at worst. But in many organizations, that is exactly what has happened. In others, the mainframe is still in place, but many mission-critical applications have been moved to networked desktop computers.

The early 1980s saw the beginning of the desktop computer revolution, which, after many fits and starts, finally took off in earnest with the introduction of the IBM PC. In the mid 1980s, a new revolution began: Local Area Networking.

Although local area networks had existed since the 1970s, they were used primarily by a few universities and high-tech companies to connect terminals to minicomputers and mainframes. The widespread use of desktop computers, however, moved LANs into the mainstream.

What started as a way of connecting a few PCs together for information and resource sharing has become the preferred method for creating large, complex computing systems. Today's LANs include IBM PC-compatibles, Apple Macintoshes, UNIX workstations, file servers, database servers, time-sharing minicomputers, and gateways to mainframes. In fact, the LAN has become the universal data system: it allows connection to virtually any and all available data processing resources.

The use of LANs has grown in the desktop computer environment because data and information do not exist in a vacuum—they are almost always created to be shared in some fashion. The floppy disk, the original method of sharing PC data, quickly proved to be inadequate to the task. It is fine for one-way transmission of data, but when files are moved back and forth between PCs in this manner, they soon get out-of-sync, with older versions getting edited instead of the most current ones.

In addition, floppy disk exchange doesn't allow for concurrent database sharing and updating, so building a PC-based company or departmental database was impossible.

To alleviate these problems, and also to allow sharing of printers and other peripherals, users installed LANs. Even though those early systems were not without problems, they did make information sharing easier.

Over the years, LAN hardware and software has become much more reliable. We are now no longer trying to just make the technology work—we are trying to add functionality.

But just as we need to share information with those within an office, we also need to share with others outside the office. We need to share information with, among others, branch offices, customers, and suppliers.

Just as desktop computers created the LAN revolution, LANs are creating a revolution of their own—Wide Area Networking. Yes, wide area networks have existed for some time, but the need for LAN-to-LAN communication is expanding the market dramatically. As WAN usage is going up, new companies seeing new opportunities are entering the WAN market. This increased competition is beginning to force the costs of WAN hardware, software, and connections down. At the same time, new technology, the result of competitive forces, is providing increased bandwidth—the ability to carry more data at higher speeds.

Until recently, the world of wide area networking has been somewhat elitist—reserved for the anointed few who understand the terminology and technology and can find their way through the myriad pieces of hardware, software, and communications links needed to establish a wide-area connection.

This point was brought home to me a few years ago when I attended the now-defunct Interface Show. Three technologies were displayed under one roof: voice communications, wide area data communications, and local area networking. This could just as well have been three different shows, however, because the three groups had such different vocabularies that there was no communication between them. For me, with my personal computer and LAN background, it was impossible to find a common ground from which I could start a meaningful conversation with a data communications vendor.

This is changing. Data communications terminology is finding its way into the PC and LAN literature, and LAN administrators, designers, and installers are educating themselves about wide area technology.

At best, the equivalent of bumpy back roads now form our wide area networks. Narrow and full of potholes, they make our cross-country data trek slow and difficult. This too is changing. Those back roads are being pushed aside as we build the interstate highways of data communications. Our individual networks are becoming part of a global internetwork, connecting nearly all data systems at reasonably high speeds.

This interconnection and globalization of networks will not be without problems—one being data security, another being bandwidth, and a third being product compatibility. When local networks are connected to the global network, the opportunities for unauthorized access are increased. For evidence of this, read Cliff Stoll's book, *The Cuckoo's Egg,* which documented the activities of a West German cracker as he broke into computers connected to the Internet.

As the use of available wide area connections increases, bandwidth available for each given user will decrease. New services will become available, but there will be a lag between demand and delivery.

For product compatibility, the third problem mentioned, vendors of bridges, routers, and multiplexers have traditionally attempted to lock their clients in by using proprietary approaches. Industry standards, both *de facto* and *de jure*, are helping to alleviate this problem.

There are many bottlenecks in the wide area path, both technological and political. Among the bottlenecks we face are the local telephone companies. The telcos, as they are called, are promoting switched 56Kbps service and Integrated Services Digital Network (ISDN) as the ways to solve your data communications problems. Unfortunately, often these services are available only at some locations, and usually not your locations. These services also are too slow for most LAN-to-LAN communications.

While fractional T-1, frame relay, and other moderate-to-high-speed services are being provided by long-haul carriers at nearly affordable prices, the local connection to those services, where available, is usually prohibitively expensive.

The telcos seem locked in the past, still thinking in terms of mainframes and terminals rather than LANs and PCs. They seem to think in terms of a few connections at a high price rather than a lot of connections at a low price. The regulatory agencies don't seem to be a lot of help in this area, usually listening to the telcos, rather than the users, for guidance.

If the telcos continue to drag their feet on delivering cost-effective, interoperable digital services, others will see opportunity and find a way to deliver high-speed data services to your door. If the cable television providers, whose territory is being invaded by the telcos, were smart, they would be looking at this.

The biggest problems, however, will not be technical or political; they will be cultural. The global data network has the potential of creating vast cultural changes throughout the world. It will change the ways companies do business and the ways that individuals work. For information-based businesses, location of companies and individuals becomes less important. Telecommuting, or working from home while exchanging data electronically, a practice currently available to a limited few, could become widespread. Distributed workgroups and distributed offices may become common. Network directory structures, such as ISO's X.500, Banyan's StreetTalk, and Novell's NetWare Directory Services, make distributed computing even easier.

If this occurs, it will have a direct impact on the environment and the economy. When it becomes easier to transmit data electronically than it is to print it and distribute it on paper, the "paperless office" might become a reality. Fewer people commuting to and from the office could mean less air pollution. It also could mean that fewer cars will be built, which would have a definite impact on the economies of the industrialized nations. Of course, every major technological change has had similar impact—look at what the automobile did to the horse and buggy business, or what FAX has done to the postal service.

If the location of a residence in relation to a workplace becomes less important, it could create a major impact on the structure of cities and suburbs.

Will these changes make the world a better place? Like other major technological changes, there probably will be both positive and negative effects. We can only hope that, overall, the benefits will outweigh the drawbacks.

Where do we fit in? We are participants in the beginning of a new era. Our actions can influence the structure of the global network.

Should we drive on the left side or the right side of the road? Should we use a steering stick or a steering wheel? What will be the rules of the road? Those questions were answered for us by early users of the automobile. As early users of the global data network, we will be providing similar answers for those that follow us.

As users of wide area products and services, there are several things that you can do now:

- Don't accept closed, proprietary solutions that lock you in to a single vendor.

- Put pressure on the telcos and regulatory agencies to deliver the services that meet your needs, not the services that provide the most profit.

- Try before you buy. Arrange with the hardware vendor, software vendor, and the carrier for a trial. Make sure what you plan to buy works as promised and meets your needs.

Remote Maintenance and Support of Networks

by Michael S. Dell
Chairman and CEO, Dell Computer Corporation

Author Bio

Michael S. Dell founded Dell Computer Corporation in 1984 with $1,000 and an unprecedented idea in the computer industry: sell PCs directly to end users, bypassing the traditional approach of selling computers through retail stores.

By using this innovative direct-marketing approach and by taking pioneering steps such as offering the industry's first unlimited toll-free technical support and next-day, on-site service programs, Dell Computer Corporation has established itself as one of the largest manufacturers of personal computers in the United States. In just eight years, the company's sales have grown from $6 million to $890 million.

The company's corporate customer database includes two-thirds of the companies on Fortune's list of 500 largest American companies. With the recent addition of Dell Computer Corporation to this list, Mr. Dell became the youngest CEO of a company to earn a ranking on the Fortune 500.

Mr. Dell has earned the title of "Entrepreneur of the Year" from *Inc.* magazine (1989) and from the Association of Collegiate Entrepreneurs (1986-1991).

Mr. Dell attended the University of Texas at Austin. He is an advisor to the Innovative Technology Management Association at the University and serves on the Board of Directors for the Greater Austin Chamber of Commerce.

Executive Summary

More and more today, customers of all sizes are looking for complete networking solutions. Successful vendors must integrate hardware, software, configuration, and maintenance services into cost-effective, customized solutions. Because many customers do not have the resources to manage their networks, they are looking outside their own businesses for cost-effective network support and maintenance.

This effort is assisted by emerging software and hardware technology which gives improved maintenance and support from remote, centralized locations. These technologies enable nearly every aspect of network maintenance to be conducted remotely over telephone lines.

Today's personal computer networks offer customers unprecedented capabilities for sharing resources and information. But many small- and medium-sized businesses lack the expertise to support and manage their own networks, while the largest companies require new approaches which match their requirements to their capabilities.

At Dell Computer Corporation, our experience with small, medium, and large customers has shaped our customer offerings and our own corporate networking approach. More and more today, customers of all sizes are looking for complete networking solutions. Successful vendors must integrate hardware, software, configuration, and maintenance services into cost-effective, customized solutions. Because many customers do not have the resources to manage their networks themselves, they are looking outside their own businesses for cost-effective network support and maintenance. This effort is assisted by emerging software and hardware technology which permits improved maintenance and support from remote, centralized locations.

More hardware vendors today are offering integrated solutions than ever before. At Dell, for example, we preconfigure networks and install operating system and application software at our factories. Larger customers find these services help off-load work from their internal information system employees, freeing the IS employees for more strategic tasks.

Companies offering integrated solutions also help their customers get new networks up and running much more quickly, especially in small offices or remote locations. These services enable smaller businesses to network their computers, where otherwise they would not. Other services that are growing in popularity among customers include factory installation of custom software and hardware, such as special network management applications. We also see growing demand for start-up consulting services and ongoing maintenance for multivendor networks.

Here is the message: Customers want to receive systems that are ready to plug into their networks and be productive as quickly and easily as possible.

For many small- and medium-sized businesses, just getting started with a network can pose a major challenge, even with preconfigured systems and cabling.

Although technical support is available from the hardware and network operating system providers, initially these customers often lack the information even to ask the right questions. It's a catch-22.

Recently, we have worked with selected small- and medium-sized businesses in the process of installing local area networks with Dell PCs. Many of these customers had been reluctant to install a network because maintenance and support spending often would exceed hardware and software costs, especially on smaller LANs. These would-be LAN customers often found they would need to hire new people, or pay for expensive outside consultants to set up, maintain and administer their networks. Many small customers just can't justify the cost of training in-house network administration and maintenance personnel, and besides, they are not in the business of maintaining a LAN. They need to be free to focus on their core business.

The solution to these problems can be centralized, remote LAN maintenance and support. Our experience at Dell with direct sales, service, and support of PCs through a centralized facility and staff in Austin suggested we can offer cost-effective, centralized LAN support in much the same manner that we have offered other technical support. On an experimental basis, we established a telephone LAN support operation in Austin and staffed it with networking experts. Then, we worked with selected customers to understand the benefits and costs of this arrangement.

What we found was remarkable. Customers were able, with a telephone lifeline to Dell in Austin, to get their LANs installed and operating quickly and with a minimum of hassle using their existing staff to do the work. Often, they selected one person, such as a secretary, to lead the installation and serve as the contact between their company and Dell.

The ability to support remotely a customer's local area network is becoming easier with the emergence of very sophisticated hardware and software that enables nearly every aspect of network maintenance to be conducted remotely over telephone lines. Today, for example, workstations can be added, files can be backed up and software can be installed from a remote location. System problems also can be diagnosed and resolved quickly with the proper tools at a remote location.

Dell offers start-up network consulting services which have shown that customers can get their networks up and running without hiring expensive staff or consultants. At the end of the 30-day consulting period, we have found that customers usually are self-sufficient at routine network administration tasks. For ongoing support, customers can arrange network maintenance and support through optional service contracts. These typically cover on-site service as well as remote telephone network support.

Some in our industry have scoffed at the idea of a hardware vendor using a centralized support staff to provide network administration and support. But these are the same people who scoffed at the idea—now widely accepted—of selling and supporting PC hardware by telephone. We believe the same model can work for network maintenance and support.

Remote diagnostics also can work for very large companies, especially those with widely dispersed operations and branch offices which need network support. The cost of maintaining on-site support at every location would be excessive in many instances.

Our own experience with the Dell corporate network proved the point.

A large company like Dell has thousands of nodes, which are typically wired into numerous local area networks. We have LANs throughout the world, in each of our European country offices, for example. To move information effectively, the LANs are connected into wide area networks, many of which are managed remotely, saving on the expense of on-site administrators.

The hardware and software tools for managing these large "networks of networks" are just beginning to emerge and will improve with experience. In the meantime, one approach we take is a hub-management system. Through a single control point, or hub, maintenance and support can be remotely conducted for multiple connected LANs. Our European country LANs, for example, are supported through a maintenance hub in the United Kingdom.

We are about to enter a new era of networked computing. As millions of personal computers, minicomputers, and mainframes are connected to optimize the flow of information, more sophisticated diagnostic tools and support methods will be needed. Large companies also will face the challenges of efficiently connecting and managing thousands of systems in client-server computing systems to optimize the movement of information on a worldwide basis.

In the meantime, PC vendors must strive to maintain compatibility with industry standards as they introduce emerging technology and cope with increasingly complex but powerful network operating systems. Only by providing complete solutions and cost-effective support and maintenance options will the PC industry be able to meet customers' expectations for seamless and productive network computing.

The Age of the Enterprise Server

by James Edwards
President and CEO, Tricord

Author Bio

James Edwards, president and CEO, brings 27 years of management and sales experience to Tricord. Mr. Edwards spent 15 years at IBM in various management roles, including division director and general manager of the Biomedical Systems Division and in other roles reporting to the chairman of the board. Prior to joining Tricord, Mr. Edwards also served as the president of AT&T Computer Systems. At AT&T, Mr. Edwards was responsible for all facets of the company's computer line, which included research design, development, marketing, and sales channel management for all software products and services.

Executive Summary

Industry forces are driving the creation of a new product, the Enterprise Server. Get ready: The Enterprise Server will change the way you think about networking.

The history of the computer industry has been consistent: revolutionary changes followed by extended periods of evolution. The revolutionary changes have been clear: the mainframe, the minicomputer, the workstation, the PC, and the PC LAN. Each of these revolutions created billion dollar companies such as IBM, DEC, Sun, Apple, Compaq, and Novell.

Today, we are in the midst of a new revolution. Industry forces are driving the creation of a new product, the Enterprise Server. This product promises to change how you think about network computing, and it promises to become a multibillion dollar market.

Industry Forces Setting the Stage for a New Market

Industry forces are working to transform the network computing market. I group these industry forces into three categories:

- Customer Demand
- Market Drivers
- Product Vacuum

Customer Demand

A Russian proverb states, "Where necessity speaks, it demands." The necessities of corporations today are demanding a new class of networks.

In the 1980s, networks were typically departmental in scope and were used for simple tasks such as word processing and spreadsheets. The demands on networks rarely went beyond the need for simple file-sharing. Today, this state of affairs is changing.

Companies, concerned with the burgeoning cost of network administration, are consolidating departmental LANs into a small number of enterprise networks. IDC estimates the average number of nodes per network will explode by 400 percent over the next few years.

At the same time, companies are starting to use the LAN for more robust tasks. Mission critical programs, once the sole domain of the mainframe or minicomputer, are starting to appear on LANs. This trend, known as downsizing, is gathering steam. Forrester Research estimates 80 percent of Fortune 1000 companies are planning on downsizing one or more applications.

Market Drivers

Until recently, customers found LANs to be an inadequate platform for downsizing. The tools needed for creating and running mission-critical applications were missing. Today, industry leaders are providing those tools.

Network operating systems—for example, NetWare—have become much more robust, with features such as system fault-tolerance and multiprocessing finally arriving. An exciting new generation of 32-bit network operating systems—such as UnixWare, Solaris 2.0, and Windows NT—are just around the corner.

Powerful, network-ready, relational database systems from companies such as Oracle, Microsoft, Sybase, Informix, Ingres, and others are finding their way to the LAN. Powerful internetworking products from companies such as Wellfleet, Synoptics, and Cisco are extending the range of networks as well.

These are the enabling technologies of downsizing. The demand for downsizing is combining with the presence of these enabling technologies to drive the downsizing market.

Product Vacuum

Companies are uneasy with yesterday's proprietary solutions such as mini-computers and mainframes. True, these products have ample power, scalability, and reliability. Their proprietary design, however, has been unable to keep pace with the rapidly evolving network market.

Conversely, traditional PC-based servers are inexpensive and, because of their open design, are able to evolve quickly as technologies change. The problem with PC-based servers is that they lack power, scalability, and reliability. They lack the I/O bandwidth needed to handle large amounts of data. Their lack of scalability limits network expansion. Finally, and most importantly, they lack the circuitry needed to provide the levels of data integrity and reliability necessary for running mission-critical applications.

Rx: The Enterprise Server

The combination of customer demand, availability of downsizing tools, and the lack of an adequate networking platform is driving a new market: the Enterprise Server market.

Analysts are predicting rapid growth for the Enterprise Server market. IDC predicts this market will grow more than five times as fast as the PC-based file-server market between now and 1995. Analysts expect the Enterprise Server market to top $2 billion by the mid 1990s.

Anatomy of an Enterprise Server

Customers are demanding a platform for LAN consolidation and downsizing. This platform must be *high-performance*, *scalable*, *reliable*, and *open*. The machine that delivers on each of these demands is the Enterprise Server. Its design is familiar and exotic at the same time.

Power

Some vendors assume they can address the demands of enterprise networking simply by boosting each of the components of a standard PC. The result looks like PCs on steroids—more RAM, more disk storage, a faster CPU, a faster disk. The problem with that approach is that it ignores balance. What good is a faster CPU if the RAM cannot keep pace with it? What good is a faster disk if the system bus is too busy to accommodate the increased traffic?

The Enterprise Server takes a more balanced approach to power. True, it does contain some very powerful components (the fastest CPUs and disk subsystems). And, true, it does have a vast amount of capacity. But these components are balanced, so as not to lose their capacities to needless bottlenecks.

A true Enterprise Server begins with a high-speed, mainframe-style system bus. By itself, a high-speed system bus can increase the speed of a server by reducing disk and communications traffic bottlenecks.

However, systems designers have found a way to further enhance performance by adding separate disk and communications subsystems. These subsystems run independently of the main system bus, freeing the system bus of performance-stealing bottlenecks. Yet, by using industry standard designs for these subsystems, openness is preserved.

The result? Balanced power that vastly outperforms traditional PC-based file-servers.

Scalability

Companies investing in an Enterprise Server need scalability because their needs grow over time. Manufacturers must design the Enterprise Server to accommodate those changes. It is not acceptable to require customers to start over each time their needs grow. Thus, Enterprise Servers are typically scalable in such key areas as RAM and disk storage capacities, number of communications slots available, and number of CPUs.

Reliability

PC vendors don't build fault-tolerance into their PCs, but Enterprise Servers must be fault-tolerant. Enterprise Server vendors have borrowed heavily from mainframe designs to achieve a high degree of system fault-tolerance.

The most important area of reliability is data reliability. RAID technology is used to design high-performance, high-reliability disk subsystems. This concept is extended to system-critical components, such as the power supply, to provide longer MTBF ratings. Finally, Enterprise Server designers ensure reliability by using the highest quality components such as RAM.

Openness

The first three requirements, power, scalability, and reliability, are attributes long associated with mainframes and minicomputers. What distinguishes the Enterprise Server from its larger brethren, however, is openness. There are two reasons why openness is an absolute must: availability and cost.

Experience shows that openness speeds availability of new technology. Third-party manufacturers create products first for the most popular platforms. Next, they port to second-tier platforms. Finally, if the market isn't large enough on a given platform, they may license their technology to the vendor of that platform and let that vendor port the technology. Those customers running on an open platform enjoy the highest availability of new technology.

Of course, cost also is tied to openness. Competition is more fierce for products competing on open platforms, which drives prices down. The worst possible case is when the vendor of a proprietary platform is the only supplier of a given technology.

In today's market, open means PC-compatible for hardware and Intel-based for software. It is in this arena that the Enterprise Server parts company with mainframes and minicomputers.

The Age of the Enterprise Server

I began by writing about the industry's history of revolution followed by evolution. The Enterprise Server is just such a revolution. I believe this new market will enjoy the same type of explosive growth as those that have preceded it. Although the vendors of Enterprise Computers undoubtedly will flourish, the real winners will be the customers of Enterprise Servers. It is the meeting of their needs that is driving this new market.

The Hazards of Today's
Expert System Technology
in Network Analysis Systems

by Jeff Erwin
Founder, Vice President of Engineering
ProTools, Inc.

Author Bio

Jeff Erwin is the founder of ProTools and VP of Engineering. He was previously founder and president of a computer consulting organization that also specialized in network interfaces.

ProTools Inc. develops and markets network analysis software for distributed networks. The company, founded in March 1990, offers both stand-alone and distributed versions of its Network Control Series software for network analysis. These products were designed to educate users and to promote proactivity in network management. ProTools hopes to help users discover potential problems *before* they occur. Thus, Network Control Series products utilize a graphical user interface; an innovative, high-level, and intuitive approach to network analysis; a built-in guided problem-solving system; and many automatic features designed to keep administrators thoroughly informed about their networks.

ProTools Inc.
14976 NW Greenbrier Parkway
Beaverton, OR 97006
Phone: 503-645-5400
Fax: 503-645-3577

Executive Summary

This paper attempts to separate the marketing hype from the practical realities of applying expert technology to network analysis systems. We make the claim that the approach toward expert technology used by some vendors today misses the mark: that expert technology is best applied to *solving* problems rather than *finding* problems.

The reason is that finding all problems is much harder to accomplish with today's technology, given the randomness of network glitches and the uniqueness of each network. However, there are companies that claim to "make network management easy" using this approach. What in fact happens is that users are lulled into a false sense of security when the so-called expert system doesn't find many problems. It simply can't find them all.

A different and better application for expert technology is in solving problems. Because network administrators are usually the first to learn about new problems when they occur, finding the problem is not the hard part. Quickly solving the problem is where the value can be added, and this is the better place to apply expert analysis. Administrators can be led down a decision tree of symptoms through a series of simple questions and explanations, and very quickly they can be pointed in the direction of key probable causes so problem resolution can begin.

As the technology improves, expert analysis should be applied to finding problems as well. But for today, the most effective use of this technology is in quickly solving them.

In a recent article written by a protocol analyzer supplier, an alluring analogy was made between Expert System Network Management and applications in the medical industry. It goes something like this: Expert technology combines the X-ray machine, the technician who interprets the X-ray, and the diagnostic role of the doctor into one tidy package—streamlining the data collection, diagnosis, and corrective-action process. Sounds great, doesn't it?

However, such a tidy package is possible only if the system is always 100 percent correct. Anything less and you have a system that delivers a false sense of security and still requires the technician and doctor—or, in the case of your network, the network administrator—to be intimately involved in the process. Think about it. When was the last time a computer did the diagnosis of your X-rays?

So how realistic is the promise of expert technology in the network management arena? Should we be adjusting our expectations for this technology as it is applied to network management?

The problem centers around the confidence level you have for an expert system when it's indicating everything is OK on the network. If the system can identify only a portion of the wide variety of problems that occur on your network, then the network administrator still needs to be heavily involved in problem detection, resulting in very little productivity improvement. Is it realistic to expect expert system technology to tackle the challenging task of uncovering network problems, much less solving them?

Expert systems have been most successful in deterministic environments, such as auto repair. The diagnosing of an automobile engine that is not running well can be performed with the application of a set of well-defined rules. You can apply a rule (is there fuel in the tank?), and, with the resulting answer (yes), you can branch to the next possibility (does the fuel get to the carburetor?). In this way, an expert system can walk through the application of the rule tree (assuming the expert system has the capability to test and gather results) and reach a conclusion. In the case of an automobile engine, it is a bounded application in which you eliminate the fuel system, then the air delivery system, and finally the electrical system to determine in which domain the problem lies.

The reason an expert system will work in this environment is that there is a finite set of rules to be applied to a known problem. The car engine is a well-defined, closed system. Computers and computer scientists have not yet reached the point where they can deal with more than a well-defined set of rules.

This brings us to your network. If your network is a typical installation, you have many different types of computers communicating with each other and to file servers, print servers, and database engines. You add routers, bridges, gateways, wide-area links, different protocols, and application-specific traffic from the tens of thousands of applications that can run on your network. You then begin to recognize another construct in physics emerging: the chaotic system.

A true chaotic system is typically defined as a system that has so many permutations and variables that it begins to exhibit randomness in its behavior. In other words, you cannot reliably predict what will happen next based on current activity. The example most often used to describe a chaotic system is the weather. The weather system is unbounded and open. It exhibits true randomness, making it difficult to predict future climate stages (such as the severity of the approaching winter) based on current variables, despite the application of the largest and most powerful computers humans have ever designed.

The most common description used by the experts that study chaos theory is the "butterfly wing" example. According to this hypothesis, the weather in New York can be affected by the beating of a butterfly's wings in Chicago. This conjecture illustrates that the number of forces acting on the system are too great to model and analyze.

On a smaller scale, your computer network exhibits much the same variant behavior. Your network behavior and performance can be changed by something as small as a new version of a spreadsheet used by three people in the accounting department. There are more variables and permutations than we know how to handle.

Expert system technology in network management raises two serious issues. First, it can detect, due to technological limitations, only a very small subset of the problems that actually occur on a network. Even if a system could detect 200 different specific problems, this is 200 out of a range of millions for all practical purposes. (I won't even begin to address the numerous "problems" these systems detect over and over again that don't really exist.)

The second issue has to do with perceptions of the user. If the user believes, based on the hype behind expert technology, that the system is doing a nearly complete job of problem detection, the user is lulled into a false sense of security that will lead eventually to significant network downtime.

Am I saying that expert systems is the latest marketing hype and is impractical for the network management industry? No. Just as expert system technology plays a productive role today in medical applications, it can play a powerful role in managing networks—when correctly applied.

To stay with the medical analogy, expert systems succeed in medical applications because they assume that the ultimate expert system is in the mind of the doctor doing the diagnosis. In the same fashion, a "user-guided expert system" can assist the network administrator.

This distinction is subtle, but important. Rather than have the analyzer initiate problem detection and isolation, a user-guided expert system would have the user initiate the analysis based on a specific problem. The expert system then focuses on a finite set of issues, specifically problems on the network as defined by their symptoms. Apply true, knowledge-based expert system technology to finite problem resolution, and the result is a very practical, productive management environment. The administrator gets immediate assistance on corrective alternatives, and problems are solved quickly.

Here's an example of how this application of expert system technology works: A network administrator gets a call from George User on the ninth floor complaining that he cannot access his spreadsheet files on the fifth-floor server during lunch.

Our version of a user-guided expert system would enable the network administrator to tell it, "Someone can't access a file!" The system might respond, "Who can't?" "George User on the ninth floor" might be the response. "Which server?" "The one on the fifth floor."

The system would look out onto the network, perform an analysis based on several MIB agents on different subnets and on the bindery (or equivalent) in the server itself, piece the situation together and come back with the response, "You are right, and here is why. The bindery has turned off access rights to the files for George User during lunch on Tuesday. Do you want me to adjust the bindery to allow access?" This is a user-defined problem, not one that an expert system could identify. The expert system has access to a complete help system about bindery access rights, backups, servers, routers, or even some statistics about George User and the amount of time he spends on the fifth-floor server. The next time a user calls with a similar problem, the system "remembers" the previous situation and presents this as one possible alternative. But the true expert system, namely the network administrator, solves the problem—and much more quickly.

This is one example. If you close your eyes and try to count the astounding number of problems, and permutations of those problems that can occur on a network, you begin to understand why the so-called "expert system" LAN analyzers being offered today offer more hazardous hype than actual network management productivity.

So how realistic is the promise of expert technology in the network management arena? If expert technology is expected to identify problems, users should realistically expect the technology to find only a handful of all the possible problems found on today's complex networks, resulting in little productivity gain. If expert technology is targeted at resolving problems, it is much more valuable. For problem resolution, user-guided expert technology assists network administrators in understanding the network and fixing problems quickly. This approach matches the current capabilities of today's expert technology in a productive manner and, over the long term, will lead to the meaningful application of the technology.

Expert Systems Increase
Help Desk Effectiveness

by Gail M. Foster
Independent Consultant

Author Bio

Gail M. Foster specializes in the application of technology to support business goals in network and system management, including help desk productivity tools. Her areas of expertise include network and distributed systems management, expert system technology, and new product development and marketing. She is an independent Boston-based consultant, and can be reached at (617) 232-6910.

Executive Summary

Never before has the pace of business and technological change been so rapid. Businesses are reassessing service delivery with an eye on quality, cost, and speed. Companies are creating market-focused organizations which are fast, flexible, and tuned into the requirements of customers. Tasks that previously took several days to complete, such as order processing, are now being done in hours by responsive firms. The result is an increasing burden for operations staff responsible for running and maintaining the networks, systems, and applications. In organizations, the help desk was created as the first point of contact between the network and computer users and the support team. The help desk, previously responsible for answering calls and logging problems, is evolving into a critical first-line support function for the organization. Their role has become to decrease problem resolution time, increase network and system availability, and increase user satisfaction. Help desks are being pushed to perform better and, at the same time, to increase the user-to-help-desk-operator ratio (another way of saying that they must support more with the same or fewer human resources).

The next great boost to productivity may well come from the next generation of products becoming available that incorporate expert systems technology. These products support complex functions and assist in problem diagnostics and recovery. Unlike problem management software, which primarily logs and records problem information, these new products inform, advise, and assist the operator in problem resolution by leveraging information and expertise dispersed throughout an organization. This article is a brief tour of the help desk's role in the organization, a look at the kinds of expert systems available, and information about what to look for when evaluating expert systems.

Expert systems have been around in research labs for many years. They have been used in commercial applications such as financial evaluation and medical diagnosis. Attempts in the 1980s to apply the technology to network and system management had little success, largely because the understanding of technology was too new, and the problem to which it was applied was too broad and complex. The frequent result was slow applications that were often hard to maintain and out of step with network changes. The products now coming to market are being applied to assist the help desk in problem determination and resolution of real-time faults. In looking at these product groups, we will use the term knowledge-based to encompass intelligent search and retrieval, case-based reasoning, rule-based expert systems, and neural networks. They are knowledge-based in that they capture and disseminate the knowledge that previously was held by only a few specialists within an organization.

Major Functions of the Help Desk

The functions of the help desk go beyond simply helping users resolve problems. Their role within a company can have an impact on customer relations, the prioritizing of the company's resources, and the minimizing of future problems.

Managing the Customer Contact

In the past, only customers and in-house personnel were on the network. Today, vendors, suppliers, distributors, and alliance partners may have direct access to critical applications. Ford Motor Company, for example, gives its dealers direct access for credit authorizations for customer car financing. The help desk is the first point of contact and support for this diverse user base. The help desk conveys information from the caller to the organization, and relays status and results back. They must do the following:

- correctly identify caller, problem, priority, and impact of problem

- provide a consistent log of information to assist technical staff's problem resolution

- manage information flow between problem solvers and caller

- track and report status

- de-escalate problems

- generate management statistics

Their ability to be informed about the caller, to track and report status on open problems, and to resolve problems quickly reflects directly on the company's image and cost efficiency by providing improved and informed service with reduced downtime.

Service Provision

Help desk personnel are the customer advocates within their organization. The technical engineer who can resolve complex problems often may want to work on the problem that is interesting, complex, or has greatest system impact. It is the help desk's role to persuade the organization that the seemingly insignificant problem is a major issue for the customer. One company I worked with believed this so strongly that when problems were prioritized internally, it was the customer support group that had final say on priority.

Problem Tracking and Management (Problem Control)

Consistent standards for problem identification, characterization, documentation, and reporting, facilitate the flow of information among diverse parts of the organization and promote a common understanding of the problem. Help desk operators also share information among themselves on types of problems outstanding, sensitive problems reported, new or known problem fixes, and new or known troubleshooting techniques. Everyone knows how frustrating it is to call a help desk, log a problem, talk through some initial diagnostic tests, and then receive a call back from someone else who asks the same questions. By applying a common methodology to problem characterization and troubleshooting, this problem can be reduced significantly.

Where Can Knowledge-Based Systems Net the Most Advantage?

There are several broad categories of intelligence-based systems (Figure 12.1). Neural nets are a relatively new approach and aren't really commercially tested as yet, but product implementations do exist for all the others. Products like Apriori (Answer Computer Corp.), an intelligent search and retrieval method, CBR Express (Inference Corp.), a case-based tool, and Heat (Bendata Corp.), a rule-based system, are being used by companies to improve problem management, develop common and consistent troubleshooting methodologies, and broaden the knowledge base within the organization.

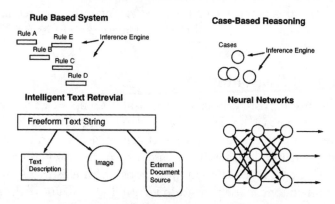

Figure 12.1. Categories of intelligence-based systems.

Also, there are hybrid systems like Expert Advisor (Software Artistry) which use a mixture of case-, hypertext-, and rule-based approaches. These hybrid systems apply different technologies to the specific aspects of the problem-solving task. The hypertext support allows users to pull up additional information, while the expert system base steps users through diagnostics and recommends or initiates action to resolve problems. Users can expect to see more and more of these hybrid-type approaches.

Intelligent Text Retrieval

Intelligent text retrieval systems (ITRs) are essentially keyword search text retrieval systems. They are extremely helpful tools for the help desk because they can replace the many dry, never-looked-at manuals stored someplace in the data center. Users can jump from one section to another quickly to get information while the caller is still on the phone. Products like Apriori support commands such as up, down to a deeper level, across scrolling, and a jump command (allowing users to jump across a conceptual link to new information or new presentation format). In Expert Advisor, this new information might be text, graphics, or sound. For example, clicking on the word reboot for a modem might jump the reader to a picture of the modem front panel or to detailed reboot instructions or to symptomatic diagrams of causes. ITRs provide flexible, loosely structured access to information, getting away from the purely linear access provided by online document systems. With their short set-up time and low maintenance requirements, they are well suited to some real-time fault-management issues.

Case-Based Reasoning

These systems are based on cases of real-life examples. Each case has a number of attributes which can be weighed to permit quantitative comparison between cases to determine the next likeliest case. When a new problem occurs, the operator describes it as a case, which the system then compares to its existing case base. The system responds with existing, similar cases which the operator can use to assist in identifying the cause of the problem and the action to take. To take an example from the real estate world, a case might be a description of a house including number of rooms, baths, location, offer price, taxes and so forth. When they come in, house buyers identify the things they are looking for. The case base can search for nearest matches to their criteria and pull up the listings. The house buyers can then narrow down their search based on the subset of information before them. Because the cases can be written by relatively nontechnical staff, maintenance and support are easier, and a library of cases may be built up relatively quickly. The more cases available to the system, the higher the probability the system will find a match to the input data. This methodology is well suited to fault and performance management in small- to medium-sized networks.

Rule-Based Expert Systems

Rule-based expert systems (RBES) are known as procedural systems because the knowledge bases consist of identified problem-solving procedures. RBESs store complex information in a system where the relationship between data items is as important as the data itself. Conventional databases are not well suited to handle these cases. Rule-based knowledge bases are often arranged in a hierarchical structure with data contained in frames. Frames are a network of nodes and relationships with high-level descriptions providing prototypes for actual occurrences. The inference engine steps through the hierarchy and tracks where the user is in the diagnostic procedure. The system walks the user through a predetermined set of steps (or executes them automatically if the user so desires) and matches the results against expected results. If there is no match, the system may begin working down a different path. Each step taken is documented, and expert users can use shortcuts (which are also documented) to bypass steps. When a problem is handed over, all diagnostic procedures run, and their results are available. There are two basic approaches these systems can take, forward chaining and backward chaining. In the former, the system begins with the error conditions described to it and then looks for solutions that match. In the latter, the system poses assumptions about the problem cause and then tests against its assumption. Both approaches suffer from increasing unmanageability as the knowledge base grows and the complexity of knowledge base design. These systems are suited best to relatively small and static environments where the expertise is readily available to input the information and where there is access to skilled staff to maintain the knowledge base. In large environments these systems become unwieldy to maintain and risk being constantly out of date.

Neural Networks

This area is one of the most recent under study. Neural networks are based not on reasoning, but on pattern matching, an approach that grew out of research in neuroscience and mathematics. They are designed to mimic the common sense logic—knowledge based on past experience—that most people apply to problem solving. Neural networks also learn from experience, a fundamental differentiation from the types of expert systems previously discussed. They are "trained" by being presented with data input and the correct data output. The system then compares its results to the correct results and adjusts its internal systems accordingly. There is great hope that these experience-based networks will be able to handle complex environments with increasing accuracy. The current drawback is the complexity of training the neural nets correctly.

Checklist for Evaluating Knowledge-Based Systems

What knowledge-based system will be best for your organization? There are a number of factors to consider before making a decision:

- the technological approach of the application
- the ease-of-use of the user interface
- the costs of maintenance for the knowledge base
- connectivity options
- vendor support

Applications

Most of the products available today are focused in the area of fault management. Figure 12.2 gives relative weight to the different technological approaches as applied to five functional areas. Some approaches are better suited to particular areas, while others may be overkill. For example, case-based reasoning is finding success in fault management (provided the environment is not too complex or rapidly changing), but because it approximates the likeliest match, it is poorly suited to highly precise applications like accounting and security. Rule-based, or procedural, systems can be very useful for security checking and configuration planning, but the complexity of designing and maintaining the rule base is a hindrance in applying them to fault management.

	F A U L T M G T	P E R F O R M A N C E	C O N F I G U R A T I O N	A C C O U N T I N G	S E C U R I T Y M G T	Application of Knowledge-Based Systems
Intelligent Retrieval	3	0	1	2	1	
Case-Based Reasoning	3	2	2	1	1	
Rule-Based Logic	2	1	2	2	3	
Neural Networks	3	3	0	0	1	

Scale:
3 = Well Suited
2 = Moderately Suited
1 = Poorly Suited
0 = Not Useful

Figure 12.2. The value of different technological approaches in relation to five functional areas.

User Interface

Navigating around a system should be easy. Ideally, this would mean having a system that included a graphical user interface (GUI), help menus, and the ability to support multiple screens. That is, it should be easy to see where you are in a hierarchy or search, easy to jump out or back up a step, and easy to take short cuts if you are an experienced user. Expert Advisor, from Software Artistry, uses a graphical user interface that enables users to point and click to obtain information or to execute a command. Users will become more demanding of this type of interface as they become more and more accustomed to GUI interfaces on their other applications.

Knowledge Base Maintenance

The larger the network and the greater the number of rules or cases to be maintained, the greater the effort to change or modify the knowledge base. Some tools, like CBR Express and Heat, enable the user to update the knowledge base. This gives an organization the flexibility to decide how and when to update and validate the knowledge base. Several systems tell the system administrator which cases were infrequently used and that are, therefore, candidates for deletion. Regardless of which system is evaluated, talk to the vendor and to other customers about the amount of time involved and the level of expertise required to maintain the system. Generally, expert systems and neural networks will require significantly greater maintenance than text retrieval products like the one from Answer Computers (Apriori). In some cases, most of the effort and cost of the system is associated with ongoing maintenance (Table 12.1).

Table 12.1. Where does all the effort go?

	Pre-installation Planning	Knowledge Base Creation	System Maintenance	Operator and Expert Training
Intelligent Retrieval	Medium	Low	Low	Low
Case-Based	Medium	Medium	Low	Low
Rule-Based	High	High	High	High
Neural Network	High	High	High	High

Integration with Other Applications

If there is one weakness in most systems, it is the lack of connectivity and interoperability with other applications. While integration with the ACD and problem management applications like InfoMan (IBM) or PNMS (Peregrine Systems) is a welcomed start, the help desk user will quickly be looking for integration with other applications like configuration and inventory management. Today's crop of products are unable to share knowledge with other systems, which can become a significant drawback in large environments. While stand-alone products will begin to provide immediate productivity gains, over the longer term, their ability to exchange information with the other applications will reduce setup and maintenance time and will provide substantially increased benefit at reduced cost.

Vendor Experience

The role of vendor experience too often is overlooked or downplayed. When adopting a new technology that will radically affect the way information is disseminated in an organization, it is particularly important to have a vendor who is knowledgeable about both the technology and the problem arena. For example, if you are trying to manage a Novell network, you ideally want a vendor who understands the technology (case, rule, neural, text retrieval) *and* Novell networks, or at least PC LANs. An experienced vendor can significantly reduce the time it takes you to get up and running. With case-based and rule-based systems, you also may need help with system setup and administration. If your vendor does not have appropriate experience but you really are set on their product, there are two other sources of help. One is from other users in active vendor user groups. The second is a start-up company like KnowledgeBroker, Inc., located in San Juan Capistrano, CA, which plans to broker knowledge bases. For a fee, their plan is to connect you with a company using the same product (CBR Express, Expert Advisor, and so forth) willing to license you the knowledge base they developed for Novell networks. This brokerage concept, by providing a national pool of existing knowledge bases, could significantly reduce start-up costs for companies hoping to implement knowledge-based systems. Companies that develop knowledge bases could begin to generate a new source of revenues through these licensing agreements.

Help Desks Can Realize Substantial Benefits

Knowledge-based systems capture expertise and make it available, giving third shift operators access to the same expertise as the first shift. Knowledge-based systems put more information at the hands of a larger group of people than was previously possible, a critical requirement where staff turnover is high or expertise is scarce. The help desk can increase problem-solving accuracy and reduce recovery time because the systems impose a standard methodology for problem solving and documentation on diagnostics performed and results generated. Knowledge-based systems can make recommendations to operators, allowing help desk staff to solve more complex problems on the first call. One help desk using a case-based product is able to solve 80 percent of the problem calls received. Others, using ITR systems, have been able to get new help desk operators up and effective in a matter of days rather than months. Because knowledge is captured and consistently accessible, these systems can be effective in troubleshooting problems that might only occur rarely. One beta customer experienced significant benefit when the system assisted in the diagnosis and recovery of a failed LAN device (the customer's expertise was only in SNA).

The final consideration on the use of knowledge-based systems concerns the complexity and rate of change within the environment. For large, complex, rapidly changing environments, there will be significant effort required to maintain the quality and accuracy of the knowledge base. At the other end of the spectrum, small homogeneous environments with highly trained help desk staff will find these systems less effective because the skill level is already high and well dispersed. For the vast majority of companies that fall in between these two extremes, these products merit serious evaluation.

Integrated Connectivity: The Role of Computer Manufacturers

by Bruce Fryer
Manager of Product Strategy, Zenith Data Systems

Author Bio

ZENITH DATA SYSTEMS

A Bull Company

Bruce Fryer is a manager of product strategy and advanced planning for Zenith Data Systems in Buffalo Grove, Illinois. Mr. Fryer has been networking PCs for 10 years. He also has written several pieces for *PC WEEK* and authored the book *LAN Desktop Guide to E-Mail with cc:Mail* (SAMS 1992). Mr. Fryer has a master's degree in management information and decision support systems from DePaul University.

Executive Summary

Networking personal computers is now the norm, not the exception. Historically, the systems integrator or user installed their PCs on the network. With head count reduction in corporations, along with the rapid growth of networks, it is costly and time consuming to do the initial network installations and have them not work the first time.

Personal computer manufacturers such as Zenith Data Systems are designing computers with integrated connectivity: certified, built-in networking hardware and software to minimize the overhead associated with installation of PCs on a network.

A recent issue of *Business Week* magazine recounted the story of an east coast insurance company that spent $120 million and six years to develop a "state of the art" computer system. The magazine reported that the company had given up its quest for the "perfect" information system and turned over the entire data processing operation to an outside firm.

This little story illustrates the endemic position of most computer hardware makers: the user needs to buy the largest, the fastest, and the newest equipment/software to succeed. If computers and software were children's toys, it would be the equivalent of starting with wooden Lincoln Logs, adding a metal Erector Set, and finally bringing along plastic Lego building blocks to finish the job. While you can build something with each, trying to build one structure using all three is difficult.

The skills to accomplish this task are located in three different places: with the user, the integrator, and the manufacturer.

Integrated connectivity is a term used to describe a process where the end user wants to network microcomputers and not invest great amounts of time, money, or personnel resources to make it happen. In this process, integration begins on the computer maker's drawing board long before the first machine is unpacked or the first wire pulled.

Networking is Not Just a Niche

Networking through the use of local area (LAN) and wide area (WAN) networks in a business environment is no longer a niche used for personal computers.

Studies by Dataquest and the Gartner Group indicate that more than one-half of all personal computers in use are tied in one form or another to a network. These studies further note that the number of PCs being hooked up to networks—including existing machines—is growing faster than the sale of individual personal computers.

The movement of PCs toward networks is growing more rapidly than the number of experienced people who can configure and install them. This level of installation complexity is making it difficult to install reliable networks at a reasonable cost. These costs are growing so rapidly that currently only 18 percent of the total cost of computing is tied up in the purchase of hardware and software. The other 82 percent of the cost of computing includes set-up, training, maintenance, and administration.

Computer manufacturers can play an important role in eliminating this complexity, reducing the cost to the end user, or reducing the overhead for systems integrators. In this paper we will look at the historical role of the computer manufacturer, examine the problems of today, and show how integrated connectivity addresses this set of problems.

In order to understand where the industry is today, we need to look back 10 years and what has happened in networking DOS-based PCs. For the purpose of this discussion, we are focusing upon installation of the traditional general purpose network.

The Early Years

The pioneers of the industry tended to be the users of networks themselves. There were no rules, regulations, or past history to build upon. Very few people worked with networks at all because of the difficulty involved and a lack of understanding of the value of networking PCs.

Those who did build networks tended to develop expertise that included knowing what machines worked with which cards and with whose network operating system. Building networks 10 years ago was like baking a cake without a recipe and using only the ingredients you could find in your cupboard.

The channel (mainly computer stores) and computer manufacturers were focused on moving single user PCs into the marketplace. Some of the more experienced users moved up into the channel and started the early network integration companies.

As you can see from Figure 13.1, demand for networking was small, and the users built up their expertise to install these systems.

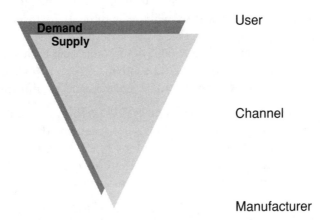

Figure 13.1. Installation responsibility: the early years.

The Last Five Years

Demand for networked PCs has grown rapidly over the last five years. The major reasons include maturity of the network components and application software which was developed to exploit networked environments (like LAN based electronic mail), along with the realization of the benefit of sharing PC resources among many users.

As the demand for networks grew, the user support organizations grew along with them. Concurrently, the channel (computer stores and systems integrators) gained more experience and provided services to install networks for those who did not have the internal expertise.

Some time in the last five years, major computer manufacturers started to provide limited network support and testing for these channels. As you can see from Figure 13.2, demand starts to outstrip the supply of experienced people. This results in more problems with users' networks, both in installation and operations.

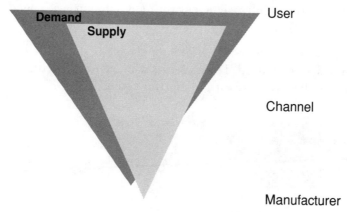

Figure 13.2. Installation responsibility: the last five years.

LAN Implementation Today

Installation demands continue to move ahead. According to research by the Gartner Group, during the next 2 years 23 PCs will be added to a network every minute of every day, worldwide.

Like Confucius' wish, networking is both a blessing and a curse. For corporate America, networks enable users to leverage expensive resources for a fraction of the cost of mainframe-based systems. However, these networks also are complicated to install properly and difficult to maintain. With the corporate downsizing movement underway, there are fewer people to maintain the networked systems. There are stories of Fortune 100 companies trying to support as many as 12,000 users with only six network experts.

Additionally, this mixed bag of blessings also hurts systems integrators. While network growth has been geometric, the supply of experienced people has expanded much more slowly. Demand is high for service, but so is the cost of overhead.

Expensive and experienced installers are spending too much time seeding cards and configuring drivers when they should be designing and implementing cost-effective, efficient turn-key solutions with appropriate network management.

As you can see in Figure 13.3, the channel has been trying to take up the slack, but it is overwhelmed. Those users who could network, did so. Those who couldn't, did anyway—with interesting results.

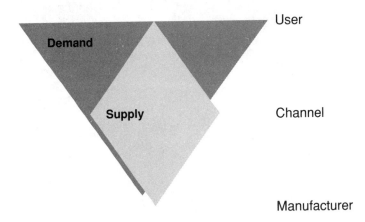

Figure 13.3. Installation responsibility: today.

Integrated Connectivity

Integrated connectivity is the way at least one personal computer maker is looking at the needs of the market place. Zenith Data Systems does not begin with a question of what hardware do you want to buy (and that which we must sell).

We ask the question, "What is it that you want to do and need to accomplish?" As a business person, you want a powerful system at a reasonable price. As a networking professional, you want to be able to bring up the PCs on the network easily and quickly.

Integrated connectivity is the process by which the personal computer manufacturer offers a certified machine that is preconfigured for network operations and has the necessary hardware and software as part of its standard features.

What does that mean to you as the end user or the systems integrator? You no longer have to install network cards, worry about IRQ jumpers, memory conflicts, or client shell configurations.

Instead, you spend your valuable time working on the delivery of business solutions running on the network.

In Figure 13.4, the computer manufacturer takes on the responsibility of providing more of the basic integration directly out of the box. This allows the channel and the user to meet the demand for new networked PC systems.

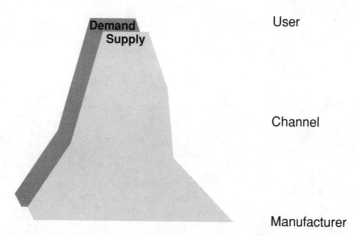

Figure 13.4. Installation responsibility: integrated connectivity.

For example, Zenith Data Systems provides integrated connectivity in their Z-NOTE notebook computers, Z-STATION desktops and Z-SERVER towers. The user simply plugs the machine into their network, answers a few questions in the automatic configuration start-up procedure, and installation is complete. And if you look at the price of the new Z Series computers, they are price competitive to PCs that are not network-ready.

Summary

Like our starting analogy of Lincoln Logs, an Erector Set and Legos, today's network experts are asked to build complex systems from incompatible components. Some of these systems were never intended to work with each other.

The value of a network is derived not from building these constructs, but by the utility the finished products provides.

Can you build a structure out of Lincoln Logs, an Erector Set and Legos? Sure you can. Integrated connectivity provided by personal computer makers such as Zenith Data Systems gives today's network I/S professional the building blocks designed to take the complexity and drudgery out of network installation.

14

The New Corporate Development LANscape

Development Issues in the Networked Environment
by Stuart Pastman and Kelly Garrett
CGI Systems, Inc.

Author Bios

Stuart Pastman: Managing Partner, CGI Systems, Inc.

Mr. Pastman is the managing partner of CGI Systems' Advanced Technologies Division within the United States. Mr. Pastman's primary responsibilities have involved consulting and education within the area of network design, acquisition, installation, and ongoing LAN management. Mr. Pastman has designed and installed LANs using all the major LAN operating systems incorporating micro, mini, and mainframe connectivity. He also has significant experience with all major network topologies. Mr. Pastman was one of the first individuals outside of Novell to receive Novell's CNI (Certified NetWare Instructor) plus CNE (Certified NetWare Engineer) status. He holds a B.A.

in mathematics and an M.A. in computer science. Mr. Pastman has spent the past 12 years in the Data Processing industry, including 5 years within the corporate environment of a major insurance company.

Mr. Pastman has lectured nationally and internationally on LANs, systems integration, end user computing, system design optimization, and host connectivity. Mr. Pastman is also chairman of the CNE Professional Association National Board of Directors.

Kelly Garrett: Sr. Network Systems Consultant, CGI Systems, Inc.

Mr. Garrett manages the Advanced Development Concepts team of CGI Systems' Advanced Technologies Division. The team's primary responsibilities include the design and implementation of large enterprise networking solutions and related development support structures. Mr. Garrett has been involved with LAN systems software engineering, distributed processing, and multi-platform application development support for 12 years.

CGI Systems, Inc.

CGI Systems, Inc., is a full-service information systems consulting firm providing state-of-the-art technology and management consulting. The Paris-based parent company, CGI Informatique, has offices located in 15 countries throughout the world, with a total staff of 4,050 employees. Our consultants specialize in CASE technologies, database management, AI/Expert systems, application development (including Client Server technologies), and teleprocessing technologies within the IBM, DEC and Bull H.N. mini and mainframe environments, and IBM-compatible microcomputer platforms, as well as local and wide area network design, implementation, and education.

We provide our clients with services in the following areas:

- Information technology management consulting

- Project management

- Application and local area network design

- Application development

- Systems programming

- Database administration

- Local area network education

- End user services

- CASE sales, support and development

Executive Summary

This paper focuses on the LAN's impact on corporate development environments. A rather brief history of PC and LAN penetration into the corporate environment is provided to lay a foundation. We briefly explore the PC development mindset and the effects of rapid technological and conceptual advances on the development effort. The role of LAN Systems Software Engineering resources within the corporate environment is presented as a solution to these development and operations challenges.

The impact of LAN systems on the entire corporate development methodology is presented within the contexts of "PC/LAN Centric" and "Enterprise Computing Platform" philosophies. The role of LAN systems personnel is explored within these contexts to provide a framework for exploring the importance of such resources.

From the end user point of view, computer systems are basically tools used to handle the tasks related to doing business. Business to end users is the process of selling their product or service and supporting the organizational structure that allows this process to continue. They use applications on the system to manage the information involved in doing their jobs. When

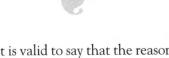

viewed in this manner, it is valid to say that the reason for the information system's existence is totally application centric. For this reason, many larger organizations rely on custom development of applications, or processes, tailored to suit their particular needs. Even off-the-shelf solutions are expected to need some form of custom tailoring or configuration to more closely match the organization.

How Things Used to Be

In the good ol' days, when large centralized systems were the only available solutions, this customization or development process was confined to a single processing environment. This single-vendor approach simplified the development cycle by restricting it to the capabilities of this single environment. This is not to say that these systems do not have a broad range of capabilities; these capabilities are merely provided within the unified philosophical approach envisioned by the vendor. Because of the size (cost) and nature of these systems, and their dependence on in-house application system development, organizations invested in the human resources required to fulfill the intended mission. This meant that they needed development personnel in addition to the operations staff. These development resources would need to include people with a wide range of developmental skills, from systems software engineers and designers to high-level language programmer-analysts. It is these resources that compose what we have come to call the MIS or Information Systems department, a very important part of every major organization in the free world.

The Personal Computer "Revolution"

The advent of the personal computer, at first, had very little impact on the MIS mission. These small systems, with their limited capabilities, were used by smaller organizations and individuals to perform some basic business functions. The fact that IBM called its system *personal* is an indication of what impact it expected the product to have on the market. The applications available were generic programs for word processing, spread sheets, and structured accounting suitable for the targeted market.

Competition from the clone manufacturers caused prices to fall and sales to soar. There was now a large market for software from third-party vendors. Lower prices also meant affordable development systems for those wishing to enter the software market. The unholy, unwashed, T-shirt-wearing masses now had access to technology and markets they would not have had access to otherwise. Powerful and unique applications were becoming available for the so-called personal computer that could rival those available on the mainframe. The PC was starting to penetrate larger corporations at the departmental level, filling niches that MIS could not or would not fill.

PCs became familiar in the corporate environment, and it became apparent to departmental managers and users that some custom applications and utilities could be developed quickly and cheaply on them. There was always someone on staff who could whip up the quick BASIC program to search or sort. The fact that the implementation schedule and resources were under the control of the department had obvious appeal to managers. Eventually, each department had its own PC guru who slowly found himself responsible for developing departmental PC programs and PC support in general. Departmental development eventually became a fact of corporate life after acquiring the needed dedicated personnel and resources. Still, the application-centric users had no intent to replace the main system for integrated business operations.

The Advent of the LAN

As the departments started connecting their PCs together and using multiuser database and e-mail applications, a profound change occurred. Important business data was migrating to the PCs, via the LAN. Each department was becoming its own data center with mission-critical data existing outside the main business system that had been used for years. Information was being "stolen" from MIS; files were being transferred from the main system to the LAN, reformatted, and merged into LAN databases. There were instances of entire departmental applications migrating to the LAN! The PC users were also starting to feel the impact of growth. Lack of standards and new technologies were starting to complicate their efforts, especially with interdepartmental integration and application development. Their application-centric mindset determined that this was their current need. They had no intention of replacing the main system for integrated business operation; certain integrated functions just evolved in the LAN environment.

Use of networks by larger organizations was having an impact on the evolution of the LAN. Most LAN technology vendors were PC centric and concentrated on the business needs of smaller organizations. This philosophy was responsible for complete solution approaches that would satisfy the needs of smaller organizations while limiting the integration flexibility needed by the larger institutions. Vendors are just now starting to address the scalability and flexibility issues that are important to these larger clients.

New Development Challenges—
PC/LAN Centric Development

If we view application development from the PC/LAN side only, we can see several areas that need attention. Many development problems relate to rapid technological improvements and new concepts available to the developers. The development environment is no longer limited to the single-user platform they are used to. The concept of multiuser access to resources is a good example. Many PC developers are not used to coordinating access to a resource and handling changes to the resource in mid-use. The developer is burdened with understanding the concept and its implications as well as the technical details involved in implementation. Tight development schedules, combined with the rapid advance of capabilities and concepts with their associated learning curves, have served to isolate developers from the true capabilities of their systems.

To many PC applications developers, the LAN is equivalent to a large disk drive hung on the end of a cable. It is merely a hardware extension of the PC that is capable of being accessed by persons other than the developers. Most do not realize that the PC's service environment extends virtually through all the resources available on the network. Ask most PC applications developers to write a program that will enable two users to communicate interactively with each other, and they will most likely do it with files as the pipeline. This is perfectly understandable, because this is the environment they are used to dealing with. They would not know how to use IPX, TCP/IP, or named pipes for this purpose; these functions are service extensions provided by the network, part of the virtual reality they are connected to.

There are those programmers, however, who would know how to use available communications protocols to perform the task. This type of person could write an abstract interface to a communications protocol that can be used by other programmers who do not have this knowledge. A few simple routines such as `OpenLink(username)`, `Send(MessagePointer)`, `Receive(MessagePointer)`, and `CloseLink()` would provide a primitive peer-to-peer interface that any application programmer could use. The programmer would not need to know or care whether IPX, TCP/IP, or named pipes are being used. This example demonstrates how a "systems programmer/analyst" would support the efforts of an "application programmer/analyst" in many organizations.

Visit any Fortune 1000 company and ask to see the system software engineers, and you would be shown a group of people. The size of the group would vary from company to company, but this would not seem to be an odd request. Ask who is responsible for LAN system software engineering, and you would most likely get blank stares or be asked for an explanation of what you mean.

The same is true, to a lesser degree, of small organizations that have grown from smaller companies with stand-alone PCs. This group represents a new phenomenon in the American business community. In the past, companies that grew to this size would have installed minis or smaller mainframes to handle the information processing requirements of their organizations. Instead, their PC-based LANs have evolved with them, fulfilling their information needs while keeping them ignorant of the large system development methodologies they require. Despite this, you would be surprised to find that many of these smaller organizations do have LAN system software programmer/analysts on staff. This may be because they follow the standard IS department models of the larger organizations, development resource divisions and all. They have the requirement for the function, even if they do not have the mainframe.

The neglect of LAN system software engineering resources at many organizations can most likely be attributed to the PC mentality. PC programmers are accustomed to doing everything for themselves and having control over all aspects of development. This was the reason for developing on the PC in the first place. This is an understandable attitude when PC programmers were a rare breed; the unholy, unwashed, T-shirt-wearing individualist. As PCs spread into the business community, demand for PC programmers increased along with demand for business applications. Many PC programmers now specialize in high-level development environments and languages such as dBASE, ObjectVision, and database form tools. Like their mainframe counterparts, many have no knowledge of assembly language and the intricacies of the machine or operating environment they are using. They have become commodities. The lack of formalized training in PC and LAN systems software development makes individuals with this knowledge rare.

Typical MIS departments view PC programming rather simply. Most believe that development tools for PCs handle all of their needs. In fact, many mainframe programmers are amazed at the capabilities of the PC development tools. They relate LAN development with PC development, seeing the LAN as a disk drive hung on the end of a cable.

This PC mentality is basically correct, until you throw in the LAN and the processing requirements of large business application systems. The mere connection to a LAN extends the resources of the PC environment into the realm of mainframe capabilities. Value-added servers of all imaginable types, communications protocols, gateways, message services, domain reference resources, management functions, and resource utilization statistics are but a few of the resources available for the mere asking. This new environment is just as new to the PC programmer as it would be to the mainframe programmer. Connect the LAN to the mainframes using APPC/APPN or other mechanisms, and these resources *are* available to the mainframe programmers.

To achieve the same level of LAN development that is currently done on the mainframe, the organization must reevaluate its view of the LAN. This complex and powerful platform must be accorded the same resources as any other large-scale development environment. This includes creation of

LAN software systems engineering and related support positions and the organizational structure to manage the development efforts and requirements of the departments. Many organizations have done this or are in the process of doing so. As more and more organizations adopt a professional approach to LAN systems development, the demand for skilled LAN systems professionals has increased. Many are discovering that they must provide access to external training and aggressive in-house skills development to develop these resources from their current staff.

Using this standard development organization, the LAN systems programmer/analysts can provide the abstract access to the LAN services that the PC applications developer needs. This process also serves to isolate the application from system-level changes. In the case of the simple peer-to-peer abstract mentioned earlier, the application would be isolated from the protocol being used. The application could be moved from a Novell platform using IPX to a LAN Manager platform using NamedPipes very easily. The LAN Systems programmer would provide a NamedPipes interface, using the same procedure architecture as before, that would be relinked into the application (or that would replace the DLL in the case of Windows or OS/2). A robust implementation of the interface would automatically determine one of many protocols to use and use the appropriate one, allowing the same application to be used on many systems without relinking.

New Development Challenges— the Enterprise Computing Platform

If we consider the LAN as a connectivity mechanism for all the resources in the organization, we can achieve additional benefits. In this Enterprise Computing Platform view, the resources of the PCs, workstations, LAN, minis and mainframes are available to everyone from anywhere. Imagine a PC application using DB2 data from the mainframe and Oracle information from a LAN-based database server to output a JES pick-list in a remote warehouse with a mainframe attached printer. After the items are picked, a mainframe application accessed from a terminal at the warehouse updates the DB2 and Oracle data to reflect the change in inventory and client billing.

A subtle change has just occurred. Besides the obvious capability to access data across diverse platforms, there is the subtle change in the mission of each platform. Instead of each platform competing for users in the organization, they are free to provide those services best suited to their design or implementation. Mega-massive databases remain on the mainframe, accessed by anyone who needs the information and has the right to it. Specialized departmental data and services reside on the PCs and database servers, accessed by anyone who needs the information or resource and has the rights to it. Remote single-terminal offices can access departmental databases from their mainframe terminals. Inter-platform animosity can be greatly reduced, as each platform can retain its core services regardless of the entry point into the Enterprise Computing Platform the users may select.

This Enterprise Computing Platform approach requires a high level of interaction between the systems software engineering resources of all the platforms involved. Connectivity and resource access subsystems will have to be developed along with applications interfaces for each platform. The applications development personnel will need to be involved in the process to help design the interface abstractions that will best fit their business unit requirements. Training of the application programmers on the use of the new interface system will have to be provided.

The level of abstraction will have to be decided. The interfaces could be rather specific and primitive, modeling the I/O and operating system calls the developers are currently used to. They could become totally abstract and object oriented, modeling the way the business units see data and processes, such as "send a bill of lading of customer X's backorders to shipping." In most cases, abstraction usually progresses from the former to the latter as everyone becomes accustomed to the new environment. In essence, the abstraction is the Enterprise Computing Platform.

By isolating the business applications from discrete technologies, the core MIS systems resources can concentrate on improving services. The business units benefit by reducing the impact of technological changes on their applications. If a database server system is not capable of handling the rising workload, it can be replaced with a new system without changes to affected applications code. The abstract interface to the new system remains the same, although relinking and testing will be necessary, as well as conversion of existing data to the new system.

Meeting the Challenge

The importance of LAN systems software engineering resources and application programming support methodologies is obvious. Whether you take the PC/LAN Centric view or the Enterprise Computing Platform view, a professional approach to LAN enabled software development must be taken to effectively use the power and promise of the LAN. The same approach should be taken for any other platform in use within the organization for the same reasons.

The vendor community must also react to these needs. The current approach of attempting to provide complete solutions will not easily fit within this new reality—it does not fit well within the old reality, for that matter. Clients increasingly need access to technical references and formalized training on systems-level development on the platforms they are using. Every aspect of a solution needs to be opened to enable clients to follow their own design requirements. This is especially needed in various management functions that are currently available only through utility applications provided by the vendor. It is extremely frustrating to have to debug a gateway or bridge management utility to replicate a function that an application or subsystem will need. Those vendors providing complete APIs for their products will have a definite competitive advantage, an advantage that must be enforced by the client community's refusal to purchase products without them.

Development systems vendors need to provide user-extendible programming environments. This is very important in the object oriented environments that organizations will be moving to. Many available today do not allow the integration of functions into the normal environment; the user additions are treated as external things that are not manipulated in the same way as the standard functions.

In all fairness to the vendor community, it must be remembered that they respond to demand. The increased costs of providing functionality that the user community does not know how to use are not in their best short-term interests. Clients cannot demand something if they do not know that they need it. When the user community begins to implement a professional development organizational structure, they will know what they need and will start to demand it.

Microsoft Windows NT
Operating System

by Bill Gates
CEO of Microsoft Corporation

Author Bio

William H. (Bill) Gates III is chairman and chief executive officer of Microsoft Corporation, a multinational company that offers the most advanced family of microcomputer software, and which has a mission to put a computer on every desk and in every home.

Gates stared his career in computer software at an early age. Both Gates and Microsoft cofounder Paul Allen worked as consultants in the mainframe/ minicomputer programming field during their high school years in Seattle, Washington. In 1974 Gates, then an undergraduate at Harvard University, worked with Allen to develop a BASIC programming language for the first commercially available microcomputer, the MITS Altair. After successful completion of the project, the two formed Microsoft to develop and market software for the merging microcomputer marketplace.

In the years that followed, Microsoft has gone on to set standards for the software industry in languages, operating systems, and applications software. Mr. Gates continues to provide the company's vision on new products and technology. He is also actively involved in significant operating and strategic decisions, and he plays an important role in the technical development and management of Microsoft.

Founded in 1975, Microsoft has become the worldwide leader in software for personal computers. The company offers a wide range of products and services for business and personal use, each designed with the mission of making it easier and more enjoyable for people to take advantage of the full power of personal computing every day.

Microsoft finished the latest fiscal year in June 1991 with $1.18 billion in revenue. The company employs more than 10,000 people worldwide. Mr. Gates believes that Microsoft's success is highly dependent on its ability to attract and retain qualified employees.

Executive Summary

The Microsoft Windows NT operating system is Microsoft's platform for high-end computing needs for the 1990s. It combines the ease of use and broad application support of the Microsoft Windows operating system and the advanced capabilities of a new, high-end operating system, with support for MS-DOS, Windows, and 32-bit Windows-based applications, as well as OS/2 character-based and POSIX-compliant applications.

Introduction

Microsoft's long-term vision is *Information at Your Fingertips*. The results of this vision will be to give personal computer users access to more information and a simpler, more intuitive way of working with information.

The Microsoft Windows operating system will deliver this vision. Today, Windows provides an easy-to-use graphical interface and superb application availability, and it enables personal computer users to share information easily between applications.

An Evolutionary Path

Microsoft will extend the Windows operating system along an evolutionary path toward the *Information at Your Fingertips* ideal, constantly adding to its capabilities while retaining the benefits preferred by the millions of people using Windows today.

As personal computers become more diverse in terms of capabilities and configurations, it is no longer clear that one operating system is suitable for all systems or all users' needs. However, keeping a unified interface and common application platform is as important as ever. Microsoft's solution is to use Windows' scalable architecture to create multiple implementations that take maximum advantage of the expanding range of underlying hardware and applications. Microsoft's current and planned implementations of the Windows operating system fall into two broad categories.

Mainstream Windows Releases

These releases will run on current and future versions of the MS-DOS operating system and will include the features needed for the majority of desktop users. They will retain the basic model of being dependent on MS-DOS. Microsoft Windows version 3.1 is the most recent of these releases, making PCs easier to use while offering improved speed and reliability.

A High-End Implementation of Windows

Microsoft will also extend the Windows operating system to exploit advances in PC hardware—including 32-bit CPUs, RISC architectures, multiprocessing, high capacities of RAM and disk storage—and to make it a platform for advanced, line-of-business solutions. This new implementation, the Microsoft Windows NT operating system, is not based on MS-DOS. Instead, Windows NT is built on a new operating system kernel. Windows NT will take advantage of the latest and upcoming hardware and will provide the enhanced reliability, scalability, and security required for line-of-business solutions—all while retaining the strengths of Windows on the MS-DOS operating system platform. Most important, Windows NT will run the widest selection of applications for any platform today, by running MS-DOS- and Windows-based applications, as well as new 32-bit Windows-based applications, OS/2 character-based applications, and POSIX-compliant applications.

Building on the Strength of Windows

Microsoft Windows is the operating system of choice for millions of personal computer users today. Users choose Windows for its ease of use, application availability, productivity, and smooth integration into existing MS-DOS environments. The Microsoft Windows NT operating system will retain and build on these strengths.

Productivity and Ease of Use

The Microsoft Windows operating system, licensed to more than 10 million users, has changed the way PC users work. The ease of use of Windows and Windows-based applications has increased the productivity of millions of users.

Windows is easy to learn and use. It shows your work on-screen just as it appears when printed. Users can access more information than ever before: the Windows operating system makes it easy to share information between applications.

Windows NT will have the same familiar and proven graphical user interface as Windows 3.1.

Application Availability

Users of Windows have their choice of a vast and rapidly growing number of applications and tools. More than 5,000 Windows-based applications are currently available, from more than 1,500 software vendors. In every major category, you can choose from several excellent Windows-based programs.

Windows NT extends this availability. Not only will Windows NT enable you to run MS-DOS- and Windows-based applications on both Intel and RISC platforms without modification, it also supports new 32-bit Windows-based applications, character-based OS/2 applications, and POSIX-compliant applications.

Compatibility with MS-DOS

Windows operating system 3.x is built on top of MS-DOS and uses MS-DOS to access hardware. This provides tremendous benefits to the millions of PC users who have licensed the MS-DOS operating system: you can move up to the Windows graphical user interface without losing the benefits of your existing systems. You can still run your MS-DOS-based applications, often more easily than ever before.

Although Windows NT is not built on top of MS-DOS, it too supports MS-DOS-based applications, on both Intel and RISC platforms.

The Power of a High-End System

Microsoft's goal for Windows NT was to create a high-end PC operating system that supports access to high-performance, scalable hardware and provides the underpinnings needed for secure, distributed computing. The system would be able to run both Windows-based and MS-DOS-based applications and other applications based on systems such as POSIX. Furthermore, the system would have to allow for advances in computing, such as enhanced file system functionality and object-oriented technology.

The Genesis of Window NT

The Windows NT team designed a modular operating system as shown in Figure 15.1. In this scheme, similar to the *Mach* system designed at Carnegie-Melon University, the basic operating system functions are provided in a foundation layer (the *Executive* in Windows NT). This foundation supports the activities of protected subsystems, which implement services such as operating system services, environments, and APIs. Through these protected subsystems, Microsoft Windows NT will support programs based on Windows (including 32-bit applications), MS-DOS, POSIX, and character-based OS/2.

Portable	Desktop	Workstation and Server
Applications for Windows		
Microsoft Windows 3.1	**Microsoft Windows NT**	
MS-DOS		
Simpler, Smaller Intel-optimized Single Processor	**High-capacity Portable (Intel and RISC) Multiprocessor Secure (C2-level)**	

Figure 15.1. Windows NT's modular operating system design.

Windows NT is remarkable for its ability to deliver this flexibility without compromising any of the general requirements for a high-end operating system: performance, robustness, responsiveness, high capacity. And at the same time, Windows NT provides the scalability to take advantage of high-end hardware and built-in networking support.

Performance

Windows NT is designed to provide maximum performance, on whatever platform is used. It has full 32-bit architecture with a flat memory model.

This increases performance by providing 32-bit operations and a 32-bit data path. Its flat memory model eliminates the overhead associated with a segmented memory model.

Windows NT also provides processes with fast interprocess communications. Windows NT's *local procedure calls* deliver high performance, as well as clean design.

By supporting symmetrical multiprocessing, Windows NT performance can be scaled upward by adding an additional CPU to a Windows NT machine.

Robustness

Deploying business-critical applications and solutions requires confidence in the platform's stability and integrity. The Windows NT operating system prevents data corruption and helps ensure data integrity through *memory protection*. It provides the operating system and other processes with their own memory spaces. No process can bring another process, or the operating system, down.

Windows NT provides *application isolation*. Only system code can run in the most privileged execution mode. Applications cannot directly access hardware; applications make hardware requests to the Windows NT operating system.

The Windows NT file system (NTFS) provides advanced file system features, including hot-fix and a full recovery system to quickly restore file integrity: NTFS maintains a transaction log to ensure the integrity of the disk structure even if the system fails unexpectedly. Additional *fault tolerance* capabilities such as disk mirroring, drive duplexing, striping, RAID (Redundant Array of Inexpensive Disks), and support for uninterruptible power supplies will be available in LAN Manager for Windows NT (available separately).

Responsiveness

As part of Microsoft's vision of *Information at Your Fingertips*, PCs will become information appliances that bring information from diverse sources to the user. Providing this type of communication requires a responsive operating system, one that can access other platforms to retrieve data while simultaneously processing other data without losing messages.

The Windows NT operating system provides this needed responsiveness. With preemptive scheduling and an asynchronous input/output model, the operating system and the user, not the application, are in control. Reactive to the needs of the desktop user, Windows NT automatically gives applications running in the foreground high priority, as well as giving priority to processes receiving input or completing input/output operations. Multiple (per-process) threads of execution allow applications to be more powerful and responsive. With Windows NT, it is not possible for a single application to tie up the keyboard or mouse, even while that application is initially loading. This means that the system is always accessible to the user.

Windows NT accomplishes this by desynchronizing the system message queue from the per window message queue (the message queue associated with a particular application). This benefits both users and application developers. For users, it prevents an application from blocking the personal computer's entire user interface and making other applications inaccessible. Users can switch from one application to another, even if an application is printing, hung, or involved in a computationally intense task. For developers, it eliminates the need to insert interrupt polling routines into the applications.

Windows NT can also support tasks requiring constant processing availability, such as communications packages, with a sophisticated preemptive scheduler. This scheduler allocates processing time to threads based on priority and can preempt any thread at any time. The scheduler can allow very high priority tasks to run and maintain control, until an equal or higher priority task arrives.

All these together give Windows NT the responsiveness required for you to run processor-intensive applications such as CAD/CAM applications in the foreground while performing asynchronous communications in the background. For example, you can simultaneously draw a wire-frame diagram of an airplane wing while downloading engineering cost data for that wing.

High Capacity

PC users and developers alike benefit because Windows NT takes full advantage of their hardware resources. Windows NT can access 4G of RAM, and multiple terabytes of storage using 64-bit addressing. This means that you don't have to worry about your files growing too large for your PC to handle. And applications such as relational databases, which demand large amounts of RAM for optimal performance, can access more virtual memory (2G per application) than before. Windows NT's 32-bit architecture and 64-bit addressing eliminate any architectural limits on processes, threads, handles, and other system resources.

To take advantage of its high capacity, Windows NT automatically tunes itself to take advantage of whatever RAM is available: it dynamically balances RAM between paged memory and a file cache. The Windows NT cache manager uses available memory for disk caching, delivering significant benefits for input/output-intensive applications, such as databases.

Hardware Support

Windows NT will support a full set of disk drives: ST-506, ESDI, SCSI, CD-ROM, and WORM; video displays: VGA, Super VGA, XGA, 8514, and TIGA; network interface cards, including many 32-bit adaptors; tape drives: SCSI, 4mm, 8mm, 1/4"; and printers. Windows NT also supports the hundreds of printers supported by Windows 3.1.

Portability and Scalability

The Windows NT operating system will run on hardware ranging from desktop 80386 systems to high-end multiprocessing systems, giving access to some of the most powerful hardware available today. With Windows NT, there is no worry about applications and data outgrowing their platform. Windows NT runs on both 32-bit Intel CPUs (that is, 80386/80486 and above) and RISC CPUs. Because Windows NT supports symmetric multiprocessing, additional CPUs add computing power.

Portable Design

Unlike previous PC operating systems, which were designed and hardcoded for only one platform, the Microsoft Windows NT operating system is portable across platforms. It will run not only on 32-bit Intel system, but also on RISC architectures.

Windows NT's layered architecture is crucial to its portability. Within the Windows NT Executive is a compact, 50K *micro-kernel*. The micro-kernel handles low-level, machine-dependent functions, multiprocessor synchronization, thread dispatching, and kernel objects. In general, the portion of the Windows NT code that has to be changed when porting to a new type of CPU is located here and in the hardware abstraction layer (see Figure 15.2).

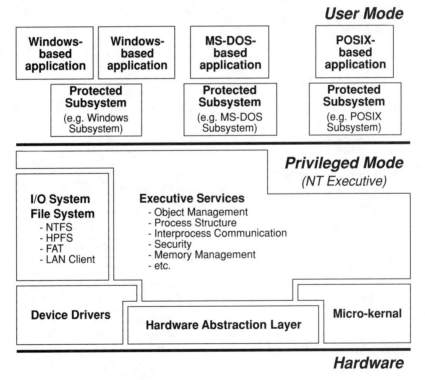

Figure 15.2. Windows NT's layered architecture

Symmetric Multiprocessing

The Windows NT operating system can deliver extraordinary performance and exceptional value by taking advantage of multiple CPUs. It is designed from the ground up to support symmetric multiprocessing. Each additional processor delivers a linear increase in performance. Windows NT can allocate threads within the same process to different processors and can allocate not only application threads across processors, but system threads as well.

Once again, it is Windows NT's modern design and layered architecture that make this possible. The micro-kernel (part of the Executive) services the rest of the Executive, which is fully preemptible, multithreaded, and reentrant. Through this design, not only do applications receive the benefit of multiple processors, so does the operating system.

Windows-based, 32-bit applications run without modification on symmetric multiprocessing systems and automatically take advantage of multiprocessing when available. Users benefit from improved performance and transparent scalability.

Security

The Windows NT operating system meets the high security standards of the U.S. government and will provide all the security you are ever likely to need. Sensitive personal or business information can now be confidently placed on a desktop or server machine. In Microsoft Windows NT, security is built into the operating system at a low level; it's not an afterthought.

Privileges and Users

Unlike many current PC operating systems, in which resources are freely available to whomever has access to the keyboard, Windows NT privileges can be assigned to particular users. This means that two people could serially (one after another) use the same Windows NT-based workstation and have access to different sets of resources.

All users, whether accessing machine resources at the console or across the network, must authenticate themselves before accessing a Windows NT system. Even after authentication, users have access only to objects and resources for which they have the appropriate permission. The operating system protects all objects and resources using access control lists. Users cannot delete Windows NT system files or critical configuration data.

Process Security

All process management, local procedure call activity, and even thread initiation are routed through the security subsystem in Windows NT. This means that applications cannot defeat the security model.

Certifiable for C2-Level Security

Windows NT will be certified at United States government C2-level for secure environments. In fact, its architecture will allow special versions of the Windows NT operating system to be certifiable for B-level security in the future.

Built-in Networking

An important part of the *Information at Your Fingertips* vision is to make it easy for PC users to share information with each other and to exchange information with non-PC platforms. Windows NT has secure peer networking capabilities built into it, both server and client, so it's easy to share and access information.

Built-in Secure File-Sharing and Print-Sharing

All Windows NT-based workstations can act as servers, sharing files on local hard drives with people running MS-DOS, Windows, or Windows NT operating systems. The tight security of Windows NT provides controlled access to important and sensitive information. Windows NT can share local printers with other users on the network. And Windows NT includes powerful workgroup application services, such as an integrated mail system.

To access and share information on local networks, as well as remote networks, Windows NT will support both local area network transports, such as NetBEUI, and the industry-standard routable TCP/IP transport.

Platform for Distributed Applications

It's not enough to share files and printers in today's world. The Windows NT operating system will make it easy to develop true distributed applications, by including a remote procedure call (RPC) that is compliant with the Open Systems Foundation's Distributed Computing Environment (DCE) standard. Because this RPC is DCE-compliant, distributed applications for Windows NT can connect to a wide range of other systems. This means that Windows NT applications written to the Windows NT RPC service can communicate and integrate with DCE-compliant servers running Windows NT, UNIX, VMS, and other systems. Of course, Windows NT will also support NetBIOS and named pipes, the industry-standard interprocess communications used by leading client-server applications today.

Open Network Interface

Bringing information to users is an important component of Microsoft's vision of *Information at Your Fingertips*. To this end, Microsoft is working closely with other leading network vendors such as Digital, Novell, and Banyan. Through the Windows Open Systems Architecture (WOSA), Microsoft is defining a standard, open set of interfaces for network services such as file-sharing and print-sharing, electronic mail, database access, administration, and configuration. WOSA allows users of Windows to access information and services across a multivendor computing environment.

Through WOSA, users of Windows NT can connect to enterprise computing resources from a wide range of industry-leading vendors. For many of these services, Microsoft will also provide a solution.

Access to Non-PC Resources

Microsoft's solution to connect to SNA resources is the DCA/Microsoft Communications Server. Through DEC Pathworks, users of the Windows NT operating system can take advantage of VMS and ULTRIX resources; DEC intends to support Windows NT as a Pathworks server and client. And through LAN Manager for UNIX, Windows NT users can take advantage of UNIX resources, including AFS, RFS, and NFS volumes.

With the Windows NT Services for Macintosh (available separately), Macintosh users will be able to share information with people using Windows NT, MS-DOS, and Windows operating systems.

Platform for Advanced Network Computing: LAN Manager for Windows NT

Although every Windows NT workstation will be able to share files and printers, and support RPC, there's an additional need to manage large networks. Microsoft LAN Manager for Windows NT (available separately) will provide the services needed to handle the largest and most complex PC networks.

LAN *Manager for Windows NT*

LAN Manager for Windows NT is an enterprise server going beyond the peer networking capabilities of Windows NT. It will provide advanced administration capabilities: just as Microsoft LAN Manager introduced the concept of *domains* to the PC LAN, making managing groups of servers as easy as if they were one server, LAN Manager for Windows NT will make it easy to manage multiple domains. With a single user account and password, a user will be able to access the resources of the entire network, not just a single domain.

After logging on to one domain, a trusted server can pass through a user's authentication to other domains. These trust relationships enable administrators to provide controlled access to users throughout the enterprise and give segmented privileges within portions of the entire network.

LAN Manager for Windows NT will also support advanced fault-tolerance features, including disk mirroring, drive duplexing, striping, RAID, and support for uninterruptible power supplies. It includes a NetView Alerter and supports SNMP (Simple Network Message Protocol) for network administration in TCP/IP environments.

Remote Administration

With LAN Manager for Windows NT, administrators can manage the network from any Windows NT-based workstation. Windows NT-based machines will provide administrators with configuration data and error messages remotely and can be rebooted on a fully remote basis. Administrators can even remotely install applications.

And with the Remote Access Service for Windows NT (available separately), administrators will be able to access and manage the network across phone lines and x.25 networks.

Integration with LAN Manager Networks

If you have Microsoft LAN Manager and LAN Manager for UNIX today, you will find it easy to integrate LAN Manager for Windows NT into the network. If you want to migrate from LAN Manager 2.1 to LAN Manager for Windows NT, Microsoft will provide you with tools and services to make this a smooth transition that can be as gradual or quick as necessary.

The Benefits of Windows in a High-End Operating System

The Windows NT operating system delivers the productivity, ease of use, and broad application availability of Microsoft Windows in a high-end operating system. Windows NT is a scalable, robust, and secure operating system, poised to deliver the power of PC hardware advances in the 1990s.

- *Windows User Interface:* Windows NT delivers the proven and familiar user interface of the Windows 3.1 operating system, which makes PCs easy to use and learn.

- *Broad Application Support:* Windows NT will run popular MS-DOS- and Windows-based applications on both Intel and RISC-based systems without modifications, as well as new 32-bit Windows- based applications, OS/2-character applications, and POSIX- compliant applications.

- *High-End Operating System:* Windows NT is a modern, high-end operating system. As a full 32-bit operating system, it takes full advantage of advanced hardware. Windows NT is a robust system, complete with memory protection, hardware isolation, and fault tolerance to provide the utmost in reliability. It is highly responsive and delivers enormous capacity on a PC platform.

- *Portable:* Windows NT runs on both Intel and RISC-based architectures.

- *Scalable:* Windows NT supports symmetric multiprocessing— effectively eliminating any ceiling on PC performance.

- *Secure:* Windows NT meets U.S. government security standards and provides all the security required to place sensitive and line-of-business information and solutions on desktop PCs and network servers.

- *Built-In Networking:* By providing file-sharing and print-sharing, workgroup application services, and a set of powerful IPCs, Windows NT brings networking into the desktop operating system.

System Requirements

The Microsoft Windows NT operating system will run on 32-bit Intel CPUs (80386 and higher) with a recommended configuration of 8M of RAM and 100M or more of disk space, as well as on similarly configured RISC systems.

The information contained in this document represents the current views of Microsoft Corporation on the issues discussed as of the date of publication. Because Microsoft must respond to changing market conditions, it should not be interpreted to be a commitment on the part of Microsoft, and Microsoft cannot guarantee the accuracy of any information presented after the date of publication.

Microsoft Corporation • One Microsoft Way • Redmond, WA 98052-6399

Portables on LANs—Now and Tomorrow

by Dirk I. Gates
President and CEO, Xircom

Author Bio

Dirk I. Gates is responsible for Xircom's technical vision, strategic product development efforts, and marketing direction. He has served as president and director since incorporation in November 1988 and has also served as CEO since October 1991. Before cofounding Xircom, Gates directed Advanced Development at Pertron Controls where he led a team of hardware and software engineers in the design of industrial control systems.

Gates earned his bachelor's and master's degrees from California State University, Northridge in electronics and communications electronics, respectively. He also holds a master's degree in business administration from Pepperdine University in Malibu, California. This year he was honored as Entrepreneur of the Year in High Technology for the Greater Los Angeles Area.

Executive Summary

The portable computing revolution promises to change the way we work, play, and communicate, bringing new challenges and opportunities to a worldwide audience. Identifying key technological advancements and market demands in the computer industry has given users the flexibility to work wherever necessary—at the office, at home or on the road.

Dirk I. Gates examines this trend, which is having a profound effect on the way people work. He also looks at the ways in which people are using portable PCs, what their real needs are, and what solutions are available to satisfy these needs.

In the ever-changing world of PC computing, one trend stands out as having a profound effect on the way we work: portable computing. As we look around, we see the continued proliferation of portable, laptop, and notebook PCs in virtually every facet of today's business. It is no longer sufficient to be bound by computers that only let us work at our office. As the technology and the market demands have evolved, these portable workhorses have given us the flexibility to work with our PCs wherever we may be—at the office, at home, or on the road. But with this new world of "mobile computing" has come new challenges and new opportunities.

In companies worldwide, small or large, local area networks (LANs) have become an accepted, almost required, part of doing business. They allow us to work cooperatively by sharing information and programs, by communicating more efficiently using electronic mail, and by sharing expensive resources such as printers, modems, and fax equipment. While we recognize the strategic importance of LANs, it has not been obvious how to connect the growing number of portable PCs to them. We need to look at the ways in which people are using portable PCs, what their real needs are, and what solutions are available to satisfy these needs.

Unlike the early portables that lacked the power to be the primary PC for the majority of users, today's portables, mostly notebooks, rival desktops for all but the most demanding of specialized applications. They have powerful 386 (and now 486) processors, large disks, ample memory, and high-resolution displays. No longer just for the frequent traveler, today's notebooks have become efficient tools for all users, whether they travel often, or simply need to take their PC home at night or on the occasional business trip. Although the needs of these diverse users vary, they still have to connect to the network when they return to the office.

The issue concerning connecting notebook PCs to LANs is a simple one. Since notebooks lack the internal card slots of desktops, they can't accept the same standard network interface cards. As a result, other methods must be used in order to achieve the kind of network connectivity required by notebook PCs. Though the issue is simple enough, the answer takes a bit of analysis.

There are two types of solutions that are available today for linking notebooks to LANs, docking stations and external LAN adapters. Each has its own set of advantages and disadvantages, with neither being the perfect solution for all applications. Two new technologies, credit card-sized LAN adapters and wireless LAN adapters, will expand the growing notebook-to-LAN market by providing additional networking solutions for new portable platforms in the future.

Docking Stations—Not for Everyone

Many of today's notebook manufacturers are offering docking stations as a means of providing additional expansion capabilities in an attempt to further bridge the gap between desktops and notebooks.

Docking stations offer the maximum in expansion capabilities. They also offer additional convenience because external connections are made to the docking station itself rather than the notebook. However, docking stations sacrifice in the areas of compatibility, portability, and price.

One advantage of docking stations is that they accept the same internal network cards as desktops. This benefits a department or company with both desktop and notebook PCs because it reduces the number of different solutions to support. Because docking stations can use the same network cards as the desktops, the performance should be the same. Furthermore, these slots also can be used for other purposes, including mainframe access, high-speed modems, high-resolution display adapters, and CD-ROM controllers. Plus, the docking station's drive bays can increase disk storage capacity beyond that of the notebook itself, providing for even more expansion.

Although docking stations have many advantages, they also have some drawbacks that limit their effectiveness for many users. First, docking stations are proprietary in nature. They are designed to be used only with specific notebook PCs and are not interchangeable among different PC manufacturer's products. Therefore, if you change notebooks as newer and more powerful models become available, you may also need to buy a new docking station as well. With many companies using different models of notebooks from different manufacturers, the number of docking stations to support can become a management problem. In addition, docking stations are not available for all notebooks, and many of the notebooks don't have compatible docking stations.

The installation and setup of docking stations should also be considered. Most typical internal network cards must be properly configured for IRQ, I/O address, and memory base address. This is usually accomplished via either jumpers and switches or a separate software program. In either case, the configuration will require someone with a reasonable level of network expertise. In addition, many network operating systems, such as Novell's NetWare, require a separate procedure to generate the actual network driver (a NetWare IPX shell, for example) as part of the configuration process. While vendors are making this step easier, it can still be a tedious and often error-prone task. Several docking stations also have switches for power settings and other options that must be set to ensure proper operation and which also require the user to open up the docking station. In general, configuring a docking station will require all of the necessary steps for an internal card used in a desktop, plus the unique installation and setup procedures needed for the particular docking station.

As a desk bound solution, docking stations are not very portable. As more locations have LANs available, it is becoming increasingly attractive to be able to connect to the LAN at a remote site as well as the home office.

For mobile users who have such a need, docking stations don't provide all the flexibility they might want.

A final area of consideration with docking stations is price. A typical docking station, including the appropriate network interface card, can cost in the range of $1,000—$1,500, making docking stations the most expensive of the solutions.

While docking stations have been a popular notebook-to-LAN solution over the past few years, there has been a trend toward another, more flexible alternative—external LAN adapters. Offering many advantages over docking stations, external LAN adapters have been steadily growing in popularity, a trend which will continue as the market for mobile computing expands.

External LAN Adapters—A Universal Solution

The solution that has continued to gain widespread popularity for linking notebook PCs to LANs is the external LAN adapter. Pioneered by California-based Xircom, external LAN adapters connect through the parallel port found on all notebooks and perform the same function as traditional internal cards.

Essentially, external LAN adapters are typical network interface cards that differ only in the way they connect to and transfer information to and from the PC. They use the same kinds of LAN chips (such as National Semiconductor's Ethernet and Texas Instruments' token ring chips) as internal cards, and they appear to the network just like a desktop PC with an internal card. However, external LAN adapters use the PC's parallel port both as a connection and a replacement for the actual bus (ISA, EISA, or Micro Channel) found in desktops.

Although not originally intended for such use, the parallel port serves as an excellent vehicle for network traffic to and from the notebook. Using software loops to control the orderly transfer, data packets are typically passed one byte at a time through the parallel port similar to the way they are passed through a desktop's bus. While this requires special low-level driver software that can communicate with the parallel port, the high-level network drivers, the network applications, and the network itself do not see the difference. In fact, even industry standard network management and diagnostic will not view an external adapter as anything out of the ordinary.

External LAN adapters typically cost one-half to one-third less than docking station and an internal card. They come in both pocket-size versions and larger desktop versions which contain an additional parallel port and can provide support for multiple media types in a single adapter. They're available from several vendors for Ethernet, token ring, and ARCnet networks as well. External LAN adapters offer some unique advantages that help explain their growing popularity.

First, by utilizing the parallel port, external LAN adapters offer a universal solution and are compatible with any notebook or desktop PC. This frees users from selecting a particular notebook PC simply because it has a docking station available, and allows them to select the one that best suits their needs. In companies that have notebooks from several manufacturers installed, this compatibility allows the network administrator to support a single solution for all notebook PCs. Today, as more companies purchase different notebooks from a number of different vendors, this feature becomes even more important. This universal compatibility has an additional advantage as well. As users change or upgrade their notebooks to newer and more powerful ones, they can continue to use the same external LAN adapter on the new one, thereby protecting their investment.

Installation and configuration are also areas where external LAN adapters excel. They don't have the configuration switches or jumpers found on internal cards for setting IRQ, I/O address, memory base address. This not only simplifies the process, but also eliminates the kinds of interrupt or address conflicts that can occur with internal cards, particularly as additional peripherals are added. Most external LAN adapters are self-configuring so they automatically determine which parallel port they're on. Many come with pregenerated drivers for popular network operating systems, making configuration even easier. Some take it another step by supporting multiple media types (thin-wire coax, UTP, and AUI connections, for example) in a single unit. These adapters automatically sense which type of wiring is attached and configure the adapter accordingly.

Another advantage of external LAN adapters is portability, particularly with the pocket-size versions. Slightly larger than a package of cigarettes, external LAN adaptors are easily carried with the notebook and can be connected to LANs at remote locations such as company field offices or client's offices. The desktop models, although larger than the pocket-size ones, are still quite portable and offer the added benefit of multiple media support in a single unit.

On the other hand, external LAN adapters aren't as fast as internal cards. This is primarily due to the maximum throughput that can be achieved through the parallel port. In measured performance tests, external LAN adapters are about 20 to 40 percent slower than their internal counterparts. For applications that require unusually high levels of data traffic, or where frequent transfers of large files are performed, the reduced performance of external LAN adapters can be a problem. However, external LAN adapters provide more than adequate performance for most typical workstation applications, and users probably will not notice the differences.

A recent development that has increased the performance of external LAN adapters is the Enhanced Parallel Port (EPP), developed jointly by Xircom, Zenith Data Systems, and Intel Corporation. EPP emulates a traditional ISA bus through the parallel port, and yields comparable performance. EPP emulates a standard ISA bus in firmware and provides an enhanced method of transferring data through the parallel port. Rather than requiring a software loop (which can be 6-12 instructions/byte) to transfer each byte through the port, EPP allows a byte of data to be transferred using a single I/O instruction. This significantly reduces the parallel port's overhead. EPP allows "repeated string I/O," whereby an entire string of bytes can be transferred through the parallel port still using a single I/O instruction. It is this reduction in the overhead/byte that gives EPP its increased performance. Using an industry-standard performance test, an EPP-capable notebook with an EPP-capable external LAN adapter tested faster than a popular 8-bit internal card.

An additional advantage is that EPP is backward compatible with conventional parallel ports so that it can be used with non-EPP peripherals such as standard parallel printers. Intel has incorporated support for EPP in the 82360SL I/O subsystem chip that is part of their 80386SL chip set. As a result, many of the new 386SL-based notebook PCs on the market are already EPP-capable, and even more of the recently announced ones will support EPP.

One additional potential drawback to external LAN adapters is local printer support. Since these adapters connect through the notebook's parallel port, the port is no longer free to connect to a local printer. While most users prefer to use the network's printers which are often high-speed laser printers, some still require a local printer, often a dot matrix printer for multipart forms or labels. Fortunately, there are solutions to this problem. First, desktop versions of external LAN adapters typically include an additional parallel port specifically to address this need. This additional port looks like a standard parallel port (either LPT1 or LPT2) and can be used transparently by all applications.

What's on the Horizon?

While external LAN adapters offer the most flexible, universal solution for notebook-to-LAN connectivity today, there are two new technologies on the horizon that will provide additional options for networking tomorrow's portable PCs.

The first are credit card-size LAN adapters that meet the Personal Computer Memory Card International Association's (PCMCIA) 2.0 standard. PCMCIA has been adopted by leading PC manufacturers as the newest technology for adding peripherals such as modems and LAN adapters to notebook, palmtop, and pen-based computers.

Unlike an external LAN adapter that uses the parallel port, a credit card LAN adapter (sometimes called a PC Card) fits into a PCMCIA compatible slot in a portable PC. PCMCIA is an industry standard rather than any vendor's proprietary solution, and as such, both notebook PCs and peripherals that conform to it will be able to interoperate. This universal interoperability will be one of the major factors in the widespread adoption of PCMCIA on portable and desktop PCs alike.

Unlike the parallel port used by external LAN adapters, PCMCIA uses an interface that offers the same performance as traditional internal cards.

As a result, credit card LAN adapters will not compromise performance in comparison to internal cards. Unlike external LAN adapters, credit card LAN adapters do not require an external power supply, which reduces the number of components the user must deal with.

With all of the advantages of PCMCIA, users should expect to see virtually every manufacturer of portable PCs, including notebooks, palmtops, pen-based Personal Digital Assistants (PDAs), and many desktop manufacturers introducing products that support PCMCIA in the near future. With Xircom leading the way in credit card LAN adapters, you also can expect to see a full range of PCMCIA memory and peripheral products as well.

Getting Rid of the Wires

While external and credit card LAN adapters and PCMCIA cards offer convenient, universal connectivity solutions for notebooks PCs, they still place limits on the user's ability to be mobile by requiring a wired "tether" to the network. As mobility becomes more important, solutions that support the mobile, or "tetherless," user become essential. With smaller, lighter notebook PCs, palmtops, pen-based PCs, and PDAs, the trend toward portable computing tools is clear. Nomadic users, however, still require access to the information and resources that are provided by their corporate networks and cannot be limited by physical wired connections.

As a result, we will see the emergence of "tetherless" LANS, not as a replacement for wired LANs, but rather as a complement to them. "Tetherless" LANS provide convenience as well as mobility. Users will be able to move freely about a building or campus, send and receive electronic mail, and access resources such as printers, all with no wired umbilical. Participants in a group meeting will be able to use their notebook (or other portable computing machines) to share information among themselves and the wired network without having to find a wired connection for each one. The applications are limited only by the imagination.

The Data Center
Takes Control of LANs

by Greg Gianforte
President, Brightwork Development, Inc.

Author Bio

Greg Gianforte is president and founder of Brightwork Development, Inc., a manufacturer and developer of local area network (LAN) support tools. He is a frequently featured speaker and contributing author to many trade publications. He formerly held positions at Bell Laboratories and AT&T Computer Systems Division, where he acquired LAN software products for AT&T private label. An engineer by training, Mr. Gianforte completed his Masters in Computer Science and thesis on local area networks in 1983.

Executive Summary

For the IS staff accustomed to managing a data center, the job of managing decentralized local areas networks can be challenging. This paper examines the five primary ways in which LAN support is different from traditional minicomputer or mainframe support.

At a recent industry event, more than 250 IS professionals packed a conference room to learn about successfully supporting LANs. Most had not been involved in the initial LAN installations at their firms, yet they were now being asked to take over support for the LANs. A computer is a computer is a computer, right?

Well, not quite. What many of these IS managers are finding is that there are some significant differences between supporting host users and supporting LAN-connected PC users. For the most part, LAN support can be much more expensive than host support. Thankfully, these higher support costs are offset by the drastically reduced expenses associated with the LAN system itself. But you will probably need to lobby to get some of the savings diverted to support functions so you can do an effective job. This article will give you the justification you need.

Software Diversity and Freedom

The first major difference between minicomputer and LAN support is how software is installed and managed. On a host system the IS department traditionally has a well-thought-out plan of execution to install and implement software. It is impossible for an end user to go out at lunch time and pick up a magnetic tape at a local shopping mall and come back to the office and load it on the mainframe without anyone authorizing it. Yet this is a daily occurrence on most large LANs.

One IS manager recently promoted to MIS manager (now with a window office overlooking the company parking lot) was appalled to see the diversity of local software-store bags being carried into the building every day after lunch. End users believe it is their privilege to load whatever software they feel is sufficient to perform their daily functions, without thought to any consequences it may cause.

Such activity presents several potential problems for the IS manager who traditionally did not have to deal with such end-user freedom:

- Legal exposure due to noncompliance with software license agreements

- Compromised system reliability

- Higher support load due to software diversity

What to Do

Decide what your software policy is and state it in writing. It should answer questions such as

- Which packages will you support?

- Can users load their own package on the LAN?

- How will you protect local hard drives against viruses?

No matter what your policy is, it takes periodic audits of your LAN to determine what you have installed. Electronic means are now available to do this.

Vendors, Vendors, Vendors

LANs are comprised of many vendors. Typically, more than 50 vendors are involved in supplying all the components for a single LAN: PCs, hard drives, monitors, mice, adapter cards, application software, utilities, cabling, backup devices, and so on. With all the dip switch settings, the software options, and the other particulars of your LAN configuration, ask yourself, "Who certified our configuration?" Generally, the answer to this question is no one. This fact adds a level of uncertainty to LAN support.

Successful support relies on a process of elimination. With too many variables in the equation, such a process can be difficult to implement.

What to Do

Standardize as much as possible. Select a minimum number of vendors and configurations in each required area. For example, configure all machines that will run Windows with 6 megabytes of RAM even if not all users will require it, because the machines will be interchangeable when something breaks. Or create classes of machines such as secretarial, manager, software developer, and so on, each having particular characteristics for the user but not a lot of diversity within the class. The extra money you spend on a machine will be made back in eased support and system reliability because the components are interchangeable.

Do a configuration audit when you first get control of the LAN to standardize as much as possible. For example, the file structure on each file server should be similar; users should generally configure their memory managers in similar ways. Doing this greatly simplifies the troubleshooting process when something does go wrong.

One Person per Hundred Users

It's a fact: LANs take more people to support than mainframes do. Expect your LAN to require one support person for every 75 to 125 users. You can do a few things to adjust this number, but support is intensive.

One airline was able to support an 800-node LAN with only three people. This was accomplished by implementing diskless PCs and only one application. Users were unable to load any new software. This is a luxury most of us will be unable to sell in our organizations.

What to Do

Agree on service levels with your users. For example, will you support all applications they can drag out from under a rock? If so, you will need more people. The more you agree to support, the more people you will need.

Participatory Support

Get users involved in the support process. Fifty or more years ago, AT&T did a projection which showed that given the rate of growth of phone usage and the amount of time required to connect telephone calls, by the year 2000 everyone in North America would have to be a telephone switchboard operator. Guess what? It happened. Every user of a phone participates in the old switchboard work. A similar occurrence will happen to LAN users.

Getting users involved in the support process, if done properly, can actually *reduce* your support load. Also, as LANs grow, not doing so can set you up to have your resources totally consumed by increasing support loads.

Here are some steps to get you started:

1. Designate departmental LAN coordinators for every 15 to 30 users. Choose people who have a desire to learn and want to increase their PC aptitude. These people already exist within your companies and are helping users daily in the various departments. You just need to get them on your team. They might do nothing more than hand out software manuals initially, but they will be invaluable later as your advocate on the front lines. The job should not take more than 20 to 30 percent of their time.

2. Get your departmental LAN coordinators together once a month. Make them feel special. Give them LAN knowledge through monthly training—for example, how to use multiple fonts in the word pro-cessor or how to access a new application on the LAN. They can then share this information with their departmental users and gain satisfaction from having special networking knowledge. Also, at your monthly meetings distribute written solutions to LAN problems that have occurred in other departments. Select problems you feel your departmental managers might be able to solve on their own.

3. Direct departmental people to these managers as a first-line support. If it is simple cockpit error or one of the problems you have documented, they will then be able to handle it, and this will reduce the calls to your central help desk.

The objective is to create a support pyramid in which only the most difficult problems reach your most experienced support staff. Enforcing a support structure like this leaves your users better able to help themselves, they receive faster turnaround on simple problems, and your central staff deals only with problems that require their attention. As your departmental coordinators become more knowledgeable, they will be able to handle more difficult problems.

Moves and Changes

Ever have someone walk off with a cluster controller? Probably not. Ever have someone move a PC without telling you? A daily occurrence on a LAN. User-initiated moves and changes are a major headache.

It is impossible to support a LAN unless you know what you have installed. The first step in getting control is taking a site survey. Without detailed knowledge of what is installed and where it is, it's close to impossible to effectively support a LAN.

Suggestions for Taking Control

- Document what you have installed, and monitor changes in software and hardware.

- Standardize as much as possible, and minimize the number of vendors and configurations you have to support. Bundle major groups of users together into classes and instruct them on those standards.

- Shift savings to support. Define the level of support you will provide. Determine what services the user department will bill-out for support and which portion you will provide. Look at the savings you have received from moving from a larger system to LANs and how much must be allocated to LAN support.

- Empower users to assist in support. Set up a support pyramid that enables users to participate in the support process. This will reduce the support load on you and make your users more self-sufficient, leaving you time for strategic planning and evolution of your systems.

The MIS manager who doesn't use the PC talents of nontraditional MIS personnel are closing the doors to 'free' end-user support...and opening the floodgates for high expenses trying to find 'qualified, traditional' personnel to support LANs.
—name withheld, LAN Manager

The Once and Future NOS

by Robert Gill
Vice President, Gartner Group

Author Bio

Bob Gill is a market analyst/consultant with Gartner Group in Stamford, Connecticut. His research focuses on network computing, with emphasis on network operating system (NOS) vendors, technologies, products, and trends. Major attentions focus on the current and future impact NOS technologies will have in creating a logical infrastructure for next generation network computing applications.

Mr. Gill has 14 years experience in communications and networking, and has help-management and technical positions at Western Electric and a number of AT&T marketing, product management, and laboratory organizations. Prior to joining Gartner Group in 1989, Mr. Gill served in network planning in AT&T Communications' Concept Development Center.

Mr. Gill holds a master's degree in management information systems from Stevens Institute of Technology and a bachelor's degree in business administration from the University of Notre Dame.

Executive Summary

Tempering the enthusiasm over the Network Operating System's role in network computing, alternative technologies appear to threaten the very viability of the product category. We propose that over time, surviving and relevant LAN NOS technology will be driven to commodity as the demand for interoperable solutions increases and standards-based model for distributed computing gains acceptance. Ultimately, the surviving NOS offerings in the late 1990's will be viewed as a coordinated set of distributed computing services, built largely from then-commodity modules. The future NOS sheds the image of a server technology and becomes the manageable "glue" or "plumbing" of network computing.

As operating systems such as Windows NT and Apple System 7 gain networking functions, file and print protocols such as Sun's NFS and Microsoft's SMB become commoditized, and consortia such as the OSF seek to establish open and available sets of technology for distributed computing, the future market demand for NOS products is seemingly in doubt. If file and print services are indeed commodities and client/server processing is separate and distinct from today's NOS functionality, the future role of the NOS in network computing remains questionable.

What is NOS's Role Today?

Despite the excitement surrounding LAN-based client/server, the majority of today's LAN applications still revolve around serving DOS and Mac applications and providing physical transport to host systems. While it is true that many advanced implementations feature robust application servers with client-based presentation services, such systems are still in the minority. We believe 1992 will be remembered as the year that LAN-based, mission-critical applications first moved into the mainstream, with vendors such as Sequent, Hewlett-Packard, Oracle, and Sybase providing the core application-server technology to make such systems possible. We also believe that the magnitude of the installed base of applications and data makes it extremely difficult for an entirely new processing model to be inserted into an IT plan. Therefore, in order for client/server computing to become mainstream during the planning period, coexistence with and migration from existing applications is paramount.

The role of today's NOS is to continue providing file and print services while offering the manageable transport "glue" to tie "legacy" DOS clients to an exploding array of application servers. As newer and more powerful clients emerge (Windows NT, OS/2 2.0, and UNIX, for example), the NOS will need to provide an even higher degree of application services integration. Vendors such as Banyan, Novell, and Microsoft will provide such services by the end of 1992. As a result, the key role of today's NOS technology is to facilitate the *migration* of today's processing model toward client/server computing. Network computing is the superset of services and procedures that allows this migration.

Will Today's NOS Technology Be Driven to Commodity?

As we leave the decade of "years of the LAN" and enter the decade of network computing, NOS vendors face two dramatic challenges. The first is the increasingly sophisticated application or use of the NOS (far beyond simple file and print) and the associated platform demands . Many planners are questioning if the NOS is even the right platform for client server computing given the complex demands of distributed computing and the current paucity of NOS benefits. The second challenge is the widespread commoditization of the very technology that each vendor has so closely guarded. Mirroring the LAN interconnection market's relentless drive to incorporate higher layers of protocols into silicon or public domain source code, NOS technology is also being commoditized up the ISO protocol stack, with no obvious end in sight (see Figure 18.1).

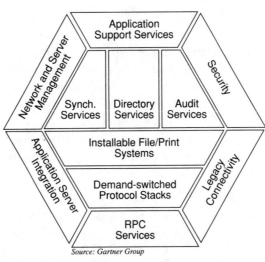

Source: Gartner Group

Figure 18.1. NOS technology commoditization.

Later in this paper we will examine the likely future role and structure of enterprise-serving NOS offerings, which we refer to as CNOS (Corporate NOS) products and services. Key to the CNOS concept is an orientation toward sets of manageable network services as opposed to specific departmental "server boxes." For heterogeneous devices and configurations to make use of NOS technology as the "glue" in network computing, it is vital that many of these services will be common across offerings, allowing interoperability between mixed client and server populations. We believe that this vendor focus on commonality and, therefore interoperability, will give way to the sharing and ultimately the commoditization of these services, thus reshaping the market.

The trend toward aggressive competition through commoditizing one's own technology (known in LAN folklore as "Anthemizing,") now extends to core NOS technology with a clear goal in mind: expanding the overall market for LAN software while creating nearly insurmountable survival hurdles or barriers to entry for less aggressive players.

Concurrent with the self-imposed drive for "better, faster, cheaper" technology, today's NOS vendors are also challenged with meeting user expectations of the LAN NOS as a distributed application platform. The inclusion of such advanced (and as yet non-commodity) technologies as directory, authentication, and management services finally offers hope for the NOS as a "systems platform." Interoperability between "legacy NOS" platforms and the resulting ability to migrate to the more advanced systems platform are key to vendor sales and user implementation success. The combination of such advanced platform services in conjunction with the above mentioned, ubiquitous "multivendor installable services" such as file systems will prove to be the cleanest path for users toward tomorrow's network computing environments. Accordingly, vendors will be forced to adopt such a product planning model to maintain their relative market positions. For NOS dependent corporations such as Novell and Banyan, a business model that proposes growth at current rates perpetuates increasing reliance on non-traditional NOS revenues, perhaps from providing communications services (Gateways and protocol stacks), network management platforms, and even integration services.

In the short term, we believe virtually *all* of today's NOS services will become commodity modules by 1996, either as installable options or through a "black box" API emulation approach. In addition, network and resource management, packaging, distribution, and support will become the primary differentiators of the NOS in 1997. Even such elusive services as network and systems management will become "commodity-like" as higher-layer management platforms such as Hewlett-Packard's OpenView and Sun Microsystems' SunNet Manager mask many of the unique properties of vendor-specific management applications. The ultimate winner is the user, who will finally obtain a services-rich, distributed application platform with a clear migration path from today's technology. While a reduction in the number of vendors could imply a reduction in technology diversity and, ultimately, slow innovation, new pressures from other market segments such as traditional operating systems vendors (USL with UNIX and Microsoft with NT, for example) will forestall NOS vendor complacency. Perhaps the greatest irony is that by the end of the planning period, interoperability— how well a product works with competitors' products—will become the key differentiator *between* products.

We urge planners to begin viewing NOS offerings as strategic *sets* of common services, favoring the products (and corresponding service sets) that will best connect existing and planned clients to server resources. A market analogy for these services can be found in the TCP/IP market, where companies such as FTP software and Wollongong have been extremely successful in selling packaged TCP/IP protocol stacks into a market base that could obtain such technology via the Internet. While specific advanced services such as directory, security, and management will continue to be vendor-unique for several years, a services orientation will avoid the short-sighted, departmental-box buying that has led many users to technological dead ends.

What Exactly is NOS's Future Role in Network Computing?

Network computing has been and will continue to be possible without the use of a PC NOS. Vendors, such as Sun Microsystems with ONC and HP-Apollo with NCS, have developed complex applications using workstations and UNIX servers for nearly a decade. In these cases, advanced protocol mechanisms and programming interfaces attempt to shield the developer and user from the underlying network. Unfortunately, the reliance on operating system communications extensions for network computing assumes a considerable degree of homogeneity between a small set of client and server options, as well as integration expertise on the part of the user. This advanced layer of "network richness" must and will be provided for heterogeneous configurations by Microsoft, Banyan, and Novell by early 1993 in order to move "PC LANs" beyond PC disk sharing and establish the next generation NOS as the Network Computing foundation.

Eventually, we believe that the majority of network computing applications will not be NOS server-based at all, but will be developed on general-purpose application servers and mainstream front-end client operating systems. The key distinction is that today's image of a file and print service PC NOS bears little resemblance to the corporate NOS emerging role. The primary reason we believe the NOS is critical to network computing is that it is already offering established, ubiquitous transport for the majority of the millions of PCs and workstations in the installed base. A technology that can provide managed transport—the basic "glue" today—and evolve to meet the more demanding connectivity needs during the planning period provides a cost-effective, politically palatable means of migrating users to more complex processing models.

What's Next?

By mid-1993, the availability of these network computing application services and the availability of more powerful clients such as Windows/NT and UNIXWare will drive a new focus for the NOS vendors: evolve products to CNOS capabilities, or face dwindling market share in a shrinking portion of a growing market. Successful CNOS implementations will provide unique combinations of both commodity and proprietary elements, enabling heterogeneous multivendor network computing. While the OSF DCE model is a viable framework and shows the types of services widely distributed computing will require, we believe a successful CNOS of the mid-1990s will be a superset of such a model, with differentiation arising from the CNOS integration capabilities and backward compatibility (see Figure 18.2). The CNOS will support the requisite elements of models such as ONC and DCE, but will extend beyond these through vendor-specific management systems, backward compatibility for multiple client types and host systems, and multiple installable file systems and protocol stacks.

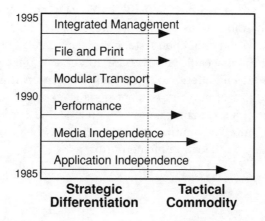

Figure 18.2. CNOS reference model (source: Gartner Group).

Is There No Room for Innovation in Traditional NOS Servers?

Concurrent with the evolution of the CNOS to framework status, the very nature of the data being stored and retrieved in a file-and-print system is evolving. Storage of advanced data objects, whether they be high-resolution images or graphics, or even multimedia speech and video, will place new stress on the storage, retrieval, and output systems traditionally thought to be the domain of the NOS. In this instance, even supposedly stable file/print protocols and services must undergo radical change. An orientation to predictable digital data streaming rather than probabalistic packet switching is indicated for the handling of multisession, continuous video, while algorithms for compression, aging, and long term storage of huge images will change even the most basic of NOS foundation technology.

Bottom Line

To a cynical top-down eye, the LAN NOS was and will be a passing PC communications fad that will never achieve the power or respect of legacy operating systems such as MVS, VM, or VMS, and therefore has no place in enterprise computing. While hard-core NOS enthusiasts may argue these specifics, the debate is myopic. Network computing applications will be served on application servers, including those based on the operating systems mentioned (and their open systems replacements). The LAN NOS was and will be the manageable multivendor, integrating "glue" that will tie together more front-end clients to more back-end servers than any other technology. The goal of network computing is to extract the best of the desktop, NOS, proprietary mainframe and open models. In order to achieve outstanding distributed computing implementations, the CNOS must be the once and future vehicle of implementation.

Enterprise Messaging— Implementing the Company Post Office

by Steve Glagow
Enterprise Communication Marketing Manager
Digital Equipment Corporation

Author Bio

Steve Glagow is responsible for worldwide product marketing of Digital's Enterprise Communication products which include electronic mail. Steve joined Digital in March 1989 in Valbonne, France, as the business communications marketing manager. His responsibilities included marketing of Digital's electronic messaging, videotext, computer conferencing, electronic data interchange (EDI), and voice messaging products in Europe. Steve moved to the U.S. in August 1991 to assume his current position.

Before joining Digital, Steve was the manager of Strategic Business Services with Coopers & Lybrand. Steve was responsible for marketing and management of major domestic and international market research projects. The technology focus was office information systems, enhanced telecom services (electronic data interchange, electronic messaging, videotext, and so forth), and network management services.

Mr. Glagow is currently on the board of directors of the U.S.-based Electronic Mail Association. While in Europe, Steve was the vice chairman

Insider's Guide to Personal Computing and Networking

of the European Electronic Messaging Association. He has been a contributing editor of *Office Systems* magazine and has written articles for several trade magazines.

Executive Summary

The electronic post office is reality today—it is at Digital and in probably 20 or more companies around the world. At Digital, internal hard copy mail has declined by more than 60 percent over the last 10 years. Digital's worldwide messaging network is complex and takes several people to manage, but the system costs less than the number of people required to manage the internal paper mail force. We were able to build an electronic post office only because everyone uses the same electronic messaging post office—the one we developed. This is not the case for the majority of corporations. This paper talks about the issues corporations have faced in deployment of the electronic post office and how vendors are helping to make this a reality for all companies.

The electronic post office is an essential asset for most organizations. The 1990s will be the decade of rightsizing, cost efficiencies, and high speed communications. Corporations must enlarge the infrastructure they developed in the 1980s by incorporating new, leading-edge technology. Electronic messaging provides a competitive edge by sharing information and data in less time than it takes to read this paragraph. That makes decision making more effective and enables a faster reaction to new opportunities. But when will everyone have the electronic post office available?

By the year 2000 every white-collar worker in the United States will have access to a global network—a network that will allow people to receive electronic mail, voice mail, access data worldwide, computer conferencing, fax, telex, and full motion multiuser video conferencing. While business women and men travel, their pocket computers will send and receive information using wireless communications. The paperless office will be a step closer—and the electronic post office will be fully operational and effective!

To achieve this vision many vendors have been working together to establish rules and guidelines for the design and development of commercial technology. Many user companies will have invested millions of dollars in industry standard compliant software and will have spent countless hours implementing those systems. There is no doubt that the investment will be worth it. The global information network will allow companies to communicate internally with staff members and internationally with their trading partners—24 hours a day.

Let's look back on how it all began. We will look at what is happening in 1992 and how we got here, what the business problems and issues are, and how the technical issues were resolved.

What Is Happening in 1992?

Desktop devices are proliferating within the Fortune 1000. Each day new Local Area Networks (LANs) are appearing in departments as small as 20 or 30 users. LANs are being connected into corporate wide area networks, and it is estimated that by 1995, 95 percent of all white-collar workers in the Fortune 1000 will have access to their corporate network from their desktop of choice.

Access to the corporate network does not necessarily mean the ability to share information or receive information ubiquitously. The end user, however, has to receive information on his desktop device the same as he would in paper form on his desk. This article deals with the issue of transparent ubiquitous sharing of information, and using the network to deliver enterprise-wide electronic mail—to the desktop of choice, on the network of choice, with the messaging system of choice.

How Did We Get to 1992?

The first computer-based messaging service was introduced in 1974. The first publicly available computer-based messaging software for internal corporate use was developed and became available in 1975. Since then both service providers and software developers have been working furiously to develop new and better messaging systems. The problem for end users was that none of the messaging systems could communicate beyond their own domain. Information Systems (IS), however, was in the process of implementing the same electronic messaging system company wide. Unfortunately, not all divisions had the same computer equipment and operating system, and the same electronic messaging system did not run across different vendor systems.

When the PC was introduced in the late 1970's, departmental managers found that they could provide personal productivity tools to their people at a reasonable price using off-the-shelf software and by not requiring corporate computing resources or the corporate MIS department. Small LANs began proliferating in the early 1980s, and PC users began to share information. PC-based messaging systems began appearing at the same time as LANs. Although people now could communicate within their own groups, they still could not take advantage of corporate electronic messaging systems.

The problem of enterprise messaging was growing more complex. Multiple incompatible LANs and electronic messaging systems were springing up in groups and divisions throughout most companies, and few were able to intercommunicate. Departmental managers were also selecting office information systems such as ALL-IN-1 and PROFS, which have electronic messaging central to their design.

In the early 1980s Digital introduced MAILbus, which interconnected incompatible, proprietary messaging systems through a series of gateways. Soft*Switch followed with their version of an interconnect tool. At the same time, vendors of messaging systems and services were gathering around the table at CCITT meetings discussing an industry standard for electronic messaging called X.400, the rules for the post office coded in electronic terms.

In 1984, the first commercially available X.400-compliant messaging system was introduced, but it had no one to talk to (like the first telephone). By late 1984, Digital had introduced MRX, the first X.400 gateway that allowed any user agent connected to the Digital MAILbus to communicate to any other X.400-compliant user agent. Since 1984, over 30 companies have developed either X.400 messaging systems or X.400 gateways allowing the interconnection of mail systems and the ability to reach trading partners beyond their own enterprise.

In just 20 years, messaging technology has evolved to the point that people can communicate via electronic mail worldwide. But there are still many obstacles to overcome to realize the vision. The first is to allow any type of information to be transferred to any system and be either recognized for processing or automatically converted. The second is the implementation of workflow across multiple platforms that can be executed by unlike workflow systems. The third is a mail-enabled application that will allow a user to access their messaging system from within any application on the desktop—allowing the user to send information transparently and quickly.

Digital has developed prototypes that address all three of the previously described obstacles. These prototypes will likely be developed into products. Many other vendors are also working on new and exciting additions to enhance the electronic post office. The electronic mail vendors have successfully worked together to develop electronic mail systems based on standards—they will do the same for the enhanced mail offerings of the future.

How Do You Get to the Year 2000?

First you need to do a complete evaluation of the present network. What is in place now? Can you diagram or map your corporate messaging network? You certainly should be able to! Understand which departmental systems are compliant with industry standards and which are not. A well-implemented, reliable electronic network is a corporate asset upon which you will build the value-added services of the future such as EDI, FAX, workflow, multimedia, and other mail-enabled applications. At Digital we have found that our worldwide electronic network is an essential part of many of our business processes and is one of our most valuable corporate assets.

When you fully understand where you are today, examine your goals for the future. Understand how *your* business environment is changing and determine the likely impact the availability (or lack thereof) of information and data have on your operations. Look toward the future and envision a network handling not only interpersonal text messaging, but a network which moves voice, data, graphics, and video and serves as the highway for mail-enabled applications.

I would suggest that this task is best conducted by a single task force at the corporate level—a task force that can define the interconnect issues between the disparate groups within your company and then make solid recommendations for resolving any conflicts. The task force needs to understand the impact and the value of international standards such as X.400 and X.500, as well as the *de facto* standards of existing proprietary systems.

Planning for the year 2000 requires an investment today. The network infrastructure our corporations are building today will influence their operations for years to come. The advantages of a flexible, reliable enterprise-wide messaging network outweighs the costs of making it happen by 10 to 1. Just ask us…or your competition!

The Hayes
Philosophy of How a
Network Should Work

by Dennis C. Hayes
CEO, Hayes Microcomputer Products, Inc.

Author Bio

Dennis C. Hayes founded Hayes Microcomputer Products, Inc., in 1978 at the age of 28. When he started the company, he already had more than 10 years experience working with large and small computer systems, telecommunications, manufacturing, and electronic product development. While attending the Georgia Institute of Technology, Hayes participated in a co-op program, working for AT&T Long Lines. Later, he joined Financial Data Sciences where he worked on systems using the first four-bit microprocessor and demonstrated the economic advantage of the new technology.

Hayes then returned to Georgia Tech to study physics and serve as a teaching assistant with responsibility for undergraduate physics labs. After concluding his studies at Georgia Tech, he worked for National Data Corporation where he was responsible for network management, overseeing operations of NDC's communications network staff. He developed micro-computer-based systems to interconnect networks and maintained the communications systems on large mainframe computers before leaving NDC in 1977 to form D.C. Hayes Associates, Inc., in January 1978.

Known today as Hayes Microcomputer Products, Inc., the company is a leading worldwide supplier of computer communications hardware and software products. The company's products are distributed through an international sales network for use in personal computer and computer communications network environments. Focusing on global availability, the company designs its products to meet the requirements of more than 60 countries. In addition, Hayes continues to maintain its leadership by entering new markets such as LANs, ISDN, and facsimile. Recognizing the company's success, *Inc.* magazine has twice ranked Hayes among the top 10 fastest growing private firms in the United States.

A native of South Carolina, Hayes is active in both community and industry organizations. He is chairman of the Georgia High Tech Alliance, a founding board member of the Georgia Research Alliance, and a founding member of the Governor's Advisory Council on Science and Technology, all of which were formed to promote growth of the high technology industry in Georgia. In addition, Hayes is a member of the board of directors of the Atlanta Chamber of Commerce and a member of the advisory council of the Association of Technology Business Councils in Washington, D.C. He also serves on the chairmen's committee of the Computerworld Smithsonian Awards.

Executive Summary

Networks should be easy-to-use, inexpensive to maintain and easy to expand. To obtain these goals, you need a powerful network designed to be more complicated on the inside so that it is simpler on the outside.

This article illustrates how the goals mentioned above can be achieved. It also outlines and illustrates other pertinent areas within the LAN industry, such as the particular perspectives in which people place networks, specific network needs required by users, underlying technology, present technology, and even higher technology.

Market segment research and an explanation about how Hayes integrated a higher, more powerful technology currently on the market into Hayes LANstep is provided.

The Network Perspective

The industry tends to view LANs from a product-oriented, technological perspective (see Figure 20.1). It talks about high-end networks and low-end networks. High-end LANs are considered to be powerful and to have the advanced features. Everyone knows high-end LANs require constant maintenance and an expensive network administrator who constantly functions as a network mechanic. The client-server model often is used when referring to high-end networks.

When talking about low-end LANs, we think of the DOS-based, peer-to-peer networks that generally are easy to install but lack many of the advanced features of high-end networks. Today's low-end LANs still require a large degree of ongoing maintenance, particularly once they begin to scale up and above a single server or a few workstations.

It is increasingly important for the industry to look at networks from the user's perspective (see Figure 20.2). New users who have limited technical expertise but who want the benefit of the network are constantly entering the market. These market-entry users just want the benefit of the network and are not really interested in the technology. With time, they may become experienced and knowledgeable users. Eventually, if they have the technical interest, they may learn enough about the technology to become advanced users. Increasingly, large numbers of customers are coming into the market who have no real interest in becoming advanced users, nor do they have the technical background.

Figure 20.1. High-end versus low-end LANs.

User Needs

The many locations that need a powerful network, but don't have the technical expertise to manage a complicated network or the luxury of hiring a network mechanic, are a tremendous market opportunity. The industry runs the risk of disappointing these customers or may entirely miss this market opportunity unless it creates products that truly serve the customer requirements of this rapidly developing market.

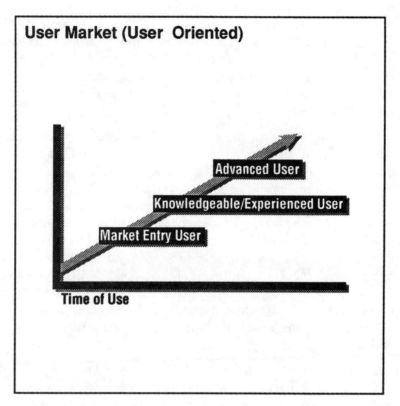

Figure 20.2. Viewing networks in terms of user sophistication.

The traditional approach has been that if you fit that customer profile, you start out with a DOS-based, peer-to-peer LAN and sacrifice the capability that you would like. At some point, you go through the conversion from a low-end network to a high-end network, picking up the cost of maintenance for that high-end network and hiring a network administrator.

Market research shows that a large segment of the potential LAN market has not been served yet by the existing typical products on the market. Over seven million businesses in North America have between 2 and 100 employees. These business locations may be small companies, branch offices, or departments of a large user. They need networks for their existing personal computers. There is an opportunity to develop this market by providing products which are powerful and, at the same time, easy to manage and inexpensive for entry-level users to maintain. These products should not require additional support personnel who must be heavily trained in network maintenance.

If a company (or even an individual) purchases a car, they do not expect to "purchase" a full-time car mechanic to keep the car running. They do realize, however, that a driver for the car is needed, while a mechanic is only needed on rare occasions when something unexpectedly goes wrong with the machine. A network purchase should be similar. Small business locations do not have the luxury of hiring someone designated as the full-time network administrator—the network mechanic. They can only afford an employee with a basic knowledge of DOS to spend a few minutes a day administering the network. The LAN industry development is limited today because there is no way for the industry to train seven million local area network mechanics. The office manager or the administrative assistant should be able to manage the LAN without having any significant technical LAN knowledge.

At Hayes, we recognized that to serve this growing market, we needed a powerful network that met the needs of the entry-level user. That's why we brought the technology that began at the University of Waterloo over 10 years ago to market as Hayes LANstep—a technology with a history in research of distributed computing and one that provides the ease-of-use required by market-entry users.

A network should be fast and simple to install. It should be self-configuring with a series of simple questions to determine the best settings for a particular user environment, giving the installer flexibility without excessive overhead.

For a network to be easy to use, it should not have complicated commands or filenames. You should be able to quickly access information and resources on the network without having to remember extra information. The network should present you with a list of choices which you have permission to use, and it should enable you to select from those choices. You should be able to give meaningful names to resources on the network so that regular users can understand them easily and can get a file without having to remember a path name or create a script to remember the path name. Take someone's files: On the network, you should be able to name a directory, for example, "Joe's Microsoft Word Documents" as opposed to a complicated file and path name like "server/sys:home/Joe/worddocs . . . /backslash, /backslash . . . /backslash."

You should not have to know where a file is stored; that is the LAN's job. You told the LAN to put something on the server; it should remember where it put that item and be able to retrieve it for you. The same is true for shared printers. You should not have to use complicated commands to access them. The network should do that for you. To compare it to the real world, when you get into a taxi cab you say, "Take me to the airport." You don't say "Go to Main Street, turn right, go five miles, and turn left." The same is true for LANs. You should be able to say to the network, "Take me to the printer."

A network should provide an interface flexible enough to be customized for particular users or applications. This interface should also address the needs of both advanced and novice users. The network should not be limited to a single interface that requires an expert or, worse yet, be so cumbersome that custom front-end utilities must be written and constantly updated and maintained to make the network usable.

Networks should offer a simple way to expand the number of users on the network, without interfering with the normal operation of the network or affecting other users on the network when new users are added. You should not have to take down the network, reinstall, or reconfigure to implement network upgrades.

People ought to be able to demand a lot from their network; the network should not demand a lot from its user or administrator.

The Underlying Technology

If you use a real multitasking network operating system, you can build a multiserver network, where servers are essentially peer-to-peer but capable of being managed as a single resource. The network operating system provides facilities to make the management easy. It tracks all the resources and services for the manager. Each server provides the server portion of the client/server advantage, such as shared programs or data files. Each station on the network delivers the ability to access the various services in a client manner.

Using the LANstep technology, Hayes implemented this simple philosophy by creating an operating system in which individual tasks or programs can communicate with each other. Almost any operating system can accomplish this function on a single computer, but LANstep allows all the computers in the LAN to communicate at this complex level.

LANstep technology gives you flexibility the to distribute the network workload over different machines. It provides the fine-tuning and load-balancing needed to fit your unique environment without sacrificing the ability to use the resources of the network easily, regardless of the machine's physical location.

The result is that the entire LAN is linked as a single computing environment that gives LAN users the flexibility to move from distributed management to central management, or some combination of both. The benefit to this arrangement is scalability. When you triple the size of your network, everything doesn't get three times slower and nine times harder to manage.

It's a much more powerful environment than the earlier approaches, and, at the same time, we can provide automated and streamlined management capabilities that make LAN management easier.

Local Versus Remote

The combination of the power of the PC with the far-reaching capabilities of the telecommunications network is expanding the network well beyond the local office. Most people think in terms of local area networks or wide area networks, but that distinction between local and remote is becoming less important to users. We must ensure that the technology once thought to be useful only locally can be used remotely, and that as the local network grows into a "planetary" network, the users see no difference in the way they make it work. This usability requires the network operating system to manage the connection between the user interface and the underlying network technology.

The Planetary Network

The combination of computer and telecommunications technology is accelerating the development of LANs and enabling new industry trends and applications. Desktop conferencing and video conferencing enable users in different locations to collaborate on the same document, which allows them to complete a presentation in a matter of hours, rather than several days. When you shorten cycle time, you become more competitive. In fact, a key application making companies more competitive is just that: sharing information through networks.

Remote connectivity is getting faster, allowing you to make the full resources of the network available to remote workstations. Technologies like high-speed modems and ISDN play an important role in this connectivity. With the appropriate application software and ISDN, you can operate a PC workstation as a remote node and have the same functionality as if you were in your office on the LAN. Your access to shared resources on that network is the same. In addition, LAN functionality can be emulated on a wide-area basis over ISDN by interconnecting remote networks over a dial-up connection.

Many people think that the only way to connect networks is with a multimega-bit connection. I see that as a lazy choice.

Most traffic on a network is interaction or transaction oriented. To be smart about managing technology, use 56 to 64K connections through the switched network and make possible the connection of LANs over long distance. You will rarely try to move large data or program files over a network. Even if the file was somewhat large, you still would send it faster over the switched telephone network than by Federal Express. I'm not proposing that this choice is in head-to-head competition with the multimega-bit over wide area or leased lines, but that it offers a choice which gives you flexibility and cost savings.

Another important benefit of choosing dial-up, switched technology is "connection-on-demand." This choice means you can call whom you want when you want. No longer does the network depend on leased lines limited to connecting fixed points. Because you have access to the public switched telephone network, the world is open to you.

In the 1980s, users thought in terms of computer-to-computer communications, whereas in the 1990s, the interest is in network-to-network communications. You see the melting of the distinction between the local area network and the wide area network; the local area network is now the user's way of managing and accessing services on networks wherever they might be. A switched connection is simply the communications resource to enable physical access to these services when needed.

Upon realizing how important the LAN would be to the evolution of computer communications, we also realized that the LANs popular at the end of the 1980s would not have the architecture to take the industry forward through the 1990s.

Hayes LANstep

When introducing Hayes LANstep, we deliberately limited revealing the degree of its capability because we wanted to prove that LANstep could serve the market for small organizations that don't have a local area network engineer on staff. When revolutionary technology (like radically-advanced local area networks) is introduced into an area, it takes time for the new technology to be understood. But an understanding about the power of the approach we have taken with LANstep is developing rapidly in the user community.

Conclusion

Our goal at Hayes and our purpose for being involved in LAN operating systems is to take the mystery out of networks, just as we did with modems. Hayes is committed to making technology available to a broader base of users and creating new choices in the way they manage their business. Through innovation, we look for ways to reduce the cost of owning and managing technology, we develop ways to make the technology available to a larger market, and we provide applications that meet market needs.

The Mensch of Networking

by Tom Henderson
President, Corporate Networks

Author Bio

Tom Henderson runs Corporate Networks in Indianapolis and beats networks into submission for fun, profit, and sport. An author of seven books on computer and network topics, Henderson is editor-at-large of *LAN Magazine*, technical editor of the Network Report, and a frequent speaker at NetWorld and other computer industry events. The views he expresses are his own.

Executive Summary

Networking began as a populist movement—a response to centrist data management. The power of the desktop spawned guerilla movements of the local area network. As software increased and cofunctionality could be achieved, revolutionary armies were formed—the departmental network. Today, networks and internetworks exist in a shaky coalition government with MIS.

Networks are both nonobvious and nontrivial. Like many host-based computer systems, no two networks are identical, both for historical reasons and the fact that the computer industry makes so many compelling improvements so quickly. The original network pioneers had no idea of the impact networks soon would achieve.

Gaining control of the network has been difficult. Until 1990, few parallels to host network control existed in PC-based networks. Since then, network management protocols and services have been springing up like mushrooms. Mushrooms, you'll recall, are kept in the dark and fed a lot of poop. So, in keeping with the spirit of better network reliability and ease of implementation, I'd like to try my tainted hand at network management protocol design and propose some network management protocols, new services, and more descriptive ways of describing the reality of network implementations:

NSNMP

New Strong Nostril Mismanagement Protocol—This protocol finds network packet runts, widows, and misroutes, and then reports them by giggling through the speaker of your PC. The louder the laugh, the bigger the problem. Can use Sound Blaster boards very effectively. Makes data sausage on the side.

SNAT

Silly Nonsensical Attempt at (data) Transmission—Bound to continue to be one of the leading protocols because it is mutable at the will of a sales-person, and it's painted a loving cobalt blue—radioactive cobalt. Don't say this abbreviation quickly.

RSNP

Really Simple Network Protocol—An icon in X, Windows, or System 7. Simply nods its head up and down when an internetwork is working okay and from left to right when it's not. Click on it, and it sticks its tongue out at you.

SOLD

System Out to Lunch Detector—You always wondered, and now you know. Federal labor law mandates a one-hour lunch per day. Internetworks are known to take an annual allotment all in one week.

MIB-R

Maddening Information Bucket-Redux—The kind your great-grandmother had in her parlor behind the curtain.

HSPFP

Hand Stamped Packet Forwarder Protocol—Would clean up the unemployment problem overnight. Suspected to be the basis for X.25.

NPFS

Network Performance Flatulence Suspicion—Add white beans to network server filing systems, and what do you get?

RMON-II

Really Maddening Oligarchical Nuisance—Seizes all packets, looks for information destined to it, and forwards the rest randomly.

A New Services Proposal

Truly successful software products have always been an easy-to-understand analog of tasks performed in daily business and personal life. Networks have allowed services to be added or modified modularly, and the result is that the computer industry has become very service-centric:

Building Server

Turns on lights, opens doors, washes windows, controls union contracts, manages heating plant, runs on a PC jr. Options: random light switch pattern generator, elevator requerer. Built-in Chicago River detector.

Coffee Server

Although not popular in Utah, the Coffee Server comes in three styles: Expresso (by NetFrame and Tricord), Cappucino (a joint venture with AT&T and Olivetti), and the Canadian SFT Favorite, Double-Double. Variation: Decaf Server—sends only empty frames.

Fast Food Server

Comes in optional Kentucky Fried Pigeon, Burger Sling (home of the Slopper), Burger Doodle, Long John Sliver, White Blastle, Boy Rodgers, and of course, Blendy's Protocols. Advanced Options: Backup and Restore and, of course, fiber. Antidote: Rolaids 3.0

Insult Server

Specifically addresses computer-generated error messages. Intercepts "Unrecoverable Applications Errors" and restates them as "Buy More Memory" or "Windows Programmer Asleep at the Switch, Application Bailing." Also replaces "Bad Command or File Name" with "Spell It or Shell It." Options: E-mail hooks to applications vendors using random epithets, heritage doubters, and hot-key coolers.

Justice Server

New from Remington Software. Takes six months to ACK a reply. Requires passage of bar exam to use—the CNF medallion (Certified Network Fool). Uses Winchester hard drives. Makes your day (excellent for accounts receivable problems). Requires Process Server.

Lox and Bagels Server

Made in Manhattan. Requires dedicated T3 link to certain fishermen in Nova Scotia. Best used with sweet onions, tomatoes, cream cheese, and capers. Only up before 11:59 a.m.; down on Saturdays.

Music Server

The perfect multimedia advance. MIDI, CD-ROM, MTV, and VH-1, all rolled into a single machine. Gives a whole new meaning to the phrase "Jukebox." Options: Concurrent Orchestra Tuner and Bluegrass Protocol.

Office Pool Server

With integral database. Tracks football, baseball, basketball, and other sporting events, as well as an accounts receivable database for wedding presents, shower presents, hospital flowers, etc. Also can be used for March of Dimes, NPR, and United Way agencies. Options: Coffee Mug Output, exit interview summarizer.

Political Correctness Server

Filters all network conversations and removes all sexism, racism, and heritage doubt; replaces them with politically correct substitutions. Requires frequent updates; comes only in shades of grey.

Process Server

Used only by law enforcement agencies. Requires Sniffer. Variation: Probation Server.

Sex Server

Only for license in certain parts of Boston, North Hollywood, all of San Francisco County, and southern Nevada. Self-explanatory. Uses Twisted Sister Pairs. Option: 10BasedMe, dBasedMe. Not for sale to minors.

Shrink Server

New personnel management tool with optional e-mail analyzer. Uses a new multitasking (schizo) mode. The phrase CPU slices has been replaced with phrase "processor time management." Advanced Options: Psych Service, ex-Spouse database, virus prophylactic, and substance abuse filters.

Tennis Server

The first sports equipment to be used on networks. An excellent perk and antidote for Programmer's Paunch. Note: Insurance rates are very high. Sponsored by GTE.

Favorite Failure Modes

No other industry (except our armed forces) has a greater capacity to abbreviate than the computer industry. After installing more than 500 networks, many conditions naturally have lent themselves to abbreviation and acronym. The more important codes:

Installation

5SB3—Ordered 5.25" got 3.5" floppy format. Variation: 3SB5—Ordered 3.5" got 5.25" floppy format

DRN—DOS Revision Nightmare (also pronounced the same way)

HMCTN—Humidifier Mistakenly Connected To Network

FM—Freaking Magic (The Experience Factor)

IWLT—It Worked the Last Time. Variation: IWITS It Worked In The Shop

LMS—Local Magnetic Storm

ML—Manual Lies (see also NIM)

NIM—Not In Manual (see also ML)

NINCU—New Installation Never Came Up

NUN—NetWare Update Nightmare

OCTPLAC—Of Course The Power Lines Are Clean (also the sound equipment makes during certain thunderstorms)

OFOSS—Oceans Full Of Shells Syndrome

SIN—SCSI Installation Nightmares

SSIWW—Salesperson Said It Would Work (mumbled: what you're thinking)

TWTD—That Was The Demo

Networks

BO—Bridge Out

BOB—Blown Off Bindery (go ahead and fool with utilities)

SOL-CLV—Speed of Light-Cable Length Violation

EBO—Ethernet Bridge Out (a/k/a Campus Construction Syndrome)

GD—Gateway Down (best mumbled)

GU—Gateway Up (best mumbled, as well)

NFCHTC—Network Function Call Has Toll Charge

PE—Psychotic E-mailer. Variation: PECCA—Psychotic E-mail Carbon Copy Artist

PSFO—Protocol Stack Fell Over

QTP—Queue to Pakistan

TRCN—Token Ring Cabling Nightmare

VMFH—Voice Mail From Hell

Users

BMF—Brazen Mad Formatter (see also MF)

CCDDS—CaCaDooDoo Syndrome (a/k/a laser printer buffer overflow resulting in a ream of paper with one character strategically placed in the upper left hand corner of each page)

FSBS—Forward Slash Back Slash Syndrome. Also: File Server Bad Syntax

GIM—Ghost In the Machine (also, a terrific Police album)

IDTS—I Don't Think So (best mumbled)

MF—Mad Formatter (similar to Type A Syndrome)

NOTDWEA—Network On Three-Day Weekend Again

UBFWI—User's Been Foolin' With It

URTMAISDW—User Read The Manual and It Still Doesn't Work (usually mumbled)

UOOC—User Out Of Control

UNHMR—(pronounced unhummer) User Not Holding Mouth Right

TSBA—Tech Support Busy Again. Variation: TSBF—Tech Support Busy Forever

WITAK—Where Is The <ANY> Key?

Tech Support Problems

AFIR—All Files In Root

ATHF—A Trigger-Happy Formatter (See also MF and BMF)

BCHD—Basket Case Hard Disk

BOC—Blown Off COMMAND.COM (as "he BOC'd it")

CHHAUT—Computer Has Hands Around User's Throat

FEB—Foreground color Equals Background Color (a/k/a polar bear in a snowstorm syndrome) as "he FEB'd it"

NDDLT—Network Death During Lunch Time

NRIFL—Next-Revision-Is-Free Lie

ORDW—OS/2 Really Does(n't) Work

POMP—Phase Of the Moon Problem

PQAFU—Print Queue All Messed Up (sounds best screamed)

SLO—Smoke Let Out (on the theory that smoke is the operative element in chips and power supplies)

TCS—Trashed Config.sys

TCISUS—Tie Caught In Shredder—User Screaming

TCIP—Tie Caught in Printer (also the sound it makes)

TDTM—Tape Drive To Mongolia

TEBATS—Test Equipment Back At The Shop

TEPIGP—Thick Ethernet Plugged Into Game Port

TS900N-NVT—Tech Support Has 900 Number-New Vendor Time

YCTTTMNAIS—You Connect That Thing To My Network And I'll Scream!

Note: Some of these listings by Tom Henderson appeared in the *NetWare Advisor* (800.950.LANS) or in the *Network Report* (LANDA- 708. 279. 2255) and are used with permission. Dan Bent and Laura Henderson contributed to the abbreviations.

The Evolution of a LAN: ARCNETPLUS
A statement on Datapoint's advanced local area networking technology

by Robert Hollingsworth
Director of Marketing
Datapoint Corporation

Author Bio

Robert Hollingsworth, marketing director of Datapoint Corporation, is responsible for the strategic definition and implementation of enhanced network products.

Hollingsworth brings a unique professional experience to the Marketing Director position as indicated by his previous assignment as the Director of Engineering and Services. During his term of engineering management, Datapoint successfully initiated their transition to Open Systems Networking by introducing Intel-based symmetric multiprocessing network servers, Personal Computer network integration, and industry-standard connectivity solutions using OSI and TCP/IP.

Hollingsworth's combination of technical networking expertise along with a decade of designing and implementing multinational systems solutions provides an ideal skills mix for a member of a worldwide marketing team.

Executive Summary

The past 20 years have seen a very gradual evolution in the LAN market. This paper explores the technology and the transition that has occurred and why the growth has been far slower than for the rest of the computer industry.

The past two decades of new technology design and implementation have been a process filled with the gratification of completion followed by a rapid replacement cycle. New and better ways to accomplish the same objectives are being discovered daily. The local area network (LAN) is one area where this cycle has been accomplished more slowly than most. In the late 1970s, both ARCnet and EtherNet found commercial success as they were introduced into selective marketplaces that were slowly accepting the transition from centralized computing to distributed, networked systems. By 1991 these two "ancient" technologies accounted for almost 67 percent of installed LAN connections.

Integration and Cost Investment

The staying power of these pioneering technologies is quite remarkable considering that faster products have been designed and made commercially available in the intervening years. The continued commercial success of these initial products can be attributed to the fact that the basic concepts have remained unchanged over the years and there has been continued technical investment in both products to retain and expand their viability in the marketplace. Most of this investment has been used to increase product integration at the building-block level, thereby reducing the costs of products incorporating the improvements. A second major contributor has been the proliferation of wiring systems supported, including coax, fiber, and Unshielded Twisted Pair (UTP) cable.

Performance Investment

Until 1992 the only commercially successful LAN to undergo a performance enhancement occurred through the release of the IBM 16M Token Ring Network (TRN/16). The original 4M Token Ring Network (TRN/4) was introduced in the marketplace as an alternative to ARCnet and EtherNet but was never widely accepted. The lack of industry interest led the TRN developers to create a solution that raised the network bit rate performance from 4 million bits per second to 16 million bits per second (Mbps).

With the introduction of the 16M Token Ring Network came the decision to make the original 4M product obsolete. This determination was necessary because of the TRN signalling architecture whereby each data packet has to be processed by every node on the network.

All the nodes can receive and send data only at exactly the same rate—therefore, the slowest node defines the maximum bit rate performance of the entire network.

The only means available to improve LAN bit rate performance before 1992 was based on a replacement and obsolescence strategy. Discussions regarding a similar strategy for EtherNet surface in the trade press periodically, but the potential problems for such a large installed base appear to be insurmountable. EtherNet's success and market share appear to have frozen the data rate performance at 10M per second.

Another Approach to Multispeed Technology

When ARCnet performance improvements were first discussed, no consideration was given to a replacement or obsolescence strategy. The power of ARCnet in the commercial marketplace lies in the free range of the technology components and the ability to interchange products and components between suppliers.

The original designers of the ARCnet protocol, Datapoint Corporation, were committed to a development strategy of upward compatibility for all products. Under the guidance of the ARCnet Trade Association (ATA), any performance improvement to ARCnet would be acceptable only if the original products would continue to interchange data and share networks with the enhanced products.

ARCNETPLUS

Within these guidelines, the concept of ARCNETPLUS was born—a faster version of ARCnet capable of total compatibility with previous ARCnet products.

ARCNETPLUS is a 20 Mbps LAN that has been designed and implemented to offer performance and service to meet the applications requirements of the 1990s. Prime characteristics of these applications include

- Large command files with a great deal of programming space and high memory utilization

- Frequent data access and storage requirements

- Larger networks than ever before and more competition for the server

- Graphics on the desktop and images in the applications

- Higher overhead and more flexible standard protocols

Combined, all of these elements create a network-level bandwidth requirement that greatly surpasses the applications needs of the past 15 years. Incorporating such large data and application traffic—as well as a multitude of small messages—requires a network designed to optimize the small messages and also support large information blocks. ARCNETPLUS, a high-integrity, high-performance LAN, is the first product that combines multispeed economic benefits with record-setting performance.

The unique features and performance of ARCNETPLUS reflect a systems solution for the use of LANs based on the experience and commercial success of ARCnet.

The new ARCNETPLUS features are enhancements that have evolved through an understanding of how a properly designed and implemented network can become a virtual Information Technology tool for an end user.

ARCnet's Success in the Marketplace

The success of the ARCnet technology in the marketplace can be measured in various ways. There is the obvious commercial success—nearly 4 million nodes shipped to date. (See Figure 22.1.) Then there is ARCnet's economy and reliability, the reasons customers buy and suppliers sell ARCnet. Both customers and suppliers are interested in customer satisfaction and future implications relative to business systems. Since its 1977 introduction, ARCnet has provided users with a low-cost economic solution and long-term benefits, such as ease of expansion and configuration flexibility.

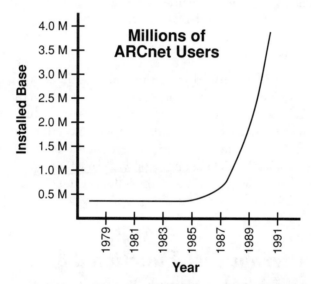

Figure 22.1. The commercial success of the ARCnet technology.

Another reason for the wide acceptance of ARCnet as a primary LAN solution is the availability of ARCnet-compatible products from various sources. This is a direct result of the fact that the primary ARCnet design elements are encapsulated as elemental building blocks, guaranteeing compatibility at the network level. This concept has enabled systems component manufacturers to concentrate on opportunities for performance and feature enhancements without jeopardizing the integrity and compatibility of future additions that could be sourced from an alternative supplier.

As a result of this concept, ARCnet has been driven by customer and commercial needs. With ARCnet, the customer has held the key in determining future enhancements. This has enabled suppliers to be more effective in terms of selling products. The resulting continuity and compatibility of products has provided a highly stable environment for ARCnet customers and resellers during the years of product evolution.

During the past three years, an increasing level of network bandwidth requirements has emerged for many users in the ARCnet community. Network performance demands have also increased in certain application sectors, whereas they have remained constant or have even decreased in others. This conflicting level of requirements has led many previously satisfied ARCnet customers and resellers to seek higher performance networks as a general solution.

The high level of network integrity and flexible network expansion enjoyed by ARCnet users is certainly compromised through the incorporation of alternative network segments. Even in cases in which wiring and network management has been mastered, the network performance achieved has been largely disappointing. To a great extent, this is because even with its modest bit rate, ARCnet has always provided users with a consistent and deterministic performance level over the full spectrum of commercial uses. (See Figure 22.2.)

LAN Alternatives: Functional and Economic Implications

It may be helpful to consider some of the LAN alternatives to ARCnet and evaluate both their functional and their economic implications.

EtherNet

The advent of 10BaseT wiring alternatives has significantly improved the appeal of EtherNet as an alternative to an existing ARCnet network. The capability to wire a facility in a star configuration for a higher degree of network management and troubleshooting capabilities, coupled with the dramatically reduced cost of PC adapters, has led many users to experiment with this technology in situations in which network performance has become critical to user productivity.

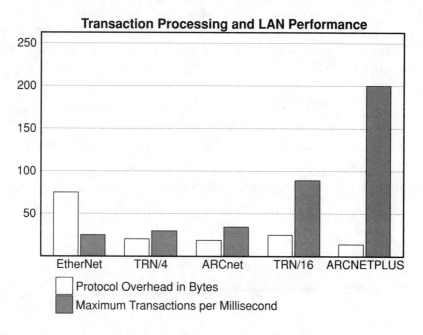

Figure 22.2. Transaction processing and LAN performance.

The first negatives encountered in a wholesale replacement scenario are cable length limits (100 meters maximum) and configuration complexity (how many 10BaseT hubs can be added before active concentrators also must be added?).

The next concern involves measuring performance gains, especially as a cost differentiator between ARCnet and EtherNet. In small, simple networks, some gains are obvious. But in larger systems, the often-forgotten implications of network packet collisions in transaction-based situations suddenly become quite real.

16 Mbps Token Ring Network

The IBM-sponsored 16 Mbps Token Ring Network (TRN) is an alternative that offers several attractive replacement benefits to a current ARCnet user. The wiring scheme—although it requires radically different and much shorter cables—is generally consistent with ARCnet's. And the even distribution of network bandwidth through the use of a logical token for packet transmission is accepted as a viable mechanism for a self-managed network.

In addition, TRN's 16 Mbps data rate, combined with a deterministic performance profile, can actually produce an improvement in raw network performance and help to justify the significant expense of the transition.

From an economic standpoint, converting an existing ARCnet to either TRN/16 or 10BaseT EtherNet involves new expenses in four key areas:

- New PC adapter cards

- Replacement of hubs

- Network redesign

- Replacement of cabling plants

Partial Additions of TRN or EtherNet

Most real-world customer network performance problems are best resolved with a partial system change. Many ARCnet users are well served by the existing ARCnet LAN solution—parts have been purchased, wires are in place, training has been completed, and expenses have been absorbed. The needs of users whose productivity and application requirements demand and justify an increased level of LAN performance should be addressed individually. Both TRN/16 and EtherNet solutions have negative implications relative to a more "perfect" alternative.

The partial introduction of a new network topology into an existing LAN environment requires the use of several systems design techniques that drastically complicate network management and expansion. Network segments must somehow be bridged to allow continued access and sharing of common data and communications resources—the primary reasons networks exist. (See Figure 22.3.)

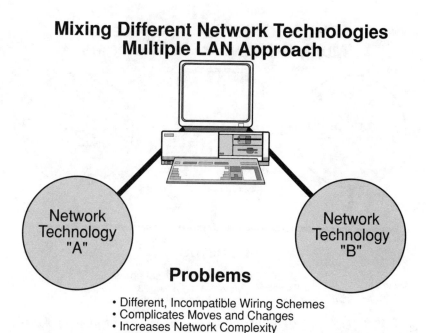

**Mixing Different Network Technologies
Multiple LAN Approach**

Figure 22.3. Mixing different network technologies: the multiple LAN approach.

The complexity of systems configuration and the management implications of introducing multiple segments into a network must be factored into the overall equation as a cost. Both immediate and future costs related to restrictions that such hybrid systems place into the planning cycle are important considerations for network systems administrators.

ARCNETPLUS: A Better Solution

ARCNETPLUS—the first multispeed LAN—provides the performance benefits users demand, and it retains ARCnet's topology characteristics. These benefits, which have been ARCnet's strengths for the past 15 years, are attained through the use of a single wiring scheme and allow upgrades to be made simply by making changes in the user's workstation. This separates the issues of building wiring and performance. (See Figure 22.4.)

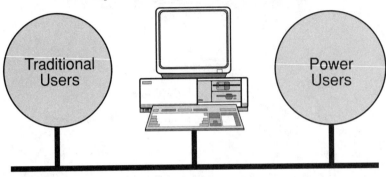

Figure 22.4. The ARCNETPLUS approach: multiple network technologies

ARCNETPLUS represents the implementation of five highly creative intellectual concepts, some of which are patented inventions, never before applied to the LAN environment. The first is the idea of a LAN with multiple, but interoperable, capabilities. Simply put, this means the LAN exhibits multiple performance characteristics—higher data transfer rates when exchanging information between faster partners, and compatible lower data rates for exchanges between slower partners. The LAN's capability to identify and adapt the data transfer rates in a manner that is transparent to the upper-level operating systems and applications systems is a key to the commercial acceptance of such a product.

Beyond the multiple data rate functionality, there is another significant intellectual concept featured in ARCNETPLUS. It involves the capability of dynamically accomplishing data interchange determination supporting a wide variety of potential alternatives, including

- Data rate and packet compatibility for both ARCnet and ARCNETPLUS nodes

- Data rate with small packet support for ARCNETPLUS nodes

Support of these alternatives creates a wide level of systems compatibility, including operation in existing networks without changing network operating system software. This significant capability results from the design of an interface directly into the ARCNETPLUS LAN Controller integrated circuit that provides compatibility for the original ARCnet software interface. This enables all software drivers written for ARCnet to be capable of immediate execution when coupled with a properly designed ARCNETPLUS network interface card.

Perhaps the most significant marketing implication of integrating ARCNETPLUS into an existing LAN environment is the capability to use existing star-based coaxial ARCnet wiring. This means ARCnet coaxial wiring rules are supported as a function of network design when ARCNETPLUS is implemented to enhance network performance. ARCNETPLUS is the only product set introduced for commercial use that allows use of 2,000-foot, copper wire network segments at the node and wiring hub level.

ARCNETPLUS's analog design will enable future product enhancements to incorporate support for unshielded twisted pair and fiber optic interfaces, as is the case with the original ARCnet wiring scheme.

Another important intellectual aspect of the design and implementation of ARCNETPLUS is the multibit amplitude and phase modulated LAN transceiver. This allows for both wiring plant and signalling compatibility. (See Figure 22.5.)

The importance of characterizing ARCNETPLUS as intellectual property to both customers and resellers is twofold:

- System compatibility, as with the original ARCnet technology, can be facilitated by the establishment of a standard protected at the basic intellectual level whenever the term ARCNETPLUS is applied to any product in the marketplace.

- Patenting the base technology allows Datapoint to offer the key ARCNETPLUS components and technology concepts to the general marketplace for improvements and enhancements vital to the evolution of network solutions in the PC, factory floor, process control, and other yet-to-be-explored environments.

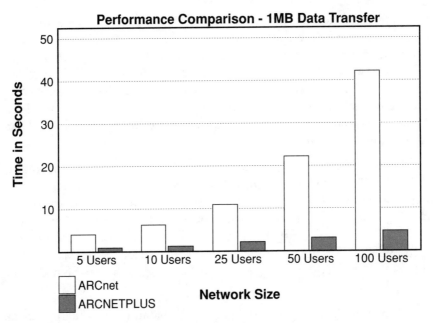

Figure 22.5. ARCnet versus ARCNETPLUS.

Standardization

In today's marketplace, a major element in the design, sale, and acquisition of commodity technology is the support and development of standards.

As a *de facto* standard, ARCnet has been commercially successful for the past 15 years. But the absence of an accepted international standard designation has played a major role in the recent slowing of ARCnet's growth.

To address this situation, the ARCnet Trade Association—which was designated an American National Standards Institute (ANSI) standards development body in September 1991—is chartered to have its ARCnet standard reviewed and approved by ANSI. ATA plans call for taking the same route to standardization for ARCNETPLUS. (See Figure 22.6.)

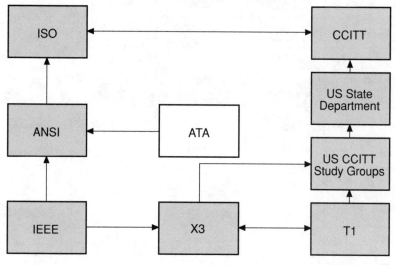

**USA and International
Standards Relationship**

Figure 22.6. USA and international standards relationship.

ANSI's confirmation of the ATA as a LAN standard development group—and a peer to IEEE—provides an appropriate alternative solution that enables both organizations to continue with their chartered activities. Conformance with the communications model established by the International Standards Organization (ISO) as the Open Systems Interconnect (OSI) model is the key to attaining an international standard designation. The OSI model shows the placement of ARCnet, ARCNETPLUS, and other formal and *de facto* LAN and WAN solutions based on this standard. (See Figure 22.7.) The primary consideration is compatibility with upper-level software and systems protocols which can be achieved through any of the documented alternatives.

Layer		OSI Product	Other Norms	Other LANs				Function
Application	7	X.400, X.500 FTAM	LU 6.2	NOSs				Application Processing, EMail, Networks, Directory Services
Presentation	6	X226 X216	3270, NCS Videotex	NetWare LANMan POWERLan 3COM+ Vines Others	FTP	SMB		Syntax rules for message definition
Session	5	X225 X215	SNA DNA					Service associated to starting and restarting a session.
Transport	4	X224 X214	VTAM	SPX IPX		NetBIOS		Point-to-point transmission
Network	3	X.25 I451	SNA DNA		TCP/IP			Data transfers
Data Link / LLC MAC	2	I441 HDLC	SDLC	FDDI				Formatting data fields and address controls
Physical	1	I431, V24 X.21, RS232		IEEE 802.3, 802.4, 802.5 ARCnet, ARCNETPLUS				Physical and electrical standards

Each of the seven layers in the OSI Model has a specific, independent function, but which is logically linked to its closest neighbors. Services provided in this format offer a means of demonstrating the complexity of designing systems to accomplish information exchange and access.

Figure 22.7. The OSI model.

The proper placement of ARCnet—and now ARCNETPLUS—into this hierarchical structure has been delayed because of a lack of systems software solutions that exploit ARCnet at standard protocol levels. The only generic protocol that has been available for ARCnet in the past has been the IPX service module defined and implemented by Novell through its NetWare-supported network adapters.

Recent developments have greatly extended this level of support to include the *de facto* standard Internet Protocol (IP). For the first time, this has enabled ARCnet users to gain access to application solutions based on the Transmission Control Protocol/Internet Protocol (TCP/IP) software standard.

In addition, a major change has occurred in the area of network hardware support, enhancing opportunities for both ARCnet and ARCNETPLUS to gain service access to present *de facto* standards and future formal connectivity standards. System software suppliers are now offering network adapter Packet Driver standards for public use. These products mask and make transparent the actual physical nature of both LANs and WANs in use in any specific customer systems solution. (See Figure 22.8.) Standard network adapter packet drivers include

- The Open Driver Interface (ODI) from Novell

- The Network Driver Interface Specification (NDIS) from Microsoft

- Clarkson Packet Driver from Clarkson University

Multi-Protocol Packet Drivers			
Network Services	File/ Print	Named Pipes Comms	TELENET NFS
Network Protocol	Novell Network	Microsoft LAN Manager	TCP/IP
Network Packet Driver	Open Drive Interface	Network Driver Interface Specification	Clarkson Packet Driver
Network Interface Card			
Physical Network	ARCnet ARCNETPLUS	EtherNet	TRN

Figure 22.8. Multi-protocol packet drivers.

The implementation of these packet drivers throughout the industry will result in the availability of general service access to local and wide area network services—including transparent data packet interchange—through all network adapter technologies where these drivers have been incorporated. For the consumer, this trend represents the capability to mix and match diverse network segments selected according to a specific economic and systems architecture requirement based on the supported applications.

When this level of internetwork service is combined with the intranetwork functionality offered by the multispeed LAN environment available with ARCNETPLUS, the real winner is the end user. Systems enhancements march in step with the evolutions in base LAN technologies that offer the most benefits in terms of flexibility and economy.

Environmental and Physical Considerations

Environmental and physical elements must also be considered when designing a customer LAN solution. These elements include

- Wiring distance limitations
- Electrical interference
- Cost per linear foot
- Cost per connector
- Troubleshooting tools
- Multimedia support connectivity
- Standard protocol support, IPX, IP, Vines, Lan Manager, UNIX
- Connectivity
- Gateway support, NETBIOS

Before making any recommendation regarding a LAN performance upgrade to any customer, a competent systems analyst will first become comfortable with the customer's requirements and then determine an appropriate solution.

Making the Decision for ARCNETPLUS

The primary concept of a network is the provision for sharing business information in a way that is transparent to the individual user. The variety of requirements imposed on the networked system through the demands of the users creates a level of complications that tends to be inconsistent with the geography of the typical business environment. Network decisions therefore have to accommodate the mechanical requirements for long-range planning and the individual requirements for varying levels of applications performance.

Into this complex equation comes ARCNETPLUS, which for the first time enables a purchasing decision for the LAN to incorporate multiple levels of performance within a single systems wiring scheme. Comparisons of price and performance become issues to be resolved at each user level as opposed to becoming issues that have to be imposed on the entire network because of the higher performance requirements of a few specific users.

Selecting a high-performance network solution for a specific set of users can now be placed into the same category as the selection of color screens, local disks, increased memory, or higher performance CPUs. In each of these cases, the management decision to acquire high performance is based on the individual needs of the users and their contribution to the goals of the total organization. Now, for the first time, the same concept has been extended to the LAN. Installation of a common wiring scheme, coupled with a high-performance ARCNETPLUS LAN Adapter in the server, provides a multispeed LAN environment. As user application requirements demand higher performance network service, individual purchasing decisions can be made in the same way as other high-performance add-ons to the computing environment.

ARCNETPLUS

Based on ARCnet, the world's first commercially available LAN technology, ARCNETPLUS truly offers a sensible alternative to the other LAN technologies available in the marketplace. ARCNETPLUS has been designed to meet the latest in application requirements—database, image, graphics, and windowing services. And with its unique multispeed performance capability, ARCNETPLUS offers far more than simply the best alternative LAN solution.

ARCNETPLUS, combined with existing ARCnet technology, offers a unique, price-competitive solution to the problems posed by today's multifunctional network components.

ARCNETPLUS offers existing ARCnet users a unique opportunity to test and evaluate high-performance networking in a production environment—the Test DriveSM. Because the ARCNETPLUS components are 100 percent compatible with existing ARCnet installations, users can assess their purchase requirements by simply installing ARCNETPLUS into key network nodes and exercising their applications in a production networking environment. The simplicity of the ARCNETPLUS upgrade combined with the Test Drive capability make ARCNETPLUS the first LAN to evolve beyonds its roots in the world of high-performance networking.

Certain ARCNETPLUS components are covered by one or more of the following U.S. patents, by U.S. patents pending, or by corresponding patents pending in other countries: No. 5,008,879; 5,048,014; 5,050,189; 5,077,732.

Network Management Today, Tomorrow, and Yesterday

by Scott H. Hutchinson
Saber Software Corporation

Author Bio

Scott H. Hutchinson currently develops LAN Administration Netware Loadable Modules for Saber Software Corporation. In the past Mr. Hutchinson has developed products for many facets of the networking industry, from protocol analyzers to mid-level network management software. He can be reached through CompuServe at #70523,2467.

Saber Software Corporation is a leading developer and manufacturer of software-based LAN administration tools. Its family of products includes the Saber Menu System for DOS, the Saber Menu System for Windows, the Saber LAN Administration Architecture (LAA) Console/RT, the Saber LAA Agent Toolkit, the Saber LAN Administration Pack, and the Saber Windows Print Manager for NetWare. Since the company's launch in 1986, it has won many prestigious awards, including LAN Times Readers Choice, LAN Magazine Product of the Year, InfoWorld Buyers Assurance Seal, and LAN Technology Network Specialist Preferred. Saber's products are sold around the world through a network of distributors, resellers, and dealers. For more information on the company or any of its products, contact Saber at 800-338-8754 or 214-361-8086.

Executive Summary

The lack of interoperability and common user interfaces in most of the network administration tools on the market today makes the task of being a network administrator more difficult. In this paper the author traces a path from the early days of network administration and management to the current state of the art and beyond. This paper goes on to show the problems that exist with most of the network administration and management utilities.

Where are we going with network administration and management? Why is it costing us more to maintain and administer our networks than ever before? Networks are growing in size, and the business of selling networking utilities is growing as well. Vendors are coming out with a wide variety of network management and administration utilities. Most of these utilities are very useful. However, very few of the vendors are working together to build applications that interoperate. This makes it more difficult for the managers to maintain their networks, because they usually need to pull together information from two or more places to get "the big picture" of their network.

There are currently two major types of network management: low-level protocol management and high-level application management. In the past these have been separate entities, each dealing with different issues. Lately, low-level protocol management systems have been growing in complexity and moving up to manage higher level protocols. The high-level management systems have been growing in complexity as well and moving down toward the low-level protocol level. There is still a gap between the two, but this gap is shrinking and will continue to shrink as time goes on.

What this means to network administrators is that they currently need at least two network management and administration solutions: one to manage the high-level applications and to perform network administration tasks, and one to manage the low-level physical network. Having multiple solutions can be expensive. Often the budgets provide for only one solution, so network administrators and managers are forced to choose between the two when both are really needed. Also, most of the solutions available tend to be single-purpose and nonintegrated, requiring network administrators to manually combine the information from many sources to both solve problems and do routine administration tasks on their network.

Down on the Wire Five Years Ago

Five years ago there was a whole group of low-level network management tools designed to manage and maintain the available physical network cable. These tools used to be limited to cable and protocol analyzers. Cable analyzers, cable scanners, time domain reflectometers (TDRs), and protocol analyzers were all available, from simple software packages to full-blown high-end protocol analyzers capable of capturing and decoding all packets being transmitted on the network.

These tools were extremely useful for installing and maintaining the physical network cabling, bridges, and routers. Cable analyzers and TDRs both provided information, such as cable length and whether the cable was shorted or open, and they were usually fairly inexpensive. These tools proved to be helpful when network cabling was being installed. After the cabling was installed, however, these devices were not helpful in diagnosing network problems. They usually could look at only the physical network cable, and often the problem was at the application layer and not in the cabling. The next logical step up the protocol stack was a device called a protocol analyzer.

Protocol analyzers started out as a logical extension of cable analyzers and logic analyzers. They connected to the physical network, captured the packets they saw, and decoded them. This provided network managers with a low-level view of the traffic on their network and enabled them to see which nodes were sending packets out onto the network. It also enabled them to decode those packets and view the actual data being transmitted. These tools were very powerful for the experienced network manager and were one of the few tools that could diagnose low-level problems. For example, if you had a node that was sending corrupt packets out onto the network, you could, by looking at the packets, see which node was causing the problem. Without an analyzer the only option available was to diagnose a problem through trial and error, unplugging one system from the network at a time until the problem went away. Several problems existed with protocol analyzers, however. They were expensive and difficult to use, and you needed to be an expert on the protocols involved to successfully diagnose problems.

Cable scanners, TDRs, and protocol analyzers dealt with the lowest level of network management. These products helped network managers manage the low-level networks in their installation. After the network was installed and functioning, these products did nothing to help administer a network. That was a task left up to the high-level network administration utilities.

Applications Five Years Ago

Five years ago there was a limited selection of high-level network administration applications. The few available were in the form of individual utilities or groups of utilities that helped network managers administer their networks. These utilities performed various administration-related tasks, such as disk usage reporting, printer management, remote machine control, and menuing. These utilities were nonintegrated, had different user interfaces, and had virtually no form of communication among them.

Network managers and administrators could load these utilities onto their file servers to administer various parts of their network servers. They could learn to use each utility to receive reports for whatever information was needed. They could then gather the different reports in different formats and spend a lot of time manually putting together all the pieces of information. For example, to build a complete network report, the network administrator could buy a package to report disk usage by user, then purchase and install another package to gather information about the different users, and then use yet another package report to administer the different printers. Then the administrator was forced to learn each of the packages and the data formats that the packages used in order to collate all the information manually. By today's standards, this was an extremely crude way to administer a network, but it was state-of-the-art at the time.

Bridging the Gap

A couple of years later, a series of mid-level packages came out that provided connection-oriented information about users and the physical network. They gave the network manager information about network connections and user information, enabling the manager to track problems dealing with network cards and configuration. These packages used connection diagnostic facilities, such as the Novell Diagnostic socket that became available with Netware 2.0, to gather their information. These packages were the first to combine user-level information with protocol-level information in one package. Like the earlier high- and low-level packages, they were also standalone and nonintegrated. These mid-level packages have been surpassed in functionality by today's protocol analyzers, which now do a lot more than watch the low-level cable.

Down on the Wire Today

Currently, there are many protocol analyzer packages on the market that perform functions very similar to their earlier counterparts. These packages, which have gotten much more sophisticated, are beginning to combine information about the physical network with information about the application software running on top of the network. The best example of this is probably the Expert Sniffer from Network General Corp. This product combines all the functionality of a low-level protocol analyzer with an expert system that automatically interprets the information and provides both high-level diagnostic information (such as whether a file server is running too slow, or a node is corrupting data on the network) and low-level product decoding.

Many other protocol-level analyzer products are on the market that will give some level of user information and interpretation of the data packets they collect. However, these packages still require the network manager to have a strong knowledge of the physical network in order to diagnose problems. Although these products are much improved over their earlier counterparts, they still tend to deal only with the low-level network, thus requiring the network administrator to have other products to help administer the high-level applications as well.

Moving from the Wire toward the Applications

The wiring closet management software that is available from most of the networking hardware vendors provides most of the current-day mid-level management. These applications provide management information to the network administrator, usually on the port level, regarding such things as error counts, packet rates, and so on. This information can be useful in load balancing and fault isolation. However, because the information is rarely integrated with the high-level applications and users, and it rarely gets down to the packet level, its usefulness is limited. These packages have a few problems, the largest of which is that they are extremely expensive, adding to the per-node cost of a network sometimes by several hundreds of dollars. This would be acceptable if the packages provided a complete solution, but currently they do not because they deal only with the management of the wire. These packages do nothing to help administrate the high-level functions of the network.

High-Level Administration Today

Currently, there are a large number of packages on the market that provide a wide variety of functions to the network administrator. Most of these packages tend to be geared toward single-purpose problem solving. In other words, these packages usually will fill only one need and are still not integrated. Most of today's network managers have a number of these packages at work on their network. The services these packages provide are as varied as the number of packages available. There are packages to manage the disk space on your network, manage application usage, track network errors and usage, watch for viruses, and so on. Most of these packages have nice clean user interfaces and can help administer most facets of your network. The problem most of these packages face is that they all have different user interfaces, thus forcing network administrators to learn several different packages. Very few of the packages interoperate with other packages to integrate all the information into one coherent interface.

For example, suppose a new network administrator finds that the server is running out of disk space, and he needs to find out who is using a specific package that uses a lot of disk space. He might also like to know which users have local hard disks capable of storing the data files created by this application. With most of the packages available today, this network administrator would have to purchase a metering package to find out which users were running that application. He would have to install the package and learn how to use it. He would then need to find a hardware inventory package to find out which users had local hard disks. With most packages this would mean a different installation procedure, a different user interface, and a whole new learning curve.

This whole process of purchasing different packages with different user interfaces, and learning each of these user interfaces, is both inefficient and time-consuming. It leads to confusion and problems for network administrators ("To exit this screen do I press F10 or Esc, click on Done, or press Enter?"). At the very least, it's time-consuming and confusing to the inexperienced network administrator.

Where Do We Go from Here?

The cost of installing networks has been decreasing, and the cost of maintaining networks has been rising. Networks are becoming simpler to install, and high-end machines are beginning to emerge that are "network aware" right off the shelf. Networks are providing better resources to end users at less cost than ever before. The number of networks and the size of existing networks are growing faster than ever before. With this increased growth of networks, there has also been an increased growth in the number of products available to the network administrators and managers. These products need to be integrated into a coherent network management and administration architecture so that network administrators can manage their networks more easily. Unfortunately, the industry is far from having a comprehensive strategy for network management and administration.

Several companies and groups have come up with network management standards: SNMP, CMIP, and Novel's NMS, to name a few. These standards are beginning to pull the information from different vendors together, but they are far from complete. Most of the standards on the market today are geared toward mid-level management, or the management of the cable and connections. Although this is important, it cannot be the end solution unless the standards are expanded to include the high-level administration tasks as well.

In a recent survey done by *Computer World*, 86 percent of the network managers surveyed said that adherence to standards was one of the most important issues they had when defining their network strategies. The survey also found that more than two-thirds of the respondents felt that multivendor interoperability and network management hindered their full networking implementations within their companies. This is the opposite of the way it should be. Network management and multivendor interoperability should be making the networking implementations simpler and easier, not hindering those efforts. The network managers I have talked to are using a wide variety of applications and architectures. However, they have been united in wanting coherent standards and interoperability between vendors of networking hardware and software.

The Growing Role of Removable Storage in Networks

by Michael Joseph
Vice President of Product Marketing, Iomega Corporation

Author Bio

Michael Joseph is the vice president of product marketing for the Iomega Corporation.

Iomega Corporation is rapidly establishing itself as the premier removable storage company in the fast-growing personal computer market. Founded in 1980, the company makes two removable mass storage products: the Bernoulli drive and the Iomega TAPE 250 drive. The Bernoulli drive incorporates a technology based on a physical phenomenon discovered by Swiss mathematician Daniel Bernoulli in the eighteenth century. Bernoulli drives use cartridges that look like floppy disks in compact, removable cases, which combine the removability, transportability, and security of low-performance floppy drives with the high capacity and performance of Winchester hard disks.

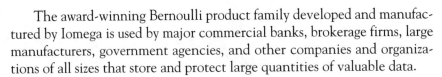

The award-winning Bernoulli product family developed and manufactured by Iomega is used by major commercial banks, brokerage firms, large manufacturers, government agencies, and other companies and organizations of all sizes that store and protect large quantities of valuable data.

The Iomega TAPE 250 drives are the first one-inch form factor products based on a floppy disk interface and the first QIC tape drives able to read Irwin and QIC media. Iomega is the first to design this technology, the first to manufacture these products, and the first to market this type of tape drive.

Iomega is a public company, and its stock is traded on the NASDAQ National Market System under the symbol IOMG. Revenues for the fiscal year 1991 were $136.6 million with income of $12.3 million, compared to revenues of $120.4 million with income of nearly $14 million in 1990. The company has shipped more than 650,000 drives and more than 3,750,000 cartridges worldwide.

Iomega has two wholly-owned subsidiaries: Bernoulli Optical Systems Company, located in Boulder, Colorado, was founded in 1986 to investigate and develop removable optical and other advanced storage technologies such as floptical technology; and Iomega Tape Unit, located in San Diego, California, was established in March 1990 to expand the company's product offerings to include backup tape systems and drives.

In addition, Iomega recently acquired Springer Technologies, Inc., a company specializing in film head technology in Fremont, California. This technology will require significant development work by Iomega teams both in California and Utah for proprietary applications in future mass storage products.

Executive Summary

Removable disk storage is becoming an increasingly valuable enhancement to network environments. Changing user needs such as offsite, non-network computing, security for sensitive data, multiple users on one PC connected to the network, growing storage demands on the server, and disaster recover have generated this growth.

Bernoulli removable disk storage has the unique ability to provide hard disk performance and capacity while offering inexpensive removable disks. This unique ability allows Bernoulli to meet these emerging needs in the market.

Traditional, removable disk storage in networks appears to be an oxymoron. However, just the opposite is happening: removable disk storage is becoming an increasingly valuable enhancement to network environments. Changing user needs spawn this growth. These needs include the following:

- Offsite, non-network computing

- Security for sensitive data

- Multiple users on one PC connected to the network

- Growing storage demands on the server

- Disaster recovery

Bernoulli removable disk storage has the unique ability to provide hard disk performance and capacity while offering inexpensive removable disks. This unique ability allows Bernoulli to meet the emerging needs of the market.

At Iomega, we have been intimately involved with such applications for over 10 years. Our Bernoulli Box product provided the first real solution for users who needed to transport or share information through and around the networks. In fact, we helped coin the phrase "sneaker net" to describe this process.

The Satellite User

Just as the lunar landing module went to the moon and returned to the mothership when it completed its mission, there are users who spend much time offsite conducting business and doing their computing at home, on planes, in hotels, and so forth, and then return to the mothership of the company network to complete their tasks. Networking a remote computer is not practical or cost effective, but communicating information still is important. Removable disk drives, however, allow users in such situations to take their environment with them. Imagine working on the network with a Bernoulli disk as the primary storage device. When users need to move to their home or offsite location, they simply take their Bernoulli disk with them. It contains their environment, which they re-create by rebooting their new location. When they return to the mothership, they bring their environment and new data back to the network. The Bernoulli removable disk becomes a seamless extension of the network users without causing serious compromise to the network.

Following are examples of environments where this extension of the network has appeared:

- Insurance companies—The growth in personal computers at individual agent sites, the need to update data quickly and accurately, and the expense of remote network communications between the home office and the remote sites have created a growing need for removable disk drive solutions.

- Home office—The increasing number of people who work at home because of work habits or family commitments or who are small business owners or consultants create demand for a system that provides primary online storage, backup, and transportability.

- Onsite activities—Accounting firms, consultants, and so forth, who need to conduct a portion of their work at the client's site face the need for rugged, transportable computing to access updates and client files and to share information with related business units in their organization.

As the power and capability of the computer grows while the relative size and price shrinks, the number of applications and remote locations where computers can provide productive help will continue to increase. As these sites become more remote from the network because of people moving computing closer to the need, the challenge of providing "extended" network support to the user will continue to grow.

Sensitive Data

Removable storage is the ideal answer for sensitive data management on a network. The device appears as another volume on the network, and it provides similar performance to the main server. It takes five seconds to bring the device online for the project and does not require a dump or restore to the main server since it is a random access device (that is, like a hard disk). Users communicate with it just as with other devices on the system. However, at the completion of a project, the disk can be removed and returned to a secure location. This reduces risk in several ways:

- The physical data is removed from the system, thus significantly reducing the risk from hackers.

- The data is not on the main server and is not at risk should the server go down or become contaminated.

- The data would not be backed up to the general tape backup device, thus further protecting it from unauthorized access.

Multiuser/Single Computer

Although the number of PCs is growing, there still are more users than PCs. Removable storage provides an ideal solution for environments where more than one user will be on a PC attached to a network. The concern in these cases is how to protect each user's data. With a removable disk for each person, users can log on with a complete environment. This provides full protection for each user's files, password, and applications. Now, each user can do the following:

- Create a unique set of files, directories, applications, and startup configuration to meet particular needs

- Be fully protected from access by other users of the PC

- Access the network from PCs as needed by booting from the Bernoulli disk

The Bernoulli drive provides a very cost-effective solution for providing adequate storage for each user, protecting their data and applications, and reducing the risk to the network from users modifying or enhancing node software.

Growing Storage Demand

According to Cary Lu, noted computer writer, there exists a six-month rule for network file servers. The rule states that no matter what capacity storage device you select for your server, it will be filled in six months. The introduction of removable disk drives provides a fast, convenient incremental storage device to cope with excess data on the server. The removable device offers the following options:

- Storage is fast and easy to access. Data is no more than five seconds away.

- It frees up the server for key database and application tasks.

- It provides a fast, convenient way to manage excess data that does not depend on the main server through a series of dump and restore actions.

This role will continue to grow as users become more and more dependent on the network as their primary work tool.

Disaster Recovery

No one wants the server to go down; and once it is down, everyone wants it up and running. Cost of lost productivity can approach $100,000 per hour for a major network. However, many managers don't realize that tape backup is not enough. When restoring a downed system with tape, it actually can require several days to reinstall the operating system and restore backup files. Bernoulli offers several key tools to provide a quick recovery process (takes just seconds) that gives the network administrator time to properly restore the system.

All in all, the Bernoulli removable random access device provides a powerful addition to networks. It enhances the remote site user, the security user, and the network administrator. That is a significant value to leading companies.

Online Complex Processing: A Powerful Alternative to OLTP

by Philippe Kahn
Chairman, President, and CEO, Borland International

Author Bio

Philippe Kahn founded Borland International in 1983, and currently serves as its chairman, president, and CEO.

Kahn, a French mathematician, studied in Zurich under Niklaus Wirth—one of the most influential computer scientists of the last decade. Kahn founded Borland in 1983, to design and develop innovative, high-performance software for microcomputers. Turbo Pascal was Borland's first product and today is the *de facto* Pascal programming standard worldwide.

Kahn is a sought-after speaker at industry events and business conferences. He is an accomplished musician and sailor and won the Pacific Cup race from California to Hawaii in 1988.

Executive Summary

Recent indications suggest that the 1990s will be the decade of the interactive database user. Powerful PCs and workstations provide users with access to highly interactive graphical user interface (GUI) applications for data access that are connected through local and wide area networks to several databases.

The online complex processing (OLCP) multigenerational architecture is ideally suited to truly interactive database applications. OLCP combines data entry and decision support, and balances performance and consistency.

In contrast, online transaction processing (OLTP) architecture has successfully brought batch-style data processing online, with its potential for processing large volumes of short update transactions. Decision support users can be reasonably supported by traditional OLTP systems only in isolation from data entry applications. This fundamental limitation will have to be addressed as these systems are introduced to the desktop data environment in the near future.

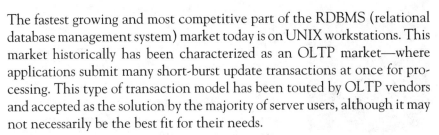

The fastest growing and most competitive part of the RDBMS (relational database management system) market today is on UNIX workstations. This market historically has been characterized as an OLTP market—where applications submit many short-burst update transactions at once for processing. This type of transaction model has been touted by OLTP vendors and accepted as the solution by the majority of server users, although it may not necessarily be the best fit for their needs.

The InterBase Server from Borland takes a different approach to transaction processing by providing a database architecture that supports OLCP—where applications submit many long-duration transactions consisting of both reads and updates for simultaneous processing. This transaction model extends the OLTP model by providing excellent support for both high concurrency and high consistency.

These two server models represent two radically different architectures, each designed to address distinct database application models. Currently many applications can benefit from the OLTP approach for short-duration, traditional data processing applications. However, this approach is not conducive to more complex, interactive applications, as proven by consistent InterBase sales wins over Sybase, Oracle, and Informix in the high-end UNIX RDBMS marketplace.

Most importantly, the desktop of the 1990s needs OLCP. The next high-growth RDBMS market already has been identified by all the major vendors: it's the desktop. Client/server and workgroup database solutions on PC LANs are part of many, if not most, corporate MIS plans. Only OLCP, with its balanced performance, support for browsing and updating, and high availability is in tune with the data management requirements rapidly emerging on the desktop.

OLTP: A Solution for Traditional Data Processing Problems

roots of OLTP RDBMS products lie in the traditional minicomputer and mainframe data processing environments, whereas database management was primarily concerned with efficient throughput of large volumes of short-duration data entry transactions. Consequently, almost every SQL (structured query language) database server has been built to support data entry applications, and all do so by offering the same performance/integrity model. Throughput of short-burst update transactions is optimized while preserving a consistent view of the database for each transaction (isolation level 3).

Significantly, all OLTP SQL servers today achieve this level of concurrency control with a common underlying record storage, record locking, and transaction management architecture. A single version of each data record (the most recent version) is stored in the database. Concurrent access to that single data copy is governed by a read-and-write locking scheme; readers can obtain share locks and simultaneously view data, but writers obtain exclusive locks and have sole access to data items. Transaction integrity is maintained by retaining locks through the life of a logical database transaction. Recovery is achieved through the parallel maintenance of write-ahead log (WAL) containing intended record updates for active transactions.

Transaction processing benchmarks based on UNIX systems indicate that the OLTP architecture provides good support for the traditional data entry model. These servers are designed to maximize throughput of short update transactions, and this is what benchmarks such as the TPC/B measure. The recent spate of OS/2 and NLM TPC/B vendor trials clearly indicates an effort to define the emerging PC LAN client/server database market along the traditional OLTP axis.

This effort will fail, however, because OLTP is not what desktop database users require. The slow growth of SQL servers in desktop environments—only 50,000 units to date, representing less than five percent penetration—points to a fundamental mismatch between current PC database application requirements and the OLTP transaction model.

Desktop Database's Next Generation

The PC database world today is a far cry from OLTP, SQL, or even client/server. Ninety-five percent of the PC desktop data is managed by single-user- or file-server-based DBMSs such as dBASE and Paradox. These systems provide an entirely different transaction model to PC applications, one that gives excellent support for long-duration, complex transactions that include both reads and updates. PC applications need this complex transaction model, for users typically want to do things like the following:

- Browse through large data sets one record at a time, updating some records based on a consistent view of the database (all records from the same point in time)

- Generate long-running reports on large data sets based on a consistent data

- Perform complex and lengthy analysis—selecting and aggregating, and perhaps updating large data sets, based on consistent data

PC data managers have succeeded where OLTP systems fail in providing support for these kinds of complex, long-duration transactions.

Of course, there is a catch. PC data managers do a great job supporting data consistency for long-duration transactions, but have been able to cheat on the concurrency side. For years, single-user database access dominated the PC market, and so users have enjoyed the best of both worlds. Concurrency is (trivially) maximized, since there is only one active transaction at a time. And data consistency is maintained no matter how long the transaction lasts, since no other users are interfering with the data.

Although this seems obvious, it is a crucial point, because it is this high-concurrency/high-consistency combination that has been historically provided to PC database applications. PC applications have been designed to take full advantage of this complex transaction model, offering users free-form and highly responsive interaction with large sets of consistent data.

What is forcing otherwise happy PC database users toward client/server RDBMS servers is a need to share data. The moment desktop users pool their data, two things happen: there is more data to be managed in one place, and there are many simultaneous transactions to be executed against the shared database. Remember, the transactions are still complex, spawned by the same PC applications which expect a consistent view of the database throughout the transaction. What do desktop users need in a LAN database server?

- Multiuser performance on shared data

- Complex transaction consistency

- Support for popular PC applications

Unfortunately, neither file-server-based data managers nor OLTP database servers can meet these three requirements. File-server architectures cannot typically take advantage of economies of scale to provide acceptable multiuser performance and have relatively primitive transaction and integrity models when compared to RDBMS servers.

OLTP systems can provide data security, integrity, and excellent scalable performance, but only for short transactions. Because OLTP systems store only a single copy of any record (the most recent version) in the database, the OLTP concurrency model is like a revolving door—everything works as long as no one goes through the door too slowly.

In a mixed-use transaction environment (reads and updates), database consistency is achieved by serializing access to a data record. Each transaction more or less waits its turn. Users with complex transactions may have to wait a long time. Worse, higher concurrency can be achieved only by compromising transaction integrity by allowing "dirty reads"—where active transactions simultaneously access and manipulate a single copy of data. Alternative isolation levels (cursor stability, uncommitted read) have been proposed and implemented in this vein, but do not provide the consistency required by complex transactions and PC applications.

In other words, OLTP systems only offer long-running transactions the choice between data consistency and high concurrency—choose one. But desktop database applications and users require both—high concurrency and data consistency. The answer lies in OLCP systems.

OLCP: High-Performance Database Servers for Complex Transactions

OLCP RDBMS servers are not new or foreign to the RDBMS market. InterBase has sold effectively for the past five years to the same customers and on the same UNIX platforms as the OLTP system vendors. Complex transactions are not the exclusive domain of PC desktop users; they are commonly encountered in "high-end" applications areas that range from engineering/scientific to financial trading applications that mix OLTP-type transactions with larger, data-intensive, analytic transactions. OLCP systems like InterBase will continue to support uniquely these application segments as they downsize their systems to PC LAN environments.

However, the major source of growth in the OLCP RDBMS server market will be tied to the eventual migration of PC desktop users seeking high-performance, shared-data platforms to client/server database solutions. It is remarkable how closely aligned the complex processing requirements of PC users are to those of current high-end OLCP system users. Where OLTP fails to satisfy the complex processing consistency and concurrency, OLCP succeeds entirely. The difference lies at the very core of the OLCP record storage, record locking, and transaction management architecture.

The InterBase OLCP performance/integrity model supports complex, long-duration transactions with high-concurrency and high-data consistency. A single-version record database approach simply cannot achieve this. InterBase provides high concurrency with a unique approach—based on a multiversion record architecture proposed in the database literature in 1980 by Bayer, Heller, and Reiser (ACM TODS 5, No. 2). Referred to often as the InterBase multigenerational architecture, the system bears little resemblance to traditional OLTP systems.

The first difference in the OLCP architecture is that multiple versions of data records are stored in the database—right on the data pages. Record versions are chained together to provide a change history. The ability to maintain multiple versions of the same record in the database immediately offers new and powerful high-concurrency mechanisms.

The second OLCP difference is the employment of a semioptimistic locking scheme—readers do not have to obtain any lock (shared or exclusive) to access record. This means that database reads always proceed unimpeded and that database writes are never blocked by readers. Multiple long-running and complex transactions can be working on the same logical records at once, and all the changes are recorded, becoming potentially available in the database immediately.

Changes are "potentially" available because high-data consistency is maintained at the same time. A given transaction can find the appropriate collection of data record versions, with respect to the time the transaction started, by following the record version chains, even if the records have been changed multiple times by simultaneously active transactions. Moreover, record versions are logically linked to active transactions that created them by a transaction inventory vector—also stored right on the data pages—so that database integrity is maintained in the event a set of transaction updates is aborted.

The third OLCP difference is the absence of a separate transaction logging system. All transaction recovery information is available within the data pages and is based on the combination of record versions logically linked to the transaction inventory vector.

Summary

Multiple-version record storage, semioptimistic locking, transaction management and recovery based on the data pages rather than logical logs—each of these OLCP architectural elements is fundamentally different than the corresponding OLTP approach of single-version record storage, pessimistic locking, and WAL-based transaction management and recovery. Most importantly, the OLCP approach represents a unified set of architectural components in the database server that is interdependent and complementary. It is unlikely that these elements can be retrofit into OLTP systems to provide an effective OLCP/OLTP hybrid.

All recent indications suggest that the 1990s will be the decade of the interactive database user. Powerful PCs and workstations provide users with access to highly interactive GUI applications for data access, all connected by local and wide area networks to lots of databases.

Network Management Tools: Complex to Simple

by King R. Lee
President and CEO, XTree Company

Author Bio

King R. Lee joined XTree Company as president and CEO in April 1987. Under his direction, the company has experienced 1,700 percent growth. Previously, he was vice president of sales and marketing with Fifth Generation Systems, a leading software utility vendor. Other positions include president of the Marketing Resource Group, a sales and marketing management company whose clients included Lockheed Corporation, Excello Corporation, and TITAN Technologies. Lee also held marketing positions at General Mills and Lever Brothers. He attended California State University at Los Angeles.

Executive Summary

Network Operating Systems are becoming more complex. This trend, in combination with desktop operating system evolution, can signal tough times for the technicians and managers called upon to handle any problems that might arise.

Fortunately, these problems have given rise to an entire industry. Network management tools are coming out from many familiar names as well as some new players on the network scene.

As the networking environment becomes more complex, you need to obtain tools that start with the big picture, help you keep it simple, anticipate problems, solve what it can, and aid you in the rest. It all boils down to having solid tools that keep your network running and your users happy. This paper discusses the criteria you can use to judge which tools are the right tools.

As we move forward in the local area network (LAN) arena, there is no question that network operating systems (NOS) are getting more complex. This trend, in combination with desktop operating system evolution, can signal tough times for the technicians and managers called upon to handle any problems that might arise.

Managers are under increasing pressure to ensure several things:

Constant uptime—unlike the "good ol' days" when people expected the mainframe to be down for some scheduled maintenance or offline for a backup, the PC revolution ushered in much higher expectations. Today, people simply won't except anything less than 24 hour availability.

Experienced technicians—the LANs of today require people with more technical and interpersonal skills than ever before. No longer do people stick boxes of cards into the "back room" expecting to find the results stuffed in their mailbox in the morning. LANs and the operational aspects associated with them are people intensive.

This is also the result of the PC revolution. The end user is now "in control" and has much higher expectations than before.

Fast fixes—partly as a result of uptime expectations, users of today expect (demand) that problems be fixed right away. In the days of big-iron, users dared not question the incantations performed by the support staff. After all, it was beyond their comprehension. Today, the user sees the LAN as a series of PCs strung together—no problem!

Easy access to everything—those of us in the PC/LAN business have been saying "power to the people" for years. Now they have it, they like it, and they expect even more.

Cheap, cheap, cheap—for years, users have been bombarded with the promises, marketing hype, and slight of hand surrounding the issue of how much cheaper operations would be when everybody downsized and worked with PCs. Surprise! The PC/LAN world has costs of its own and somewhere along the line, the end-user community got left off the mailing list.

Given all the above, the prospects for more complicated systems continues to frustrate many in the LAN management world.

Fortunately, this is America. Rules here are quite simple. Create crisis and give rise to an entire industry. Looking out over the next several years, LAN managers can take some comfort in the fact that the network management software industry has everyone's attention. Products are coming out from many old friends as well as some new players on the scene.

Which Tools to Choose?

The first obvious question is will the tools be as complex or more so than the base OS (operating system)? Simple answer: No. Again, good ol' Yankee ingenuity comes to the rescue. Today's network management tools are doing a reasonable job of helping the manager cope with problems. To be sure, there are many "not-so-good" tools out there. They tend to make the job harder than if the tool was not used at all. So how does one figure all this out? Let's take a look at some of the criteria you should consider when looking for management solutions.

Does It Fit?

By fit, we refer to the OS and the surrounding environment. Today, you might be using the good ol' DOS prompt. In a NetWare environment, C-Worthy type interfaces are something many people are familiar with. For the LAN Manager/LAN Server folks, you are used to the character-based CUA type interfaces. But that's today. Many companies are moving toward a graphical user interface and have an expectation that the tools will move in this direction as well. Talk with your vendors and look to see if the products will fit into your environment today and in your future environment.

Moving Parts

Another term is "nickel and dime." The products of today become features of tomorrow's products. This presents an interesting balancing act for you to deal with. For example, if you have an accounting product, the functionality of which becomes "a feature" of other similar products, what is the migration path for your bean counter software and the vendor who supplied it? Do the products belong to a family? Do they fit together to form a larger solution? There are many important questions that you need to ask up front. Many vendors are single product folks. This takes nothing away from the product. In some cases of serious specialty, it is the only way to go. Make sure you understand the product and its fit into the total solution.

Help?

When you look at management tools, ask yourself if you will learn anything from the product. Can it teach you something about your system or how to manage it? Will it point out information that you wouldn't have known about? A good network management software product should help solve the problems but should also teach you something about that network as well. This is an important value that you should look for in your selected products.

Prevent Defense

Can a product warn you of a problem? Today there are many programs that will page you in the hot tub when you are going to run out of disk space. Many will take a preprogrammed action based upon some decision process. The real challenge for the vendors is to add the depth to the warning by providing long range planning and anticipation. It is one thing to set a threshold in remaining disk space, but it is quite another to have software track the usage, purge/archive the old, advise of the trends, and keep you readily informed about the "health" of the disk and its space.

Development of the Future

Figure 26.1 shows the "camps" of development activity being done today.

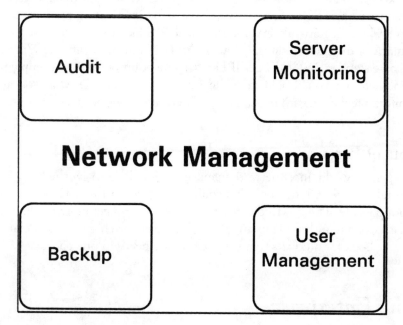

Figure 26.1. The development areas.

For the most part, you have to choose a focus and go after the tool that best meets the need in that area. While this can be done, it presents the manager with some issues and potential problems.

"It's Not Our Fault, Call..."

This is what happens when you have to use a different vendor's product and you have a problem with the products talking to each other. This is a time-consuming and sometimes fruitless exercise. You now have the original problem combined with tools that don't talk/work with each other. Not fun.

"Standards, Huh?"

Standards is a four letter word that gets uttered in the hallways but never spoken about until after the disaster. Assume, for example, each product you buy keeps a database of information. Great, right? What format? Btrieve? Paradox? Xbase? SQL? Suppose you have some monitoring products that watch when the network server starts to feel ill. Super, right? Now, you want to monitor the hubs, routers, gateways, bridges, and workstations. What is the base standard? SNMP? CMIP? Freds? The point of all this is simply to point out that you should take the initiative and decide what you are comfortable with regarding standards. Then, try to get products that fit.

Lots of Parts

In a perfect world, most network managers would love to get the Network OS and manage with the tools that come with the OS. Most of the time, this is not possible. The downside of having to go out and get more products is the issue of having lots of moving parts. This, of course, has issues associated with it. Look for products that can meet many needs in one package.

The Enterprise

Figure 26.2 shows where management and the tools are going. Today, managers are realizing that they must think of the "network" as more than just the server running NetWare or the Cabletron box. They must think at the next higher level: the enterprise.

To effectively manage the enterprise, network management software developers are going after design goals that meet this high level view. Let's review just a few of those goals.

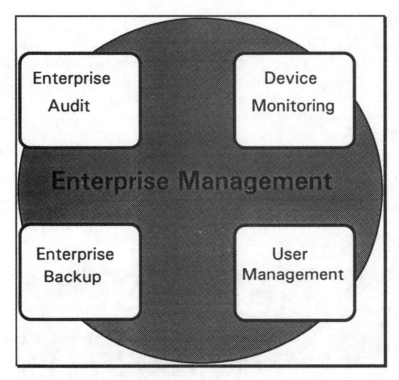

Figure 26.2. The higher level view.

Big Picture

When you bring up the management software, think NASA or, if you like military analogies, a Command Post. From your seat, you should be able to get a big picture of what is happening in an overall sense. This is the enterprise view.

Drill Down

As a problem crops up, you should be able to "drill down" and find out the cause and possible solutions. Good software will point out a problem, great software will suggest a fix, and excellent software will have already fixed the problem and sent you a note regarding the problem, what was done, and what the current status is.

Stay In Your Seat

An important design goal is to keep the manager in the seat. The manager should be able to deal with as many network issues as possible from the command console. Think of it this way: if we can send a billion dollar satellite a trillion miles away and control it, we should be able to fix many problems on the network without a trek to some back room or a grouchy ol' user's cubicle.

Advice

Figure 26.3 shows the worst case. A message and a really wonderful "bang, you're dead" message. This is available in many software packages and this feature is called advisory messages. Super.

Figure 26.3. Bang, you're dead.

Next, there is the advisory message with "extended help." This is where you are still told that you're dead, but now you get a reason why you're dead. As shown in Figure 26.4, you can get some help, but it will mostly confirm that you are dead.

Figure 26.4. *You're dead, but, heck, we can talk about it.*

Where the tools are going, however, is toward the approach shown in Figure 26.5. Depending on the situation, the system can either do something about it or at least give you some options.

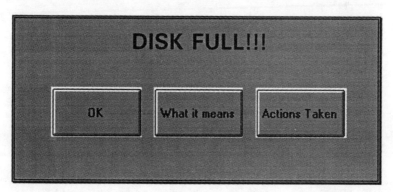

Figure 26.5. *Where we should be going.*

Summary

Many vendors will offer solutions to problems. As things get more complex, you need to obtain tools that start at the big picture, help you keep it simple, anticipate problems, solve what it can, and aid you in the rest. It all boils down to having solid tools that keep your network running and your users happy.

This is a tall order, but vendors like XTree are striving to fill it with products like the XTree ProLine series of professional network management solutions, designed to help the network manager handle today's problems as well as to help the manager move into the future.

The Myths and Realities of Network Management

by Howard E. Lubert
President, HEL Inc.

Author Bio

Howard Lubert is president and founder of HEL, Inc., a systems integration company specializing in the delivery of turnkey LANs and high level connectivity projects. As an independent reseller and consultant, Mr. Lubert has installed more than 150 networks, worked with all topologies, and has handled the "total integration" approach to successful network implementation.

As a nationally recognized speaker, Mr. Lubert has presented custom-developed courseware to over 5,000 clients on topics such as "Introduction to Local Area Networks," "Network Management and Troubleshooting," and "Printing and Communicating with Novell LANs" at PC EXPO and NETWORLD events as well as smaller, regional expositions. As an educator, Mr. Lubert has led formal classroom instruction for over 1,000 would-be CNEs. He often serves as a beta tester for LAN- and network-related products and was one of the first resellers in the country to install Netware 1000.

HEL's "typical" corporate assignments include the design and testing of a 6,000 user network, as well as the implementation of unified standards under DOS, Windows and OS/2 platforms in an 800-plus LAN environment with IBM and DEC connectivity.

HEL, Inc., is located in Wayne, Pennsylvania, a suburb of Philadelphia. Mr. Lubert can be reached there at (215) 293-1855.

Executive Summary

"The Myths and Realities of Network Management" can best be described as a position paper on the philosophy and positioning of network management rather than the tools and skills required to manage and implement the network. Network management is discussed not as a product but as a hierarchy. Each of the four levels of the hierarchy is described, and each builds on the previous level.

Readers will come away with a practical approach to the management of networks, big or small, and ideas of what it takes to implement the management at each level. Although the author specializes in the implementation of networks attached to Novell LANs, the discussion is generic in nature and can be applied to any size network or LAN.

Network management is the new hot button of the industry. It's fashionable today to discuss what tools you are using to manage your networks. Everybody, and I mean *everybody*, is jumping on the network management bandwagon with both feet. IBM has Netview, the industry has SNMP, and who knows how many others. We are deluged with confusing options and don't know which way to turn. To make matters worse, now we can't even figure out where our network management should reside! Should it be server or router based? Mainframe or minicomputer based? Integrated? In or out of band? On a Windows or OS/2 platform? Or maybe we should stick it in a slot in a concentrator or MAU? Come on now...enough is enough.

Let's look at the realities surrounding the issue of network management. My assertion here is that network management falls into four categories. Each category can be identified, defined and described. Every one of us is already involved in network management on at least one of these levels. The following pages will help you decide which level of management your environment matches and how deeply involved you are in the network management process. By the way, if you are expecting a list of the latest and greatest network management tools with a "how to" tutorial on implementation, you will be disappointed by the following pages. While many network management tools will be mentioned, this article is not intended to recommend or provide installation techniques for these tools. If, on the other hand, you are interested in a philosophy of network management, then read on—the adventure begins.

Abraham Maslow (the psychologist in me comes out) described a hierarchy of needs for man. Network management also comes in a hierarchy. The difference is that when you get to the top of Maslow's hierarchy you "self-actualize." When you get to the top of the Network Management Hierarchy your network begins to manage itself.

There are four levels of network management. The table below describes each level and the associated type of network activity associated with each level.

Let's examine each of the levels of network management and determine what activities take place at each of them.

The Network Management Hierarchy

Level	Name	Activity
4	Managed	Actualized
3	Monitored	Proactive
2	Control	Reactive
1	Rudimentary	Reactive

The bottom level of the Network Management Hierarchy is called Rudimentary. We can best describe this level of network management as *laissez-faire*. Did you know that better than 40 percent of networks don't have any security? "Passwords? What's a password? I log in at 9 a.m., do my work all day and turn off the machine at 5 p.m. when I leave. Isn't that enough security?"

Networks at this level provide application and peripheral sharing services. Owners of these networks have not caught on to the single most important philosophy behind networks: "The Data on the Network is the Most Valuable Asset of My Company!"

Along with this concept come several related ones:

- The data is valuable

- It belongs to my company

- It is *not* to be fooled with

- I have a responsibility to protect the data from users and abusers

I am constantly amazed at my management seminars how foreign these concepts are to so many people. Users and managers of networks, big and small, still haven't fully embraced "The Data is My Most Valuable Asset" concept. Let's net this to the bottom line.... There are numerous examples of business failures due to catastrophic data loss. This is why we're discussing network management in the first place!

The Rudimentary Level, or Day-to-Day as I call it, requires almost no planning or network management awareness. The network is managed on an as-needed basis. Users are added, but almost never deleted. Applications are relatively static and installations are generic in nature. This is a reactive management mode. Security, as we think of it, is virtually nonexistent. Users have IDs and possibly passwords, but the supervisor account has been overlooked and offers an open door to potential havoc. None of the enhanced security features of the NOS have been implemented. Here at the bottom of the Network Management Hierarchy, life is simple—not secure.

Tape backup, if present at this stage, is haphazard and no real plan for disaster recovery exists. It would amaze you to know that many of these sites don't even backup, and most of those that do, don't have off-site tape storage.

Most people believe that this represents most of the small "mom & pop" LANs scattered around out there. That just isn't so. At a security audit for a Fortune 10 corporation a few years ago, I found an ARCnet network with four servers and almost 200 users. Good backup program, servers in secure rooms with non-master key locks, and 47 accounts with supervisor equivalents! As the pointed man from the pointed forest said, "Having a point in every direction is like having no point at all!" There is no way to secure a network when 25 percent of the users are supervisors. It can happen anywhere.

Now I know what many of you are thinking.... This isn't my LAN. We're safe from these kinds of oversights. Are you sure? Have you checked? When did you perform your last security audit? Have you ever performed a security audit? Do you know what a security audit covers? Here's a free start. Contact the Computer Security Institute and ask them for a free copy of their PC LAN Security Checklist.

Some of the myths associated with the Rudimentary Network environment include the classics such as...

- "It will run itself!"

- "Of course it's secure...isn't it?"

- "We don't need network management, our users are self-sufficient!"

The second level of network management is called the Control Level. At this second level of the hierarchy, networks are tightened up. The concepts of security are not new here, but sometimes users are confronted with security controls that inconvenience them and inhibit some productivity. These networks are easy to recognize. Servers are secure, users are forced to change passwords on a regular basis, and data backup is implemented in a very regimented manner with off-site storage. A security audit in this network environment would prove to be extremely effective. There may be a hole or two, but it is a tight environment. This is the hallmark of the Control Network: tight security, strict software implementation programs, a formal pecking order of control, and possibly a system manager or LAN administrator in charge.

The Control Network management arena includes LAN utilities to control the LAN from a security perspective. This environment probably has a utility like "NetOff" to log off inactive workstations. There may be a copy of "LT Auditor" from Blue Lance Software to audit and track software utilization and monitor who is using, modifying, and deleting files.

Networks running at the Control Level are tightly controlled at the expense of the user. While this meets the data integrity requirements mentioned earlier, it does not endear the network to the users. On the other hand, the network administrator has provided a stable environment. The simple growth options built into a well-managed net make the Control Network the most common network environment in existence today.

Contrary to popular belief, the administrator in a Control Network knows very little about the actual network. Users, security, servers, and other platforms in the network are well-known, but little is known about what is actually happening on the network. Performance issues are not addressed in this environment until a failure takes place. These characteristics classify a Control Network as a reactive network environment.

The third level of network management is the Monitor Level. At the Monitor Level the network administrator has moved to a proactive mode of managing the net. Utilities to monitor the network provide management with information regarding performance, problems, and security matters. This network requires an additional investment of time and money to install. The administration and performance of this network are constantly being evaluated.

The Monitored Network provides an almost perfect environment for users. Security is tight but seamlessly integrated to be unnoticeable to the users. Applications are integrated and individually configured to provide user preferences and high levels of productivity.

"Novi" from Foundation Ware probably protects the network from virus infection. Because the software scans for specific types of activity and not specific signatures, it does not need to be updated after every new virus makes its way into the world. Network administrators have enough to do in this environment without having to worry about infections from virus software. Strict software and diskette policies exist and are enforced in this network. Users never install applications on the network; the support staff does. No software is introduced to this environment that hasn't been checked by the support staff.

In the Monitored environment there are formal policies on software use/abuse. End users are aware that software piracy is not tolerated in this environment. Although this environment is very solid and builds on the layers below it, there are a number of myths associated with it worth mentioning. The concepts of "security at any price" and "damn the users, the network comes first" are two of the myths that come to mind. Network managers need to remember that the network exists to serve the users within some relatively easy to define parameters. The Monitored Network, then, is the Control Network with a liberal dose of human awareness thrown in. This couples with the proactive management functions to provide a wonderful network environment.

As good as the Monitored Network environment is, there is a fourth and final level of The Network Management Hierarchy. I call this the Managed Level. At the Managed Level the network informs its administration of the day-to-day health of the environment. Monitrix from Cheyenne Software and/or Early Warning System/Frye Utilities from Frye constantly monitor the network for problems. LAN Automatic Inventory from Brightworks and some help desk packages serve the support staff in their roles as administrators and facilitators of network resources.

Standards are a *fait accompli* in this environment. Network administration in this environment includes short- and long-term planning, not putting out fires. There are occasional fires, but all in all the "self-actualizing" network normally is well behaved. User groups meet regularly with network management and serve on and voice opinions on network activities. A true partnered relationship exists between the users and the support staff. Administrators concentrate on expanding their environments as well as making newer, more powerful applications available to their users. This environment is fully integrated across all associated platforms, and users access data from these platforms with little or no regard for where the data resides.

Working in this network environment is a constant challenge. Users are looking for ways to expand their access to information, and this results in a need for constantly bigger and more powerful applications.

The desktop environment, largely ignored until now, is standardized in this environment. All users have the same "look" to their desktops although they don't all access the same applications. In this environment, standards are enforced to guarantee growth capabilities and future compatibility. Users with unusual software and or hardware requirements must present a business case to the user committee. This committee is charged with the approval or denial of these special cases based on the business case presented versus the potentially adverse effects on the homogenous network. This may sound restrictive, but the Monitored Network needs these standards to maintain its self-control capabilities.

The most humorous myth of the Managed Network is that it runs itself. Even with all of the information provided automatically by the network, administrators are deluged with information. Growth plans along with monitoring activities must be weighed to ensure a trouble-free environment. Network administrators are constantly fighting the budget battle because they are always looking for new and more powerful tools to do their jobs.

So where do you stand on the Network Management Hierarchy? None of the levels of the program are perfect, and most people would agree that a combination of features is the ideal environment. Some very large networks attempt to apply the "KISS—Keep it Simple Stupid" method of management, and some small networks have management tools up the kazoo! There is such a thing as too much management. The happy medium for you is out there. Now all you have to do is find it.

The Open Systems Approach to Enterprise Computing

by Nina Lytton
Editor and Publisher, Open Systems Advisor

Author Bio

Nina Lytton is editor and publisher of *Nina Lytton's Open Systems Advisor*, a monthly newsletter analyzing major issues in the movement toward multivendor computer systems, and president of Open Systems Advisors, Inc. (OSA). OSA performs market research and consulting in the computer and communications industry and conducts executive-level conferences and seminars.

In addition to open systems, Ms. Lytton's research and consulting interests include the organizational side of technology implementation and the quantification of market opportunities. She was the creator of the Executive INTEROP Conference and is a regular columnist in *Open Systems Today!*

Prior to founding OSA in early 1989, Ms. Lytton spent four years with the Yankee Group. She was responsible for the Distributed Systems Planning Service, and prior to that, for the Manufacturing Automation Planning Service. She also served as editor of the *Yankee Conveyor* newsletter, directed two national surveys of computer and automation buyers, and organized numerous conferences. She is the author of five Yankee Group research reports on computer-integrated manufacturing covering technology trends, market projections, vendors' market strategies, and users' organizational and implementation issues.

Prior to joining the Yankee Group, Ms. Lytton worked in product management for a PC software firm. She began her career on Wall Street and held several positions in financial analysis and commercial lending.

Ms. Lytton holds a bachelor's degree in economics from Princeton University and a master's degree in management from the Alfred P. Sloan School of Management at MIT.

Open Systems Advisors, Inc.
268 Newbury Street
Boston, MA 02116

Executive Summary

This paper provides a guide for threading one's way though the confusing claims of "open systems vendors." It discusses definitions, outlines the basic business benefits of open systems, explains the tradeoffs of various approaches, outlines practical caveats, lists criteria for judging vendors, and offers guidelines on getting there from here.

Although "open systems" is one of the latest buzzwords, the industry has been moving in this direction for some time. The open systems movement started with the IBM plug-compatible vendors and the UNIX operating system. It continued with the Internet Society's and the International

Standards Organization's models of multivendor communications, and received a kick in the pants from large users, GM and Boeing, with the establishment of the MAP task force in the mid-1980s. By then it was evident that an open systems business model was providing the rocket fuel for the PC industry's growth. Around the same time, European computer vendors founded X/Open, an industry consensus standards organization which integrates standards into a multivendor architecture for portability and interoperability. X/Open's Common Application Environment, specified in a document called the X/Open Portability Guide (XPG), now rivals SAA in comprehensiveness.

In 1988, the traditional computer vendors realized that UNIX was strategic, and they founded the Open Software Foundation as a counterbalance to AT&T and Sun. A year or two later, Unisys, ICL, Digital, and HP announced they would migrate their traditional operating systems into compliance with the X/Open XPG. Even as the public standards process accelerated the pace and widened the scope of its efforts worldwide, special-interest standards groups formed to fill the gaps. In 1991, IBM made a 100-product open systems announcement. In 1992, there was a spate of open systems announcements by the PC Team, such as Apple's Open Collaboration Environment and Microsoft's Windows Open Services Architecture. In 1992, X/Open will release the fourth version of its XPG.

Much Ado About Definitions

Today, the open systems movement is pervasive in the computer and communications industry. But all this support adds up to many competing claims. Computer buyers are getting the same dazed sensation they do in the supermarket where it seems that all food can be described by some combination of the words "fresh," "natural," and "cholesterol free." When you see an all-natural granola bar, for instance, you don't know without reading the fine print whether it's a candy bar or an organic convenience meal for vegetarians. As with groceries, the same holds true with computer hardware and software: communication at cross purposes is the side effect of buzzwords and other forms of verbal shorthand. Although they're both marketed as open systems, for example, there's just as much difference between Microsoft Windows and SCO Open Desktop as there is between a fresh-and-natural beef steak and a fresh-and-natural tofu burger. And there's about as much similarity between the HP 9000 and the IBM AS/400 as there is between a cholesterol-free cucumber and a cholesterol-free donut. (Yes, they really do exist!)

There is really no need for all this confusion. All the various definitions of "open systems" can be understood with respect to a single reference point, the IEEE P1003.0 definition. According to the IEEE, an open system is a system that implements sufficient open specifications for interfaces, services, and supporting formats to enable properly engineered applications software to:

- be ported with minimal changes to a wide range of systems

- interoperate with other applications on local and remote systems

- interact with users in a style which facilitates user portability

The IEEE accompanies this definition with two explanatory points:

- "Open specifications" are public specifications maintained by an open, public consensus process to accommodate new technology over time; they also are consistent with international standards. Specifications originally developed by private companies and consortia become open specifications when maintenance is transferred to a public consensus process.

- Application environment profiles and suites of standards appropriate to specific user situations are being developed by the IEEE to define what open systems specifications are "sufficient."

This definition won't satisfy everyone, but it includes the two basic elements of any definition of open systems: standard interface specifications and benefits. When you're confronted with a strange new breed of "open system," there is no need to feel like a blind man confronted with an elephant. Just ask "which benefits" and "whose standard interface specifications." The following discussion will help you answer questions such as "Is Microsoft Windows an open system?" or "How open is IBM's AS/400?"

Open Systems Benefits

There are two basic benefits of open system: portability and interoperability. Portability is the ability to move applications, data, and people from one vendor or computer systems architecture to another. Interoperability is the ability for people and programs to exchange information in a meaningful way. Physical connectivity used to be a synonym for interoperability, but connectivity alone is not enough to accomplish useful work.

Together, the technical benefits of open systems combine to produce four business benefits:

- Freedom of Choice—Individuals and operating units can, without compromising overall organizational synergy, make the best I/T purchase decisions to support their missions by choosing from a broad portfolio of hardware and software provided by multiple vendors.

- Flexibility and Change Management Over Time—User organizations are free to recombine and redeploy their open systems applications and I/T infrastructure as business needs dictate. With open systems, perfect foresight isn't required. Users can focus on buying or building the best application, knowing that it can be moved, if required, to several different hardware platforms over its useful life.

- Lasting Value—Open systems provide an insurance policy against being locked into a single vendor's software or hardware. Because open systems enhance the ability to compare and substitute one component for another, individual system components are priced competitively and will stay that way over time. Enhancement and upgrade options flow from a free market pool of innovation, not just a single vendor.

- Investment Protection—Open systems provide investment protection for the big-ticket, long-lifecycle items: software and training.

There are a couple of things to remember about the benefits of open systems. First, achieving the business benefits listed above depends on both portability and interoperability. This should be self-evident to user organizations developing applications in house (and then maintaining/enhancing them each year). Yet "information embolisms" (bottlenecks where information cannot flow to the end users who need it) typically make interoperability today's burning issue. Users who purchase applications rather than develop them are prone to summarily dismissing the importance of portability. But users, before you settle for an interoperability-only solution, remember that the useful life of an application could be 10 to 20 years. Do you really know where you'll need to run the application in that timeframe? Are you really sure you'll be satisfied with one vendor for so long a duration? Portability plays a vital role in the degree of freedom of choice, flexibility to manage change, value, and investment protection you will enjoy in the future.

The second thing to remember is not to get a false sense of security from checklists. When you buy a computer platform that supports open systems interfaces, you do not automatically get interoperability and portability. Applications are automatically portable, for example, only to the extent that they actually use standard application programming interfaces and that other programs they rely on, such as database management systems, are available on other platforms.

As a corollary to the point above, buying a platform that adds value to standard interfaces like Apple's AUX doesn't automatically mean you have given up portability. It is the *use* of vendor-specific interfaces or extensions (not their presence) that ties an application to that vendor's platforms. But if you buy a platform that offers POSIX or XPG interfaces and you buy or build applications using vendor-specific interfaces instead (for example, Apple's Inside Macintosh), then you have locked yourself in to that vendor. Doing so may be justifiable. If so, justify it. Don't do it by accident.

Benefits: A Matter of Degree

Another thing to consider is that the benefits of open systems are, and always will be, a matter of degree. First, at any point in time, some standards will be solid as concrete, others will be right around the corner, and others will be in the experimental stage. Interoperability of electronic mail systems is a good example of this phenomenon. E-mail for text has well-established standards; standards for exchanging compound and multimedia documents are emerging. Thus, application developers can't always confine themselves to available standards and must use standards extensions or vendor-specific "supersets." This reduces portability and interoperability, but does not eliminate them.

The use of open systems standard interfaces affects the speed and ease of applications' portability the way bar codes and scanners affect the time you stand in line at the supermarket check-out counter. The more produce items you have, the more items there are without bar codes and the longer it takes to process the order. Even with half a basket of fruit and vegetables, scanning the other half is still much faster than ringing in the whole order manually. The same is true with open systems standards. Even if you don't use them 100 percent of the time, you'll still benefit from a degree of portability.

As technology continues to advance, buyers will always have to evaluate the merit of new, nonstandard features relative to the flexibility foregone in implementing applications that use these "standards-superset" features. For some applications, the benefits won't be worth the costs; for others, the benefits will be overwhelming. Applying the discipline to think through these tradeoffs is essential to realizing the benefits of open systems.

Open Systems Standards

There are two key issues to understand about open systems standards. First, there is more than one kind of "public consensus process" at work selecting standard interface definitions. Second, there won't always be "one" standard in a given area, and this isn't cause for a crisis of confidence.

The IEEE definition of open systems focuses on the official public process that results in *de jure* standards. As a practical matter, *de facto* standards, those established in the market, are equally important. The source of a *de facto* standard interface specification is usually (but not always) the vendor of a best-selling product such as Novell NetWare. The "public consensus process" of making these interfaces into standards is that of buyers voting with their dollars. I join the IEEE in disputing the openness of these vendor-defined standards. Although Microsoft would probably dismiss me as a gnat and dispute the relevance of the IEEE's POSIX except as a check-list item, a *de facto* standard is often a one-way street.

I don't want to knock vendor-defined standards entirely. After all, when a vendor "opens" its interface definitions to cloning or licenses its source code for enhancement and resale, it opens itself to competition. But vendor-specific standards can also be used to protect the market position of the originating vendor, like allowing buyers to make certain choices but not others. Specifically, the objective can be to allow the buyer to switch everything else but the *de facto* standard product. For example, Microsoft's Win32 API is a *de facto* standard that encourages choices of hardware and applications but not of operating systems. IBM's Systems Applications Architecture and Apple's Inside Macintosh are *de facto* standards that facilitate applications choice but not hardware vendor choice. In all of these cases, dependency on the vendor originating and maintaining the specification is extreme. Software and hardware clones are an option, but they are always a generation behind. Users must decide whether the advantages of single-vendor standards are worth the sacrifice in flexibility.

Both *de jure* and *de facto* standards have major shortcomings. *De jure* standards are slow to be defined and then established in the market. Typically, commercially available implementations lag far behind the state-of-the-art choices users must make when implementing competitive-advantage systems. Individual vendors can establish *de facto* standards rapidly, but they can enhance choices in one area by limiting choices in another. Historically, vendor-specific *de facto* standards have evolved slowly once established. This is no surprise to economists: the standard bearer has no effective competitive pressure and is, for practical purposes, a monopoly. Monopolists are complacent and slow-moving by definition.

But when *de facto* standard products are cloned (the interface definition is independently implemented) or when a countervailing force gathers, the monopoly price umbrella is threatened. Then, the originator of the standard has typically gone into engineering overdrive and taken steps to ensure that the independent implementation stays a generation behind the "real" standard. Often this is accompanied by marketing fanfare, sometimes by legal action. Sudden leaps into activity are common as monopolists are jolted out of their complacency.

Consensus: The New Approach to Setting *De Facto* Standards

Open systems-minded vendors and users have tried to achieve the best of both worlds with a third approach to establishing open systems interface definitions: consensus standards developed by consortia or *ad hoc* groups of companies. Consensus standards are tested in the market, and, if successful, become *de facto* standards. Some are percolated through to the *de jure* standards process. The Internet protocols and the X/Open XPG are the standards that proved the viability of the consensus method.

The Internet suite of protocols is the *original* open systems standard for worldwide messaging. Work first began on "TCP/IP" about 20 years ago for a Department of Defense network called the ARPANET, and the protocol was subsequently used in the National Science Foundation's NSFnet. Today, the "Internet" is most commonly used to refer to the Internet mail community. Active users number about eight million, almost 10 times the size of the Compuserv user base. Although the number of Internet users is more than respectable, the fact that they are all interconnected is amazing. In April 1992, some 750,000 host computers were connected to the Internet through a backbone of more than 5,000 interconnected subnetworks in 70 countries around the world.

The Internet first became popular because it was the only source of badly needed wide-area internetworking functionality. Today, federal subsidization covers only a small fraction of the total cost. There are a number of commercial Internet providers such as AlterNet, CERFnet, Performance Systems International, Advanced Networking Services, and SprintLink. There is also a Commercial Internet Exchange (CIX) which allows private providers' customers to exchange traffic.

The Internet standards process is a best-of-all-worlds approach which combines the practical focus of the PC Team with the rationality and order of a more formal process, and adds these elements to the Internet Community's strength in practical wide-area internetworking technology. Most recently, this process produced the Multipurpose Internet Mail Extensions (MIME), a multimedia mail standard that is nondisruptive to the installed base.

The development of Internet standards is governed by the Internet Activities Board (IAB), a group of invited volunteers. The IAB meets regularly to approve standards and allocate resources such as network addresses. User concerns are addressed by another group of volunteers, the Internet Engineering Task Force (IETF), responsible for short-term engineering. The Internet Research Task Force (IRTF) is responsible for longer-term research. The IAB bodies are open to input from all quarters: anyone can design, document, test, and implement a protocol for use on the Internet.

Protocols are documented in the Internet Request for Comments (RFC) series. Because most RFCs are informational, ones in the standards track are also placed in the Internet STD series. The Internet standards track consists of three "states"—proposed standard, draft standard, and Internet standard. States are assigned by the IAB after review of the interface definition and the implementation experience. To progress to a full Internet standard, there must be several implementations and deployment experience sufficient to provide a basis for an evaluation of interoperability.

X/Open's value added is as a standards integrator, consolidating and harmonizing input from many sources, working proactively with *de jure* standards bodies and special interest groups like the X.400 API Association (X.400 APIA) and the Object Management Group to expedite the process of moving to *de facto* and *de jure* standards. This might sound like a slam-dunk of desktop publishing. In reality, it is anything but that. First, the specification of a standard frequently contains a maze of options, many contradictory and incommensurate with those found in other specs. Occasionally, specs are even self-contradictory! A fine-toothed comb is required to get everything straight. Second, there are many holes between standards, and special interest groups don't exist in every area, forcing X/Open to form its own in many cases. Thus, X/Open is a participant in and the coordinator of an enormous, multivendor engineering effort.

The X/Open process of establishing interface definitions begins with primary research into user requirements by the "Xtra Process." This research is both qualitative (focus groups) and quantitative (worldwide surveys). With user input in mind, X/Open staff and shareholder representatives discuss proposed standards with three advisory councils composed of users, software vendors, and system vendors. The specification of X/Open's "Common Application Environment," contained in a series of documents called the X/Open Portability Guide (XPG), are prepared by the X/Open staff and ratified by a consensus of the shareholders.

Computer systems (hardware and system-level software) that comply with the XPG are evaluated by an extensive test suite before being granted the X/Open brand. Because no test suite is 100 percent comprehensive, vendors with branded products are legally bound to correct any noncompliance that subsequently arises. As alluded to above, there is an abundance of branded hardware: all X/Open shareholders—which include all the mainstream computer vendors, even IBM—are committed to offering systems bearing the X/Open brand. And shareholder companies, of course, are not the only ones who can (and do) implement the spec. The X/Open XPG is the standard interface definition that unifies virtually all versions of UNIX at the source code level and has become popular enough to spread to traditional operating systems such as DEC's VMS.

By purchasing or writing applications that comply with the X/Open XPG, users can stay flexible on all three dimensions—hardware, operating environments, and applications—without investing extensive effort in developing a standards profile from scratch. There is one caveat to the XPG, however. Although it is the open systems industry's greatest common denominator, the XPG is not a panacea. As a consensus organization, X/Open can't give guidance on issues for which there is no semblance of agreement.

Today, the consensus standards approach is widely used by special interest groups. Sometimes consensus standards are proposed in competition to a proposed extension to a *de facto* standard, or vice versa. One example of this phenomenon is the Open Software Foundation, which competes in UNIX technology with the UNIX System Laboratories. Another is the Microsoft Mail API (MAPI) and the Vendor-Independent Messaging (VIM) API put forward by Lotus, Apple, Novell, and Borland. Both arose as "refinements" to the X.400 APIA's work. It will be up to the market and the public standards process to weigh and, if possible, resolve the differences between multiple proposed standards.

Whether proposed by a consensus process or by an individual vendor as an extension to a *de facto* standard, interface definitions generally get some modification in the process of acceptance as consensus or *de jure* standards. For this reason, and because there is never a guarantee that a proposed standard will actually win acceptance, it is important that users do business with vendors who commit to migrate their products into compliance with international standards on an ongoing basis.

Multiple Standards Are Inevitable

Even if some proposed standards don't catch on, there is usually more than one survivor in any given area. Multiple standards exist in the market because the world is a big place, inhabited by different communities with different needs, different skills and biases, and different economic interests. What is suitable for the PC community, for example, may give the mainframe community a bad case of the heebee-jeebees. The way the PC industry tackles something is quite different from the way the UNIX industry will tackle the same problem. The "PC Team" will usually take a pragmatic, incremental approach to establishing standards, putting them forward as compatible steps forward (not leaps forward) from existing products. But where Microsoft will solve a *specific* problem with a spec for Object Linking and Embedding, the UNIphile-dominated Object Management Group will go after the *general* problem and reconceptualize the entire architecture for distributed, object-based computing. The third reason for the existence of multiple standards is vendors' economic self-interest. The *de facto* standard setter wants to retain its monopoly as long as possible. Its competitors pool their resources to mount a credible alternative.

So why aren't multiple standards all that bad? First and foremost, competition is good for the customer. The coming clash between Microsoft and the UNIphiles is a good example of Adam Smith's "invisible hand" at work: each side has spurred the other to greater efforts. Second, within each community, a standard serves as a leverage point for the investments of multiple vendors, a springboard for innovation. Between communities, standards serve as opposite ends of the bridges to portability and interoperability of applications, data, and people. The existence of multiple standards within a single organization does raise the system and network management challenge but is warranted when it meets the legitimately different needs of multiple user constituencies.

Open Systems Vendors

Generally, vendors fall along a continuum with respect to open systems. At one end of the continuum are vendors like Microsoft, Apple, and the AS/400 division of IBM. These vendors see themselves primarily as the generators of *de facto* standards on an ongoing basis. They pick their spots for compliance with international standards as they evolve. They emphasize interoperability and don't recognize portability to other operating systems as a requirement beyond perfunctory compliance with checklist items. At the other end of the continuum are vendors like HP, NCR, and SCO. They see themselves primarily as collaborators. They pick their spots for innovation carefully and are unambiguously committed to migrating their offerings back into compliance with international standards on an evolving basis. They emphasize the users' right to stay portable as much as they emphasize interoperability. Vendors like Univel and SunSoft are somewhere in between. Compared to the Microsoft, Apple, and the AS/400, SunSoft and Univel offer far more portability to other operating systems. But SunSoft is the volume leader in the workstation arena, and Univel has the backing of the UNIX System Laboratories. Each—unlike SCO, NCR, and HP—is determined to set the *de facto* standard for UNIX single-handedly.

But just as vendors differ, so do users' needs. Openness is in the eye of the beholder, and every user organization must select the vendors that are open on the dimensions and to the degrees that best meet its overall business needs. As discussed previously, users need to consider which benefits are provided by the *de jure*, consensus, or *de facto* standards they are subscribing to: Freedom to chose what? How much flexibility? Value on what dimensions, achieved at the expense of what other dimensions? Protection for which investments?

And users also need to consider their vendors carefully. There are several factors that distinguish the openness of so-called open systems vendors. We recommend that I/T decision makers use the following five-point checklist to size up their vendors' commitments to open systems:

1. Open business practices, the willingness to participate—on a "100 percent best-efforts basis" by all personnel—in the sale, integration, and support of open, multivendor hardware and software systems

2. Track record of maintaining a compatible upward migration path for the installed base

3. Proven commitment to verified compliance with *de facto* and *de jure* interoperability standards as they emerge

4. Proven commitment to provide portability by migrating products into verified compliance with international consensus and *de jure* standards as they evolve

5. Open innovation practices—demonstrated ability to use existing standards as a springboard for innovation, incorporate innovation from the outside where expedient (rather than reinventing the wheel), and make innovations available on platforms from multiple vendors

As with open systems benefits, open systems vendor qualities are a matter of degree. I can't think of any vendor today who doesn't possess some of these qualities, at least to some extent. Mustering a halfway decent story on Points #1-3 (open business practices, upward compatibility, and interoperability) is a prerequisite for getting in the door at major accounts today. However, realities differ considerably, so these points should be evaluated thoroughly.

Adherence to Point #4 is a much bigger step. It means that a vendor is willing to keep its products in the mainstream of the whole industry's innovation/standardization/innovation loop. For their customers, this means "the world's your oyster." Because it is so much easier for customers to switch, vendors who comply with Point #4 need to stay good enough so customers won't *want* to switch. All the same, look carefully at prospective vendors' financial stability and support track records. Switching is not your objective, it is your insurance policy.

The ability to incorporate innovations from their erstwhile rivals is important to a vendor's ability to stay competitive in the rapidly evolving open systems world, and depends on Point #5—open innovation practices. Open innovation practices benefit the vendor and the customer alike. The vendor gets additional revenue when it licenses an innovation to competitors; when a vendor licenses an innovation from a competitor, customers get the benefit without having to do the system integration. Here, because what goes around comes around, look for a vendor which has good working relationships with its peers.

Getting There from Here

The benefits of open systems—freedom of choice, flexibility and change management, lasting value, and investment protection—are compelling. Here are 10 steps information technology executives can take to begin realizing them. The first three steps are just plain common sense. They are here to emphasize that achieving business objectives is the *end*; open systems provide the *means* to do so in a rapidly changing world.

Ten Steps to Open Systems

1. Keep an open mind.

2. Focus on the business mission.

3. Consider the whole system. Technology exists in the context of business strategy, culture, education policies, and the organizational structure. You can't solve problems effectively by treating symptoms.

4. Identify "information embolisms"—the bottlenecks where information is not flowing where decision makers need it. These are good opportunities for open system pilots.

5. Invest in education. Start with UniForum's Guide to Open Systems Procurements. Find out what guidance organizations such as NIST and X/Open can offer and what specifications are available for procurement purposes. Pilots are an excellent form of education.

6. Put your plan in place. Fix systemic I/T problems with an open-systems architecture approach. The need for information flow between departments or functional groups and across organizational boundaries is continuously increasing. A policy of patching systems together cannot keep up.

7. Participate in setting priorities and defining functional requirements for needed standards. Participate in the X/Open "Xtra" market requirements process and consider joining the X/Open User Council and other user forums. Be an active buyer.

8. Specify standard interface definitions, not vendor brand names, and insist on ongoing standards compliance from your vendors. Don't fall off the wagon without a good reason. Be a disciplined buyer.

9. Buy now what is mission-critical now, but use the five-point checklist in the previous section to make sure it is as open a system as possible. Be pragmatic.

10. Manage your internal development for interoperability and portability. Use the XPG for as much of the pilot application as possible, and have programmers work from it rather than from vendor-specific manuals. Avoid vendor-specific features unless they are essential to accomplish the business purpose of the application.

These guidelines are for the realistic, not the impatient. Getting to an enterprise-wide open systems infrastructure will take some organizations a decade. Even then, there will be selections to be made from among nonstandard alternatives at the leading edge of technology. But remember, just like bar codes and scanners in the supermarket checkout line, open systems benefits aren't an all-or-nothing issue. Put your priorities in order, put your plan in place, put your educated judgment to work with discipline, and don't worry. You'll have the flexibility to deal with whatever the future brings.

Images in the '90s: Fax and Network Technology Come Together

by Josh Mailman
Product Manager, Jet Fax, Inc.

Author Bio

JetFax, Inc.

Josh Mailman has been involved in the PC industry since 1985. Before joining JetFax, Inc. in 1992 as product manager, Mr. Mailman was president of MVR Inc., a database consulting corporation specializing in software for the banking industry. Mr. Mailman is regularly published on database, networking, fax, and general computer issues. He is also a frequent speaker at industry conferences and user groups. Mr. Mailman received his graduate degree in 1986 from the Anderson School of Management at UCLA.

Executive Summary

Network faxing is an industry in transition. Although the technology exists for network faxing, the current implementation is fairly complicated, negating the principal benefit of fax communication: simplicity. The challenges for network faxing are:

- to create standards that will make it as easy to fax within a network as it is to fax from a standard fax machine

- to develop software interfaces that are as intuitive to use as standard fax machines

- to deliver this capability to the network community at a reasonable price and without overburdening time-crunched network administrators

Network fax is a nascent industry. During the 1990s, all indications have pointed to a surge in demand for network fax services; BIS CAP study indicated that at least 45 percent of users surveyed had a strong need for network fax. However, the market has not reached expectations. Although the industry is beginning to grow—IDC reported a 52 percent growth rate in 1992, over a 17 percent growth rate in 1990, for LAN fax—the industry lags behind market predictions for a number of reasons.

Background

Fax became the instant communications venue of choice because of its simplicity and reliability. The speed and simplicity of walking up to a fax machine and dialing a phone number made it ideal for any level of user. Even technical people appreciated not having to learn complicated routes to communicate instantly.

In addition, the fax standards established by the CCITT fax committee were adopted quickly by fax manufacturers, making seamless communication possible between machines of different manufacture. These standards proved very reliable. Thus, fax had three big advantages: ease of use, accessibility, and reliability. This was in great contrast to electronic mail, which requires users to learn complicated character strings and has not enjoyed a high degree of standardization.

Computers and Faxes

Computers and faxing seemed an ideal connection. In the late 1980s, vendors began developing fax boards which would enable users to send faxes directly from their PCs, presumably saving time. However, these early attempts at PC faxing proved complicated and slow. Users had to take apart their PCs, install the board, and learn how to use the fax software. They also had to tolerate slow fax printing, and because the CPU of the PC was used for much of the conversion and transmission process, considerable impact upon PC applications. As a result, most users returned to their standard fax machines.

Recognizing the promise of the computer fax market yet aware of the limitations of existing products, JetFax, Inc. was formed in 1988 with the purpose of bridging this gap. The company's first product, JetFax, (see Figure 29.1) was a printer-based fax solution that was *external* to the PC. It allowed users to receive plain paper faxes on their existing laser fax machines. The JetFax did not require any PC resource in order to operate.

Figure 29.1. JetFax II.

In time, JetFax has enhanced the product to be used as an outbound gateway providing PC and network faxing capability too. The company has recently introduced a new machine, the JetFax 8000-D, combining traditional fax machine functionality with fax server capability. JetFax is not alone in the endeavor; Gammalink, ALCOM, OAZ, Intel, and Optus have been working over the past few years to bridge the gap.

Network Faxing

Network faxing, the ability to send faxes from any workstation on a local area network, is a coveted feature. A study conducted by BIS CAP indicated that while only 4 percent of network users surveyed already had network fax capability, another 45 percent wanted it. However, a number of factors are inhibiting the growth of this market as mentioned above: the lack of standards for how to route faxes within the network, the lack of simplicity, and high price.

The current methods of fax routing are less than ideal. The most common ways are manual routing of faxes; a network administrator looks at each incoming fax and directs it manually to the proper recipient, which is time-consuming. Direct Inward Dialing (DID) requires each user to have his own fax phone number, and the sending caller must know this phone number—an alternative many users feel is too complicated. Dual Tone Modulated Frequency, or DTMF, involves the sender dialing an extra passcode, while Optical Character Recognition (OCR) relies upon OCR software to recognize the recipient's name and route the fax correspondingly. This is imperfect, since typos or other mistakes—or faxes that are sent to a title instead of a name—will probably prevent the fax from being delivered to the intended recipient.

JetFax, Inc. has tried to address these issues by keeping the process simple. In studies done by JetFax, 75 percent of all network fax users don't use the routing capability anyway, and most network managers surveyed indicated that complicated routing was a chief deterrent for network faxing. So, the JetFax product doesn't route faxes at all; it simply prints them on the network laser printer.

Another user requirement to be addressed is the need to scan hardcopy documents. According to a recent Gallup Organization study, 44 percent of Fortune 500 fax users surveyed said that less than 50 percent of their documents are PC-originated, suggesting the need for traditional fax gear with a scanner. NetFax News, which reported the finding, concludes: "This strongly suggests that a fax machine requirement will persist and indicates that fax servers might benefit by integrating with fax machines."

One Goal, Two Paths

All network fax companies want to make network faxing easy and affordable. We see two paths to this goal. The first path, adopted by the fax board manufacturers, is to drive network faxing through the computer. In time, DID will drop in price, and OCR software will be improved to the point where faxes will be delivered through electronic mail. Although this approach will work eventually, it does not take into consideration why faxes became popular in the first place—ease of use.

The second approach, and the approach we believe will be most successful, involves a hybrid of technology—marrying fax machines and fax server products. End users will have their choice of what interface they wish to choose: the computer interface or the fax machine interface. The hybrid machine would serve all the functions of computer fax solutions, and also provides all the functions of a traditional fax machine such as scanning out hardcopy documents.

We believe that making the network fax simple, accessible, and inexpensive is how this market can best succeed.

Regarding Groupware

by Jim Manzi
President, Chairman, and CEO, Lotus Development Corporation

Author Bio

Jim Manzi is president, chairman of the board, and chief executive officer at Lotus Development Corporation. Manzi joined Lotus in May 1983, as director of marketing. Later as vice president of marketing and sales, he led the company's expansion into international markets, which now accounts for more than 50 percent of Lotus' revenues. Manzi was named president and chief operating officer in November 1984, and chief executive officer in April 1986. In July 1986, he was appointed chairman of the company's board of directors.

Since Manzi was appointed president in 1984, Lotus has increased revenues from $156 million to $828.9 million in 1991, and has emerged as a leader in several business software areas, including presentation graphics, word processing, communications, information services, and groupware.

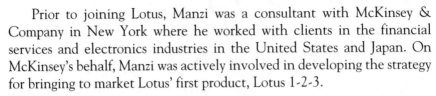

Prior to joining Lotus, Manzi was a consultant with McKinsey & Company in New York where he worked with clients in the financial services and electronics industries in the United States and Japan. On McKinsey's behalf, Manzi was actively involved in developing the strategy for bringing to market Lotus' first product, Lotus 1-2-3.

Manzi began his career as a writer for the national *Review* and later worked as a reporter for the Westchester-Rockland Newspapers, a subsidiary of the Gannett Co., Inc.

He earned a bachelor's degree in classics from Colgate University and a master's degree in economics form the Fletcher School of Law and Diplomacy at Tufts University.

Manzi serves on the board of trustees for Colgate University and for Jobs for Massachusetts, a consortium of business leaders created by Gov. William Weld to address economic issues in Massachusetts.

Executive Summary

Why groupware? Why do organizations need it? Why would large numbers of people actually use it?

The last question is crucial if you want to spend time developing something most people still don't understand. The goal is to provide individual users with a rich, seamless computing environment.

Groupware has great promise over the next decade, but that promise cannot be achieved by ignoring the past decade's revolution at the desktop. The test of fulfillment will be when you no longer worry about definitions and when the word *groupware* is not used because the line between stand-alone and group computing has disappeared.

As an industry, we have tended to wrap ourselves in our underwear over terms and definitions. The main reason is that, until rather recently, there hasn't been a lot out there to define—beyond prototypes, green house apps, and simple e-mail. You can't define anything in a void. You need context, and you need to look at what groupware can actually do in the real world.

Justice Oliver Wendell Holmes once said, "The life of the law is not logic, but experience." The same is true of groupware, and fortunately we are now beginning to accumulate some real-world experience that gives meaning to the concept.

If groupware is best defined by real experience in the marketplace, then the best place to begin any discussion is with Lotus Notes. It has been out there for sometime, and there are now more than 200,000 Notes users and 500 Notes customers. It is used for a wide range of activities— conferencing, document management and distribution, sales tracking, project management, publishing, and work-flow management.

Most important, Notes is being used to meet real, tangible business goals. One customer says, "I don't know much about groupware—we just use it to win bids."

There is no question that Notes is a full-fledged example of groupware— by any definition. With its robust communications capabilities, its ability to create an object store that can be shared by users and replicated between servers and between servers and clients, and with its rich development environment, Notes is not just another groupware product. What it does is define, in a real way, the future of workgroup computing.

I think it's worth stepping back a bit to consider some basic questions such as: Why groupware? Why do organizations need it? Is there any reason to believe that large numbers of people will actually use it?

The last question—which has to do with potential market size—is crucial to any of us who wants to spend time developing something that most people still don't understand.

The notion of groupware goes back about 15 years and from the start it has always had its strong adherents. In some ways, it has been more of a social movement than a technology—promising a better world through cooperation and sharing, much like the Shakers, the New England Transcendentalists, and the followers of George McGovern.

In truth, groupware is part social and part technology. But the question has always been: how do you go from the realm of social theory, academic research, prototypes, and toywear to the real world of experience?

The short answer of course is that you simply go out and do it. This is what we have been doing with Notes, and we believe we've gained a real world laboratory as well as a rich platform for the future of workgroup computing.

To go back to the basic questions: How big is that future? Doug Engelbart has stated that groupware is the next explosive growth area in information technology—more explosive and more promising than the PC revolution of the last decade. I'm not about to dispute him. There are certainly abundant signs that groupware is an idea whose time has finally come.

The most obvious sign has been the rapid growth in networks over the past several years. It's been estimated that about 30,000 PCs are being connected to networks everyday and that by the end of the next year more than half of the world's 100 million PCs will be connected. These are dramatic numbers for an industry that's now struggling with slower growth.

Networks of course are not synonymous with groupware, but they are a necessary condition. There is also clear evidence that networks are being used for more than just simple file sharing or connections to peripherals. LAN-based E-mail has become the fastest growing application category. *The New York Times* carried a story headlined, "The Zip's in Communications." It reported that the number of new network servers dedicated to communications will double this year to 90,000, creating a market of $2.7 billion.

Groupware is potentially a very big game, and if all of us in it can meet certain challenges, it will soon be the main game in town. Apart from such obvious signs as the growth of networks, I believe there are two basic reasons for the enormous potential of groupware.

The first reason is that groupware is not simply another application category. Its potential is much broader, more basic, and more profound. We should really think of groupware as the foundation for all other applications. Groupware is the foundation because it meets the most basic need of any organization—communication.

Norbert Weiner, an authority in the same league as Oliver Wendell Holmes, observed that "society can only be understood through a study of its messages and communications facilities." If that is true for society at large, then it's also true for such lesser entities as corporations, government agencies, business schools, and computer science departments.

The truth of Weiner's dictum today is becoming more evident as old structures—based on command and control or the organizational pyramid—begin to break down. It becomes clear that these structures were never written in stone, but were in place mainly for the filtering and distribution of information.

According to both logic and experience, it is another basic truth that the concept of information, which we like to think of as the guiding purpose of our industry, has no meaning apart from the closely allied concept of communication. The concept of information presupposed the capability of communicating information.

In our sometimes solipsistic ways, we sometimes forget that information by itself has no value. It is simply a commodity like coal. It has no value if it, in effect, remains in the ground. It has value only if it can be communicated and if this communication leads to the production of goods and services.

If we focus only on the accumulation, coding, or storing of information, then we are no wiser than the character Ring Lardner once described in a short story: "He took me into his library and showed me his books—of which he had a complete set." There is obviously more to information than that. It is obviously not static. It is meant to be shared and meant to be used by individuals and organizations.

Even though communications is basic to any organization, and even though it is basic to the very concept of information, these truths have up until recently remained foreign to most PC users and most members of the PC industry. The PC revolution is often regarded as a triumph of democracy and individualism, but the new found freedom also brought isolation from the organization—which is perhaps not a bad thing depending on your organization.

But for all the gains in individual empowerment and individual efficiency, there was no corresponding gain in organizational productivity because PCs originally were not intended to communicate. They were intended—and succeeded magnificently—as an individual tool for creating information, manipulating and analyzing information and, to a lesser extent, gaining access to information. By and large, they were asocial.

Who knows why the PC did not become a tool for communications sooner? You can argue that the technology was not quite there, but technology always has a way of responding to demand. Simple inertia is a more likely explanation. Peter Drucker argues that force of habit is so powerful that any new technology must be shown to be superior by a factor of 10 before it will be accepted.

The more important question is: Is there any reason to believe that PCs can now fulfill their obvious potential as a new communications technology?

This brings us to the second reason that groupware is now poised for a period of dramatic growth: Groupware not only meets the basic organizational need for communications, but it also can do so at a time when organizations are in the midst of profound change.

I won't bore you with a discussion of the various management theories that have gained currency in recent years. We all know them well enough by now: the need for leaner organizations, flatter organizations, more decentralized organizations; the need to stick to your knitting or focus on core competencies; the need for empowerment; the need to build in entrepreneurialism—a word so resonant that the Democratic presidential candidate is even making hay with it.

The key point is that these various theories are now reflected in a rather fierce economic reality. We are seeing massive layoffs, many of them in our own industry at such former stalwarts of job security as IBM and DEC.

Much of the turmoil is not just the result of a recession, or what Alan Greenspan calls a modest recovery, but represents a response to more fundamental, long-term change—the forces of globalization, increased competition and lower margins, which place a premium on speed in terms of market response and product cycles.

Despite all the pain and the uncertainty, this fundamental restructuring of many companies, not to mention relationships between companies, presents a tremendous opportunity for the PC industry, especially in the area of group computing.

Much of the downsizing is occurring in middle management and staff positions—those parts of the organization responsible for the filtering and distribution of information. In other words, the old information technology is being called into question. Because nature as well as commerce abhors a vacuum, there is a clear opportunity for new communications technology.

But before we can rush in we have some selling to do. Before we can expect our customers to invest in our communications solutions—no matter how good they are—we must first deal with what's known as the productivity paradox.

The productivity paradox is the failure of businesses to achieve gains in organizational productivity despite the massive investments in information technology over the past 10 years. It is a topic that has received inordinate attention—18 business review articles, 97 speeches, and 1 MTV video in just the last year.

It comes down to a tough question from customers: Now that I've spent some $300 billion on PC hardware and software (and even more on training and support), where is the Return-On-Investment? It's doubtful that anyone wants to go back to the days before PCs, but before going forward, many customers want to know what they are getting for the money they've spent.

As I've indicated, at least part of the problem has to do with the asocial nature of PCs. Until recently they had not begun to fulfill their potential as communications tools. As Arno Penzias has noted, there is likely to be a net decrease in productivity any time human beings are reduced to running errands between isolated machines.

But part of the problem has also been the database-centric view of information that has predominated at most organizations and among most IT professionals over the past 20 years. In the database-centric view, information is mainly the province of MIS and centralized support staffs. In this world, more information is always the answer. Never mind that the processing and reprocessing of information simply adds to administrative overhead, generating reports that are never read.

Paul Strassman, who was at one time head of MIS at Xerox, has written more incisively than anyone—even Oliver Wendell Holmes and Norbert Weiner—on the subject of the productivity paradox. He has several insights that have significance for anyone interested in workgroup computing.

The first is that some companies do achieve productivity gains from their IT investments. But the key factor is not how much is spent, but where in the organization it is spent. When the investment goes online to solve real business problems, there is usually a net gain. But when it goes to what used to be called administration, it falls into a productivity black hole—expanded central databases require more IT professionals and more clerical staff to maintain them, and the added staff then generates even more information. Information technology becomes like the sorcerer's apprentice rather than a productivity tool.

The second insight is that automation all too often simply encodes old business practices and makes the introduction of new technology and new practices more difficult. The corrective is to always remember that anything not worth doing is not worth doing on a computer.

The third insight is that information technology is too important to be left solely in the hands of MIS and IT professionals. Gains in productivity are achieved most often when the heads of businesses become involved and when IT investment is considered in the context of business goals.

There is nothing startling in any of these conclusions. But taken together they constitute an indictment of the way information technology—and information itself—has traditionally been viewed in most organizations.

And even more important, these conclusions are an open invitation for a new approach—one based not on inert stores of information, but on the flow of information—and approach based on communications, coordination, and network-based collaboration. In other words, it adds up to an open invitation to groupware.

Following the trail blazed by Strassman and the belief that the future lies in real experience, we began some structured research with Notes customers earlier this year to assess whether we could see tangible, measurable returns on investment.

We started with 21 customers and then selected 11 applications at 8 customer sites for detailed quantitative analysis. This was a careful study, with an emphasis on hard ROI.

We found that Notes applications have had a significant impact on our customers' business. The return on investment has averaged well over 100 percent, and often as much as 500 or more. For one Notes customer, a government agency, the return was over 2000 percent. Some would say that in the government, that's only scratching the surface.

The study also found that the payback on our customer's investments was incredibly fast—an average of less than four months.

It also showed you can achieve impressive gains in productivity without a large initial investment. Groupware does require commitment, but not to the tune of $62,000.

It's true that when we introduced Notes a couple years ago, we set a 200-seat or $62,000 minimum for the initial purchase. That was because it was new, because we felt it required a strong management commitment and because, after all, it was designed for groups.

There is no question about the need for commitment and some learning beforehand, but it has also become clear that the groups using Notes don't have to be quite so large—nor does the initial investment, especially in a recessionary economy.

Our study found that Notes can bring real gains, even for groups of five or six and with investments of several thousand dollars. So we've done away with the minimum. As I said earlier, the first law of groupware is not logic but experience.

Notes, with its ability to handle rich data types and replicate information, enables groups to filter, shape, and act on a wide range of information and have the assurance that the information will be accurate and up-to-date. These capabilities result in tremendous leverage. Metropolitan Life began with just over 50 seats in its investment department, which makes decisions involving billions of dollars.

But after a relatively small investment, and after seeing what Notes could do, Met Life has expanded its applications to include more than 500 users. The lesson is that groupware applications don't have to begin big to become big.

Met Life, of course, is by no means a small company. But we've also learned that you don't have to be a Fortune 500 company to use Notes successfully.

Harmon Contract is a Minneapolis-based construction company with 1200 employees and revenues of $225 million. Harmon began with a Notes pilot, and today it has Notes applications running on more than half of its 500 PCs.

Harmon views Notes as a way of capturing and sharing knowledge—which in the past was stored away in cabinets, was lost in the interstices of company databases, or perhaps simply stayed in the heads of individual employees.

Harmon is now using Notes not just to facilitate the flow of information and knowledge within its own company, but also with customers and suppliers—or what's come to be called the extended enterprise. Suppliers and customers are asking for Notes.

Notes—as well as groupware generally—may not yet have had the transformational effects that were once predicted. We may have let the utopian rhetoric get ahead of the stubborn reality. So heaven may have to wait—at least for awhile.

In the meantime, as our ROI study of Notes' customers demonstrates, many companies are already getting some significant returns, and we can expect the returns to become more dramatic as the use of networks and the number of groupware users and applications increases.

This is a classic case of what economists call the law of externalities: the value of groupware, or for that matter any communications technology, tends to increase as more people use it. It is just the opposite of the productivity trap of central data processing where increased investment generates still more processing and more overhead.

The transformation will come. But it will come about not because coordination and collaboration are desirable social goals, but because new ways of coordination and collaboration on computer networks can bring tangible gains in productivity.

I believe the challenges ahead lie in three broad areas.

First, we still need to learn more about the organizational context, not just of groupware but of information technology itself. We need to know more about the often subtle and complex ways that people work together and how that changes and, hopefully, can be enhanced when information and communication go electronic.

We know, for example, of the tendency for "flaming" in sending electronic messages, and how the notion of sharing information can threaten status and position in an organization. But there's a lot more we don't know.

It's much easier to build an algorithm for a computer than it is for an organization, or even a person. That's because you first have to know what a person does, or wants to do. What some people do and how certain organizations work is often a mystery. Carl Kaysen, a Princeton economist, once said, "Computers can never replace businessmen because businessmen don't know what they're doing."

That may or may not be true, but well-designed groupware can certainly take over some tasks, speed certain processes, and even provide focus on what is essential and what isn't. With this in mind, we worked closely with academic researchers in organizational theory and practice in developing Notes. As a result, we were able to build in some of the first real active agent technology. You'll be seeing even more in Version 3. This is a key area we will continue to pursue.

The organizational context is a two-way street. Not only do we have to continue to learn more about the workings of organizations, but organizations need to learn more about groupware—what it is, what it can do, and what's required to take full advantage of it.

There's always a learning curve with any new technology. Because groupware is often accompanied by organizational change, or requires organizational change to be effective, that curve can be steeper and the resistance stronger. So it's essential to follow Paul Strassman's dictum and bring people with line business responsibility into the educational process.

The second challenge is one that always comes up at every PC industry conference—the need for standards. It's been said that our industry must really be committed to standards, that's why we've got so many of them. Standards, of course, are important for PCs for the same reason standard auto parts are important for cars—it means greater choice and flexibility for customers and a potentially larger market for producers.

But if standards are important for stand-alone computing, they are absolutely crucial for the future of groupware. It's one thing for an organization to have users on different networks and different operating systems, but it becomes a real problem if you have different networks and different operating systems and you then want everyone to be able to share work and send messages to each other. And if you're an applications developer, it can be difficult to design groupware that works across different operating systems.

That's why virtually the entire industry is now at work on several competing standards for messaging. Lotus, along with Borland, Apple, Novell, and IBM, has proposed one called VIM, which is based on the Notes and cc:Mail APIs. Other standards have been put forward as well. Let me just say it's in everyone's interest that we have some standard messaging protocols to guide future groupware development.

In the foreseeable future we are not likely to have the equivalent of a Holy Roman Empire in operating systems. There will be DOS, Windows, Mac, OS/2, NT, and of course UNIX on networks, and perhaps eventually something now called Pink. That's why a key part of our strategy for Notes is to have it run across all platforms—we'll introduce a Mac client version of Notes later this year, and we'll have a UNIX version of Notes ready next year.

Notes, with its wide connectivity and rich development environment, is as much a platform as an application. It's been compared to an operating system that sits on top and runs across other operating systems. Certainly a large part of its success is due to the applications and technologies developed from Notes—first from VARs and now from Eastman Kodak and Action Technologies. We've worked with Eastman Kodak to develop imaging and optical character recognition for Notes and with Action Technologies on work flow automation technologies.

Like any good operating system company we will welcome and support all future development efforts based on Notes.

The final challenge is to meet the needs of individual users, who after all, are a basic part of the equation. Added up, they constitute the groups that groupware is designed to serve.

The growth of group computing as well as the closely allied growth of mobile computing will bring a new class of users to the PC. But in the meantime, the 100 million current PC users can't be wrong.

Too often groupware has been designed as though there was no one sitting there looking at the screen. Ease of use and innovation in user interface has in the past not been one of the hallmarks of groupware. We have tried to keep the end user in mind in our Notes development efforts, but there is clearly more to do. One of the things we've done in Version 3.0 is to take SmartIcons—the advance in GUI developed for our individual apps—and adapt it for Notes.

Future development efforts in groupware must also meet the needs of the increasing number of mobile users who are only occasionally connected, but still need to communicate with home base and gain access to secure, up-to-date information. That's why we've emphasized replication and remote capabilities in Notes.

In the not too distant future, it's possible that the line that now separates stand-alone and group computing will disappear. Users will share information and collaborate freely across networks without the operating system, the hardware, or applications as we now know them getting in the way.

In the transition phase just ahead, desktop applications will become group-enabled. The design challenge will be to provide new communication capabilities to desktop apps in a way that naturally extends the product metaphor while changing the way the products can be used. In this phase, groupware must be opened up to desktop tools to provide the communications and data-sharing capabilities of groupware systems.

The goal must be to provide individual users with a rich, seamless computing environment. The great promise of groupware over the next decade will not be achieved by ignoring the revolution at the desktop of the last decade.

There can be no doubt about groupware's promise. The test of fulfillment will be the time when we no longer worry about definitions, and no one even uses the word groupware because the line between stand-alone and group computing will have disappeared.

Windows on NetWare:
Tips for Making It Work

by Howard Marks
Chief Scientist, Networks Are Our Lives, Inc.

Author Bio

Howard Marks is chief scientist at Networks Are Our Lives, Inc., a Scarsdale, New York, network consulting and education firm. He is coauthor of *Networking Windows—NetWare Edition*, a frequent contributor to *LAN Magazine*, and to *LAN Views for Data Communications*. Mr. Marks is a frequent speaker at industry events. He has been involved in the personal computer industry since 1979 and has worked in networking since 1982.

Networks Are Our Lives, Inc. is dedicated to network education by developing and presenting networking classes worldwide. Current classes include "Networking Windows 3.x," "Solving the NetWare Printing Puzzle," "Advanced Async Solutions for LANS," and "Building a Structured LAN Cable System."

Mr. Marks can be reached at (914) 472-0879 or on MCI Mail as HMARKS.

Executive Summary

Some people believe that integrating Windows 3.x into a NetWare LAN is a black art to be practiced by an enlightened few. System administrators, planners, or users now running Windows or contemplating adding Windows to their network will find that these tips will improve the performance and stability of their systems without consulting the local guru.

By now you're probably a little tired of seeing computer magazines with "Windows 3.1. It's New, It's Hot, and We've Got It" splashed across the cover. You're tired because the article inside always says the same things: "TrueType fonts, rebootable virtual machines, and no more UAEs." We can summarize the changes from Windows 3.0 to Windows 3.1 in just 3 points:

- it crashes less often

- it runs faster (about 20 percent overall, up to 200 percent in File Manager)

- it has a few new features

After all, if it's faster and doesn't crash as often, does it really matter what the new features are? If all you want to know is whether to upgrade, stop reading and run right out to your local software store because the answer is a most definitive yes!

Windows 3.1 has some new features that you should know about because they will make your life as a network administrator much easier.

As Microsoft puts together each new version of Windows, they make network administrators' lives a little easier. Networking Windows 2.11 or Windows 386 was like black magic—you had to burn incense, face east, reformat your RAM disk, and light candles. Making Windows 3.0 work on a network was just hard work. You had to type batch files, expand the diskettes, and run setup 5,000 times.

Apparently the network administrators at Microsoft snuck into the Windows development team's Jolt Cola closet and ambushed them because 3.1 has many of the features that we've all been looking for. You can now control user's desktops, install a shared copy of Windows without running obscure batch files, update user's NetWare shell and IPX automatically in their login scripts, and create a customized installation that automatically will install Windows the way you want it on a user's workstation.

The most overdue change from Windows 3.0 to Windows 3.1 was getting rid of the EXPALL batch file you had to run to install a shared version of Windows. With Windows 3.1 all you need to do is type SETUP /a and it will copy and expand the files on the distribution diskettes; your server prompts you for each diskette.

Tip #1—Create an Automated Setup Script for Your Users

Once you expand the diskettes you can write a setup script file that makes running the SETUP program a completely automated process. Rather than going to each workstation and running SETUP so that it recognizes the particular hardware configuration and gets the programs on the user's local hard disk installed, you can just have your users type SETUP /H:MYSCRIPT.WIN. Even better, put that in a batch file called WININST.BAT so your users just have to type WININST.

In your script file you can: disable the screen with SETUP as you verify the hardware configuration, override the default configuration for a hardware driver or language, specify the directory Windows should be installed in, prevent some of the Windows options like wallpapers and games from being installed, install applications, install the default printer, and control the updating of AUTOEXEC.BAT and CONFIG.SYS.

If you'd like to write a custom setup script, get a Windows Resource Kit for $19.99 from Microsoft's sales number (800-642-7676). The Windows Resource Kit is the technical documentation for Windows 3.1, including information on how to customize the setup process, how to run Windows on different network operating systems, and what all the entries on WIN.INI and SYSTEM.INI mean. It's the best 20 bucks you'll ever spend.

Tip #2—Update Your User's Shell and IPX in the System Login Script

In your Windows Resource Kit you'll also find NEWIPX, a little gem of a program I wish Novell had written years ago. NEWIPX takes your existing IPX.COM, the driver for your LAN card, and a new IBX.OBJ and links it all into a new IPX.COM with all the same configuration options as your old one. You don't need to run WSGEN, JUMPERS, SHGEN or ECONFIG again.

All you need to do is copy NLINK and the LAN drivers from your WSGEN directory to a directory with the IPX.OBJ from the Windows distribution diskettes and NEWIPX. Then add a line to your system login script that runs NEWIPX and specifies the IPX.COM to update.

Updating ODI-based machines and the NETX shell is even easier. Microsoft and Novell have set aside their competiton and cooperated to put a new version of IPX.OBJ, IPXODI.COM, LSL.COM, and NETX.COM on the Windows 3.1 distribution diskettes. All you need to do is copy them from your shared Windows directory, where SETUP /a put them, to each user's boot disk.

Tip #3—Create a Shared Program Group to Add an Application to Many Users' Desktops at Once

Back in the good old days when you were running a DOS-based network, all you had to do to add a new application to everyone's menu was edit the menu file. When you installed Windows you found out that each user had her or his own separate desktop and you had to send out an E-mail message telling them to pull down the File menu, click on New, and so on.

If you create a program group in a directory where all your users have the Read right, they can all share it. If you add an application to that group, it will appear on each user's desktop the next time that they start Windows. You should flag the file as "read-only" so that one user doesn't decide to remove an icon from everybody's desktop.

Under Windows 3.0 your users will get an error box any time they try to move an icon out of the group or exit with the Save Changes box selected.

Windows 3.1 finally recognizes that this is a good idea and it just won't let your users move icons in a "read-only" program group.

To set up a shared group, just create the group in a shared directory through the New selection on the File menu. Move the icons you want your users to see into the group and flag the file "read-only." To make it appear on each user's desktop, edit or replace each PROGMAN.INI to include the new group.

Tip #4—Restrict Users' Customization of Program Manager

Even with a shared program group you don't have enough control over users' application usage. In a typical DOS-based network the system administrator creates a series of menus for his or her users, and the users' access to network resources is limited to only those applications that appear on their menus.

With Windows 3.0 you give up all of that control as soon as you install Windows. Once Windows is installed on a user's desktop he or she can pull down the file menu and click on Run to run any program on the network or click on New to add new applications to the desktop.

Automated Design's Windows Workstation and Saber Software's Saber Menu System for Windows both provide a centrally controlled menu system for your users, but they require some significant setup, cost more of your meager budget, and Saber Menu doesn't "look and feel" like Program Manager.

With Windows 3.1 you can get back some of your control without having to go out and buy third-party menu systems. Microsoft has made two changes to Program Manager that make LAN administrators' lives much easier: the capability to use "read-only" program groups without error boxes and the capability to restrict user's ability to customize their program groups.

The [Restrictions] section of each user's PROGMAN.INI is where you can take back some control from your users. It allows you to restrict a user's access to the more powerful, and dangerous, features of Program Manager.

Each parameter in the [Restrictions] section enables or disables a feature of Program Manager. The available parameters are:

- NoRun—A value of zero or no entry enables the Run command on the file menu. A value of one disables the Run command so your users can't run applications that aren't on their desktops.

- NoClose—A value of zero or no entry enables the Exit command on the File menu. A value of one disables Exit and prevents your user from exiting Windows by closing the Program Manager window or exiting by hitting (Alt)-(F4). Your users then can't get to a DOS prompt by exiting Windows. Be careful with this one.

- NoSaveSettings—A value of zero or no entry allows a user to save the arrangement of program groups and icons on his desktop when he exits Windows. A value of one prevents a user from saving his desktop as he exits Windows. Set NoSaveSettings to one if you want all your Windows machines to display the same desktop at startup. Good for walk-up and other shared systems.

- NoFileMenu—A value of zero allows a user to access the file menu. A value of one disables the entire file menu. A user with NoClose=0 can still exit by hitting (Alt)-(F4).

- EditLevel—The EditLevel parameter allows you to specify how much control a user should have over his own desktop.

A value of zero or no entry means that you've imposed no restrictions. A user can make any changes he wants to his program groups subject to the limitations above.

A value of one prevents a user from deleting, creating, or changing the parameters (like filename) of program groups. The user can still create, delete, and modify program items (icons for applications).

A value of two stops a user from creating and deleting program items within groups as well as prevents users from changing, creating, or deleting program groups. The user can still modify the properties of icons so he or she can change the program to which the icon points.

A value of three has all the limitations of level two but the user can no longer change the command line parameter in the item properties dialog box. The user can still change the icon, title, and working directory properties.

A value of four essentially prevents the user from changing anything but the arrangement of icons. The user cannot delete, create, or change program groups and cannot create, delete, or change program items (icons).

A typical Windows 3.1 PROGMAN.INI is shown below. Note the NETAPPS group which is shared is Group 20. The group numbers need not be consecutive.

```
[Settings]
Window=-4 0 728 440 1
SaveSettings=1
MinOnRun=0
AutoArrange=1
display.drv=SUPERVGA.DRV
Order=20 11 10 2 5 4 6 9 1 7 8

[Groups]
Group1=C:\WIN30\MAIN.GRP
Group2=C:\WIN30\MICROGRA.GRP
Group4=C:\WIN30\WINDOWSW.GRP
Group5=C:\WIN30\NORTONDE.GRP
Group6=C:\WIN30\COMMUNIC.GRP
Group9=C:\WIN30\WINDOWS0.GRP
Group10=C:\WIN30\STARTUP0.GRP
Group11=C:\WIN30\ACCESSO0.GRP
Group7=C:\WIN30\WINFAX.GRP
Group20=z:\public\netapps.grp

[Restrictions]
NoRun=1
NoClose=1
NoSaveSettings=1
NoFileMenu=1
EditLevel=4
```

Tip #5—Enable the Screen Savers for Security

Over the years we've always been looking for a good solution to the problem of user's walking away from their PCs without logging off. We've tried nasty memos, locking the account, fines, and programs that halt the PC and ask for a password or log off a user if he doesn't type anything for five minutes.

Nothing was a perfect solution. No matter how much you try, an occasional user will walk away from his or her PC. The programs that log off users when there is no activity either used such broad definitions of activity that they never logged off the user, or they triggered when a user had files open and they became corrupted. The best solution seems to be a screen blanker that triggers if there is no keyboard or mouse activity and forces the user to enter a password to gain access to the PC.

Windows 3.1, much to the chagrin of the makers of InterMission and After Dark, includes a few screen blankers that do just what we've been looking for. You can select the delay before the screen is blanked and have the screen covered with a blank screen or star field, or have the approaching stars turn into the Windows logo. When you hit the mouse or the keyboard you have to enter the password. The password is encrypted in the WIN.INI file. (See Figure 31.1)

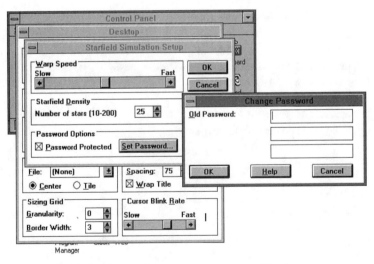

Figure 31.1. The dialog boxes that control the screen blanker.

Tip #6—Create a Permanent Swap File If You Can

When you run Windows 3.x in 386 enhanced mode, which you should, it will swap memory to its swap file to create virtual memory. If you have a permanent swap file on a drive that is accessed through the ROM BIOS, Windows 3.x will access the swap file by bypassing DOS and sending commands directly to the ROM BIOS. Since DOS isn't the fastest file system in the world, bypassing it significantly speeds up disk access.

Windows can only bypass DOS if the swap file is using contiguous disk space on your local hard drive. Once Windows knows the track, head, and sector of the first block of the swap file, it can figure out the rest. Unfortunately, this means that you cannot have a permanent swap file on a local drive that is created by a device driver like Disk Manager or Stacker, or on a file server because requests between a file server and a workstation are at the file level not at the head, track, and sector level. If you use a program like Stacker to compress a disk that is also accessible through the BIOS, put the swap file on the uncompressed portion of the disk.

If you don't have a permanent swap file, Windows will create a temporary swap file at Windows start time and expand it as needed. Because Windows accesses a temporary swap file like any other file, you can put a temporary swap file on any drive that is accessible to your workstation under DOS. When you start Windows it will create a 1M temporary swap file.

When a NetWare 2.x file server receives the request to allocate a 1M file, it allocates the disk space and then fills that 1M file with zeros. NetWare fills the file with zeros for security purposes. If it didn't, you could write a program that searched all the available disk space on a server by allocating a large file and reading the data that was in the space that is now part of that file. If the file is all zeros, this security hole is plugged, but starting Windows is slowed down significantly.

NetWare 3.x file servers don't actually allocate disk space when they receive the request from the workstation. They don't allocate disk space until the workstation writes to the disk. If a program requests part of the file that hasn't been written to yet, the file server returns zeros just like a NetWare 2.x file server does.

Tip #7—Turn on FastDisk

If you have a hard disk controller that is register compatible with the IBM AT's hard disk controller, Windows 3.1 will take another step in speeding up virtual memory: bypassing even the ROM BIOS and communicating directly to your hard disk controller. Since the ROM BIOS is 16-bit real mode code, using the 32-bit FastDisk feature saves some mode switching and makes Windows 10 to 15 percent faster. As an added feature you'll be able to run more DOS applications because Windows will not swap running DOS applications without FastDisk.

If you don't have a compatible controller you won't be able to run FastDisk. Most IDE, ST-506, and some ESDI controllers work with FastDisk. Most SCSI drives won't. Don't use FastDisk with a laptop computer because it can't handle trying to swap to a drive that is shut down to save battery life.

To turn on FastDisk, select the Use 32-bit Disk Access box on the Virtual Memory dialog box of the Control Panel's 386 enhanced mode icon.

Tip #8—Use Persistent Connections for Drive Mappings and Printer Assignments

A new feature for Windows 3.1 is persistent connections. If you mark a printer connection assigning a logical printer port to a print queue in Print Manager or the Control Panel and select the Permanent box, Windows 3.1 will automatically reestablish that connection each time you start Windows. You don't need to run CAPTURE. You should set up the LPT1, LPT2, and LPT3 ports to the printers the user uses most often.

Drive mappings you make through File Manager can also be declared permanent so you can have your users automatically map drive letters to specific directories when they start Windows.

These persistent connections are stored in the [Network] section of the users WIN.INI. You can just copy it from one user's WIN.INI to another.

Tip #9—Keep Windows and the .INI Files on the File Server

Recent benchmarks show that for most light or moderately loaded NetWare 3.x systems, Windows runs fastest if the temporary files are sent to the local hard or RAM disk and Windows is loaded from the server. The location of the user configuration files like WIN.INI and the .GRP Program Manager groups doesn't significantly affect performance but it does affect how much time you're going to have to spend managing your network.

A system administrator has many reasons to update his or her users' configuration files. Adding a shared program group, turning on the screen saver, and setting a user's capture status can all be done more easily if you can sit at your desk and access all the appropriate files. If the configuration files were on local hard disks, you would have to run MAP Assist or some other program to access local hard drives across the network or get on your bicycle and go to every workstation.

Even worse, most Windows applications need to add a few lines to WIN.INI or their own .INI file before they will run. Installing PageMaker for 20 users means updating 20 sets of .INI files.

Tip #10—Automate .INI File Maintenance

One of the most annoying parts of managing a Windows network is all the trouble it takes to install a new application for a large number of users. We've found two good ways to automate this process.

The first is to use a Windows batch language like Wilson WindowsWare's WinBatch, PubTech's BatchWorks, or the script language built into Windows Workstation. These programs all allow you to write a script file that copies files, updates .INI files, and calls the appropriate application.

We use WinBatch to create an icon that checks a new section in the WIN.INI file and verifies if you've installed an application already. If you have already installed it, WinBatch runs the application. If you haven't, WinBatch makes the changes needed for this application and then runs the application. It's completely transparent to the user that he just installed PageMaker for his workstation.

The other solution is to use a shareware product called Network Application Installer (NAI) from Aleph Systems. NAI's maintenance module lets you specify the changes to the .INI files, the files that should be copied, and the changes that should be made to install each application.

The user module will present your users with a menu of the applications you've set up. When they select an application and click on the install button, NAI will perform all the actions you've specified. A cute extra is that a user can also click on the uninstall button to remove files and lines from his WIN.INI.

Tip #11—Remove the DOS Prompt and File Manager Icons From Users' Desktops

If you've set a user's restrictions through PROGMAN.INI, you should remember to prevent your users from running any program they want by removing the DOS Prompt Icon and File Manager Icon from their Program Manager. The easiest way is to remove them from one set of Windows and then copy around the new MAIN.GRP. A more elegant method is to edit SETUP.INF to not install these icons in the first place.

Life Without File Servers: The Great Experiment

by John T. McCann
President, Integrity Software

Author Bio

John T. McCann is the author of many network utilities including Brightwork Development's SITELOCK. He is the author of *The NetWare Supervisor's Guide* (M&T Books) and is coauthor of the *NetWare LAN Management ToolKit* (SAMS Publishing). John also has served on Novell's NetWire forum as a lead SysOp. John is currently president of Integrity Software. John holds a master's degree in computer science from Texas A&M University.

Executive Summary

A new paradigm of network computing is rising. Over the horizon are new and different events. Of these, one proposes to change the way we think

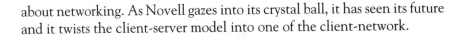

about networking. As Novell gazes into its crystal ball, it has seen its future and it twists the client-server model into one of the client-network.

Life Without File Servers: The Great Experiment

Life for many of us includes a relationship with Novell's NetWare. Over the years Novell's networking model has grown to accommodate many protocols, client types, and even differing host CPUs.

For most of us, our current LAN lifestyle embraces two fundamental entities: the client and the server. The relationship of the client and server are not so much slave to master as it is symbiotic. Unlike a truly mutual relationship, the client benefits more than the server. The server, however, is used to group clusters of users. Generally, for each server there is a specific set of clientele. Moreover, the server acts as host to its client's data. This model works well due to its naturally modular paradigm. Additional support for clients is achieved as needed through the augmentation of new servers. For LANs with separable client data the expanded server base is implemented easily.

For instance, users with their own set of word processing work could easily have it divided among many servers. On the other hand, if they shared common word processing templates, replication and coherency among the servers would increase complexity. Remember these shared files can be any file type—executable, data, definition, and so forth. Sure, a "central" server could be ordained to host the commonly shared files. Unfortunately, the reason for adding new servers in the first place was to distribute the load, not to have it fall back to one "central" server. Repartitioning of the central data will become necessary eventually. Adherence to the "central" server theory will necessitate more powerful servers. Applying laws of physics, there will either be a point of diminishing returns or a capacity limit. Thus distribution of the load at the server level, specifically in the manner which the servers offer their services, becomes paramount to maintaining network throughput and easing data accessibility.

There are many methods to achieve distribution of network load. As explored already, one method to achieve distribution includes dividing users across multiple servers and designating "central" servers. Early pioneers altered their software to utilize the network as best befitted their needs. For instance, the addition of dedicated duty servers—database, print, gateway, asynchronous communication—separated services from "file servers." This represented the early or first sign that the "do everything central server" theory would eventually erode. Focused services and efficient operation will ensure dedicated duty servers continuing well into the future.

Now that the distribution of specific services is well under way in our own LANs, there comes the next step—the establishment of networkwide "general file services." In an upcoming version of NetWare (Distributed NetWare or DNW), Novell will address this unfulfilled need.

In the next NetWare evolution, Novell plans on removing the file server designator from our vernacular. This awesome task will, by no means, be completed in the first revision of this next NetWare release. The specific physical unit, which is the file server, still will remain. Its identity, however, will be obscured. Unlike its progenitor, DNW promises to remove the file server centric "bindery." In DNW the connection between user definitions and specific file servers is severed, thus creating a distributed name space. Instead of binding users to file servers, they will be grouped in administrator-defined families or partitions. These families will not be required to be uniquely disjointed from each other. More importantly, the "membership records" of these families will be stored, in replicate, on all file servers de-fined as home of the family members. Herein remains a reference to the identity "file server." As another example of the underlying importance of singling out specific file servers, Novell's bindery will be emulated in DNW. This is especially important for Novell's Service Advertising Protocol (SAP) which will remain indefinitely as a means to locate specific services (servers). In a retrospective way, Novell's SAP was NetWare's first truly innate distributed database. Consequently, its continuation is natural.

Remember Novell's first augmentation of a distributed "bindery"? It was called the NetWare Name Service or NNS. This precursor (in idea only) to

DNW is no longer needed. NNS was released as an interim scheme only to be completely usurped by DNW. However incomplete NNS was, it did allow those early adopters a taste of NetWare's future. The ideas of a "network login" and "domains" remain on the forefront of DNW's feature list. Unlike NNS, DNW has been derived from the CCITT's X.500 Recommendation.

Upon the true implementation of a "serverless" bindery, DNW will be poised to provide "serverless" file services. Heading for this ultimate mutation of file server to network is a DNW goal. In succeeding releases data will be scattered among physical entities (referable as servers) as it is scattered among a file server's disk drives today. Note that whole files will be scattered. In specific exceptions only, actual files would not be divided between physical servers. The illusion of a "network" entity will be complete when "saving" a file and not truly knowing where it is physically stored; in other words, the creation of the distributed file system.

To increase the robustness of this distributed file system, two methods could exist to ensure file availability. Both methods include the administrator "hand picking" which files are to be duplicated. The first—complete file replication—allows the administrator to select the physical servers in which to store the chosen files. The actual servers used could be determined dynamically by the network or chosen statically by the administrator. The second method increases the automation the network assumes, namely the scattering of files, not the whole file, but pieces of the file across multiple physical servers *a la* RAID (Redundant Array of Inexpensive Disks) style. Such scattering of selected files' data would provide the ability to "access" the whole file even in the event of a server failure where the file was (partially) stored. This latter method somewhat reduces the need to keep multiple copies of a file in sync because the file is not completely replicated at any one server. Also, this second method allows for split reads of the file since its data is scattered among many servers, some of it redundantly scattered. This would enhance performance when the file was being multiply accessed.

No one has invented algorithms to locate data in a distributed file system as appropriately as possible among a network of servers. Such algorithms would not yield static results, rather they would need to take in to account the relocation of files when network throughput needs demand it, such as in "load balancing." Not only would dynamic relocation be necessitated by a distributed file system, but complete replication of files and their associated synchronization (to remain coherent with its other copies) may be the decision of such dynamic algorithms. The latter may be reserved for database files only, and more notably would not actually be a duty engaged by DNW; rather it would be left to another application with a singular focus in such matters. Remaining, however, would be the dynamic placement of files to best affect network throughput responsiveness.

Examples of file activity requiring absolute responsiveness abound. Witness your current local LAN requirements. Take the simple login script. Most users have or share one. For DNW to offer "networkwide login," a copy of the login script must be available on a local server (as physically defined). Changes to these login scripts must be replicated throughout the partition in which they are defined. Also, loading and running of applications need to be provided for in the most timely manner possible; after all this is the hallmark of NetWare. In a truly distributed file system, the act of locating a data file that is out there somewhere becomes a task in and of itself.

The goal of a distributed file system is to quickly locate and transmit a requested file. To accomplish any less would diminish its usefulness. In a single server situation this goal is readily accomplished. In a multiple server situation with self-contained file systems (your current NW386 3.1x or less LAN, for example), the solution is also resolved quickly by simply preceding the filename with a file server designator. However, this system quickly becomes inadequate because the user requesting access to the named file must already be logged into the designated file server. Without networkwide logins the inbetween step of logging in becomes a hassle—if not impossible. The promise of networkwide login is the ability to attach/detach automatically (login/logout) to any required server. The actual server no longer matters because its access is automated behind the scenes. Furthermore, coupling networkwide login to an index of file locations (relevant to a physical server acting as host) completes the automation loop that allows for files to be accessed regardless of their physical location. In fact, even the location of the "file pointer" index is dynamic in a distributed file system. The goal of all of this is to make file location lookups as instantaneous as possible. The index itself might even be cached at local servers to achieve this rapid lookup.

All this automation magnifies the need for high-speed connections between server entities. A likely demand of the client-network model may well be a high speed "server-only" backbone. Protocols utilizing bandwidths of 100Mbps or more might well be a prerequisite for accommodating all this extra interserver communication. And as backbone needs increase, required power of the server entities increases. This power is realized by two major components, fast CPU(s) and lots of RAM. Together, high-speed connections and high-power servers will provide an environment which is suitable for client-network computing.

It is clear that the client-server model must evolve toward a client-network model. This is not to say, however, that the client-server model has outlived its usefulness—it will remain the model of choice for certain applications. Nevertheless, to achieve a distributed name space as well as a distributed file space (system), a new client-server paradigm must evolve.

Solving Our Customers' Challenges

by Microsoft Corporation

Author Bio

Founded in 1975, Microsoft has become the worldwide leader in software for personal computers. The company offers a wide range of products and services for business and personal use, each designed with the mission of making it easier and more enjoyable for people to take advantage of the full power of personal computing every day.

Executive Summary

The electronic mail industry is entering an exciting period, defined by a new generation of messaging technology. First-generation electronic mail systems provided a basic text link between users and introduced a valuable communication tool to organizations. Although such an alternative to the interoffice paper memo remains important, today's e-mail technology can deliver far greater efficiency. Just as the postal service can deliver more than just typewritten letters, the right e-mail technology makes it possible to deliver a wide variety of interactive "packages" of information. In the coming years, users will work together across buildings or across the world, sharing data of all types—from graphics to spreadsheets to sound—all made possible by electronic messaging.

As the e-mail industry enters this period of rapid and important change, it is crucial that organizations understand the many issues involved both in setting up a new electronic messaging system and in enhancing and consolidating existing e-mail systems. At Microsoft, we have carefully considered electronic messaging issues and have developed a comprehensive messaging strategy.

In this paper, we'll discuss the key issues facing organizations using electronic mail. In addition, we'll explain Microsoft's electronic messaging strategy and how it addresses key requirements for a reliable architecture (or "messaging infrastructure"), support for workgroup applications, open and customizable systems, and vendor support.

Customer Challenges

Connectivity—How can I connect various e-mail systems running on mainframes, minicomputers, and PC networks in the highest-quality fashion?

Migration—How can I consolidate multiple e-mail systems or move from a host-based system to a PC LAN-based solution without too much cost or disruption to my organization?

Leverage—How can I leverage my existing resources and my investment in the new e-mail system?

Strategic E-Mail Issues

Many organizations are now making critical decisions about their electronic messaging capabilities, whether they are purchasing their first e-mail system or enhancing existing ones. Whatever their situation, organizations should consider three primary issues affecting their e-mail strategies. These issues are the rapid growth in the number of e-mail users, the proliferation of PC LANs, and the emergence of new productivity-enhancing workgroup applications.

E-mail User Growth

Electronic mail is quickly becoming an essential tool for organizations around the world. A recent study by the Electronic Mail Association (EMA) predicted that e-mail use will nearly triple by 1995, with 25 million users transmitting nearly 15 billion e-mail messages each year. The EMA's findings also show that organizations currently using e-mail expect to add an average of 23 percent more users per year and that 25,000 new sites will be using e-mail by 1994.* While organizations face tremendous e-mail growth within their own buildings, they must also prepare for the emerging need for intercompany and international electronic communication that accompanies this growth.

PC Local Area Networks (LANs)

The growth of LANs is increasingly influencing e-mail strategies. Some analysts predict that the number of PCs connected to LANs in 1995 will be greater than the total installed base of business PCs in 1991. Today, many organizations are trying to open communication among their islands of LANs. Some are struggling to connect new LAN-based e-mail systems to existing host-based systems such as IBM PROFS. And other organizations are trying to determine how to downsize from host-based to LAN-based systems. Because of their high performance, low cost, and flexibility, LAN-based solutions will continue to grow rapidly.

EMA study cited in a November 11, 1991, editorial in Network World.

Workgroup Applications

Electronic mail networks are quickly becoming more than a simple link for text messages. More organizations are looking to their e-mail system as the foundation for workgroup applications, an emerging category of software that enables users to work together and share all types of data—not just simple text memos. Just as the fax machine revolutionized telephone technology by turning it into a visual medium, so too will new workgroup applications transform e-mail systems into much broader channels of communication. In the coming years, these applications will change the way users work together.

There are growing numbers of e-mail users, powerful PC LANs, and new workgroup applications. These and other issues will significantly influence the electronic messaging strategies of organizations in the next decade. Given the complexity involved, most organizations are simply trying to determine what questions to ask as they define their strategies for electronic messaging. They know that the e-mail system they select will have a major, long-term impact on their operations. As both a leading vendor and a user of electronic mail, Microsoft also understands the critical nature of this decision. Our strategy for electronic messaging products focuses on delivering the best solutions for today's communication problems while providing a solid foundation for the future.

An Electronic Messaging Strategy

As a developer of key operating systems and applications, Microsoft is positioned to be a technology leader in strategic electronic messaging and workgroup applications. Shared next is our strategy, which we hope will assist our customers in moving forward with this exciting technology. This strategy applies to the global issues of moving forward and should be helpful regardless of the products you select. Our electronic messaging strategy uses the powerful design of host-based systems as the model for our LAN-based architecture. Built on extensive input from our worldwide customer base, our electronic messaging strategy includes four key commitments:

- To provide the best LAN-based messaging infrastructure

- To develop a line of modular, tightly integrated workgroup applications that leverage the services of the messaging infrastructure

- To deliver superior programmability and openness throughout the e-mail system

- To offer expert vendor support with consulting, training, and troubleshooting

Before discussing each of these, we should first discuss the cornerstone of any electronic messaging strategy: the messaging infrastructure.

What Is a Messaging Infrastructure?

In light of the rapidly changing advances in electronic communication, it is important to look at an electronic mail system as a comprehensive messaging infrastructure. Microsoft's entire electronic messaging strategy is built on this understanding.

A messaging infrastructure provides an integrated, enterprise-wide architecture for communication that encompasses the following:

- A message store facility to securely house critical data and information in the form of messages, documents, and folders

- A message transfer agent (MTA) to route messages among e-mail servers and other systems

- Gateways to provide connectivity to other e-mail and communications systems

- Administrative tools to manage users, the e-mail system, and any gateways

- Directory services to enable users to easily send messages to anyone in the organization

Interpersonal communication within an organization is only one reason a messaging infrastructure is important. Another reason is that electronic messaging is an "enabling technology"; that is, it drives other technologies and applications within an organization. These include workgroup applications for group scheduling, automated forms processing, project planning, and much more. Consequently, establishing a reliable messaging infrastructure today creates significant advantages in the future.

Microsoft's LAN-Based Messaging Infrastructure

At Microsoft we recognize the strategic importance of the messaging infrastructure in solving our customers' current problems and meeting their long-term communication and workgroup applications needs. The goal of producing a high-quality infrastructure has always guided the development of our Microsoft Mail products.

As a result, we offer the most reliable messaging infrastructure available for LAN-based e-mail products. Microsoft Mail for PC Networks and Microsoft Mail for AppleTalk Networks include a full range of e-mail clients for the major desktop platforms: the MS-DOS and Microsoft Windows operating systems, the Apple Macintosh, and OS/2 Presentation Manager. Microsoft Mail is a leader in supplying native e-mail servers optimized for PC and AppleTalk networks. In addition, we provide a comprehensive suite of gateways tightly integrated with Microsoft Mail for communication with virtually any e-mail system within our customers' organizations.

Microsoft Mail version 3.0 for PC Networks significantly enhances our messaging infrastructure. Version 3.0 offers automated, fault-tolerant global directory synchronization across Microsoft Mail and with external e-mail systems as well as powerful administration facilities for managing larger networks. Global directory synchronization significantly reduces routine administration activity by automatically integrating directories from multiple e-mail systems into the MS Mail directory. The fault-tolerant synchronization process also ensures that each Microsoft Mail server has received all requested updates through reliable serialization and thorough error checking.

In addition, version 3.0 of key Microsoft gateways supports sophisticated messaging capabilities such as backboning and message encapsulation. For more information on our advanced gateways, refer to our discussion on connectivity later in this white paper.

Version 3.0 also includes new clients for Windows and OS/2 Presentation Manager. These clients provide an updated graphical user interface and advanced e-mail features that enable users to easily communicate more effectively. The client for Windows also employs a transport-independent architecture designed to work with other e-mail servers. This creates significant advantages for customers who are migrating to Microsoft Mail or who want to use this client as a universal user interface to other e-mail systems.

In the future, we plan to further enhance the messaging infrastructure by delivering a native X.400 message transfer agent (MTA). X.400 is emerging as an important international electronic messaging protocol, especially for interorganization communication. Embracing this important standard will enable Microsoft Mail customers to connect directly to X.400based e-mail systems. We will also leverage advances in operating systems. We believe that in the future, operating system vendors will provide more components of the messaging infrastructure, such as directory and user authentication services, and we do not intend to erect artificial or proprietary barriers to prevent our customers from accessing these advances. Our customers will continue to benefit as Microsoft Mail and our workgroup applications take advantage of these operating system services.

The messaging infrastructure provides the important foundation for workgroup applications because these applications use the directory and transport services of the e-mail system. Customers will be able to leverage their messaging infrastructures over and over with more powerful workgroup applications instead of starting from scratch with every new networked application. This is why an organization's ability to adopt the best workgroup applications in the future is closely tied to its choice of an e-mail system.

Workgroup Applications Commitment

Increased networking is bringing people closer together, making it easier than ever to cooperate, work more efficiently, and produce better-quality work. As a result, workgroup applications are another key component of Microsoft's electronic messaging strategy. Workgroup applications, also described as messaging-enabled applications, enable coworkers to easily share information and collaborate on projects electronically. They not only make individuals more productive, but they also make groups and organizations more productive by improving information flow and work processes.

Workgroup applications extend beyond simple messaging. Examples of these applications include

- Messaging-enabled personal productivity applications, such as word processors and spreadsheets, that enable users to send e-mail and file attachments while working within the application

- Integrated voice mail and e-mail systems that enable the e-mail system to notify users of new voice mail messages or enable the voice mail system to play e-mail messages over a telephone

- Group scheduling systems that are integrated with e-mail to facilitate the scheduling of meetings of workgroup members

- Intelligent forms-routing applications, such as insurance claim or loan processing systems, that use e-mail to automate work flow

Today, application products exhibit many of the messaging-enabled characteristics of workgroup applications. For example, users can send Mail messages from applications such as Microsoft Excel and Microsoft Word and automatically attach the file they are working on. With this capability, electronic communication jumps to a new level of productivity.

But today's messaging-enabled applications are just the beginning. Microsoft is pursuing an integrated strategy that will produce modular, best-of-breed workgroup applications that leverage the Microsoft Mail messaging infrastructure. Customers, however, won't be restricted to using only Microsoft products. Our support for open application programming interfaces (APIs) will enable our customers to build on the messaging infrastructure with their own custom workgroup applications or with products developed by third parties.

Open and Customizable Systems

Key to any electronic messaging strategy is a commitment to truly open systems, recognizing that no one vendor can meet all of a customer's application needs.

Customers increasingly demand the ability to integrate their e-mail systems with existing PC applications and new workgroup applications. In addition, customers want the ability to customize their e-mail system, for example, by installing special commands in the menu structure that enable them to access other applications and services quickly. The e-mail system must be "open" so customers and third parties can easily extend its services and accommodate new applications and customized options.

Some vendors will attempt to meet this demand by supplying programmability and flexibility within the framework of a single, all-encompassing product. But such a monolithic approach offers "openness" only within that vendor's own system. This can result in compromised product capabilities, an inability to use third-party products, limited options for adopting new technologies, and little integration with other applications or with the users' familiar operating environments.

Microsoft offers open programmability by supporting industry-standard APIs, specifically, the Microsoft messaging application programming interface (MAPI). MAPI gives Microsoft, our customers, and third parties rich access to services in the messaging infrastructure for customizing e-mail and developing advanced workgroup applications.

MAPI offers a transport-independent architecture for both e-mail systems and messaging-enabled applications. Customers can use any MAPI-enabled application, such as an e-mail client or a group scheduling product, with any e-mail system that supports MAPI, including Microsoft Mail. As a result, our customers will have superior freedom of choice because they can select the best MAPI-enabled applications and the best MAPI-compliant e-mail system. And because MAPI has been designed and developed with the input of many independent software vendors, customers can expect a wide variety of messaging-enabled applications to choose from.

Superior Vendor Support

A final component of an electronic messaging strategy is a commitment to provide unsurpassed vendor support. As the developer of a customer's e-mail system and gateways, Microsoft is accountable for the complete LAN-based e-mail solution. We offer various support services to help customers formulate a messaging strategy, manage its implementation, and support users and administrators.

Microsoft Consulting Services (MCS) provides expert assistance in defining an optimal enterprise-wide e-mail configuration and in leveraging that messaging infrastructure with future workgroup applications. MCS can show customers how to integrate Microsoft applications and systems to create comprehensive, high-quality office automation systems. MCS professionals have extensive knowledge and hands-on experience with the messaging problems faced by large organizations.

Microsoft Product Support Services (PSS) offers many technical support options for Microsoft Mail and gateway products. These options are designed to meet the differing needs of our customers. PSS has a dedicated, knowledgeable staff of engineers who focus only on Microsoft Mail and gateway product-support issues. These engineers can be accessed by telephone or, electronically, via the Microsoft Online for Windows communication software.

Authorized Microsoft Mail Resellers can also provide technical support by bringing their configuration and troubleshooting expertise directly to customers' sites.

Finally, a messaging solution isn't complete until the new e-mail system is being used to its full potential. Our customers can attend classes at Microsoft University (MSU) that train both users and administrators on Microsoft Mail. MSU courses are designed to help customers get up to speed with the new e-mail system as quickly as possible.

Conclusion

As organizations develop their electronic messaging strategies for the 1990s, they are addressing today's communication problems such as connectivity and migration while planning for tomorrow's changes. Organizations understand the critical importance of these decisions because electronic messaging can fundamentally change the way they operate. After an electronic messaging product has become an integral part of an organization, the financial and management costs of replacing it may become prohibitive. As a result, organizations need to consider many significant technology issues when selecting and implementing a long-term messaging solution:

- Reliability, integration, and evolution of the messaging infrastructure

- Openness, flexibility, and customizability of the entire messaging framework

- Opportunities to leverage both existing investments and new technology

Selecting the best vendor is just as critical as choosing the right technology. To make the best choice, customers need to consider whether a vendor offers

- A long-term strategic vision

- Technological leadership and support for industry standards

- Financial, developmental, and support resources to deliver the strategic vision

Microsoft has made a significant corporate commitment to develop electronic messaging and workgroup applications products. We have also invested in a knowledgeable consulting and technical support staff to assist our customers in optimizing their electronic messaging solutions. As a leading developer of personal computer software, Microsoft is uniquely positioned to help its customers implement advanced messaging and workgroup solutions in the 1990s and beyond.

Network Software Licensing

by Microcomputer Managers Association
White Paper Committee

Author Bio

The MMA is a national, not-for-profit professional association of micro-computer managers. Established in 1982 for the purpose of professional exchange of information, research, and communications, its members represent major organizations in both the private and public sectors. The MMA sponsors an annual conference and chapter seminar meetings. The MMA also publishes a bimonthly newsletter.

Neither the MMA nor anyone connected with the organization endorses any company to the exclusion of any other. The views expressed in this paper do not necessarily reflect, in any way, the views of the entities with which the authors may be affiliated, and the agreement of those entities with the views expressed in this paper has not been sought.

Microcomputer Managers Association
P.O. Box 4615
Warren, NJ 07059
908-580-9091

The Microcomputer Managers Association White Paper Committee

D. Keith Herron, Co-Chair
Manager of Microcomputing
Weil, Gotshal & Manges

Joanne T. Witt, Co-Chair
Senior Technology Analyst
Siemens Medical Systems

Sam Blumenstyk, Esq.
Dave Chan
Jenene Karamon
G. Jeffrey Knepper
Steven Mayner

Executive Summary

In the fall of 1990, the Board of Directors of the MMA chose software licensing as one of its monthly meeting topics for 1991. In the winter, the board was approached to lead a panel discussion on Network Software Licensing at Spring Comdex in May. From the success of these two meetings, the MMA's Board of Directors instructed the White Paper Committee to publish a paper on network software licensing. They asked Keith Herron and Joanne Witt to chair the effort, and three members of the New York Chapter joined the committee: Sam Blumenstyk, David Chan, and Jenene Karamon. Two members-at-large also joined the committee: G. Jeffrey Knepper from Washington and Steven Mayner from Dallas. Keith and Joanne worked with Jenene to add questions to the annual MMA survey to gather opinions from all members on the subject.

Through these public forums, survey data from our membership, discussions with managers from various types of corporations, and software publishers, we developed the issues confronting the two groups and our recommendations for solving the problems we both face.

Corporate America is not in compliance with its software license agreements. Not because microcomputer managers want to be out of compliance, but because

- They have too many conflicting licenses to administer; every software package has a different license.

- They often do not have the mandate from upper management.

- They have users who are ignorant of copyright and shrink wrap law.

- License agreements are difficult to understand and clouded by legal language.

- License agreements are too difficult to monitor and enforce.

Corporate America is not compliant because managers do not have the time or the tools to police the variety of license agreements in use today.

Microcomputer managers are not police. It should not be necessary for us to spend extensive time ensuring adherence to the various license agreements. If microcomputer managers were expected to do that with the existing cornucopia of license agreements, they would need to increase their departmental head count just to keep track of and manage them.

Businesses believe that they should pay for all the software they use. They invest a significant amount of money in supporting application software, hardware, training, and in-house support personnel. They feel they deserve to have a network software licensing agreement in place that is understandable, easily managed, and fairly priced.

This paper presents findings from case studies submitted by members of the MMA and from our 1991 membership survey. We identify problems faced by both microcomputer managers and software publishers. We offer recommendations to both groups that bring us closer to a consensus on how software should be licensed on a network.

The MMA

The Association was founded in 1982 by microcomputer managers who realized that an organization was needed to address their common needs to the microcomputer industry.

Based in New York, the Association offers membership to individuals whose primary responsibility is managing microcomputer technology in their organizations. It presently has more than 1,000 members representing most of the Fortune 500 companies, government agencies, and other large microcomputer users.

The MMA also works closely with members of the industry's vendor community through its various sponsorship programs. Participants receive the MMA's Newsletter, which addresses microcomputing issues. They enjoy the privilege of submitting material to the membership under certain arrangements.

Microcomputer managers come from many types of organizations: small and large, controlled and flexible, centralized and decentralized. The MMA includes representatives from all types of companies.

Licensing Methodologies

There are many different ways to license software. The most frequently encountered types are per machine, per user, concurrent use, per server, and site license. We'll use the following scenario to examine these licenses: You are a network administrator for a single server LAN with 100 users. Of those users, 80 use WonderSpread, a new spreadsheet. There are 60 machines attached to the file server, and there are two shifts of workers, so that only 40 users use WonderSpread at any one time. How many copies of the software should you purchase? It depends on the license agreement.

- Licensed per Machine—This license requires that you purchase a license for every machine on your network. Since there are 60 machines attached to the file server, you would buy 60 copies of WonderSpread. Types of software that seem to lend themselves well to this type of license are operating system software and memory management software, which need to be on every station.

- Licensed per User—This license requires that you purchase a license for every person who could use the software. In our hypothetical case, that would mean buying 100 copies.

- Concurrent Use—This license requires that you purchase licenses for the number of people who will be running the software simultaneously. You would purchase 40 copies of WonderSpread to comply with this license.

- Licensed per Server—You need a single copy of the software residing on the file server under this license agreement. That single copy serves as many nodes as are attached to the file server.

- Site/Entity License—Typically, these licenses are individually negotiated with the publisher and vary widely in their provisions. A single license of WonderSpread would be purchased. This license allows the user to have an unrestricted number of users either within a specific site of an organization, or throughout an entire company or entity.

Problems with the Current Environment

Both software publishers and microcomputer managers have problems with the way software is currently licensed. Because the two groups are on opposite sides of the product—one being the producer, the other the consumer—they often clash on what they see as problems.

Problems with Licensing Methodologies

We will use our hypothetical scenario once again to examine what a LAN manager must do under the various licensing methods to provide the most value for the company.

Licensed per Machine

If the company wanted to buy only 40 copies, for the number of persons who would run the program simultaneously, the manager would have to restrict, by node address, or other means, which nodes had access to the software on the network. This requires a great deal of planning on the manager's part: Are the same 40 nodes used on both the day and night shift for WonderSpread? Do all nodes have access to the correct printer or printers? When the network grows, how are the 40 nodes redistributed? When employees change offices, how are the WonderSpread nodes redistributed? What happens when a network card goes bad; must you change which node has access? What if the entire station develops problems; can you substitute a working machine in its place, or must you again enter the management module to tell WonderSpread which node should have access? Although this method may work for some stand-alone software, it becomes a managerial nightmare on a network. In a multiserver environment, the headaches can grow exponentially.

Licensed per User

The manager can restrict access to the software to just the 80 people who use it, thereby obviating the need for 20 copies of the software. He or she could restrict access to just the 40 simultaneous WonderSpread users by having a day and night shift worker share a sign-on and password and restricting that sign-on to one logon at a time. However, the administrative overhead in this method would be enormous. Any personnel change would require changing access privileges. Temporary workers would have to be accommodated in some fashion. Sharing sign-ons and passwords invalidates most audit trail information and also presents a security issue.

This license is difficult to police if workers have computers at home: Can they legally load and run the software on their home systems or their laptops? Can they do this if their sign-on is being used at the office? Again, this method might work in a stand-alone environment, or outside a corporate setting, but it has no place on a corporation's LAN.

Concurrent Use

This method has analogies in life outside the computer industry. Consider a library that might purchase a number of copies of a popular novel for lending. When those copies are lent out, the librarian doesn't copy the book for the next person to request it, but makes that person wait until one of the books is returned, or the library buys another copy.

Concurrent use licensing works in this fashion. A number of copies are purchased and "lent out" as they are run. When the number of licenses in use exceeds the number purchased, the "librarian" refuses to give the requestor a copy of the software until another license is obtained.

For this method to work, and to prove to the WonderSpread publishers and to the Software Publishers Association (SPA) that you have only 40 users at a time running WonderSpread, you need a "librarian." The function of the "librarian" in this case is performed by the metering software. The microcomputer manager need only tell the "librarian" how many licenses are available. After telling the metering software that 40 licenses of WonderSpread are available, the manager's job is completed. He or she need not place any restrictions on where or by whom the software is run. She or he doesn't need to watch and make sure only 40 persons are running the software. If a computer fails or personnel changes occur, the network administrator need make no changes to accommodate them.

This method is much easier to administer than the previous two, but it requires that you have metering software for all your programs. Although there are third-party packages on the market that perform this function, some applications come with their own proprietary meter.

In a library, you have a single way to check out books, whether they are biographies, reference books, or novels. Similarly for metering software, there should be a single package that handles the "lending" for all your software.

Concurrent use also can be less expensive for a company. In one of our case studies of a large accounting firm, the firm determined that in a 150-user LAN, they required about 25 concurrent spreadsheet licenses and 40–50 concurrent word processing licenses. The firm enjoyed a considerable cost savings over purchasing 150 copies of each program.

Licensed per Server

This license is one of the easiest to administer and verify and works very well for network operating system software or electronic mail. This license makes it very difficult, however, for publishers to price the software because they don't know how many users will be attached to a single file server.

In practice, this license is often not very different from the concurrent use license. One network operating system (NOS) company prices its software based on the largest number of users that can attach to a file server. They provide licenses priced for 20, 100, 250, and 1,000 users. The net result would be similar to having a concurrent use license for 20, 100, 250, or 1,000 users—even locking out the 21st, 101st, 251st, or 1001st user—except that the number of licenses would already be set in the built-in metering software.

Site/Entity License

The Site/Entity license is the simplest license to administer since it is easy to prove that you are compliant. If a person is an employee of the company and located at the site covered by the license, that person has the right to use the software covered by the agreement.

Practically, however, this license is difficult or impossible to obtain unless your company has strong central control and is one of the Fortune 500. Software companies have largely stopped offering site licenses and can be convinced to negotiate one only by a very large company. Although they require enormous efforts on the parts of both the software publisher and the purchaser to negotiate a settlement, users want this type of license because it is easy to manage compliance with the software license.

Case Study Concerns

From the case studies we collected and the conversations we have had with microcomputer managers, we have identified a number of concerns.

Pricing of network software—Software publishers assert that network versions of their software cost as much to develop as stand-alone versions. Therefore, they say, network versions should sell for as much as, or more than, stand-alone versions. This argument leaves out one important point, however. Although development costs of network versus stand-alone software are roughly the same, support costs are not. A network implies central control and central support. When a software publisher sells 100 copies of a network package to a company, they will not receive support calls from 100 individual users as they might if they sold 100 stand-alone packages, but more likely from one or two support individuals within the company. The software publisher also will receive far fewer total calls since the bulk of the questions from individual users will be handled by the local support desk.

Upgrading to network nodes—One of the problems when moving from stand-alone machines to a network environment is the cost involved in moving from single user licenses to a network license. Users should be able to upgrade their copies in the same way they upgrade to the next version of the software.

Uncouple manuals/licenses—Software companies have started selling LAN packs of their software. These packs often come with 5, 10, 20, or more licenses and some number of manuals. Usually there are fewer manuals than licenses. The publishers do this to cut costs and because customers have told them that not all users need manuals. Managers like LAN packs because they reduce bulk and because manuals don't have to be stored or destroyed.

What makes more sense, however, is to price the licenses separately from the materials (disk media, manuals, templates, tutorials). Managers can then purchase exactly what they need, and publishers can cut down on needless shipping expenses. This position is also environmentally sound since unwanted materials occupy valuable space only until they are hauled to a landfill.

Consistency among license agreements—The largest single problem facing microcomputer managers is the lack of consistency among license agreements. Not only do users have to maintain records of software purchases, hardware purchases, and users, but they must compare these numbers differently for every piece of software. The more consistent that license agreements can be made, the less time managers spend doing police work, and the more compliant the end users will be.

Simplify language of license—Users cannot comply with something they don't understand. Oftentimes legal departments, called in by baffled microcomputer managers, cannot tell what is and is not allowed by some license agreements. For this reason, licenses must be written in plain language the average person can understand. In addition, a grid called "Truth in Licensing" should be printed on the license (similar to the grid that appears on credit card applications showing credit terms) which spells out exactly what is and is not allowed under the terms of the license.

Need for auditing—Audits are imperative to ensure compliance with license agreements. Microcomputer managers simply do not have the tools, for the most part, to know whether they are in compliance. At one Texas insurance firm where they thought they were legal, an audit revealed that barely 52 percent of their software was paid for. After purchasing licenses to bring themselves into compliance, they instituted policies to stay legal from that point forward. They educated nontechnical upper management on licensing issues, began ordering software as they ordered hardware, and mandated periodic and annual audits of software purchase and use.

Local copy—Many users would like to have a copy of a program on their hard drives even though they normally use the software from the network. That way, if the network fails, they can continue to work with the copy on their local drives. Some managers argue that this local copy is their backup copy that is allowed under Copyright Law, and therefore does not figure in when determining the number of copies in use. This creates problems for verification if the software is licensed for concurrent use. The metering software could not lock out the person running the software from his or her local drive.

The need for metering—To utilize concurrent licenses, metering software must be available to verify that companies are abiding by their license agreements. A number of third-party products perform this metering function. Some application software also has this feature built-in or provided with the package.

Although it is convenient to have the metering software provided with the application, there are problems associated with this approach. First, each application would have its own interface for its metering software. Second, there would be multiple programs which might require that administrative information be entered. It makes much more sense to have a single package provide the metering for all application software on the network.

If we concede this point, however, software publishers have a problem: with which of the metering packages on the market should they be compatible? To overcome this problem, the metering should be done by the NOS. Users have been clamoring for more and better management features from the NOS for some time, and metering is just one of the features that must be provided.

Instant licensing—A very real problem is the "it has to be done yesterday" syndrome. The ability to provide solutions quickly can mean the difference between profit and loss for a company. Therefore, giving managers the ability to set the number of licenses for concurrent licensing is very important. LAN managers can work with their vendors to provide licenses in the most timely manner.

There are also software delivery mechanisms available for LANs. These delivery systems will install and update all associated files (AUTOEXEC.BAT, CONFIG.SYS, WIN.INI). This alleviates the requirement for human intervention, provides a way to control licenses, and lowers overall support and management costs.

Several software distributors are delivering licenses and software through electronic means. A company would not have to wait for the morning's overnight service delivery to have software delivered, but could download it from the distributor almost instantaneously.

Survey Data

In a 1991 MMA survey, members responded to whether or not they understood their current software licensing agreements. They also indicated which type of licensing they preferred to see on the network and why.

Of those responding, almost half said they did not understand all of their license agreements.

Our members preferred the following types of licenses:

Machine	1	percent
Individual	0	percent
Concurrent Use	31	percent
File Server	22	percent
Site	45	percent
Other	1	percent

The most important reason cited by the individuals preferring file server and site licenses was that it made compliance easy. As we've seen from our earlier discussions, the concurrent use, file server, and site license agreements are much easier to administer and police than any other. Those choosing concurrent use felt they saved their firms money by making licenses "pay as you use."

Conclusions

Microcomputer managers are not, nor should they be, the software police. We don't have the tools to enable us to do that job in addition to the duties we already have. Under some license agreements, it would be a full-time job just to manage their implementation. Microcomputer managers do not find it in their job descriptions to handle that kind of task.

Our membership clearly believes that site licensing is the preferred solution for network software licensing. It removes from the manager the burden of proving license compliance.

Almost as popular was the concurrent use license. Although more of a burden to administer (since metering software is a necessary part of the license), it eliminates the need to negotiate an agreement with a software publisher.

File server licenses fall somewhere between these two other types in the software license continuum. Some consider it a slightly simplified version of a concurrent use license; others, an easier-to-negotiate partial site license. In the present environment, file server licenses are priced more like concurrent licenses than site licenses.

Microcomputer managers seek control over the software they support. They must manage who uses the software, how they use it, when they use it, and where they use it. Concurrent use, file server, and site licenses make it easier to carry out these tasks. Metering software and network management tools make them easier as well.

Managers also have economic concerns. They must provide the most value for their employers; the most productivity for the least cost. This is in direct conflict with the publishers' wish to maximize their profits. Because the file server license is difficult to price and few publishers want to negotiate site or entity licenses, concurrent use licenses afford the most common solution between managers and software companies.

Managers have many different software packages to support. Because every manufacturer has a different license agreement, it becomes a management nightmare to comply with them all. Standardizing on a concurrent use license will greatly simplify the manager's task of compliance. Making the license understandable will make the task even easier.

Recommendations

The MMA has compiled the information for our position from many different sources. Panel discussions were held in April 1991 and at Spring Comdex in May. We have incorporated the views of our full membership as reflected in our annual survey during the summer of 1991. We have conducted discussions with network managers, software publishers, and the SPA and reviewed articles in the trade press on licensing issues.

In light of the previous discussions and our extensive research, we make the following recommendations to software publishers and microcomputer managers in order to establish a consensus on network software licensing:

- Application software on a network should be licensed for concurrent use. Organizations should be able to purchase licenses for the number of copies that are intended to be run simultaneously on the network.

- There should be metering software to track how many licenses have been purchased for each software package on the LAN and how many are in use at any given time. It must lock out, or prevent, a program from running if a license is not available. An unauthorized user would receive a message indicating that all licenses are in use.

- This metering software should be integrated with the NOS. NOS publishers should standardize on a common Application Programming Interface (API) which application software publishers will use to allow their program to work with this metering software.

- The license agreement should be written in plain language and incorporate a "Truth in Licensing" summary box, which clearly states what is and is not allowed by the license.

- Documentation should be uncoupled from media or licenses. In other words, licenses, installation media, documentation, and all other materials should be priced separately and sold to organizations in the numbers they require.

- Organizations should be able to upgrade from stand-alone software to network versions of the software. The costs involved should be comparable to those when upgrading from one version of the software to the next improved version.

- Microcomputer managers should make a concerted effort to educate their users about software licensing and illicit software. They should encourage their firms to adopt a policy against illegal copying of software and establish reasonable but tough sanctions for a failure to comply. They should adhere faithfully to the license agreements they enter into. Their organization should conduct a software audit at least once a year.

Summary

This paper represents the viewpoints of our organization's members and incorporates a clear guideline for software publishers that both managers and publishers can live with and follow.

These recommendations, if adopted by software publishers, will enable microcomputer managers to comply with their license agreements. In turn, this will ensure that publishers are paid a fair price for the software in use in corporations.

These recommendations are specific, yet broad enough to allow publishers to continue to use license agreements to distinguish their own products from their competitors'.

Over the past year, many of the recommendations set forth in this paper have been adopted by software publishers. This is apparent in an almost industry-wide move to concurrent licensing, simplifying the compliance issue. New software delivery mechanisms, such as electronic distribution through the software vendor or through a third party package on a LAN, has gained popularity in larger organizations.

Software vendors have developed new licensing methodologies that provide mechanisms for controlling costs and ensuring compliance. The new licensing methodologies are aimed at large centralized organizations and by in large do not take into account many of the decentralized and smaller organizations that are faced with problems outlined in this document.

The MMA, in conjunction with the SPA, developed the Licensing Service API (LSAPI) that is incorporated in the Microsoft WOSA standards. The LSAPI provides a standard way for applications and licensing systems to communicate. The specifications for the API are available through the MMA, SPA, or Microsoft.

Although site licensing is gaining in popularity, very few vendors have implemented the "Truth in Licensing" grid. It remains as true today as it did a year ago, that licensing agreements are unclear. Software publishers should give serious consideration to rectifying this problem.

By in large, documentation and media have been uncoupled from the licenses. We expect this trend to continue. Attractive upgrade prices from stand-alone to a network version has not been widely adopted.

Microcomputer managers firmly believe that software companies deserve to be paid for their products. These recommendations provide us with the tools we need to ensure that publishers are paid a fair price, and paid for every copy used.

The Telecomputing Office Environment

by James J. Mulholland
Director of Channel Development, Triton Technologies

Author Bio

James Mulholland has a Bachelor of Science in Economics from Jacksonville University. In August 1985, Mr. Mulholland formed Triton Technologies together with David Saphier and Floyd Roberts.

In seven years, Triton Technologies has evolved into a leading US and international supplier of remote access and file-transfer communication packages for IBM-compatible PCs, LANs, and wide area networks. Triton's cornerstone product, CO/Session, has been critically acclaimed as the fastest remote-control software product and was recently selected as *PC Magazine*'s Editors Choice.

Executive Summary

Providing remote access to data and programs on a network is becoming more popular and can lead to increased productivity and employee morale. By carefully researching and planning a telecomputing strategy for your company, selecting and implementing the proper technology will be much easier.

Fueled by the growing popularity of lightweight notebook computers, office workers with home PCs, and the number of employees working from home regularly or part-time, requests for remote access to programs, data, and gateways located on a LAN are increasing at a rapid rate.

Planning and implementing a telecomputing strategy for your network and company does not have to be difficult. With a minimum of careful planning, you can provide all remote users with the proper access and performance to enhance your employees' productivity and to safeguard valuable company information.

In designing a telecomputing strategy, your first challenge will be to understand the various terms and technology that different vendors offer. The two most popular approaches currently available to offer users remote LAN access can be described as "remote control" and "remote node." The two approaches described are typically used with standard dial-up telephone lines and asynchronous modems.

In a "remote control" environment, a remote user takes remote control of a local PC on the network and passes screen updates and keystrokes back and forth between the "host" and "remote" locations. All processing is conducted on the host PC, and the amount of data transmitted over the telephone is minimal. For each remote user connected to the network, a host PC on the local area network must be available for remote dial-in.

Transferring files from a remote user to or from the network is accomplished through a file transfer menu. Some products, such as CO/Session and pcAnywhere, provide remote users with a very friendly file transfer menu. Both CO/Session and pcAnywhere offer a file transfer menu that displays names and sizes of files located on the local and remote drives simultaneously on a single screen. Transferring a file from one location to another is as simple as highlighting a file with your mouse and pressing a single key.

Typical retail costs for remote control software is $179–$199 for one remote and one host package. These software products are easily available at substantial discounts through mail-order software shops. Examples of remote control products include Carbon Copy Plus from Microcom, CO/Session from Triton Technologies Inc., and pcAnywhere from Symantec.

In a "remote node" environment, a remote user does not take remote control of a PC on the LAN but instead functions as a new node to the LAN. Instead of dialing into a host PC on the network, remote users instead dial into a single station router on the LAN. All processing is conducted on the remote PC, and the amount of data transmitted over the telephone line is substantial because the programs, data, and network protocol are all sent over the telephone.

A major advantage of remote node products is that you don't have to dedicate host PCs on your LAN for remote dial-in. The disadvantage of this type of technology is that instead of dedicating a PC to locally process and talk to the file server, the remote node must instead use the telephone line just like a network cable. This means that a remote node on a Novell network is now sending IPX packet at modem speed versus at the high speeds usually operated at by network interface cards.

To optimize performance when using a remote node product, it is extremely useful to have each remote user load onto his local hard disk any programs he may want to use when accessing data on the network. By doing this, the remote user can then eliminate long delay waiting for a 400K program to be remotely loaded. For each remote user connected to the network, a single station router must be available.

When a remote node product is being used, transferring files from a remote user to or from the network is accomplished via the DOS copy command because the remote user is in fact an actual node on the network.

Recent product introductions from Microtest, UDS, and Shiva have produced a hardware product that basically combines a network interface card, a high speed 14.4 bps modem, and a single station router into one box with a suggested retail price of $1,699–$1,999.

For most installations, remote control software products will produce superior performance, additional flexibility, and lower costs, although Shiva's NetModem/E product does offer substantial advantages when using DOS and Macintosh computers together on a network.

Another advantage for LAN Administrator when using a remote control approach versus that of a remote node is that maximum performance can be achieved with all software application located on the file server versus on each individual remote node. This translates into easier management of software updates and licensing issues.

In devising your telecomputing strategy, it is also important to note which types of programs and data remote users will need to access. If your remote users will be running non-Windows spreadsheet, word processing, or database and they do not require the capability to display EGA or VGA graphics, your system requirements will be vastly different than if the remote users need to run Windows-based or VGA-based graphical application programs.

For text-based applications, users of remote control software products will find performance to be acceptable with 2400 bps modems and very good with 9600 bps modems. For running Windows-based application programs, standard VGA is acceptable at 9600 and Super VGA at 14400. For optimum performance, it is recommended that you use a modem capable of 57600 bps.

With remote control software products, the power of the host PC is also an important factor. For nongraphic programs, using a PC with a 12MHz 80286 processor is usually acceptable. It is recommended that when running Windows, you use an 20MHz 80386 or faster processor.

Memory is also a major issue with remote control software products. Most remote control products requires between 60K and 80K of memory on the host PC. To provide users with the maximum amount of memory for running programs remotely, equip your host PCs with 80386 processors, at least 1M of RAM, and DOS 5.0. Then load the remote control software along with your network drivers "high."

Security issues for remote access can be controlled through the use of your current networking security system plus enhanced by password protection, dial back, directory access restrictions, and file transfer rights. A useful tip in setting up your telecomputing strategy with remote control software is to have the host PC reboot after each disconnect. This feature will ensure that all remote users will have to log in and enter their network password each time a connection is made.

For allowing multiple users to dial into your network at the same time, it is also wise to set up with your telephone company a group of phone numbers on a rotary system. This enables you to give out just one telephone number, and if that number is busy, it will automatically roll over to the next available line.

And just in case the thought of stacking up 20 PCs in a closet somewhere scares you, vendors such as Cubix Corporation and J & L Information Systems provide a much neater and more professional solution by allowing you to purchase PCs on a card, and a chassis capability of storing 48 or more PC processors for dial-in access in a single tower.

The technology for remote LAN access has been with us for many years now. In the past 12 months, great strides have been made in increasing performance, overcoming the challenges of remotely running Windows, and making the software easier for the nontechnical users to learn and cope with.

The benefit of remote LAN access can be directly traced to a company's bottom line.

Outside salespeople equipped with a notebook computer and modem who can check office e-mail, stock availability, and price have a tremendous advantage over outside salespeople without current information.

Mothers returning from maternity leave or opting to work part-time can still keep in daily touch with the office and gain access to all information needed to be productive and informed.

Managers tired of working late or arriving home after their children are asleep can opt to go home and finish up monthly forecasts or weekly reports after the children have gone to sleep.

Faster modems, lower costing PCs, changing lifestyles, and government regulations to reduce the number of people driving to work each day will continue to fuel the rapid growth of remote LAN access for many years to come.

Companies implementing a telecomputing strategy can also help to improve employee morale and contribute to improving the environment by helping to reduce the number of cars on the road daily commuting to work and adding harmful pollutions to the air we all breathe.

In many densely populated areas such as Los Angeles, Boston, and New York City, proposing a corporate work schedule of four days in and one day home would reduce by 20 percent the problems and pollutions caused by the daily rush-hour traffic jams.

Future technology advancements will enable companies to easily allocate PCs, modems, and other network resources dynamically to handle the network needs for remote access and dial out access to information services such as CompuServe and Dow Jones.

Open Systems Are Now Open To DOS Users

by Therese E. Myers
President and CEO, Quarterdeck Office Systems, Inc.

Author Bio

Therese E. Myers is president, CEO, and cofounder of Quarterdeck Office Systems, Inc., a technology leader in the development of software products that enhance the performance of DOS-based personal computer hardware and software. Quarterdeck develops, markets, and supports multitasking, windowing, and memory management software designed to bring innovative, cost-efficient computing solutions to business and individual personal computer users.

Prior to forming Quarterdeck in 1981, Ms. Myers was vice president of product development from 1974 to 1980 for Axxa Corporation, a subsidiary of Citicorp, where she pioneered the development of integrated, multiuser office workstations.

Ms. Myers received a master's of science degree in industrial administration from Carnegie Mellon University, a bachelor's degree in economics from Newton College of the Sacred Heart (now part of Boston College), and is also a certified public accountant.

Ms. Myers is a director of Advanced Logic Research, Inc. and serves on the board of directors of the High Technology Industry Group for the City of Hope. In 1991, The Institute of American Entrepreneurs named her "Entrepreneur of the Year" and made her a lifetime member.

Quarterdeck Office Systems, Inc.
150 Pico Boulevard
Santa Monica, CA 90405

Executive Summary

DOS users are no longer left out of open systems computing. Therese Myers discusses how the X Window System, an international graphic standard now tailored to DOS, gives DOS PCs on a network powerful workstation capabilities. The new architecture allows DOS users to take full advantage of distributed and multiplatform computing.

There is a lot of talk about client/server, distributed computing, and open systems these days. That's because of the availability of low cost/high performance PCs and workstations, advances in network technology to support different hardware platforms and operating systems, and the emergence of hardware and software standards. The result is a new way of thinking about software architecture and an economical way of preserving the legacy in computer hardware and software. The benefit to computer users is the ability to integrate the old with the new while taking advantage of the advances in computer technology.

The era of network computing has introduced to the workstation and mainframe market the concept of splitting applications into multiple parts.

This concept splits an application's front-end (its graphical interface) with its back-end (the part that performs calculations, manages data, and so forth). Depending upon the application, the back-end may be running anywhere on the network (for example, on a Sun SPARCstation, an IBM RS/6000, a DEC VAXstation, or on a powerful mainframe). And since the front-end of today's workstations supports windowing and multitasking, one workstation can display and manage the back-end of multiple programs running throughout the network on different hardware platforms and on different operating systems—thus making the open system a reality.

The foundation for doing remote computing on a network is the X Window System, an international graphic standard designed by MIT and funded by the X Consortium, a group of companies that includes AT&T, IBM, Digital Equipment, Hewlett Packard, Sun, Sony, and others.

The X Window System consists of two main parts. An X Server controls a computer's display screen, drawing windows, text, lines, pictures, and circles according to the requests from an application. An X Server may handle the screen drawing for multiple applications concurrently—each application typically displaying information with one or more windows on the screen. The second part is an X Client. This is an application program (such as a spreadsheet) that communicates with the X Server and instructs it what to draw. A well-defined messaging system links the two parts—either over a network or within a single machine.

Most X Window System implementations are currently on UNIX (the Sun SPARCstation, the IBM RS/6000, the Silicon Graphics Indigo, the HP 9000 Series, the Data General Avion) or on VMS (DEC VAXstation). X Window System implementations on DOS have been limited to only a portion of the system, the X Server—until DESQview/X. DESQview/X is a full implementation, X Server, X Clients and X Toolkits on DOS.

At Quarterdeck we have focused in the last 10 years on creating DOS enhancement software that brought workstation power to DOS. This focus led us to create products that provide memory management, preemptive multitasking, windowing, data transfer, and customization capabilities on DOS PCs—and most recently to bring to DOS the X Window System (server, clients and toolkits).

The result is a DOS PC that can display, simultaneously, X programs that are running on a remote workstation on the network with other DOS programs and with other Microsoft Windows programs. Conversely, remote X workstations can display DOS and Microsoft Windows programs that are running on the DESQview/X DOS PC.

To network users this means that DOS PCs now have the same capabilities and interoperability as powerful workstations. Programs that require a fast processor or megabytes of memory can run on the machine most suited for them. Files can be transferred between nodes on the network. Support staff can install software remotely and even train users remotely. Software on different hardware platforms or operating systems can be used without the user having to understand new operating systems or getting new equipment. With this architecture, computing power can be placed where it will be most efficiently used. Data and processing can be spread across several systems. But most of all it means that DOS is not an isolated system. Instead it fits all the criteria of an "open system."

To developers, a full implementation of X on DOS means the ability to develop software on one platform that can be ported easily and quickly to another platform. To corporate MIS directors it provides an evolutionary way to migrate to other computing platforms. It also provides a way of integrating central and end user resources simply.

And to DOS users in general it means once again that DOS is by no means "dead."

Distributed Computing from the Desktop

by Art Olbert
Personal Systems Director of LAN Systems, IBM

Author Bio

Art joined IBM in 1969, and worked on the design, development, test, and maintenance of four DOS releases. From 1972 through 1986, he held various jobs in development, headquarters, and management. In 1987, he became director of the Endicott Programming Lab, responsible for VM/SP, VM/IS, and related communications products.

In 1989, Art became Enterprise Systems Director of Client/Server computing. He was appointed to his current position in 1991. His responsibilities include worldwide market planning, systems strategy, and development for PS software offerings for LAN systems, including OS/2 LAN server, NetWare from IBM, and Notes from IBM. He graduated from Hunter College in the Bronx, New York, with a B.A. degree in history and mathematics.

Executive Summary

While more and more corporate data is finding its way onto the LAN, the degree to which organizations entrust it as the sole or major repository of their information will depend on the LAN's ability to deliver on the promise of providing the best of both workstation and host environments.

Technology providers face three significant requirements: delivering LAN systems at least as robust, reliable, serviceable, manageable, and secure as the current generation of host systems; giving the transparent networking capability to enable true client/server applications that execute across heterogeneous platforms; and providing a staged and easy migration to evolving technologies.

While much has been written about global competition, decentralization, flat organizations, and the knowledge worker, little has been done to define an orderly migration toward the information infrastructure that will support organizations as they move from the demands of today to the promise of tomorrow.

The source of that change—the tremendous pressure on today's organizations—has little to do with technology. Whether the pressure is because of the changing demographics of the workforce, increased competition, globalization, company sales, acquisitions, or strategic alliances, the bottom line is the same: Market and world forces are stretching and reshaping organizations, forcing them to change in order to remain viable—even to survive.

In response, organizations are shrinking, reducing layers of middle management that once served primarily as information conduits. As a result, these employees have new levels of power. They understand company goals and are empowered to make decisions that can dramatically impact the organization. These individuals are not the generalists of earlier decades; instead, they are highly-skilled specialists who bring a great deal of expertise to bear on a given problem. To add the breadth necessary, they work in flexible teams or workgroups that are formed and disbanded based on the nature of the problem or opportunity confronting an organization.

Bottoms-Up Requirements

These highly skilled individuals are both more and less than computer literate. They understand technology and rely on it to improve their efficiency. But they are unwilling to become computer experts. They see computers and systems as tools which must bend to the wants of people. Many are mobile, not tethered to a given workplace, and impatient—demanding easy access to all the information they need to get their jobs done, regardless of where they are and where the information is when they need it.

Accordingly, individuals rely on desktop systems for their individual needs because only desktop systems can provide the power, specific applications, end-user interface, and malleability people require. The teams formed by these individuals are supported by local area network (LAN) systems for connectivity and servers for shared capabilities. The desktops become clients. Wide area networks (WANs) are used to link LAN teams together and provide access to existing host-based data and applications.

This grass-roots demand for information will be a major factor in helping redefine organizational networks. From the bottom up, these specialists are fueling the local area network's transition from data sharing—file, print, and relational—to a new generation of industrial-strength networks that will enable transparent access to critical resources wherever they reside, inside or outside the organization. This will provide a platform for robust, client/server line-of-business applications.

Moreover, their demand for access and connection will continue to grow. According to WorkGroup Technologies Inc., Hampton, NH, in 1990, the average number of workgroups in major corporations was 14. By 1993, that number is expected to more than double to 35. In the same time frame, the average number of clients per server will triple from 15 to 45. But more importantly, the average number of applications requiring communication beyond the workgroup will grow from 18 percent to 45 percent.

People and organizations drive LAN systems, and technology with its function and price performance enables them. This is a truly virtuous circle of productivity and competitiveness. While the requirement for connectivity beyond the workgroup is being driven, at least in part, by the user, cost pressures and investment protection are driving another set of requirements.

Traditional Tops-Down Requirements

While more and more corporate data is finding its way onto the LAN system, the degree to which organizations entrust it as the sole or major repository of their information will depend on the LAN's ability to deliver on the promise of providing the best of both workstation and host environments. This transition also will depend on the LAN system's ability to enable migration from and coexistence with existing applications and systems. Technology providers face three significant requirements:

- They must deliver LAN systems that are at least as robust, reliable, serviceable, manageable, and secure as the current generation of host systems.

- They must invest in the transparent networking capability to enable true client/server applications that execute across distributed platforms, regardless of which vendor's hardware and software is in place.

- They must provide a staged and easy migration to evolving technologies.

A New Generation of Hardware

During the past five years, dramatic improvements in graphics performance, ease of use, microprocessor speed, and memory size and cost have dramatically changed the desktop. At the same time, the connection has changed, and LAN and WAN bandwidth has increased to the point where distributed systems are possible. LAN systems support hundreds of thousands of organizations and departmental teams in large enterprises and whole corporations in small enterprises. In fact thus far, LAN systems are more accepted in small organizations than in large, host-experienced organizations. Yet, nowhere will you find a more dramatic shift than in the industry's perception of a host.

Depending on your viewpoint from the glass house, LANs may be thought of either as a new class of subsystem for existing mainframe and minicomputer systems, or, as an increasing number of MIS managers and industry analysts see it, as the new focus of the enterprise system with host resources being reassigned to serve LAN-based users. Although in many cases the host may continue to be a large mainframe or minicomputer, there will be more and more instances where the "computer" is a connection of desktops and servers—a single entity wherein each one of the components also may be a computer, a Dell running OS/2, an Apple Macintosh, or a PS/2 with NetWare running its own software as well.

This powerful mix of computer systems means that large organizations can meet both the bottoms-up and tops-down demands, connecting users to data and applications that are running on the most cost-effective platform. While some applications rightfully run at the desktop and some applications rightfully run at the host, many applications will run at the LAN system, distributed between clients and servers, because the LAN offers the best of both worlds—the ease of use and accessibility of the desktop and the high-volume processing and storage capacity of big iron. With cost pressures continuing to increase, the top-down pressure to make more effective use of all forms of technology will continue to mount.

In some cases, this push may mean upsizing, moving from a non-computerized solution to a computerized solution—once the capabilities and cost of the technology justify the decision. One customer referred to this decision as a migration from plywood and magnets, the company's manually controlled resource management system. Downsizing, on the other hand, refers to moving applications and data that once resided on a mainframe or minicomputer onto the LAN. And rightsizing means exploiting the full spectrum of technology to put data and applications where they can be accessed, processed, and managed most effectively.

As competitive and organizational pressures combine, they will force an evolution from workstations as personal productivity tools to workstations as part of true distributed applications. The requirement for a robust, easy-to-use, transparent interconnection that gives users access to all the information they need regardless of where it resides is forcing new requirements in terms of network reliability, availability, serviceability, manageability, security, and performance.

The Software Platform Comes of Age

To fulfill the requirements of the major organizational conduit of information, LAN systems—including the client, the server, and the interconnection—must be as robust as shared logic systems like Data General's MV/10000 with AOS/VS, the VMS Systems on VAX hardware from DEC, and the IBM AS/400 and ES/9000.

Systems such as IBM OS/2 2.0 and AIX as clients or servers have made dramatic advancements in their ability to exploit the capabilities of 32-bit hardware. OS/2 2.0 delivers enhanced crash protection, preemptive multitasking, an easy-to-use, object-oriented graphical user interface, and advanced networking capabilities. That situation, however, is not the case with traditional network operating systems—a new generation of technology is required. The software must enable the paradigm shift from desktop-focused sharing to network-focused distributed applications.

In addition to the power of the individual clients and servers, LAN systems must be reliable. They must deliver better "up time" than a mainframe or minicomputer, without losing the attractiveness of PC/workstation technology. This means performance as well as ease of use. Today, the impatient populace of computer-literate users expect their networked computer to deliver better response time than their local hard disk. Tomorrow, they will demand more availability than they get from a host.

In addition, LAN systems must provide the infrastructure for security and systems management. Security has many facets. Controlling access to applications and data is one. While current networks usually rely on simple password protection, password protection on individual systems becomes irksome in a distributed system with tens of different applications and servers. Tomorrow's network of thousands of nodes demands a more robust and manageable form of authentication. In the network that is evolving, security mechanisms must be sufficiently trustworthy to control access to valuable network resources such as high-capacity computer servers or printers with specialized capabilities like the magnetic ink character recognition (MICR) printers—used for issuing checks.

As many organizations have found already, systems management capabilities will be critical. Users are not interested in systems management issues. They do not expect to worry about backing up files, getting to a printer, configuring a server, or gaining assistance if there is a problem. Some organizations already live by the dictum "Don't distribute what you can't manage." Others will back into the dictum after untangling complex and crippling distributed systems management issues.

In its simplest form, systems management means a set of procedures and programs that supports configuration, installation, and distribution (CID) of both clients and servers. CID enables automatic configuration on the desktop—not only the operating system, but also the applications an individual wants at the workstation. CID capabilities will end an organization's reliance on "sneaker net" by automatically distributing and installing software over the network, either from a server in the department or from a host to a server to the desktop—without human interaction.

Systems management issues already are complex enough in a relatively static network environment. Yet, in the very near future, systems management issues will grow exponentially as dynamic network environments evolve with users having access from workstations, laptops, and personal data assistants (PDAs). These new LANs will be interconnected by telecommunication links for wide area access, and as prices for new equipment like computers and printers continue to drop, the network will remain in a constant state of flux as equipment is added and removed from the network on an hourly basis.

Delivering Open Systems

The potential of client/server computing and powerful distributed systems management will dramatically affect organizations as they begin to exploit

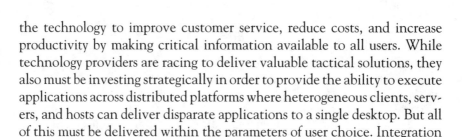

the technology to improve customer service, reduce costs, and increase productivity by making critical information available to all users. While technology providers are racing to deliver valuable tactical solutions, they also must be investing strategically in order to provide the ability to execute applications across distributed platforms where heterogeneous clients, servers, and hosts can deliver disparate applications to a single desktop. But all of this must be delivered within the parameters of user choice. Integration of the system must retain the individuality of user and organizational choice.

As a corporation, IBM has committed to delivering products—clients, servers, and hosts—that are built on open, industry standards. One set of standards is being driven by the Open Software Foundation (OSF), an organization that IBM and six other major computer vendors helped to form. The goal of OSF is to enable users to implement computing environments where systems and applications work together, locally, and globally, regardless of which vendor hardware and software is chosen.

Since its inception, a number of other corporations have joined OSF, and together these organizations are working to create an open system where critical components are consistent across platforms. Consistent technologies for key functions such as remote program execution, network time, security, and global directory services will enable true, cross-platform client/server capabilities—where it is possible to run a piece of an application here and a piece of it there, while still providing the ability to manage and support it with full problem determination capabilities.

To complete their responsibility to customers, technology providers must not only begin to migrate away from proprietary technologies toward this open environment, but also they must involve users in the evolution.

IBM has chosen to take a leadership role in developing key components that will become the foundation of the open environment. We also will take the first OSF technology and combine it with a number of other components into Distributed System Services (DSS), the core of a network that will support client/server computing on a LAN or across an enterprise. DSS will permit applications and data to reside any place that an individual or an organization decides.

Some pieces of DSS will come from IBM, like the way relational databases communicate with each other. But even in this area the solution will not be IBM-unique, as Oracle, Informix, and a number of other vendors have adopted or said they will support that form of database-to-database communication. Other components of DSS will include components created through industry consortia, vendor independent messaging (VIM), for example.

IBM's direction in client/server computing is to provide a distributed system infrastructure that can be used to access resources from any desktop or application, whether it is running on a client, a server, or a host—on DOS, AIX, OS/2 with LAN Server, NetWare, or another LAN-operating system, or on MVS or OS/400. The goal is to help protect our customers' existing investments in hardware, software, applications, and data while enabling the new capabilities of distributed computing.

The Need for APIs

In order to support the development of cross-platform, client/server, and distributed applications, technology providers also must provide stable industry-standard application programming interfaces (APIs) for the use of independent software vendors and other developers. These APIs should enable an application to execute on the workstation, the server, or the host without requiring the developer to worry about how the applications are realized.

In a distributed database application, for example, the stub of code in the client can give access to an SQL database, while the actual database can be resident on a client, server, or host. As long as the APIs are constant and industry-standard, it should not matter where the database or application is running. One advantage of this approach is transparent access to resources. From the application view, it will not matter where the database resides, and databases can be changed or substituted without affecting the application program.

In addition to a single set of constant APIs, the offering must include an API framework so that its services can be obtained transparently—even to the application programmer. For example, with an open API framework, an application could obtain relational data from OS/2 Database Manager, Sybase SQL Server, SQL/400, DB/2, and so forth, with no change to the

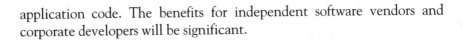

application code. The benefits for independent software vendors and corporate developers will be significant.

The Next Frontier

After providing systems management solutions and strategic investments in open systems and platforms, vendors must grapple with the challenge of providing a staged and easy migration to the future. One characteristic of that future is the hardware of PENs and PDAs which will alter the ratio of humans to clients in the network. Another is object-oriented distributed systems.

Today, a single person is most often represented to the network as one system. As hardware technology advances and supports connected systems, PEN capabilities and PDAs will dramatically alter the network system environment. A single person will "be" multiple systems. Yet, that person will expect transparent access from any system, expecting the network to handle security, access, sharing, and management.

Another frontier, object encapsulation, provides key capabilities such as code reuse and easy extendibility, offering the promise of major improvements in programmer productivity as applications are reengineered to exploit the distributed LAN environment.

Next-generation technologies will enable completely distributed objects to be implemented, allowing access to objects located anywhere in a network. The goal is to provide a path to a completely object-oriented system, where industrial strength APIs permit transparent access to objects. This provision will enable customers and independent software vendors to optimize their productivity through reuse of these objects. It also will enable end users to develop sophisticated custom applications to meet their needs, without requiring an in-depth knowledge of programming.

A Paradigm Shift

Although technology and service providers tend to get caught up in the connection mechanisms, users will force them to stay focused on the core issue of providing people with the information they need, brought to them in a form they can use and understand.

Grappling with implementation issues is a tremendous challenge for technology providers; the pressure is reshaping the computer industry. There is movement from proprietary to open systems. Companies that compete now also work together, and the line between customer and supplier often blurs.

The key is to choose a service provider that will support an organization through its entire transition from today's environment, of stand-alone applications linked together to share data, and into a world where the full power of distributed computing is realized. That means choosing a provider that is not tied to a single technology, but instead is committed to the vision of interconnected workgroups functioning together in an open environment to provide users with all the information they need to do their jobs effectively, efficiently, and competitively.

Networked Databases:
A Key to Computing Vitality

by *Richard Rabins*
Co-Chairman, Alpha Software Corporation

Author Bio

Richard Rabins founded Alpha Software Corporation in 1982, to develop a PC-based software that brings the highest degree of functionality and ease of use while recognizing existing industry standards.

Rabins came to the industry as a management consultant and marketing executive for Management Decision Systems, Inc. (MDS), a vendor of decision-support software based in Waltham, MA. At MDS, he devised marketing strategies for companies such as R.J. Reynolds, Kimberley Clark, and Carnation Foods.

Rabins holds a master's degree in both engineering and business administration from the Massachusetts Institute of Technology, Cambridge, MA.

He is also one of two cofounders of the Massachusetts Software Council and is currently serving as president for the organization. Rabins is a frequent speaker and panelist at industry conferences.

Executive Summary

Databases can be one of the most challenging, yet rewarding, applications to offer within a networked environment. A company and even a department can gain much through shared data access. The database you select to handle your company's critical information and the way you handle data are crucial to the success of your database, because they can aid or impede all of your data operations. However, a number of risks are associated with sharing data on a network. When these risks are known and understood, they can be addressed and eliminated.

A company's critical information is typically housed within its database management system. This information may range from customer records, to sales and receipts of products, to customer satisfaction, to internal shipping records or inventory control. In order to function efficiently, all the data must be accessed by many users simultaneously. That is why the Networked Database is so important to day-to-day operations. Without it, the company could not function. How this information is handled, therefore, is of tantamount importance. And how information is handled depends greatly on the database management system selected.

The database you select to handle your company's critical information is even more important than how you handle your data because the database can aid or impede data entry, data access, data update, and data storage. Certain database characteristics, however, help to simplify the process of information-handling over a network. These characteristics range from ease-of-learning, to ease-of-use, to end user empowerment.

Ease-of-Learning

As networking makes databases accessible to more and more end users at the departmental level, the task of bringing an entire department up-to-speed using the database can be frightening . A lot of risk is at hand, and a lot of time is involved. The risky situations cannot be avoided, but they can be diminished. Additionally, although the time to train cannot be eliminated, it can be greatly reduced.

Ease-of-learning not only affects users initially, it also can extend positive effects to advanced users ready to tackle more complex steps within the program. An easy-to-learn database makes it possible to have more users at the higher tier of product knowledge so that you can build a base of advanced users as well as competent ones. The time involved to learn a networked product doesn't increase necessarily over its single-user cousin. Because the networked database is accessed by numerous users with varying skill levels, however, finding a system with a learning curve acceptable for beginners and a feature set rich enough for expert users is no small feat.

Ease-of-Use

Ease-of-use becomes increasingly important, again, because of the sheer volume of users. If not well monitored a large number of users can create a real strain on the MIS department. A database that is at once intuitive, simple, and powerful is the one that will gain greatest use on the network. Because of the wide range of users, the database easiest to use will be the most beneficial one to all who use the network.

Even skilled programmers appreciate the ability to select the right tool for the job when faced with a basic application development task. Writing code may not be necessary when designing a simple mailing list. Developing an application by outlining it may be the simplest, most efficient solution in some instances, while at other times, a more complex database programming solution is required.

An easy-to-learn, easy-to-use database adds up to an independent community of users within an organization capable of learning and using a powerful product to create robust database solutions. This computing self-sufficiency allows MIS to focus on projects that usually demand cross-corporate integration and that require programming capability.

Empowering the End User

What kind of solutions can the newly liberated computer user design? With the advent of the relational database available across a network, even novice users can build elegant database solutions for themselves and their departments, even the whole company. End user computing is no longer contained to the simple word processing or spreadsheet package. With pull-down menus, buttons, and dialog boxes, users can push the envelope of database design.

Today network users are fully capable of building slick, powerful applications previously reserved for the programming elite. However, in order to design the robust database applications required, users need a system with powerful features accessible through a logical menu-driven interface.

A database designed for the business user provides everyone with quick access to solutions. Those at the department level now are able to help themselves, and those with solutions that honestly require programming can demand attention from MIS. The net effect is a diminished backlog within MIS and a pool of happy database users.

Information Handling

Installing an easy-to-learn, easy-to-use database is only the first step (although a major breakthrough) in developing a secure data system. Still to come is the responsibility for proper information handling. Several instances during the data handling process can be looked to as critical points in maintaining data integrity. We will focus here on some of the issues necessary to ensure successful handling of the information housed within a corporate or departmental database.

Data Entry

The data entry process represents the greatest risk for human error. In a networked environment, the process is challenged by many users entering data at the same time. The more people responsible for data entry, the greater the chance for error. However, if designed properly, the database can incorporate certain checks that help to prevent data corruption. For example, you can design field rules that make data entry faster and more accurate, look-up tables that contain field options, trigger events that automatically occur in response to an entry, and templates that require fixed characters in a field. Also, you can add required fields so that all the pertinent information must be entered before the record is saved. By specifying criteria in the application's design, the data entry process will be faster, easier, and, most importantly, more accurate to protect the integrity of the data at that initial step.

Other crucial aspects of the multiuser database management system include protecting confidential information and ensuring that data is not lost or files corrupted when multiple users access and update the same databases simultaneously.

File Access

Perhaps the most widely recognized advantage of networked databases is simultaneous access to files across the network. The convenience of accessing shipping records while looking up part numbers is a great boon to productivity. This convenience is not without its complications however. One safeguard on a networked database is to install various levels of password protection. This way, information that may be confidential to the accounting department cannot be accessed by other departments. By designing a tiered password-protected system, only authorized personnel will have access to sensitive information.

Record Updating

If file access is acknowledged as the great boon to networked database management systems, surely record updating is recognized as the biggest challenge to successful networked computing. Networked database designers have taken every care to maintain the integrity of the data, not only through the use of passwords, but also through other methods such as record locking and global updating.

When more than one person is working on a database, record locking is essential! Record locking automatically prevents multiple users from making changes to the same record simultaneously. Once the record is accessed in the change mode, that record is "locked." Other users will be able to view the record, but will be unable to change that record in any way.

Another important feature to watch for is global updating. It saves hours of data entry time and ensures accuracy by updating all the records in a database with one command.

Conclusion

Databases can be one of the most challenging, yet rewarding, applications to offer within a networked environment. A company and even a department can gain much through shared data access. Some of the rewards can range from simultaneous access of up-to-the-minute shipping and inventory information to robust sales lead tracking and in-depth analysis. The benefits of shared data on a network are apparent. Because the risks are known and understood, they can be addressed and eliminated prior to implementation.

Recycle Computers: Pass It On!

by Alexander Randall
Executive Director, East West Educational Development Foundation

Author Bio

Alex Randall and his wife created the Boston Computer Exchange. He is author of *Alex Randall's Used Computer Handbook* and executive director of the East West Educational Development Foundation. Randall also produces a weekly computer news program, SoundByte News, and writes the "Well-Wired Entrepreneur" column for *Success* magazine. Randall holds advanced degrees from Princeton University and Columbia University, including a doctorate in general systems research. He lives on Beacon Hill.

East West Educational Development Foundation
Recycling-Refurbishing-Reusing Computers
(617) 542-1234

Executive Summary

The decay in the cost of the average new computer system has reduced the value of the original IBM PC, XT, and AT to below the threshold for cash sales in the secondary market. These popular computers are now donation items. Owners of older technology are given suggestions for recycling their computers to keep them in use. They may not be worth much cash, but they are useful technology to someone with simple needs. To meet this change in the market, national donation clearinghouses have emerged. Readers are advised to seek a donation clearinghouse that can appraise their equipment, handle it, refurbish it, and place it in a new setting. East West Education Development Foundation is an example of such a clearinghouse.

Computer recycling is becoming a topic for more and more computer users. The wave of new technology and the rush forward into new systems means that you are less satisfied with the computer on your desk. What do you do with the old computer when you get the new one you want?

Don't put it in the warehouse or closet! Your computer may be old to you, but it's not old to everyone below you on the ladder of technology. With 50 million computers on the planet and five billion people, only one percent of us have personal computers. Lots of people still may think of your old, dusty turbo XT as a shot into the future.

Corporations, like individuals, need to plan the disposition of older computers and channel them to sites where they will do the most good—for the next-in-line and for the bottom line.

Five possible paths exist for the disposition of a computer that is older, used, and being displaced.

1. Add boards or swap motherboards to make the old computer as good as a new one: that's not true. Add-on components never perform as well as the same components in a system designed for them. The cost of tech and setup time raises the cost above new systems. So, this path is not recommended.

2. Pass it down to the lower level staff in your own office. Known as office trickle down, this works until the organization is saturated or you can't handle the technical incompatibilities.

3. Sell it to a staff member to take home. This works as long as the staff will take computers in as-is condition and as long as this policy won't gobble up support-staff time trying to get displaced computers to work at home. While sounding like a nice idea, it is fraught with problems—who sets the value, are software licenses included, who will take time to ensure that older computers are still working?

4. Sell it through professional services. Professionals are prepared to do this work, and depending on the level of work they and your staff perform, selling a computer in this matter can provide a significant return on the original investment. This option works as long as there are cash buyers for old equipment.

5. Donate the equipment to a national charity clearinghouse that will refurbish the equipment and place it in critical charities where it will be a "new" computer to them. This works for all levels of computers. The best organizations can take gear as-is and refurbish it before placing it. Also, tax advantages for making donations of computers might result in more value than if you assume the workload of selling yourself.

The donation option catches up with each older generation of computers. The original IBM PC is out of the market, and so is the XT. With the price declines in 1992, the IBM AT with a 286 processor joined the ranks of computers without cash buyers—it became a donation item. This is because the average system that an average office worker needs in an average office setting has fallen below $1,000. This has pushed the AT era computers out of the cash market.

The decline in computer prices for popular microcomputers has continued throughout the entire age of the industry. Computers have a 40 percent price decline on start-up and lose all but about 10 percent of their value within two to three years. They have a shelf life similar to fresh produce. Computers should be depreciated over the shortest possible time because they run out of buyers faster than any other capital investment.

What's ironic is that while computers lose their value faster than typical office equipment, they do not stop being useful or powerful tools for empowering their users. Even the oldest personal computer is still hundreds of times more powerful than the latest typewriter or calculator. What is old and over-the-hill to an aggressive user is rocket fuel to the charity or school.

While American business took to the computer like "business-as-usual," the American school system and charitable community have just begun to get the word that the future is in handling information and that computers are information utility tools.

What's needed is for all computer users, individuals, corporations, and our government, to adopt a policy about recycling computers. We should plan their reuse to ensure that the disadvantaged have access and that the schools can teach young people the rudiments of computer technology.

Computer technology is different than any previous technology and has evolved faster than any technology in history. It changed from massive room-filling monsters to palmtops in 45 years. It is generic, mind-augmenting technology. It should never be idle, but reused and reused.

Hundreds of large organizations use tens of thousands of personal computers. A PC five to eight years old, and obsolete to corporate managers spending most of their time working on a laptop, isn't worthless. It just needs a new home.

At this moment, a teacher somewhere is trying to convey a sense of the modern world with textbooks and blackboards to students raised on MTV. Meanwhile, tons of last-generation computers gather dust because their owners have moved on and put them in storage.

This country makes a big fuss about recycling five-cent aluminum cans and pennies worth of newspaper, but has no strategy for dealing with thousand-dollar motherboards.

This technology should be flowing out of corporate America into schools. It should pass through the levels of the community of users as quickly as it develops.

American corporations should be encouraged by appropriate tax deduction incentives to pass the older computers on to the not-for-profit community as quickly as the users require more powerful tools.

When the nation sees a need to improve the educational system, yet lacks the funds in the public sector to purchase the technology of the future, isn't it appropriate for our corporations to pass their just past state-of-the-art computers to the schools and the service sectors?

There are no losers in this plan. Corporations get to reach for the technology that will make them competitive; schools get the computers they have little chance of purchasing. Down the line, older hardware will pass through the donation channel to lower and lower level users.

Is Your Data Really Safe?
Will It Be Next Year?

by Lawrence D. Rogers
Emerald Systems

Author Bio

Dr. Lawrence D. Rogers, Emerald Systems' executive vice president, over-sees engineering as well as product and business development for the company. He has more than 25 years' experience in advanced computer technologies.

Emerald Systems Corporation, with headquarters in San Diego, California, and the Netherlands, provides network backup and storage management solutions for Novell LANs worldwide. In addition to a broad range of tape backup drives in 1/4-inch, DAT, and 8mm formats, the company offers innovative software that gives network administrators many advanced, easy-to-use storage management capabilities in the Microsoft Windows environment.

Executive Summary

This paper explores, by example, today's and tomorrow's problems of protecting valuable, distributed corporate data in LANs while optimizing the use of storage. It discusses the evolution of networks, the demands that these will place on network data protection/management solutions, and how the problems will be solved.

Protection of valuable, distributed corporate data in LANs is a task that commonly has fallen to inexperienced departmental network administrators. The backup, restore, off-site vaulting, and archive pieces of this responsibility are a difficult set of complex tasks—tasks that often conflict with basic human nature. As one sage assessed, "It is a technological problem with a political answer." How well are *you* doing? What is your opinion on how best to perform these data management functions in the LAN environment?

Backup Test

	Yes	No
1. Is backup always done on schedule, or is it sometimes missed or incomplete?	☐	☐
2. Are the backups always fully verified?	☐	☐
3. Are network securities fully backed up and successfully restored?	☐	☐
4. Are all nodes and LANs included in your backup/restore policies?	☐	☐

		Yes	No
5.	Are you successfully supporting all the OS/file systems on your network?	☐	☐
6.	Is the window of exposure and risk between backups suitably small?	☐	☐
7.	Does your backup time-window allow sufficient time for your backup program to complete?	☐	☐
8.	Are the backup tapes periodically tested to prove that they can be restored?	☐	☐
9.	Does your system adequately track your backup files and tapes?	☐	☐
10.	Are files restored easy?	☐	☐
11.	Have you planned for managing your disk capacity growth?	☐	☐
12.	Are you managing file clutter and keeping your disk expansion costs in line?	☐	☐
13.	Is there clear filelevel traceability to your archives and off-site records?	☐	☐
14.	Are there fully implemented backup, archiving, and disaster-protection plans, and have they been tested?	☐	☐

Test Cases

The following two scenarios are presented as samples of real-life situations at two companies that use PC LANs. Only the names are changed to protect their identity. Your challenge is to identify what could be improved in these examples. Then apply the test criteria to your own LAN. Evaluate how your LAN and your own data management practices compare.

Scenario 1: Corporation A, Los Angeles, California

The network consists of 17 local servers running NetWare 3.11, and 5 additional servers in New York running NetWare 2.15. There are 1,800 clients on the network with another seven-hundred 3270 terminals scheduled to be converted to the LAN in 1992. The local servers have 15G of data, mirrored. Only 300 of the nodes have hard disk drives. Capacity growth is 100 percent per year.

The backup system consists of seven 8mm tape drives (one for every three servers plus a spare). A workstation-based backup system was chosen because of concerns about impacting the servers. Full backups are performed nightly for simplicity. Tape mounts and tape rotation are managed manually but are sometimes forgotten because the backup duty is rotated among the supervisors.

Backups do not always occur on all servers because of the amount of manual support required. File restores are also a mess and take a lot of time. A network administrator has to perform this function for the users. There have been as many as 15 single file restores per week. Users are told to be happy if they "can even get their files back." The 300 nodes with hard disks are not backed up by the system. Those users are on their own unless they copy their files up to the server.

Scenario 2: Corporation B, San Francisco, California

The network runs on two Novell servers running version 2.15 and four Banyan servers. There are 130 nodes with 33 on the NetWare side, all of which have access to the Oracle database server running under Banyan. Total disk capacity is 6.7G on the servers and another 4G on clients. Twenty-five percent of the nodes are diskless. Capacity growth on the existing systems will be 50 percent in 1992, but another 1.5G and another 100 nodes also will be added to the LAN due to downsizing. Five branch offices are coming online, increasing the network even further.

Backup is performed on the two Novell servers using a single 8mm drive. The Banyan servers are backed up using Banyan's backup utility with 4mm drives. The Oracle server is backed up to its own tape drive with third-party Banyan-compatible software. Clients are not included. At the branch offices, the users are untrained in backup. They are currently on their own. "We do not support them," a company spokesman says. "There are virtually no single-file restores because we discourage it." Under Banyan, it takes a long time and places a heavy load on the server. "Capacity expansion currently is not a problem. Disk space is so cheap that file clutter is not of much concern. However, we do have too many instances of the Banyan servers running out of disk space because users will copy full directories to the server. We periodically do a manual file deletion, but mostly we just buy more disk drives." The Oracle server is shut down at 5 p.m. on Friday for backup. Otherwise, it is online 24 hours per day. Restores are done only by a network administrator. There have been too many occurrences of a user overwriting shared files on one of the servers.

Now look at your own situation and take the test. Think also about what it costs to manage storage in your LAN network. Do you even know? Other questions can be asked. How fast are file transfers on your network? Did you know that you can measure this? Is your backup system optimized for the performance of your network? Can you perform single file restores easily? Can your users? Are all your important, valuable corporate data well protected? Is it also off-site and current? How large is your exposure between backups and off-site archives? How good are your backups? Have they been tested? Have you exposed yourself to an independent audit? These and other critical questions need to be asked of your systems.

What Is the Problem?

The problem with backup is that there are so many issues and decisions to make that are site specific. In our two test cases, there are many faults in the backup/restore systems that should be changed. Some of the key points are these:

- Even though both companies are using "unattended" backup software, they are still manual systems that require substantial

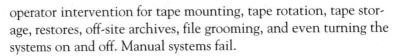

operator intervention for tape mounting, tape rotation, tape storage, restores, off-site archives, file grooming, and even turning the systems on and off. Manual systems fail.

- For many companies the backup window is closing, especially for performing full backups every evening. But incremental backups on multiple servers vastly increases the media management issues beyond the bounds of reasonable manual techniques. Automated help is available in today's data management software.

- Every network is unique in some ways. Tying together heterogeneous networks increases the management difficulties. Yet this is today's reality. Enterprise-wide solutions and services are needed—not mixed, incompatible solutions like those found in company B. Better solutions are available that use, for example, the NetWare namespace conventions to provide backup and data management functions for other network operating systems. Administrators should take advantage of NetWare's namespace capability to integrate these heterogeneous systems. Backup and other management jobs then will be easier. True heterogeneous network support is still a future event.

- Do these companies have procedures and policies in place that are right for them? It is apparent that there are large gaps in their backup strategies. For example, Corporation B does backup on the Oracle server only weekly. What a large risk! Even once-per-day backup can be inadequate. The cost to reconstruct 1M of data has been estimated at more than $2,500. How much can you afford to lose?

- Neither company has a program in place to verify the restore capabilities of their backups and archives. This is a tedious hassle, but as many companies have discovered after being unable to restore data due to incorrect procedures, it is a necessary one.

- Both companies require administrator involvement in performing restores. It is not uncommon to find each restore event taking 30 minutes to one hour. Programs utilizing a disk-based database/librarian, such as Emerald Systems' Xpress Librarian software, can reduce this time dramatically. Systems such as these are well suited to future automation of user-initiated restores that will have yet more payback.

Managing disk capacity growth is a problem for these companies. Corporation A reports purchasing on the order of $75,000 worth of disk drives per year. Corporation B reports running out of disk space "too often." What about using file-migration/file-grooming applications that will reduce this nonstop, uncontrolled growth? Many surveys have measured that 30 to 50 percent of all data files have not been accessed in more than 90 days, and most of them do not need to be on hard disk storage.[1] A number of integrated backup/file-grooming solutions are available to manage this process. Constructing a Backup and Archive Planning Profile on each of your LANs will help you see the advantages of such an approach and will help to scale the file-grooming problem. Mapping the "frequency of change" of the files on each of your servers is paramount to constructing a proper backup and data management strategy.

In summary, some key points can be made about these two examples. Both companies are spending too much time and too much money manually interacting with the backup and restore process. Explosive disk capacity growth is being tolerated as the "lesser of evils." Continuing to buy more disk drives is a "Band-Aid" approach that eventually will catch up with them. Both companies have a large degree of exposure and risk in their data management policies. Yet in many respects they are not unique.

The best of today's data management solutions, such as Emerald Systems' Xpress Librarian, would ease their problems and should be utilized. The cost of data management technology is an inexpensive tradeoff compared to the cost of not upgrading your data management practices as your LAN network grows and evolves.

Backup and Archive Planning Profile

- **Server Characteristics (per LAN segment)**
  Name, Location, NOS Type, Hardware Type, File Systems/OS Supported, Protocols Routed, Network Topology, Communication Links, Backup Device Type & Topology

[1]*Source: Peripheral Strategies, Inc.*

- **Server I/O**
  Disk Sizes, Types, Backup Speed (e.g., 5M/min)

- **Client I/O (if direct backup support is planned)**
  Disk Sizes, Types, Backup Speed (e.g., 5M/min)

- **Backup Load Determination (example numbers)**

Frequency of Change/Access	Amount of Data (M)	Backup Time* (Minutes)
Change daily	120	24
Change weekly	300	60
Change monthly	1,080	216
Change quarterly	900	180
Unchanged >90 days	3,600	720
Unaccessed >90 days	1,260	252
Unaccessed >180 days	1,800	360

*Backup time is the amount of data/backup speed (M/min).

PC LAN Evolution

The typical PC LAN network is evolving in some predictable directions, all of which are contributing to the creation of a crisis in storage management. The move toward enterprise-wide networks not only brings together multiple sites but brings with it incremental growth and complexity. In 1992, 44 percent of all business PCs were connected to LANs. By 1996, this is expected to grow to 80 percent.[2]

This means that the average number of nodes per network doubles. Although the average disk capacity per PC is relatively small, a 100-node LAN today easily will have 4G of distributed data on the clients, not

[2]Source: Peripheral Strategies, Inc.

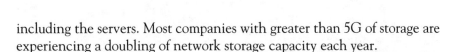

including the servers. Most companies with greater than 5G of storage are experiencing a doubling of network storage capacity each year.

How do companies deal with this growth? The universal answer is, "Buy more disk drives." Remember that users demand to have all their files online all the time. Is storage being used efficiently? All the factors of out-of-control growth, escalating costs, declining productivity, and decreasing performance contribute to the prediction that we are heading rapidly into a storage management crisis. A typical LAN with 5G of disk capacity may have 300,000 files under management. People cannot manage gigabytes of files manually. Even worse, they won't.

The option of continuing to add more disk drives eventually becomes cost prohibitive. Thus, a crisis forms. You can't afford to shut down the network to fix the file clutter problem, nor can you afford the $50,000 in disk drives for the next expansion increment.

Crisis in Storage Management

- The PC connectivity rate is driving network growth.

- Storage capacity can't keep up with the data explosion.

- Adding more disk drives is a "Band-Aid" solution.

- The overnight backup window is disappearing.

- Complex heterogeneous networks need professional management.

- The cost of network management is burgeoning.

Next-Generation Solutions

If we accept that the basic set of user needs can be summarized as follows, then what will soon be needed is a new approach and a new class of storage management solutions.

User Needs

- High data availability

- High reliability

- High-performance data transfer

- High storage capacity

- Automated, transparent background operation

- Understandable interfaces

- Easy operation

- Reduced cost of ownership

- Transparent file access across heterogeneous networks

How will this be achieved? Many events need to occur to bring all these solutions together into a set of viable products. Fundamentally, the network operating systems must enable storage management across heterogeneous networks. Novell is pioneering this evolution under the umbrella of its Storage Management Services (SMS) program. SMS is not a backup system, as is commonly believed. It is a program to put the plumbing and capabilities into the NOS to enable storage management.

In parallel, new technologies must emerge. Many new features are being added to current products to offer enhanced data management. But the real solution to the capacity, availability, and performance problem will come about when all storage media is integrated into a storage hierarchy. Every file and data set is categorized by its storage class, then stored by the system on the lowest cost media that can support its performance requirements. Backup and disaster recovery operations also are performed automatically. All of this is transparent to the user.

This capability will be enabled by a new product class called a storage server. A storage server is a dedicated application that operates continuously. Its role in the network is to provide automated network storage services. With a fast CPU, a large hard disk, optimized bus and I/O, and with an optical jukebox or a tape library, the storage server application can automate multiple storage management functions, reduce error-prone operator interaction, and optimize the use of storage while providing data availability to the user. With operating system changes, this new class of products will perform these functions transparently, requiring network administrator and user interaction only to set control parameters, not to perform all the actions.

What to Do Today

Back to the business at hand. The best advice we can give you is to begin with knowing the characteristics of your particular LAN. Take the test and address any particular shortcomings it identifies. Also, construct backup profiles and archives on each of your servers, measure your backup speeds, determine your file aging profiles, determine the costs of operating the way you are, and buy and implement the best data management software and systems that match your needs. Finally, be sure to plan for the growth and changes that will happen to your networks. Are your data management systems keeping up with these changes?

Communications Technology Overview

by John P. Rohal
Managing Director
Alex. Brown & Sons Incorporated

Author Bio

John P. Rohal is a managing director and co-head of Technology Securities Research at Alex. Brown & Sons. As a senior analyst, he specializes in the Communications Technology sector with emphasis on local area networking, wide area networking, internetworking, voice processing, and videoconferencing.

Mr. Rohal has been a technology analyst for 9 years with Alex. Brown and has previously covered the Design Automation and the Networked Computing sectors. Before joining Alex. Brown, he spent 15 years in the computer industry with IBM, Honeywell, and Martin Marietta holding management positions in sales, marketing, and planning.

Mr. Rohal has a Bachelor of Science degree from West Virginia University and a Master of Business Administration degree from the University of Pennsylvania Wharton School. He also attended Georgetown University Law Center and the University of California, Los Angeles, engineering extension. Mr. Rohal has been a guest journalist in various trade publications, including *Computer Systems News*, *Computer Graphics World*, and *Upside Magazine*.

Alex. Brown & Sons Incorporated is a national specialty firm headquartered in Baltimore with 21 offices around the country. The firm also has an office in London that serves as a base for international operations. Alex. Brown is considered the nation's leading firm in providing investment banking services to growth companies in eight key industries: technology, health care, environmental services, transportation, media communication services, energy, and consumer services.

Executive Summary

A series of powerful trends in business, government, information systems, and personal lifestyles continues to fuel the growth in communications. Although many of these trends are well-known concepts—such as globalism, networked computing, enterprise-wide systems, and third-world infrastructure development—we believe it is still early in the life cycle of their impact on communications industry growth. Our communications technology investment strategy focuses on the two most powerful forces driving growth— networked computing and productivity enhancement—each of which creates growth rates in market segments ranging from 25 percent to over 100 percent annually:

- *Networked computing*—This concept involves linking rapidly expanding desktop computers into local and enterprise-wide systems with sophisticated communications networks.

- *Productivity enhancement tools*—Because a large share of the workday is spent attempting to access information or providing information through person-to-person or person-to-machine communications, the ability to improve productivity in communicating produces powerful cost-time savings.

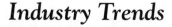

Industry Trends

We believe the long-term growth prospects of the communications industry are very attractive. As in most large industries, some market segments are mature with slow or no growth while young markets are growing explosively. Before defining the characteristics of the various segments, it is important to review the key trends that play a broad role in the growth of communications.

Globalism

Worldwide markets create worldwide companies with immense communications requirements when enterprise-wide systems are built. We do not yet know whether communications for global enterprises is a new business or an overlay integrating a matrix of existing country-defined businesses. The new global business model would provide a competing alternative to the country-based systems, that is, Cable and Wireless competing for corporate communications business in the U.S. This trend provides opportunity for communications technology vendors in internetworking and in wide area networking, but competition increases for the transmission services companies, AT&T, MCI, and Sprint.

Deregulation, Privatization, Alternative Providers, and Duopolies

Governments around the world are using a variety of measures to challenge the traditional telephone service utility. This process is creating competition for the service providers. The infrastructure of communications networks must be upgraded to stay competitive. Leading communications technology vendors will benefit from the process of upgrading network infrastructures as service providers are forced to lower costs and increase performance.

Technology

The big performance gain in moving from copper wiring systems to fiber optics systems is yet to come. We recently wrote an article titled "Zero Cost

Communications" (*Upside Magazine*, December 1990) to dramatize the likely decline in the cost of transferring a single bit of information across a communications network. As in computer memories, technology will drive the cost per bit toward zero.

The lower transmission costs and higher performance will encourage image and data communications that directly help videoconferencing, LANs, and internetworking market segments. A variety of content-rich, network-based services also should emerge.

Standards

Unlike computing, standards have played a key role in public communications networks for many years. Unfortunately, standards historically have tended to retard rather than stimulate innovation. To deal with the increased pace of technological change and expanded networking requirements, greater emphasis is being placed on accelerating the development of standards.

Standards are gaining influence over broader ranges of communications technology and increasing vendor risk as regards product conformity and transitions. Standards have increased competition in low-value-added products but have less influence as product sophistication expands.

Online Enterprise

In September 1989, Alex. Brown's technology analysts wrote the "On-Line Enterprise" report to describe events leading up to enterprise-wide information systems. By definition, the online enterprise envisions a communications-intensive environment that stimulates LAN and internetworking growth and has the following results:

- The communications traffic mix evolves from roughly two-thirds voice traffic and one-third data traffic to a new mix with data traffic representing the majority of the volume.

- With data traffic in the majority, packetizing gains stature as the transfer technology of choice.

- Data traffic continues to grow at rates exceeding 30 percent annually through the decade.

- Multimedia networking becomes a natural by-product of the online enterprise and networked computing.

Industry Characteristics

The previously listed trends stimulate growth in communications traffic volume. However, the growth comes with the challenges of increased competition, price pressure, uncertain regulatory processes, and volatile technology and standards. To deal with these challenges, most communications technology vendors focus their efforts on a piece of the overall communications network solution. Unfortunately, only a few of the communications technology market segments have reached multi-billion-dollar revenue levels. Today's communications technology industry can be characterized as follows:

- Markets tend to fracture rather than aggregate as they mature, thereby keeping segments relatively small.

- Many small, highly focused vendors operate in tightly defined markets with a few well-established vendors in the large markets.

- Alternative technology solutions often represent a greater competitive threat than the traditional competitors within the market; for example, the flexibility of routers changed the market for high-end bridges.

- Vertical product integration is more difficult than acquiring competitors for increased scale.

- Network performance and reliability are critical whether achieved with a single vendor or by integrating multiple vendors into a single network.

- We prefer vendors selling to end users rather than to transmission services providers; end users have less concentrated buying power.

- Many international markets are restricted by old regulatory processes and communications networks that badly lag current digital technology and retard growth. They, however represent huge infrastructure upgrade opportunities.

- Network integration services have been performed by users, value-added resellers, local and regional network integrators (including distributors), communications services providers, and most recently, the major information systems integrators—for example, GM-EDS and Andersen Consulting—as networks have evolved from a specialty to a functionality provided by professional services firms.

- Network management functionality has been provided on a top-down and bottom-up basis but not well integrated overall—the network management tools market represents an interesting opportunity, but it is not yet well-defined.

Industry Framework

To help investors understand how the various communications technology markets interrelate, we have developed a communications framework (see Figure 41.1). Our framework divides communications technology into four areas of interest. We use the following characteristics to define the framework:

Type of Communications Traffic

- Data—now one-third of the volume but growing at more than 30 percent annually, and likely to be the majority of traffic volume long term.

- Voice—now two-thirds of the volume, but growing at single-digit rates in the U.S.

Location of Communications Traffic

- Local network (location dependent)—the traffic is in close proximity to its origin and flows within the "local system."

- Wide area network (location independent)—the traffic leaves the "local system" to be sent through public or private wide area networks to any variety of locations that may be relatively close or widely dispersed.

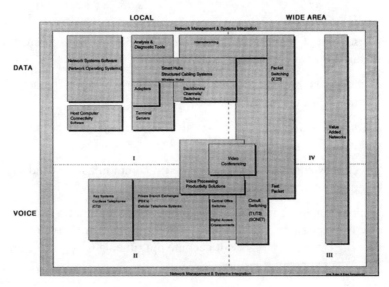

Figure 41.1. Communications technology framework.

We believe this framework provides a visual representation of how the markets and vendors relate to users' communications requirements. The typical framework used to define a computer-communications architecture, the seven-layer open systems interconnection (OSI) reference model, can act as a third dimension to define the functional roles of data communications vendors (the top half of the framework in Figure 41.1). The data communications hardware vendors, that is, Hubs, care most about the lowest layers of the OSI model whereas software companies, such as Novell, tend to move up the model, which offers increased product value-added and competitive differentiation. Many communications technology products integrate hardware and software to provide a solution. Higher software content often increases the complexity, functionality, and differentiability of the system level product.

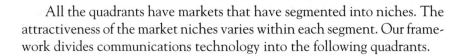

All the quadrants have markets that have segmented into niches. The attractiveness of the market niches varies within each segment. Our framework divides communications technology into the following quadrants.

Quadrant I

The intersection of "data" and "local" provides information systems tools used to gain corporate competitive advantage:

- Highest growth quadrant—benefits from growth trends in data communications and LANs.

- Attractive strategic position—deals with the large population of end users.

- Coveted by computer companies—both communications and computer companies want to own this space.

- Standards gaining importance—computing requirements provide a driving force since the transport vehicles (LANs) are private networks for data; LANs will become multimedia (data, voice and video) networks in the future.

Quadrant II

The intersection of "voice" and "local" provides personal communications productivity:

- Large but mature—technology replacement cycles provide key growth waves for the largest segment—PBX.

- Enhanced services stimulate demand—system performance and functionality expand to provide the new services and thereby generate increased network traffic.

- Productivity tools gain acceptance—voice messaging evolves toward integrating voice processing, FAX, and electronic mail applications to create business solutions.

- International opportunities abound—public and private networks must be upgraded to current digital technology and expanded to reach more of the world's population.

Quadrant III

The intersection of "voice" and "wide area" provides transmission at increasingly lower costs:

- Price stimulated growth—highly competitive carriers have driven down costs and prices, resulting in boosted traffic.

- Regulatory upheaval—Tariff 12 gave AT&T the ability to competitively price transmission services and also recapture private network traffic; this created an investors' "tariff trap" as companies built on the economics of the old tariff structure found their markets collapsing.

- Multiple technology transitions—users are uncertain regarding selection of the wide area technologies of the future and, therefore, are slow to make decisions.

- The boundary between Quadrant III and Quadrant IV continues to deteriorate—wide area networks often transport both voice and data traffic, and the trend will accelerate in the future, particularly if voice traffic is packetized.

- Weak strategic position of technology vendors—public network carriers have greater buying power and emphasis on standards (ability to exert price pressure) than the private network owners.

Quadrant IV

The intersection of "data" and "wide area" provides the big growth opportunity in transmission:

- Strong volume growth—benefits from growth trends in data communications and from competitive carriers lowering pricing; linearity of growth may be difficult.

- Vendors' strategic position weakening—public carriers are eroding the role of private networks—this may be a big-players-only game in the long term.

- Computer companies can't decide how to participate—because services in this quadrant are data-intensive, the computer companies are interested, but WANs are unlike LANs—watch for a lot of change.

- Standards gaining importance—the increased role of the public networks and the need to integrate enterprise-wide systems are driving standards.

- Big performance gains coming—metropolitan area networks (MANs) and Switched Multimegabit Data Service (SMDS) should provide the technology for public networks to internetwork LANs at LAN speeds, thereby stimulating additional LANs and internetworking for enterprise-wide systems.

Quadrant boundaries are being attacked by the evolution of technology. As mentioned earlier, the boundary between data and voice in the WAN continues to erode as users look for cost-effective transport solutions regardless of traffic type. In fact, all boundaries are likely to become "gray areas" transitioning with new technologies. For example, the boundary between Quadrant I (LANs) and Quadrant IV (WANs) is well-defined today with different technologies in each quadrant. In the future, WANs are likely to evolve toward the "connectionless" technology as WANs attempt to eliminate their performance bottleneck.

The changing market boundaries increase the investment risk. As mentioned earlier, alternative solutions can be a strategic danger competitively. This trend forces partnering and other relationships to cope with the change. These risks are lower when the market is in its early life cycle, that is, internetworking, but as it matures the boundaries surely will dictate significant change—invest early.

Both LANs and WANs will undergo significant changes in protocols and access methods as the demands increase for higher performance. Quadrant I drives the wide area performance requirements far more than Quadrant II drives the wide area. A single voice user is not performance-constrained, but a single computer user could easily be performance-constrained by the wide area network. Quadrant IV network performance levels should be multiples of LAN performance. The "rethinking" of dramatic new network strategies is occurring now but will take years to translate into new standards. In the interim, a modest evolution with frame relay is happening, and ATM (a synchronous transfer mode) technology is appearing in hub-based wiring systems for LANs prior to its move to WAN environments.

In addition to the blurring of boundaries just discussed, some market segments purposefully straddle the boundaries. Some of communications technology's highest growth markets fall into the multiquadrant category. Multiquadrant markets include

- Internetworking—tying together LANs

- Videoconferencing—visual communications system transferring voice, video and data for local and remote group meetings

- Voice processing—evolving to integrated systems with voice and data for local and wide area networking

These multiquadrant markets offer flexibility to the user in fashioning solutions to business communications problems. They are attractive to investors since they offer high-value-added systems that typically are competitively differentiated.

Surrounding the framework and tying all four quadrants together are the network management tools and systems integration services. Network management functionality should reside at all levels in the network. Most communications technology vendors provide some network management capabilities and interface—this usually forms the "bottom-up" view of network management. Users are struggling to link the various network management pieces into an integrated, "top-down," system-wide managed view of the network. To achieve system-wide network management, some users have turned to systems integrators to install the network and the related management tools. As networks become larger and more complex, the need for network management and systems integration should increase significantly. Standards such as Simple Network Management Protocol (SNMP under the TCP/IP standards effort) and Common Management Information Protocol (CMIP under the ISO/OSI standards plan) are emerging. These standards should facilitate the integration process and, more important, result in more reliable, easier-to-fix networks.

Upping the Rate of Return on Your Most Important Corporate Asset

by Harry J. Saal
President, CEO, and Chairman, Network General Corporation

Author Bio

Mr. Harry J. Saal is a magna cum laude graduate of Columbia University, where he received his Ph.D. in High Energy Physics in 1969. He then served as deputy director of the Stanford Linear Accelerator Center's Computation Group, and later as visiting associate professor of computer science at the State University of New York at Buffalo. From 1973 to 1978, he worked for IBM at the IBM Scientific Center in Haifa, Israel, and for the IBM General Products Division in San Jose. He was a project leader for the design and implementation of enhancements to the APL language and time-sharing systems.

In October 1978, Mr. Saal founded Nestar Systems Incorporated, a pioneer in local area network systems for personal computers. He left Nestar Systems in May 1986 to form Network General Corporation. His goal was to make Network General the first company wholly dedicated to the area of network diagnostics.

After less than three years, Network General made its initial public offering of common stock, in February 1989. The offering was comanaged by Alex. Brown and Sons, and Hambrecht and Quist. The company made a second public offering in August 1989.

Currently, Network General markets its Sniffer family of network analyzer products throughout the U.S. and in more than 26 countries worldwide. Ernst & Young named Dr. Saal the Bay Area 1990 Software Entrepreneur of the Year. Currently, Dr. Saal is president, CEO, and chairman of Network General Corporation.

Executive Summary

In our high-tech world, the rate of change presents a real challenge to an organization's ability to collect and manage information, often meaning the difference between success and failure. To organize the dissemination of corporate information, technology has given us an advanced method of handling data: the enterprise networks. And yet, despite the growth and importance of networks in an organization, corporations today are seriously underinvesting in maintaining and managing these networks that are the repositories of their most important assets.

It's no secret that, in today's business environment, a corporation's success results in large part from its ability to manage its assets. Although those with a leaning toward financial management may argue that means hard financial assets, most of industry's most successful executives realize that a corporation's assets extend far beyond cash in the bank, real estate, or accounts receivable.

The rate of change of our industries continues to rise, seemingly without end. So an organization's ability to collect and manage information such as marketing intelligence, business and market trends, customer preferences, competitive data, and product information in practically real time can mean the difference between the organization's success and its failure.

If we add the traditional types of data maintained by virtually all organizations, such as accounting and personnel records, we can see that, unlike the proverbial army that travels on its stomach, a modern corporation travels on its information. To speed and organize the dissemination of corporate information, technologists have provided us with a 20th-century version of the file cabinet: the enterprise network. The latest generation of information network does far more than merely connect terminals to hosts; it permits the rapid interchange of information from site to site, from one local area network (LAN) to another across town, across the country, or around the world.

Yet, strange as it may seem, most corporations spend far less on maintaining and managing the networks that are the repositories of their most important asset than they do on the salary for a typical Fortune 1000 CEO. Contrast that tiny expense with losses of up to $3.48 million employee productivity and direct revenue losses that can average as much as $606,000 per year, and we have a dichotomy that is hard to explain.

Facts and Figures

Infonetics, Inc., a Santa Clara research firm, has conducted a survey to determine the actual cost of local area network downtime. The surveyors polled 100 Fortune 1000 MIS and network managers of campus-wide and extended networks. What they found was surprising.

For example, in addition to the losses pointed out in the earlier paragraph, the survey revealed that the average network is disabled about twice a month for an average of nearly five hours per failure. Networks are growing at a rate of nearly 50 percent annually, and the bigger the networks get the more likely they are to fail. And although these companies spend an average of over $650,000 per year on network upgrades, they spend only about $60,000 annually on maintaining and managing them.

Nor is the problem unique to the United States. A study in the U.K. revealed that British corporations experience nearly the same statistics. Finally, a survey by "Computer Reseller News" and The Gallup Organization confirmed the earlier findings of Infonetics for U.S. networks. In fact, the Gallup survey, conducted in 1992, showed an increase in the amount of time networks are going down. The average Fortune 1000 company experiences 4 hours of downtime per work week, according to the Gallup survey, which is nearly double the 2.4-hour average cited in the Infonetics survey conducted two years ago. There is no question that a wide gap exists in the value of corporate information on networks and the resources expended in protecting that information and managing the networks that hold it.

Getting a Handle on the Problem

The bottom line, in terms of managing this most important of corporate resources, is that most corporations have underinvested in trying to obtain the maximum benefit of what is, perhaps, their most strategic asset: their information systems and the infrastructure that drives them. In fact, "underinvested" may be overstating the case, because most companies have simply accepted the state of network problems as if there were no alternative, and merely staffed to deal with traditional daily care and maintenance of the network.

There are several specific areas where companies can target improvements in the network infrastructure. The first, and probably the most important, is training. As networks proliferate throughout organizations, the people who are called on to administrate them often come from nontechnical or, at least, non-network backgrounds.

Usually, these new network administrators are "thrown in the pool" without adequate training. The result is that the administrator has a good knowledge of the operating system's commands but almost no understanding of networks in general or how his or her segment fits into the corporate information management picture. In short, the new administrator is prepared only to become a work group asset instead of a part of the corporate information management team.

Worse, that administrator is often expected to manage the network in addition to his or her current workload. The administrator is neither properly prepared nor adequately compensated by workload balancing to perform as a top-notch information system manager.

A second area where corporations can improve information management is in network systems design and management. Networks need to be planned and designed by trained network architects in order to meet the growing information management demands of growing companies. Too often networks "grow like Topsy" and, eventually, need to be interconnected. These unplanned and often dissimilar network architectures cannot function at peak efficiency within the corporate enterprise.

It's All in Your Attitude

When I am asked, "What is an acceptable figure for network downtime?" I invariably answer "Zero." Companies that are willing to accept any network downtime are saying, in effect, that they are willing to accept mediocre communication. If they are willing to accept mediocre communication, then there are always plenty of excuses for mediocre performance.

People's performance improves directly with their ability to communicate information to and get information from their colleagues. The company that can't manage its own strategic information cannot be competitive in its marketplace. Because corporate intelligence is no more accessible than the infrastructure that holds it will allow, that infrastructure is the key to the company's competitiveness. Effective information management begins with the attitude that nothing less than full efficiency in information management is acceptable.

Achieving zero downtime on a large network is not a trivial goal. It requires a commitment to excellence in training, system design, and network management. It means that corporations must dedicate appropriate budgets to new equipment, proper courses for network managers and support staff, enough trained support personnel, and network administrators with the time and resources to do their jobs.

It also means that information executives must develop a plan for approaching the goal. That may mean that you strive to reduce downtime by 50 percent within a particular time frame. To do that you will need to apply both budget and human resources as well as training. After you have achieved your first downtime improvement, move on to the next. Continue until you are close enough to zero downtime to make it an achievable goal.

It may take some time to reach your objective, but with the right resources, training, and support you can develop an attitude of "total quality" among your network professionals.

As companies struggle to manage the glut of information with which they must deal daily, the alternative to excellence in the area of information management is failure. It is failure to grow efficiently. It is failure to compete effectively. And it can mean, in the future, the failure to survive.

Realizing the return on the company's most valuable asset, its information, requires investing in the infrastructure that supports, manages, and disseminates it. As managers we have a fiduciary responsibility to support our company's efforts in our marketplaces. In times of high competitiveness and tight budgets, we must exercise that responsibility by examining closely our corporate information infrastructure, and that means allocating the resources necessary to help it achieve excellence. Although this does mean increasing spending in the network management area, this is probably the most highly leveraged investment you can make today.

A LAN in Every Pocket: Wireless LANs Today and Tomorrow

by Stan Schatt
Senior Industry Analyst—LANs, InfoCorp

Author Bio

Mr. Schatt tracks the LAN industry for Infocorp. He formally served as chairman of the Telecommunications Management department at De Vry Institute of Technology. He also served as president of Network Associates, a network consulting and systems integration company. Mr. Schatt is the author of 21 books, including an all-time best seller for the LAN industry—*Understanding LANs* (SAMS, 1992), currently in its third edition. Schatt has also published books on LAN/WAN integration (*Linking LANs*), network management (*A Manager's Guide to Network Management*), and two books on NetWare. Mr. Schatt's industry experience includes stints as a computer retail store manager, a network analyst for a Fortune 500 corporation, and a systems programmer and trainer. He has taught at several universities, including the University of Southern California and the University of

Houston. Mr. Schatt was a Fulbright exchange professor to Tokyo University, Keio University, and the University of Hiroshima.

Executive Summary

We are on the brink of a revolution in the wireless LAN industry. Today there are several competing technologies, including narrowband and spread spectrum radio as well as infrared. This paper examines the advantages and disadvantages of each approach. Although narrowband radio signals are virtually free of distortion, their broadcast radius is limited and signals cannot pass through most building materials. Spread spectrum LANs can broadcast through various building materials, but only Windata has achieved reasonable transmission speeds. Point-to-point infrared LANs can achieve high transmission speeds but are restricted to environments permitting line-of-sight. With the exception of an IEEE 802.11 standard, all factors required for wireless LANs to increase their market share dramatically are in place. Candidates are emerging as possible applications to spur customer interest. This paper looks at some of the more interesting wireless applications on the horizon.

The same old pattern seems to be repeating itself. I watched during the late '70s and '80s as hobbyists and early adapters of PCs gave way to small business owners and finally to corporate purchasing agents. PCs were transformed from exotic "high tech" to commodities found in supermarkets. The questions I fielded at cocktail parties also changed. "What good are those little computers?" and "How can they help me?" soon gave way to "What kind of network do you think is best?" and, more recently, "How do we link together our different networks into an enterprise network?"

With the exception of a standard for wireless communications, all the key elements are in place for a wireless revolution in the way we use computers and the way we think of networks. Apple estimates that by 1995 half of all computers purchased will be portables in one form or another. Its Newton is the first of a family of Personal Digital Assistants (PDAs) that Apple plans to link through wireless connections to enterprise networks. Some of Apple's 1993 products are expected to include an infrared link to a wireless LAN. Grid offers as one option for its PalmPad computer a built-in fax modem with an integrated limited-distance wireless radio modem that can communicate within an 800-foot radius. Olivetti subsidiary TA Triumph-Adler AG sells notebook models called Walkstations that can communicate with each other and other similarly equipped PCs using an infrared transceiver designed by Photonics. AT&T's Safari laptop contains an interface to the AT&T 3730 cellular telephone. The Safari can use this phone to dial into networks from any location. It is no longer necessary to bring along a screwdriver to unscrew a hotel telephone in order to establish a standard modem connection.

Just as the early PC landscape was dotted with competing technologies and proprietary hardware and software, today's wireless environment includes radio as well as infrared technology. Let's examine these technologies and their proponents to see who the likely winner will be.

Today's Wireless Environment

Today's wireless environment can be divided into the worlds of radio-based LANs and infrared LANs. Wireless radio LANs can be further subdivided into narrowband and broadband (spread spectrum) categories. Motorola's Altair is an example of narrowband wireless communications. It utilizes the 18 GHz microwave frequency band that requires FCC licensing to avoid interference. The company has made arrangements with the FCC to license this frequency and to allocate it to its customers. Microwave LANs utilizing the 18 GHz band can achieve relatively high speeds (3 Mbps) and produce signals that are virtually free of any distortion. Unfortunately, these signals cannot penetrate metal walls or concrete bearing walls. Distance is also a limiting factor (5,000 square feet) compared to spread spectrum technology (50,000 square feet).

Spread spectrum technology uses the ultra-high frequency (UHF) radio bands falling between 902 MHz and 3 GHz. Products falling into this category currently include NCR's WaveLAN (2 Mbps), Telesystems' ARLAN (1 Mbps), and Windata's FreePort (5.7 Mbps). Although these LANs can cover extensive distances (six miles for ARLAN, for example) and can penetrate walls and ceilings, they consume large amounts of bandwidth because they "spread" their signals across several frequencies. As long as several of these networks are not in close proximity, though, there should not be any serious conflicts. Windata's decision to utilize the 2.4 GHz and 5.7 GHz bands rather than the 902 MHz to 928 MHz bands utilized by its major competitors has enabled it to parlay this greater bandwidth into a faster transmission rate.

Infrared LANs currently fall into three distinct groups. Point-to-point infrared systems such as BICC's Infralan provide high-speed transmission but are limited to a distance of approximately 100 feet and must maintain a clear line-of-sight. BICC has EtherNet and token ring versions available that can match the transmission speeds of similar cabled systems. Low-speed scatter infrared systems such as Infralink from Infralink of America transmit signals off walls and ceilings and depend upon a room's degree of infrared reflectivity. These systems are limited today to the role of peripheral sharing. Finally, reflective infrared LANs are high-speed systems that utilize optical transceivers mounted near each workstation that are aimed toward a common spot on a ceiling or other surface. Clearly this technology's limitations define its niche market. Products such as Photolink from Photonics Corporation are limited to around a 40-foot distance between workstation and reflective spot. They are ideal for environments with high ceilings such as old offices or factories.

Infrared technology likely will become a key component for notebook and palmtop computers as evidenced by the current strategic partnerships between computer manufacturers and wireless vendors. Spread spectrum vendors such as Windata also have announced products for the palmtop market with a 1993 delivery date. The real battle for survival will take place between the narrowband and broadband radio LANs. Windata's FreePort seems a good long shot because of its key partnership with powerhouse Cabletron, but Motorola has the resources to refine the Altair product line and make it even more attractive.

The IEEE 802.11 committee continues its struggle to produce a wireless standard. The trend now is toward defining a Medium Access Control layer

(MAC) and then approving various medium interfaces in much the same way that the 802.3 standard has twisted pair and coaxial cabling options. Likely there eventually will be both spread spectrum and infrared options. Meanwhile, wireless vendors continue to try to build large enough installed bases to establish their products as *de facto* standards.

Wireless Awaits the Right Application

Because of their cost and generally lower transmission speed, today's wireless LANs are niche players. They are ideal for old buildings with asbestos, buildings without drop ceilings, companies with short-term leases, and offices in which employees frequently move from one location to another. Just as the Apple II needed the VisiCalc application and the IBM PC needed Lotus 1-2-3 to jump-start sales, the sales of wireless LANs will increase dramatically as technology for notebooks and palmtops matures and as pen-related software applications are developed. NCR cites a study by a large urban police department, for example, that forecasts a savings of at least $4 million per year if police officers are able to use pen-oriented software and notebook computers to fill out paperwork on-site. These officers would not have to return to a police station to fill out paperwork and then input their data into a computer.

The manager of a large government computer complex told me that he is seriously considering laptops and/or notebook computers with wireless LAN connections for one primary purpose—enabling staff attending meetings in different conference rooms to be able to access computer LAN database information and print this information without having to leave their meetings. AT&T intends to equip its Business Network salespeople with notebooks and modems and have them work out of their cars and homes. The company estimates a savings of 50 percent on office and supply costs and expects to see a 40 percent increase in productivity. The city of Mission Viejo, California, recently installed a wireless LAN to avoid the expense associated with frequent moves and changes. Travelers Corporation, an early adapter of wireless LANs, estimates the cost of wired LANs at $20 per node and that of wireless LANs at only $10 per node.

The Wireless World of the Future

Go Corporation has developed a version of PenPoint that runs on AT&T's RISC microprocessor called the Hobbit. The two companies hope to collaborate on handheld wireless devices that can be used to transmit phone calls, data, and images. Rather than developing just another handheld computer, AT&T and Go are betting on a single hand-held device that incorporates wireless data communications and voice communications. Xerox's Palo Alto Research Center (PARC) is developing products for what it refers to as "ubiquitous computing," an environment in which the home and office will contain hundreds of inexpensive computers, all linked by a wireless network capable of connecting with wired networks. Although it is difficult to conceive of an intelligent, meaningful conversation with a toaster or room dehumidifier, the vision of a world in which intelligent devices at home and in the office can be accessed seems valid. Imagine a world very much like the one envisioned by Isaac Asimov in his classic Foundation trilogy. Virtually everyone would have a hand-held computing device, one that was linked through wireless connection to the equivalent of several supercomputers. Knowledge from the world's libraries and databases would be as accessible by merely jotting down a question.

Motorola is advocating a worldwide satellite system that will enable users of cellular phones to access computer networks without worrying about fading out and losing their connection. Because of the growing union between notebook computers and cellular phones, it should be possible to access computer networks through a notebook wireless link from virtually anywhere in the world.

Clearly, wireless computer communications today are very much like the state of personal computing during the late 1970s. It was not clear who would emerge as the winner, but it was clear that the technology had infinite possibilities. We are still waiting for the wireless application that will have the same effect that VisiCalc and Lotus 1-2-3 had on the PC industry. The inventor might still be in high school, or perhaps today he is a very dissatisfied programmer buried in the software development department of a large conservative computer company. Meanwhile, there are network managers throughout the country who are besieged with cabling problems that often comprise as much as 70 percent of their workload. These overworked, underappreciated keepers of the network long for a wireless universe, a world where they can throw off the shackles of coax and even twisted pair and shout, "Free at last, free at last, thank God Almighty I'm free at last."

The Expanding Role of Intelligent Hubs in the Enterprise Network

by Ron Schmidt
SynOptics Communications, Inc.

Author Bio

Before the formation of SynOptics Communications, Ron Schmidt spent five years with Xerox Corporation, where he most recently was a research fellow at the Palo Alto Research Center (PARC). Prior to Xerox PARC, Schmidt spent seven years at AT&T's Bell Labs, where he was a member of the technical staff performing research in fiber-optics communications. He is a fellow of the IEEE and is currently participating in IEEE 802.3 fiber-optic and twisted-pair standards committee work.

Dr. Schmidt received a B.S. degree with "highest honors" in 1966, and M.S. and Ph.D. degrees in 1968 and 1970, respectively, both in electrical engineering from the University of California, Berkeley. He has extensive experience in planar optical circuits, acoustic surface-wave devices, microfabrication technology, integrated optics signal processing, high-speed fiber-optic links, and local area networks.

Executive Summary

Local area networks (LANs) have assumed a mission-critical role in corporate computing. How will LANs keep pace as new demand for higher bandwidth applications puts pressure on the LAN infrastructure? Where will LANs fit in emerging multi-enterprise networks as organizations move to link their networks to the networks of their suppliers, customers, and strategic partners?

"The Expanding Role of Intelligent Hubs in the Enterprise Network" examines the intelligent hub architecture as a platform for growth. Intelligent hubs will provide a means of integrating existing LAN and internetworking technologies, as well as emerging high-performance connectivity and network-management capabilities. This paper discusses steps SynOptics has already taken to ensure a smooth migration and to protect customers' investments and SynOptics' plans for integrating emerging technologies into the intelligent hub.

This is an exciting time in the intelligent hub business. As local area networks assume an increasingly important role in corporate computing strategies, intelligent hubs also are gaining in stature. For a growing number of LAN customers, intelligent hubs—which provide a platform for LAN connectivity, internetworking, and network management and control—have become the cornerstone of the enterprise network. As a result, intelligent hubs today represent a billion-dollar business—one that is expected to grow 54 percent in 1992 worldwide.[*]

Current market trends will further fuel this explosive growth. Demand for applications that handle multiple streams of different data types simultaneously to the desktop is increasing. "Multimedia" has become a catch-all buzzword, but the need to integrate data, video, still images, scanned images, computer-generated graphics, animation, and voice is becoming very real.

---

[*] *"LAN Concentrator Market Trends and Forecast"—International Data Corporation, May 1991. Forecasted growth rate is for 1992.*

Among the emerging multimedia applications are distributed document management and image processing, electronic data interchange, collaborative computing, and video conferencing, to name a few.

In addition to changing the nature of desktop computing, these applications place new demands on networks—both the enterprise network as we understand it today, which links heterogeneous domains within the same organization, and the emerging multi-enterprise, which will link organizations with their suppliers, customers, and strategic partners. These new applications require a robust and reliable network capable of growing while maintaining management and control in the face of increasing complexity.

The common denominator in all these situations is performance—to satisfy application needs, to enable network growth, and to enhance ease of management and control. Because LANs occupy such a pivotal role in the enterprise network today, all eyes are on LANs. Can traditional shared-access LAN technologies meet the performance and management challenges facing enterprises, particularly as they move to more sophisticated applications and extend their communications facilities beyond the boundaries of their own enterprise?

This is a troubling question for LAN-based enterprises because the answer is no. Shared-access LAN technologies such as EtherNet, Token Ring, and FDDI have reached the limits of their performance capabilities and will not support these new network demands. What faces architects of the enterprise network today is the jarring reality that the billions of dollars invested in LAN technologies and network designs based on LANs are running out of steam.

The discontinuity that looms ahead poses a real dilemma. There is no question about the need to adopt new, higher performance networking technologies. But what about the significant investment in LAN technologies that exist today? And what about the need to maintain the same or even greater capability to manage and control the network?

Clearly, advances in networking technology must ensure greater reliability and control, along with greater performance. The issue is how to move forward safely. This is where the intelligent hub comes in—and why the intelligent hub will play an even greater role in enterprise networks as they evolve.

The real advantage of the intelligent hub is that networks built around them employ a network architecture that provides a center for control and management, as well as a platform for seamlessly integrating new technologies. As new technologies emerge to meet the performance needs of the enterprise network, SynOptics believes that the intelligent hub is the key to incorporating new technologies while preserving the installed base of equipment, the integrity of the network's design, and the experience base of those managing the network.

To understand why, one must understand the important contribution the intelligent hub has made to networking in providing a control point in the network for configuration and management. Structured wiring, a necessary part of the hub-based scheme, creates a control point in the wiring closet, simplifying system maintenance and improving network performance.

In addition, focusing network activity in the wiring closet streamlines network management, bringing disparate access methods—EtherNet, Token Ring, and FDDI—and a variety of internetworking functionality under common network management. With network management unifying the network, new technologies can continue to be integrated seamlessly and transparently into the intelligent hub.

Historically, this is how the intelligent hub has evolved. When LANs first appeared, they represented a discontinuity to existing host-based communications systems. The intelligent hub at first provided a better way to gain control over LAN implementations. Over time, intelligent hubs integrated some of the "legacy" functionality provided by centralized computing, such as terminal servers and more comprehensive network management, giving users greater flexibility in configuring networks consisting of both old and new technologies.

But perhaps the best example of this capability to date is the integration of high-performance routing into the intelligent hub. Routing resolves some of the complexity issues of large networks. Routers have been successful at this because they are extremely powerful devices. However, routers alone are simply devices within the network and are typically managed as devices. The ideal is to integrate routers into the network itself and manage them as part of the overall network.

This is precisely what SynOptics has done in partnership with Cisco, the world's leading router vendor, and the world's leading UNIX-based network management platform provider, SunConnect—a Sun Microsystems business. The resulting product, the RubSystem, is an intelligent hub designed for use in the data center. It will complement SynOptics' existing System 3000 wiring center intelligent hubs. The RubSystem will integrate routing into the intelligent hub backplane, providing even greater visibility and control for both internetworking and connectivity.

Once again, we are faced with a potential discontinuity, as the current shared-access methods employed by LANs fail to keep pace with growing demand for bandwidth. Asynchronous Transfer Mode, or ATM, technology has been presented as a way to achieve the next level of throughput to serve enterprise networks. Although ATM functions as an access method, much like EtherNet and Token Ring, it is not a traditional LAN technology. Unlike traditional LAN access methods, ATM is not a shared medium. Because it establishes a direct, virtual circuit to occur between two points on a network, ATM can deliver a full 155 megabits per second throughput to each desktop, server, or LAN segment. Also unlike shared access methods, aggregate throughput is scalable in proportion to the size of the switching matrix used.

ATM, as promising as it is, poses special issues in the LAN environment. It can deliver enormous dedicated performance, but frankly, this level of performance is necessary for only a small fraction of desktop users today. And even though ATM can serve as both a connectivity access method and an internetworking medium, it cannot and will not replace existing LANs. So the challenges of ATM are twofold: How can companies deploy ATM cost-effectively and fit it into the enterprise network as demand increases? And how can they deploy it in such a way that it can be managed along with LAN technologies under common network management?

The logical solution is to integrate ATM into the intelligent hub, which already provides the capability to grow LANs incrementally and put disparate network resources under common network management. But can it be done?

The answer is yes, and the best example of this to date is SynOptics' integration of high-performance EtherNet switching from Kalpana, Inc., into its new multisegment EtherNet intelligent hub. The Kalpana switching technology plays a key role in SynOptics' implementation of multisegment EtherNet and is the first example of a nontraditional technology being integrated into the intelligent hub.

SynOptics tackled two challenges: First was the need to develop a high-performance solution for internetworking between multiple EtherNet segments. This challenge was solved through the co-development partnership with Kalpana. The second was the need to integrate both multisegment EtherNet and this new switching technology seamlessly into the intelligent hub. It needed to be managed under common network management. And customers had to be able to buy this new solution incrementally and continue to use existing LAN systems.

SynOptics integrated multiple EtherNet segments through a backplane upgrade in the intelligent hub rather than creating a new intelligent hub chassis. This provided a low-cost change that could be executed easily at the customer's site and that preserved customers' significant investment in EtherNet and network management modules for the hub.

EtherNet switching is integrated using a module that plugs easily into a slot in the existing system.

The adoption of Kalpana's switching technology marked the first integration of a switching technology into the intelligent hub—no doubt a foreshadowing of things to come. That SynOptics achieved this while protecting its customers' existing investments and network designs demonstrates that the hub architecture can turn a potentially troubling technology discontinuity into a smooth technology evolution.

Looking forward, intelligent hubs will certainly accommodate tighter integration of new and existing technologies. The challenge for all hub vendors is to create a migration path that maintains the billions of dollars invested in existing networks, while addressing the effects that each new development has on existing parts of the network.

In Search of the Ultimate Network Manager

by Chip Sandifer
President, VisiSoft

Author Bio

Chip Sandifer has over thirteen years' experience managing and implementing software systems. He has used his strong technical background in PCs and graphical systems to become a pioneer in the development of applications for the Microsoft Windows environment. As president of VisiSoft, Mr. Sandifer leads the teams of engineers that developed the VisiNet products. In addition, VisiSoft actively consults in areas of computer networking and Windows programming with knowledge in the specifics of Microsoft LAN Manager, Novell NetWare, NetBIOS, and SNMP. Mr. Sandifer has been instrumental in the development of network and graphical projects at well-known firms such as Microsoft, DCA, Racal-Milgo, and Scientific-Atlanta.

Executive Summary

The network management marketplace is in a state of transition. Utility vendors are rushing to market with many programs that address managers' specific information needs. But, as they are bombarded with raw data, network managers will realize the need for integrated, comprehensive, graphical tools that can make sense of all this data. The network must be viewed as a system. The greatest benefits of network management come from the ability to interact with a single graphical tool that enables the administrator to perform any task from adding a user and checking alarms to reconfiguring routers and initializing backups.

Networks today are growing wildly from single segments with five to ten workstations to large multiserver and multisegment internetworks. Keeping a network up and operating becomes increasingly difficult in this growth environment. Historically, network management has been defined by communications industry vendors as the configuration, control, and monitoring of their devices.

Network management consists of configuring, monitoring, controlling, and analyzing the resources available in the network, optimizing the use of those resources, and preventing and solving users' problems as they occur. Because of the disastrous effects of network downtime in even medium scale networks, network management is currently focused on detecting potential faults and problems before they become critical. True network management performs a broader role, assisting network administrators in day-to-day management tasks as diverse as adding new users, manipulating printer queues, and scheduling backups.

Recently, utility vendors have begun placing their products in the category of network management if they provide any information about the network. But, in reality, the subject of network management has a much broader scope, focusing on the health of the network as a single entity rather than what might be relatively unimportant data on particular devices. The administrator needs a tool that will enable him to cut through the reams of configuration information and esoteric statistics, see what is really going on, and focus on the important events. It must also issue a warning when something significant is happening.

The Need for Network Management

The way most people find out that a problem exists in their networks today is to receive a call for help from a user. This attitude can result in catastrophic failures and lost time for many end users. Most network managers have only a vague idea of the way information moves about in their networks.

Networks today are growing out of control. What had been a number of terminals tied to a mainframe has migrated to a large number of PCs tied to the mainframe, and then migrated to an even larger number of PCs tied together in a network. Many site administrators don't even know the exact number of stations connected to the network or the basic configuration of each station.

This situation is beginning to change. A number of vendors are beginning to offer utilities that provide network status, from the configuration of individual desktop PCs to server utilization, wire traffic, and error information. So, rather than purchasing network management systems, network managers are purchasing utilities for each specific application. These utilities are usually single-purpose, dedicated programs that provide no easy mechanism to share data for an integrated graphical presentation or centralized alarm recognition. While adequate for casual troubleshooting, this approach fails to address the need for unattended proactive analysis that alerts the administrator before a catastrophic failure occurs.

Making sense from all the textual, numeric, and tabular data provided by these utilities can be very difficult. In a tabular presentation, critical server statistics such as disk space utilization and average response time are given equal importance with relatively uninteresting statistics such as the number of users logged on. The administrator needs a user interface that will allow him or her to define important statistics, so he or she can easily see if action is required.

Network vendors also contribute to the confusion. Vendors provide the information that is convenient but make no real attempt to provide any interpretation of the data. For example, Novell NetWare provides a wealth of statistics on the status of the server software, tracking such critical performance metrics as percent server utilization, cache hit ratios, and disk and volume utilization information, but the manuals provided with the network operating system don't explain what these statistics mean or what represents normal and alarm conditions for each.

Because every network is different, the ideal network manager must be able to capture data and make suggestions for alarm settings. Trend analysis can be performed to determine these settings. Alarms need to be customizable because a serious problem on one network might be the normal state of affairs on another. No two networks are the same, so you can't have a mass-produced network manager with hardcoded alarm settings. Managers need to be able to customize what is and is not an alarm setting.

The Problems with SNMP

Simple Network Management Protocol, or SNMP, has been widely hailed as a quick solution to the problems of sharing information and interoperability between a wide variety of network devices. Hardware or software vendors simply develop an SNMP agent for their device or program. This agent is actually a small program that resides at the device and can transmit status back to a manager using the SNMP protocol, as shown in Figure 45.1.

The SNMP standard defines a variety of basic information that each device in the network is expected to provide, along with the capability for the vendor to define any additional custom data that makes sense for the device. In practice, most manufacturers define custom data for their devices. The SNMP standard and custom data are defined as a Management Information Base, or MIB.

For example, to monitor a Microsoft LAN Manager server from an SNMP management console, the textual description of the LAN Manager MIB extensions, often referred to simply as the LAN Manager MIB, can be incorporated into a manager's standard MIB to allow it to recognize LAN Manager-specific objects.

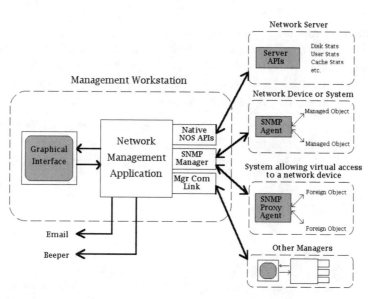

Figure 45.1. Logical network management connectivity and components.

Although this approach sounds straightforward, it places a tremendous load on the management station software that must interpret the data. SNMP has been defined to make it easy to implement agents so that most devices can be manageable. Complexities for management software aren't considered bad by the standards groups. Many of the public domain SNMP managers can simply retrieve a single status field or group of fields and display the data textually. Displaying the status of an object graphically is a complex task. A graphical icon must be defined, and the color, shape, and alarms for the object must be programmed for each individual device or subcomponent.

While SNMP is designed to provide interoperability and enable multivendor management, most SNMP managers available today are produced by vendors to manage their own hardware devices. The managers contain hardcoded references to the manufacturer's own hardware and might not even be designed to incorporate the MIBs of other devices. If it is possible to add foreign devices, they must be defined by the administrator, and the wealth of graphical features available to users of those other manufacturers' products might not be available.

It's hard to trust device manufacturers or network operating system (NOS) vendors to produce management systems capable of managing their competitors' devices as well as their own. Manufacturers aren't going to offer products that work equally well with their competitors' devices unless they believe the future lies in true interoperability.

In practice, these network managers don't address the real problems of integrated management at all. What the user needs is a system that contains predefined objects for all commonly available SNMP devices and has the capability to quickly and easily create new custom objects as they are required.

The Goal

The network management marketplace is evolving from a group of discrete, special purpose utility programs into integrated packages that perform a variety of related functions. What is really needed is a single package that can provide management of all network devices and software components from a single point. Creating this package is difficult because of the variety of protocols required to communicate with devices and software, as well as the dearth of devices with management capabilities.

The first step toward the goal of integrated management is to make every object in the network capable of reporting status to a manager. This should include not only routers, bridges, and the other obvious hardware devices but software products such as database and print servers. Often, network operational problems aren't associated with a particular hardware limitation or failure but are caused by software interactions or limitations, which aren't immediately obvious. Virtually every object in the network that provides any kind of service should be capable of transmitting at least basic status information to a manager.

In the real world, networks are managed hierarchically. The idea that a single management station will monitor and report status on thousands of PCs is absurd. Single individuals don't directly manage networks of that size; they can support at most between 100 and 500 PC end users. These individuals might report to others who are responsible for the whole internetwork, but managers at the top don't really care that the printer in one of 100 remote offices is jammed. They are concerned with the issues of overall operation of the servers, whether the internetwork communication links are functioning properly, and asset tracking and planning for the future.

Figure 45.2. shows a sample information systems organization that might be found in a medium sized manufacturing company. As in many real-world companies, the present information network models the company organization from which it evolved. Each division of the company assembled its own network, and, eventually, it made sense to link them all together to allow quick sharing of information.

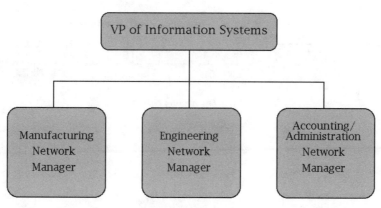

Figure 45.2. Information systems organization for a medium sized manufacturing company.

Figure 45.3. shows the logical network layout for this hypothetical company. This company is typical of many that grew into networking gradually, with different departments choosing different network operating systems and hardware topologies. The various operating systems work quite well independently, but they encounter difficulty when someone decides to connect them all together.

Each division has it's own network manager that assists users in that division when a problem arises. Because all the networks are physically located at a single site, one router links them together. In this sample configuration, four different management protocols are required: NetWare, LAN Manager, NetBIOS, and SNMP. Each manager has a management console to enable customization of the alarms appropriate for each network. Major alarms are forwarded from the division consoles to the master console.

If the network contains expensive, bridged, network links, another reason to create a hierarchy of management consoles is to prevent the transmission of management data, except for alarms, across the links. Due to this hierarchy of management, the appropriate information is available at each level to assist the network managers.

Consequently, an important function of a network management system is its ability to distribute the management data collection and alarm generation hierarchically, with each level processing the appropriate data.

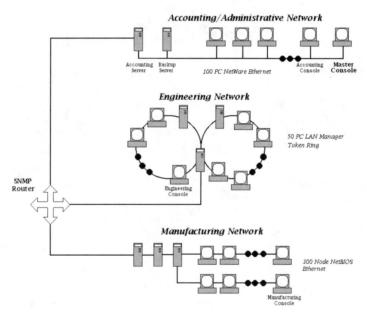

Figure 45.3. Logical network layout.

Standards

Members of the press spend considerable time debating the merits of the different standards in management today. SNMP has become the *de facto* standard for network management primarily due to ease of making an element network manageable. But the standardization process is slow, and although SNMP started off quickly, it is beginning to slow down due to the larger number of people involved in the review process. The standards for SNMP security have finally been published, but this introduction has been marred by the unexpected announcement of SMP. SMP, or Simple Management Protocol, represents an attempt by the developers of SNMP to streamline or circumvent the standardization process. It addresses many of the shortcomings of SNMP, including those solved by SNMP security. SMP has caused considerable confusion among both users and vendors because no one knows whether to proceed with the SNMP security standard or wait for SMP. Choosing a modular, easily extended management package is essential with all this confusion; if the industry suddenly changes direction, the software can be upgraded rather than replaced.

The problems associated with standardization are even more apparent in the OSI, or Open Systems Interconnection specification, defined by the International Organization for Standardization (ISO). The OSI network management standard, the Common Management Information Protocol, or CMIP, has been under development for a number of years longer than SNMP. However, very few implementations exist because of the complexity of the software. CMIP is more robust than SNMP, but at this time it is very difficult to predict whether it will be accepted and implemented by equipment vendors.

Summary

The ultimate network manager consists of a modular, configurable, open system that acknowledges extensive customization by the network manager. What we really want is a system, like the one shown in Figure 45.4., that provides a common graphical interface, for a variety of plug-in software modules, to perform network data collection or communication. Standard modules should be provided for all the common management protocols. Module interfaces should be published to enable end users and OEMs to design their own modules.

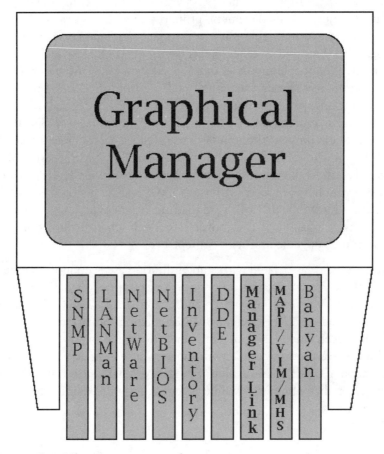

Figure 45.4. Ultimate manager architecture.

In the future when people speak of network management, I think they will come to mean distributed systems management. After all, the network is a complex system, which the manager desires to interact with as a whole, not as a group of loosely connected devices. The greatest benefits of network management come from being able to interact with a single tool that enables the administrator to add a user, check alarms, reconfigure routers, and initiate backups.

The architecture described in this chapter and the questions raised about all the approaches to network management are the result of several years' research into the field of network management, both from the academic view of the standards community and from the view of users and administrators trying to manage their own practical day-to-day problems. The design shown in Figures 45.1. and 45.4. represents the structure of the product VisiNet, which I designed. While the product, as it is shipping today, does not directly address all the issues I have raised, it is designed to provide a platform that can readily be expanded to support the emerging standards in this rapidly changing industry. The ultimate network manager may never actually exist since we set our vision at a level somewhat higher than may be practical at the present time. However, the results of this type of forward thinking are products that solve today's problems while providing the solid platform for growth, which will be required in the future.

Checklist of Features

The following checklist of network management features can be used as a basis for comparison between offerings in the marketplace today:

- Support for all popular network operating systems: NetWare, LAN Manager, Banyan, and NetBIOS systems such as LANtastic, Power LAN, 3+Share, and MS-NET

- Support for SNMP

- Sharing of data between hierarchy of managers or peer managers

- Automatic inventory of hardware and software

- Data import and export

- Graphical user interface

- User-definable objects

- User-definable alarms

- Virus detection
- Remote workstation diagnostic monitoring
- Software license metering
- Simultaneous support for multiple network protocols
- Support of NetView and other open standards
- Logical and physical network layout

46

Which OS Is for You?
It Depends

by David Strom

Editor-in-chief, NETWORK COMPUTING

Author Bio

David Strom is founding editor-in-chief of *NET-WORK COMPUTING*. He joined CMP, Inc. in July 1990 and is responsible for creating the overall editorial direction of the magazine, building the magazine's four networked laboratories, and writing a monthly column as well as occasional articles. The publication has sustained record growth in its first two years. *NETWORK COMPUTING* continues to enjoy an excellent reputation as a solid technical and practical resource for network applications specialists.

During his three-and-a-half years working at *PC Week*, Mr. Strom helped to launch the paper's Connectivity section, contributing more than 300 stories along with writing a weekly column called "The Practical Networker." Mr. Strom as executive editor also managed a staff of 15 analysts, columnists, and editors responsible for *PC Week*'s reviews, opinion, and analysis sections. He also edited several networking supplements and technical special reports during his tenure at the paper.

Prior to joining *PC Week*, Mr. Strom worked in varying roles in end-user computing. He directed new product research at Transamerica Occidental Life's Information Center in Los Angeles, where he specialized in testing micro-to-mainframe communications products. He helped evaluate and set up the corporation's first local area network. He also worked at the U.S. Department of Agriculture's Information Center in Washington, D.C.

While in Washington, Mr. Strom worked for various employers, including the Office of Technology Assessment of the U.S. Congress, the Conservation Foundation, and private consulting firms.

Mr. Strom has a Masters of Science, Operations Research degree from Stanford University, as well as a B.S. from Union College.

Executive Summary

Which is the best operating system? The answer depends on what its use will be. Strom divides the pie into three different categories: one to support graphical desktops, one to build applications, and a third concerning networked servers and applications.

Had enough of pundits, industry "experts" and other hangers-on telling you which operating system is "best"? Me too. But if you'd like hear about a new and useful way to think about how to plan your operating system purchases for the future, read on.

First, some context so that you'll understand my own biases. I currently use both a Mac running System 6 and a PC with DOS 5.0 and Windows v3.1. Both are connected to a NetWare v3.11 server. I've been a DOS user since version 1 and have also spent time in front of Suns,

VAXes, IBM 3270 terminals on MVS mainframes, and even CP/M, AppleDOS, and TOPS-20 back in the olden days (around 15 years ago).

About five years ago, an old boss of mine asked me to coauthor a book for business users on how to upgrade, plan for, and use OS/2. We wrote and rewrote it, trying to anticipate the demand for versions 1.0, 1.1, and 2.0. The book was never published. For about six months, version 1.0 was my primary operating system (which was more a labor of love than anything). So if nothing else, I've been around.

I finally got around to running System 7 during the summer of 1992. After months to test all the various System 7 apps with our network, I must say that I like its features, such as aliases and the ability to save your trashcan contents forever. I'm running Windows v3.1 for two reasons. First, Steve Morse sits in the office next to me and can get it working most of the time. It's nice having one of the experts on call. (Lucky for him, his book on Windows actually was published.) Second, I need to switch tasks frequently, and I have one mission-critical Windows application. And I'm running NetWare for two reasons too. First, it had the best support for switch hitters like me who need to go back and forth between Macs and DOS all day long. Second, it was what we all knew best when we started the magazine two years ago.

Five years ago, I used to be one of those power users who was ego-involved in my OS. I knew what every DOS command did, what the more arcane switches were good for, how to use the F2 and F3 function keys, and how to design my own ANSI.SYS screen prompts. (I still have the command that does the Texas state flag, thanks to those wild and crazy IBMers in Austin.) That's what amounted to fun back then, before we had Solitaire, SimCity, and Carmen Sandiego.

Since then, operating systems have become more complicated and I've moved on. I really don't want to know every new DOS command and switch anymore. I've got better things to do. Plus, when you are on a network, you haven't got time to learn all the ins and outs of five operating systems (System 7, Windows, DOS, NetWare, and Sun OS). Besides, any time I really need something, I've got the experts for each OS working for me and can call or e-mail them my question.

Enough context. Let's move on to my first decision point: What are you gonna do with your desktop machine? It seems to me we have three broad classes of uses:

- As a user workstation

- As an applications development platform

- As a network server

Each use has different priorities and purposes, and the trick is figuring out which sets of end users are tending toward which usage class. End users want something that can run lots of applications and can switch between them easily. These days, they like graphical interfaces because the pictures are pretty and things are intuitive (mostly). Here, System 7 and Windows 3.1 tie for first place.

The next group includes applications developers, the folks we used to call "power users." They develop in various languages, some of them the traditional programming languages such as C and COBOL and some in the newer breed of SQL databases and writing 1-2-3 macros. These folks want lots of tools such as compilers, editors, and code-debuggers. They need memory protection so that when something crashes in one window they can still get their work done in the other windows. (Users say they want memory protection, but don't actually buy operating systems based on that; otherwise, no one would buy a Mac or a Windows machine.) And they need multitasking—not just task switching—because they want to be able to launch time-intensive tasks such as a compile in the background and continue working on something else in the foreground. OS/2 2.0 wins out on these grounds, and UNIX is a close second. Surprise!

Of course, picking the right UNIX platform is another whole issue itself. It will certainly be an interesting time as Sun, NeXT, Santa Cruz Organization, and Novell/USL compete for attention against IBM, Apple, and Microsoft for the next generation of desktop buyers, users, and developers. We think these new operating systems are in for a rough ride in the short term, until applications get ported to the UNIX/Intel versions and until these operating systems run well on existing DOS, Mac, and NetWare networks.

Network servers are a whole other kettle of fish. Reliability is the number one job priority: no one wants these things to break. After that comes remote management: let's put the server in the closet under lock and key, and manage it through software someplace else (such as from a house near a nice beach). Finally, servers need to support big disks and lots of RAM, so they need the physical room inside to put this stuff. NetWare 3.11 ties with various UNIX versions here.

The reason for the tie? Well, NetWare certainly gets the nod in terms of supporting file and print services. It is the best, is the easiest to use, and has the most market presence. But in terms of building network-aware applications that require more than sharing files and printers, I would look carefully at UNIX. It's got the memory protection and multitasking that will be needed to build network applications.

Three different types of uses, three different sets of priorities. Notice that everyone is a winner in one category or another. So forget which OS is best—look at the actual use.

The next decision point is, What is the installed base and where is it going? This is important because you want to be on the winning team, but you want to call it two or three years from now. Go back 10 years and think how you would have called the DOS versus CP/M battle.

You also want to understand what is coming down the road. If every OS/2 developer you know is switching to UNIX (this is just a thought experiment, not necessarily truth), perhaps it is time for you to look at how you are going to migrate those OS/2 applications over the next two or three years.

Getting a good handle on installed base numbers is hard, mainly because no one can give you a straight answer. So you can go one of two ways on this: find a consultant or industry expert that you semi-trust and use that person's numbers, or make up your own, based on your own assumptions and educated guesses. I've made up my own (see Figure 46.1).

My favorite story with fixing installed base numbers concerns Windows 3.1. You see, several vendors, including Seagate and Zenith, bundle Windows with their products. So take the case of the user of Zenith 386 who has

Operating System	# of Users (millions)	Conventional Wisdom
DOS 5	100	Still strong after all these years. Will never die. 200 mil. before long.
System 7	15	By the time Apple is done, this will look like UNIX on multimedia.
Windows 3.1	10	And maybe 2 million actual users. Still a bear on networks.
OS/2 2.0	1	By the time IBM is done, this will look like VM. Where are those drivers?
UNIX (Various versions)	1	Stands to win the most in the IBM/Microsoft OS wars. Look out for NeXT.
NetWare v3.11 (servers)		The winner and still champ in the server department.

Figure 46.1. Who's in and who's out on the operating system scene.

a Seagate hard disk. She gets two boxes of Windows with her machine. She sticks with character-mode DOS and uses neither. And count two copies of Windows in Microsoft's sales. Go figure.

On to the next point: What are your key applications providers doing in terms of switching horses? This is a more qualitative question, and you'll need some reporting skills to get the real answers here. Often you will find out that most of the bigger shops are hedging their bets and have just about every OS platform in the works. But don't look at them. Instead, find the two or three smaller software companies that make some critical products (critical for your company, anyway) and see which way they are moving. Ask them how many developers they have on each OS platform to get a rough measure. Ask them what the VPs of development (and marketing) run on their desks to get the built-in biases of management. Count the number of times these smaller fish show up onstage at IBM, Microsoft, Sun, and Apple developers conferences.

To get a handle on OS/2, for example, look at several of the breakthrough applications providers and see what they are doing. Lotus and Sybase have NLM versions of their stuff. DCA and Citrix are building NT versions of Select Comm Server and Multiuser.

Is anyone building *new* OS/2 versions? Yes, a few hardy souls, but not many. Given this migration away from OS/2 packaged applications, it looks like I'll never get that book published. (But if you want the manuscript on disk, send me your name and address and I'll oblige.)

And the next point: How fast are the machine resources increasing to run the latest version of the OS? Here again, you'll have to do some digging. When OS/2 was first released, IBM promised that a 286-based, 8MHz AT with a 40M disk and 4M of RAM would do the trick. Don't try it with version 2.0. System 7 cannot run on 1M Macs. And the various versions of UNIX that claim to run on Intel machines will need fully loaded 386/33s or even 486s to work.

The point is that you'll need more of everything. So how hard is it to upgrade RAM and disk? Or do you just want to pass those older machines down the corporate food chain and get yourself the latest and greatest? Or maybe you should just stuff the dickens inside every new machine you buy now so that you don't have to ever open or upgrade again.

Of course, one of the reasons DOS is still a living, breathing entity is that it still runs in 8088s, like the laptop I'm using right now. But if you want something fancy, you'll need the system resources.

Take these points together and what have you got? A mess, right? You probably need to buy just about every flavor of OS at one place or another in your corporation. But at least you can plot a strategy and get started handicapping the OS sweepstakes early.

A Brief Overview of Network Management

by Chris Thomas
Manager of Core Technology
Network Management Business Unit, Intel Corp.

Author Bio

Chris Thomas is manager of core technology in the PC Enhancement Division at Intel Corp., located in Provo, Utah.

Before joining Intel, he managed systems engineering and technical support for Information Technologies Inc. and coordinated network installation and management in mainframe and LAN environments for various companies.

Since joining Intel in 1988, he has served as product manager for Intel's NetSight family of network monitoring and analysis tools, and he has worked with technical marketing and systems engineering for transmission control protocol/internet protocol (TCP/IP) and Open System Interconnection(OSI) products marketed with the Intel Fastpath controller. Currently, Thomas is responsible for unifying and integrating internal and external network management strategies. He also participates in a range of standards activities, including the Internet Engineering Task Force (IETF) and the Desktop Management Task Force.

Thomas graduated from Carroll College, Waukasha, WI, with a B.S. degree in computer science and a B.A. degree in Spanish.

Executive Summary

This document provides a brief history of the evolution of network management. It introduces desktop systems management and the current focus on providing management for local area networks (LANs) and the PCs connected to them. The document continues by describing Intel Corp.'s network management strategy and industry efforts to standardize management of desktop computers.

Network management has been a concern for corporate IS managers since the first computers with attached terminals arrived in the business world. The term originated with the large centralized mainframe environments that prevailed in the 1960s and 1970s—complete with sophisticated systems to control, manage, secure, and report on their huge data processing investments.

Elaborate management solutions could be developed fairly easily for mainframe environments, largely because this type of network is typically homogeneous. Network devices and methods of communication are well-defined and strictly controlled, with the processing and data located at a central location.

As the TCP/IP community evolved into what is commonly called the Internet, it raised new concerns over how to manage internetworked heterogeneous systems. The Internet is a national network through which any type of computer can communicate with any other, provided they use the same protocol. The more this large interspersed network grew to encompass dissimilar systems, the more it begged for a standard method of managing the interconnecting devices.

With the introduction of Simple Network Management Protocol (SNMP), the networking industry acquired an elegant management solution that was as simple as its name implied. SNMP quickly gained a strong industry following in the Internet community, and today, many network infrastructure devices such as bridges, routers, concentrators, and hubs are managed through the SNMP standard.

Local Area Networks Change the Face of Network Management

Local area networks have become critical to the operations of many companies. Industry observers suggest that the network computing industry is in the early stages of a transition in which distributed processing eventually will replace the traditional mainframe model.

The explosive growth of LANs has generated a new wave of demand for simple network management. This demand continues to intensify as LANs increase in complexity and diversity.

Management of LANs, however, is becoming much more complicated. LANs are typically composed of many different types of devices. Compounding this complexity, a particular machine may communicate using more than one protocol on the same wire.

This rapidly changing, disparate world of LANs is in marked contrast to the strictly controlled environment of the mainframe and the common protocol solution of the Internet community. Despite this contrast, corporations want to manage devices on LANs with the same expensive, sophisticated tools in which they have already invested, rather than the fragmented tools and utilities available for local networks.

The Emergence of Local Network Management Solutions

Two key factors are driving the demand for local network management solutions. The first factor stems from the existence of comprehensive solutions in corporate mainframe environments.

Corporations have become accustomed to making business, purchasing, hiring, and upgrading decisions based on the information provided by their mainframe management systems. They are also comfortable about data security, recovery, and reliability. Problems are quickly identified and resolved, and network usage is strictly monitored.

The emergence of desktop computing—and subsequently, local area networks of desktop computers—has disrupted the relatively safe, secure corporate computing environment. Valuable corporate resources and information, once secured by way of controlled access and locked doors, are now distributed across the corporation, resident on nearly every employee's desk, and frequently transported.

While the value of allowing employees quick access to information and resources is a primary motivation of corporate downsizing, there is an expectation that decision making, and management information and security tools enjoyed by the MIS departments, will be replicated for their LANs.

A second factor influencing the demand for local management solutions is the increasing complexity of the network due to the enormous volume of LAN installations and the constant introduction of new technologies using LANs.

With new technologies rapidly expanding desktop and LAN capabilities, LAN managers have an almost impossible task of keeping up with their network's ever-growing list of new and valuable functions and services. Network additions that once required change order requests and executive approval are now purchased and installed by the end user. With LANs growing at the rate of 50 percent (15 million additional nodes) per year, LAN administrators are becoming overwhelmed.

Initially, LAN management tools focused on providing reliable wiring connections and tracking basic problems. Products such as protocol and line analyzers became invaluable in isolating and tracking faults.

Today, however, as more mission-critical applications move to the local network and businesses rely on LANs for their livelihood, network management solutions need to include both tools that identify problems and tools that take a holistic approach to solving those problems.

Network management is evolving from a problem-solving science to an art. This art requires network management tools suited to specific tasks, including troubleshooting the physical network, responding to user problems, securing data, printing and faxing, tracking and managing assets, controlling access to the network, configuring and reconfiguring for changing environments, and software license metering.

Local network management tools also must provide the performance information associated with making business decisions about the LANs themselves.

State of the Industry

The state of the network management industry today can best be described as fragmented. Most of the proven tools (analyzers, monitors, and management consoles) and standards (SNMP, common management information protocol [CMIP]) focus on fault management or ensuring a reliable network infrastructure. There is a notable absence of tools that help manage the devices and services that actually use the network.

Management of the end systems themselves—as well as the services they use, provide, and share—is the challenge of the next generation of network management tools.

This management of the desktop or end system is what many industry experts refer to as the sixth area of network management. The other five areas are defined by the International Standards Organization (ISO) as configuration, fault, performance, accounting, and security management. While the traditional five areas concentrate on actual network activity, the systems management element focuses on the devices connected to the network. This makes it possible to use the network to manage components in a network-attached system that may not be network-related.

Intel's Network Management Strategy

Intel Corp. believes that while functions such as managing communications equipment and managing the LAN cabling are addressed adequately today, network vendors have largely ignored systems-level management of the desktop.

With its expertise in PC technology, its focus on workgroup solutions, and its experience in the networking arena, Intel is uniquely qualified to supply this missing element. Intel intends to integrate its knowledge of desktop PCs with proven network management schemes and development of systems-level solutions for tangible problems that plague the LAN administrator.

This enables Intel to deliver a complete local network management scheme, including more traditional network monitors and analyzers that identify network problems, and systems-level management solutions that resolve them.

Network engineers and administrators proficient at supporting their LANs with relatively complex tools want simplified and integrated network management solutions. Complex tools entail long learning curves for relatively expensive and essential support personnel. Most companies already have management consoles, policies and procedures, and personnel. They do not relish the expense, process, and training overhead of each additional solution.

Intel: Bringing Network Management to the Desktop

Intel believes that simplifying network management is crucial to the growth and development of the networking industry. It is also key to the health of the personal computing industry in general, because of the widespread interest in PC-to-PC connectivity.

Intel's network management strategy focuses on local network management. This focus involves:

- Providing solutions to manage desktop computers

- Consolidating management functions into a unified and centralized environment where all Intel products reside

- Utilizing single-agent technology

- Integrating with existing and future management consoles and strategies

- Cooperating with industry and standards efforts to solve systems-level management problems

Providing Solutions to Manage Desktop Computers

Intel's network management solutions place the emphasis on managing the workstations connected to the network. The tasks involved in this include managing applications, accounting, securing data, tracking assets, configuring and updating changing environments, and controlling end systems from a single location.

Intel has been instrumental in introducing LAN management applications that address industry needs. LANSight Support is a systems management tool that facilitates remote control, network diagnostics, workstation inventory, and other activities on network-connected PCs and servers. LANProtect protects a LAN from virus threats. NetSight products monitor and analyze LAN activity, performance, and faults. Intel's SNMP Services product bridges the gap between local and centralized systems management by mapping SNMP management requests to devices residing on the LAN.

Consolidating Management Functions Into a Unified and Centralized Environment Where all Intel Products Reside

Combining these and other LAN management applications into an easy-to-use and understandable environment further reflects the industry's demand for simplification, standardization, overhead reduction, and integration with existing management solutions. Aggressively addressing these issues, Intel has developed a unified network management offering and is working toward the development and standardization of critical elements that will facilitate both better network management applications and the ability to manage more workstation components.

Intel's unified network management offering combines a base set of system and network management functions with an environment catered to the addition and integration of other network management applications. The basic functions may be all that is necessary for the administration of a small LAN. This scalability provides a path for network management services to grow as the size and complexity of the network increases. The inclusion of applications designed for specific purposes, larger networks, or integration with centralized management solutions under the same umbrella as the base applications, unifies and simplifies management tasks.

In addition to simplifying user interfaces and adding features to existing management applications, Intel is developing a number of new LAN management applications. Among these are applications that provide asset management, performance monitoring, security and backup, and services for notification, reporting, and logging network activity.

The benefit of this approach for the LAN administrator is the convenience of a local console that controls all aspects of node management.

Utilizing Single Agent Technology

Intel is committed to providing a single management agent that can be accessed and utilized by multiple systems-level management applications such as virus protection, application monitoring, and asset management software.

In response to customer requests to limit the overhead that network management requires, Intel has developed an innovative Single Agent Technology (SAT). This technology lets management applications requiring an agent at the desktop PC utilize one small resident piece of code to facilitate management requests from any or all Intel management applications. This architecture greatly reduces the memory overhead required at each PC and eliminates the time-consuming effort of reconfiguring each desktop when new management applications are desired.

Integrating with Existing and Future Management Consoles and Strategies

Intel is mapping its products to industry-standard management consoles. The first standard supported is SNMP, today's choice for high-level management transport protocols. This mapping integrates the value of local systems-level management with centralized standards-based consoles.

Intel's SAT is instrumental in providing simple, low-impact management access by centralized management consoles. For instance, Intel's SNMP Services product uses the same SAT to provide SNMP systems management for all of Intel's networking products and PC workstations attached to the network. This mapping eliminates the overhead of an SNMP agent on each LAN device.

Cooperating with Industry and Standards Efforts to Solve Systems-level Management Problems

Intel is actively participating with both industry efforts and standards bodies to address desktop management issues. Intel is pursuing working relationships with strategic allies that further the development of the networking industry. Two efforts focused on facilitating systems management at the desktop are the Desktop Management Task Force (DMTF) and the Host Resources Management Information Base (MIB) Working Group.

Intel teamed with Microsoft, Novell, SunConnect (a Sun Microsystems Inc. business), SynOptics Communications Inc., Digital Equipment Corp. (DEC), Hewlett-Packard, and IBM Corp. to form the Desktop Management Task Force. The DMTF's goal is to develop a common set of Application Programming Interfaces (APIs) and component interfaces to facilitate the management of desktop computers.

The DMTF APIs are designed to provide a common access method for management applications, regardless of protocol, to issue management requests and commands. This reduces the overlap incurred when multiple management applications are used to manage the same network devices. It also encourages management application development by reducing the effort required at the end system. Intel expects that the result will be a generic set of functions for one generic agent—a platform upon which developers can build a suite of value-added applications.

The second area of focus for the DMTF is providing a simple interface or method that software and hardware component vendors can use to enable management of their products. The DMTF interface benefits vendors by allowing their product to be managed by any or all management applications calling its APIs. By designing a simple interface, the DMTF hopes to make it easy to retrofit existing products for management as well as encourage the development of standards for managing the multitude of products available for desktop computers.

The group intends to provide a reference implementation of the protocol-independent standard and plans to distribute the prototype at no charge to developers.

Another standardization effort under way is the Host Resources MIB Working Group sponsored by the IETF. Intel has been actively participating in the development of the draft MIB. The goal of the Host Resources MIB Working Group is to define a common set of objects that can be managed on any desktop computer. By implementing this MIB, SNMP management consoles will be capable of providing systems-level management at the desktop. This dramatically extends the function of these consoles, which have been focused on network infrastructure management.

Summarizing Intel's Network Management Strategy

In implementing its network management strategy, Intel is targeting the management issues associated with networked desktop computers. This approach leverages Intel's expertise in PC architecture and translates that experience to managing the individual PCs on a network.

Also integral to Intel's network management strategy is a commitment to developing a complementary set of products that automate the labor-intensive and fragmented aspects of the LAN administrator's job. This approach offers a number of advantages, including interoperability, multivendor support, and shorter user learning curves. Additionally, a lesser number of management products is required to manage local networks efficiently, and users gain a migration path to new products and solutions.

Another key aspect of Intel's network management strategy is a drastic reduction in the overhead required to manage the end system. Intel accomplishes this by utilizing a single agent to serve the management requirements of multiple applications. This implementation not only reduces physical memory requirements, but also eliminates the burden of managing multiple TSR (terminate-and-stay-resident) programs and performing multiple installations at each node.

As a final component of its network management strategy, Intel is providing avenues for integration with existing network management consoles. This reduces the number of management applications required and also enables the centralized management consoles to view and gather valuable information from the desktop.

Conclusion

To date, systems-level management at the desktop has not been addressed with any degree of consistency, commonality, or satisfaction because vendors have taken a piecemeal approach to network management. Thus, the focus has been on network "infrastructure" elements, such as wiring hubs, bridges, routers, switches, and cables, or on the management consoles themselves. Intel's strategy is to shift the focus to management of PC resources.

Reaffirming its commitment to making networks more manageable, Intel intends to provide a variety of robust products that make desktop management simple. Intel's product development emphasis will provide local management solutions that empower LAN administrators by automating the tasks that they now find most time-consuming and frustrating.

Further advancing the growth of the network computing industry and the personal computing industry as a whole, Intel's offerings will complement proven network management schemes and support and enhance existing and developing standards.

Serious Network Computing:
Why Superservers?

by Enzo Torresi
President and CEO, NetFRAME Systems Inc.

Author Bio

Enzo Torresi joined NetFRAME as president and
chief executive officer in January 1989. He was
previously vice chairman of the board and senior
vice president of sales and marketing at Businessland,
an international microcomputer systems integration company he co-founded in 1982. Prior to
starting Businessland, he was president and founder
of Olivetti's Advanced Technology Center in
Cupertino, California. The center developed
Olivetti's successful line of word processing and business computers. Prior to
joining Olivetti's U.S. operation, Torresi worked at the company's research
and development facilities in Ivrea, Italy. Torresi hold a Ph.D. in electronics
from the Polytechnic Institute of Turin, Italy.

Executive Summary

With the explosive growth of installed PCs (now in the tens of millions), networks of PCs have grown in size and complexity. From simple file and printer sharing applications, network servers are evolving into database, communications, and powerful application serving requirements. Computing MIPS, input/output capacity, and the need for scalable capacity are all increasing for this new generation of servers, more appropriately defined as "Superservers." Serious Network Computing is now possible with the combination of Superservers and powerful 32-bit Networking Software like Novell NetWare 3.x.

PC networking is one of the most powerful tools for computing in the 90's. The reasons are obvious: millions of graphical PCs and other desktops are now in use and users need to share data, files, mail, and often expensive devices like printers and high speed communication bridges. As PCs become easier to use through better graphical user interfaces, they also become the natural workstations to access information in a database, process a transaction, or make a reservation; easier training and fewer errors are key in the evolution of computing.

Traditionally, PC networking has been limited to file and printer sharing due to the lack of powerful 32-bit software and applications and the typical fragility of PC servers.

In 1989, Novell first introduced NetWare 386, a true 32-bit LAN Operating System capable of supporting over 200 users on a network. At the same time, NetFRAME Systems introduced the first Superserver, a true mainframe class multiprocessor server capable of enabling NetWare 3.x to provide the appropriate balance of MIPS (computing) and I/O (speed) to large networks. Indeed, large, complex, or critical networks require a good combination of powerful hardware and software and a mismatch can be the source of significant problems either on the performance side or on the downtime of the network—or both.

NetFRAME superservers were first to market, with a precise objective of providing an optimized hardware architecture that would balance MIPS and I/O, provide scalable capacity and high modularity, provide remote server management and intelligent Server Activated Maintenance (the server calls the administrator), all while ensuring 100 percent compatibility with Novell NetWare and its applications. The incredible success of this approach is evidenced by the growth of NetFRAME as a company: over 1600 Superservers installed since late 1989, sales doubled to $22 million in 1991, and doubled again in the first six months of 1992. Profitability has also made NetFRAME the first Superserver company to go public (June 1992).

Today's applications of NetFRAME Superservers are still 70 percent in file/printer sharing and 30 percent in applications/communication serving. The recent availability of powerful Database products from Oracle, Informix, Gupta, and Sybase that run as NLM's (Network Loadable Modules) on NetWare 3.x now allow the implementation of "Serious Network Computing" on LANs of PCs. This trend will change the mix of user applications as medium size companies move aggressively into client-server computing.

On these networks hundreds of users can all be directly "served" by a Superserver running NetWare. These users can have different desktops, from Windows PCs to Macs to Sun workstations. NetWare provides the connectivity among different file systems, plus the sharing of printers and mail. Concurrently, the Superserver is running a database application, possibly a 10 to 20 gigabyte bank of information, and, at the same time, providing a communication link to a mainframe. With these configurations, PCs really do what they do best—that is, run the desktop application and the user interface, and provide the "window" into the database running on the Superserver. The Superserver in these networks has to have all the attributes of a traditional mainframe, from speed to reliability to scalability, but it must also be compatible with native software for PCs, like NetWare. This is the concept behind a NetFRAME, or Network Mainframe, a key enabling technology for Serious Network Computing.

Market Research Shows Windows Will Dominate the Desktop

by Sherri H. Walkenhorst
Senior Associate, Network Associates, Inc.

Author Bio

NETWORK
ASSOCIATES

Sherri H. Walkenhorst heads the market research division of Network Associates, Inc., a public relations and marketing firm specializing in the network market. She has directed marketing and communications programs for companies in the LAN industry since 1985.

Executive Summary

The networking industry has brought more resources to the desktop than ever before. However, users must still determine which desktop operating system holds the greatest viability for network support, feature-rich applications, and simplified access to information.

Market research shows that Windows is gathering momentum as the most popular operating environment. It is clear that Windows will ultimately dominate the desktop. But the issue that remains is how fast the migration to Windows will take place.

In this paper, we'll address the factors that are driving Windows workstations onto the LAN.

Market Factors

An in-depth look at the marketplace indicates that DOS is losing market share in a migration to other desktop operating systems, primarily Windows. International Data Corporation (IDC), a market research firm based in Framingham, Massachusetts, predicts that in 1992 the market share for Windows will reach 39.5 percent to overtake DOS as the most popular desktop operating system environment. The company said DOS will claim 32.2 percent, followed by OS/2 at 10.4 percent, UNIX with 10.0 percent, and the Macintosh at 8.0 percent (Figure 49.1).

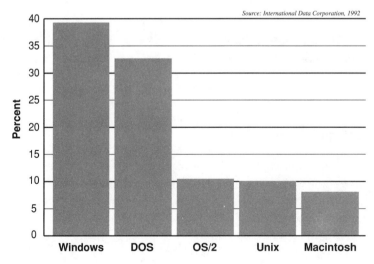

Figure 49.1. DOS market share.

Part of the reason for the increased popularity of Windows lies in software development. Windows has become the target environment for many software developers. Leading developers are designing the most powerful new applications for Windows first. Then they introduce these products to other environments such as Macintosh and DOS.

Lotus Development Corporation, for example, introduced Windows versions of Lotus Notes and Ami Pro but hasn't delivered either of these products for the Macintosh environment.

In addition, many Macintosh developers are beginning to spend time and resources in Windows development because of the growing Windows market and user demand.

For example, Claris Corporation is shifting many of its development resources to Windows and plans to introduce three Windows products by the end of 1992.

OS/2 developers have primarily concentrated on developing back-end applications such as distributed databases. Some of these developers, such as Software AG and NCR Corporation, have now moved their primary development platforms from OS/2 to Windows. Other developers continue to watch the market while developing for both environments.

Microsoft also has helped facilitate end-user development by providing a range of development tools for easy customization and for the creation of business-specific Windows applications. Products range from the easy-to-use Windows-based Visual Basic to the powerful Microsoft C/C++ for object-oriented programming.

Technology Advancements

A major factor pushing Windows at the desktop is the set of features that makes the PC easier to use than the somewhat cumbersome DOS environment. The graphical user interface provides icons and menus. Instead of learning complex commands, users gain access to resources and information by pointing and clicking. Users can also create compound documents using several applications to combine text, graphics, and even sound and animation.

The Object Linking and Embedding (OLE) protocol enables users to combine data from various applications into a single document. And users don't need to remember which tools created the various components of a report. For example, a user can embed a spreadsheet chart in a word processing document and update the chart by pointing and clicking.

Windows also provides multimedia capabilities that make it possible to create digital audio and video as well as control multimedia devices such as video disc players and digital video cards.

Finally, Microsoft's Windows Open Systems Architecture (WOSA) enables Windows users to access a variety of services and information sources without learning complicated procedures or maintaining multiple application gateways. This architecture makes Windows a friendly interface for the user.

Market Niche

Because of its graphical user interface and other features, Windows is gaining in popularity and will soon dominate the presentation graphics arena—a market previously dominated by DOS-based packages. The Software Publishers Association said that, following the introduction of Windows 3.0 two years ago, new Windows software secured 16.3 percent of the presentation graphics market.

Sales of Windows-based products grew at an incredible 170 percent, while DOS-based packages experienced an 8.4 percent decline. Clearly, Windows is the future standard for presentation graphics software.

Migration

While market factors reveal that the LAN desktop is migrating toward Windows, survey data indicates that actual use is lagging behind software development.

Network Associates recently completed a survey of LAN users, which shows that the majority of the surveyed comapanies' 286 and 386 workstations don't run Windows. In fact, most of the migration won't take place for 12–18 months. Survey data reveals also that once the migration to Windows takes place, most Windows use will occur in the LAN Manager and NetWare 3.x networking environments.

When asked to describe how the LAN users in their companies use Windows, respondents said that 31.3 percent never use Windows, as opposed to 7.0 percent who always run Windows. Rather, market analysis indicates 31.3 percent only use Windows for specific applications such as Excel, while 30.4 percent use Windows as much as possible except to run certain DOS applications.

Respondents also named several factors that prevent LAN users from using Windows. Foremost among these factors is the fact that 73 percent of users are still running DOS applications. Even with the feature-rich applications and graphical user interface available with Windows, 52.2 percent said there isn't a compelling reason to run Windows today. Other factors keeping LAN users from using Windows include the limitations of users' PCs (43.5 percent) and the poor network support in Windows (33.0 percent).

A third of the respondents cite system weaknesses inherent in the design of Windows as a reason LAN users aren't currently using Windows. These weaknesses include the awkward nature of the operating system, speed, and reliability concerns. However, Windows 3.1 has attempted to address these issues. As a result, many analysts expect user acceptance to increase in light of system developments.

Company Policy

An important factor in Windows becoming the new desktop operating system standard is a company's policy regarding the use of Windows on the LAN. Forty-four percent of respondents said their companies don't have a policy, and users are able to choose their desktop operating environment. Only 21.7 percent said their companies mandate the use of DOS. Forty percent of respondents said their companies are migrating to Windows as the standard for desktops on the LAN or have already standardized on Windows.

For those companies planning to move to Windows, the majority (32.3 percent) said this migration will take place in more than 18 months. Almost 30 percent said the move would happen in 12–18 months, followed by 21.5 percent of the respondents who expect a 6–12 month transition time, and 10.8 percent who cite 3–6 months. Only 6.1 percent said the migration to Windows as a LAN desktop standard would take place in less than three months.

Conclusions

Windows makes the PC easier to use and offers increased productivity and easy access to information. The most powerful, feature-rich applications have been developed for Windows, with more than 5,000 applications now available. In addition, most major software developers are focusing on new Windows applications.

It is evident that Windows definitely provides the most viable future for personal computing. However, its dominance will not be clearly apparent for at least 18 months.

For information on the complete Windows Report, please call Network Associates at (801) 225-7888.

Working Towards Standards of Communication

by John E. Warnock
Chairman and CEO, Adobe Systems Inc.

Author Bio

Dr. John E. Warnock, chairman of the board, CEO, and cofounder of Adobe Systems Incorporated, is known for his advanced research in raster graphics. His work includes real-time, computer-generated image systems and hidden surface elimination for rendering three-dimensional images.

Before cofounding Adobe Systems in 1982 with Dr. Charles Geschke, Dr. Warnock worked as a principal scientist at Xerox Palo Alto Research Center, where he was involved in interactive graphics research, graphics standards, and improvement of the typographic quality of computer grayscale displays.

Before joining Xerox, Dr. Warnock held management positions at Evans & Sutherland Computer Corporation, where he had responsibility for the design and implementation of real-time, computer-generated imaging systems for ship and flight simulators. He also was responsible for company research in interactive computer aided design (CAD) systems.

Dr. Warnock holds B.S. and M.S. degrees in mathematics and a Ph.D. in electrical engineering (computer science) from the University of Utah.

Executive Summary

Computers are connected to communicate information between computer systems and to provide a means for individuals working on separate computer systems to work together.

Today, computers do not share information easily, nor do they work together easily. If the computer industry works to fulfill the promise of networks and implements cross-platform standards, it will make all our lives easier.

Why would anyone want to hook a bunch of computers together in the first place?

The simple answer is: to communicate information between computer systems, or to get people who use computer systems to work together.

To look into the future, it's a good idea to keep asking ourselves the fundamental question of why we do the things we do—why we work the way we do. When we give a simple answer to the simple question, we would hope the answer describes the way the world actually works. Unfortunately, in the case of computer networking, it doesn't.

In reality, the computers we hook together today do not share information easily, nor do they work together easily. For example, suppose I have a one-page document that contains a spreadsheet table, a descriptive paragraph, and a photo. To create such a document in today's world, I would use a spreadsheet program for the table and an image-capture program for the photo. Then I would import both into a word processor to integrate the components. After completing that process, I would have files on my computer disk that accurately reflected the information in the one-page document. If I was hooked up to a computer network, I could even store these files on a file server. Now, let's ask ourselves a question: Could I use the network to send this document to anyone else? Unfortunately, the practical answer is "no." For others to use the files that I have stored, they would need many things: a similar computer system, the same fonts, the same spreadsheet program, the same image-capture program, and the same word processor. If they have all of these things and a little luck, they might be able to view or print the document and receive the information. In reality, to send the document today, I would print the document on my local printer, and then either mail or fax the document to the recipient. In doing this, I probably would not use my computer network.

Critics of this example might say that this task is too complex, one that is not a realistic goal for computer networks. They could point out that users on networks communicate all the time through common databases and that they communicate effectively with today's electronic mail. These cases, in fact, demonstrate a key point. That point, like my first question, is simple: in order for computers to communicate information, the participants must agree on standards. With the shared database, all the participants have tacitly agreed to use the same database and consistent database access programs. With electronic mail, the participants have agreed to communicate with only the simplest of text files.

In the example I gave, if you were to standardize, the standard would reduce to having the same computer systems and local environments everywhere. This level of standardization may work for very small groups, but it is certainly not going to work in a large corporation or across diverse organizations.

Now let's return to our example but let's forget computers for a while to see why the database example and the electronic mail example don't reflect how the world should work. When I come to work in the morning, my desk is stacked with brochures, research reports, magazines, newspapers, internal memos, and letters. This is the way the outside world communicates to me. The outside world also communicates by telephone calls and meetings, but these are local, more specialized communications. I also see and hear the broadcast media, but they do not represent business-to-business communication. If this is the way the world works (and not just with databases and simple messages), why is it unrealistic to want our networked computer systems to work in the same way? Why shouldn't it be possible to communicate, store, and distribute very diverse documents on all kinds of subjects?

Imagine a world in which any time you publish a document (regardless of the application used or the complexity of the document), it could be stored for anyone else on the network to read or print. This would be enormously efficient. File drawers, stacked with documents, would start to disappear. Systems designed to locate documents on distributed file servers would start to appear, and, in general, the communications promise of networked computers would start to be fulfilled.

To achieve this, critical cross-platform standards must emerge. It is not realistic to believe that the current evolution of proprietary operating systems will provide answers that will solve networking communication problems. Standards for file formats and cross-platform utility programs must appear. These standards, because they would work with different kinds of computers with different kinds of operating systems, must be independent of the specific features that are being built into today's operating systems. These standards must look to the future and account for the various abstract forms that communication might take. No hardware dependencies can be present, and such standards must be capable of evolving to a future when the document metaphor can be extended to sound and video. Said another way: We need a layer of standards that are to the side of operating systems while at the application layer of systems communication.

A communication standard such as this would be a device-independent superset of the existing operating system imaging models that would provide consistent treatment of fonts, stabilize character-encoding problems, and include extensible structures to handle all the international document problems. Such standards would have to exist at the application layer of a network, but they wouldn't have to interact with the lower layers in a network. The idea behind such a standard would be to figure out how to embody—in a single file format—all the information needed to reproduce the document without destroying (like FAX does) the information content of the document.

The first step in creating these new standards is to develop specialized printer drivers for each environment that would capture the output from applications and convert it to a single, uniform document-interchange format. With this format, users could write document viewers and printing utilities for each platform. A collection of such drivers, coupled with viewing and printing facilities, would facilitate the initial communication of documents between diverse platforms without changing existing applications.

The second step to document interchange is to build powerful applications that would use a common document-interchange format and to encourage the cross-platform sharing of object semantics that such a format would permit. These applications would demonstrate how document interchange and common editing structures could work and how the use of the extension techniques could add semantic information to the standard. If these applications give substantial value to the end user, applications developers will add new interfaces to the document-interchange drivers, and a new standard, both real and useful, will appear.

The emergence of this new standard, a paperless form of communication, would put the power of true electronic communication into the hands of computer users. No longer would business professionals waste a large chunk of their workdays dealing with paper documents. There would be no waiting while incompatible, computer-generated documents are printed out only to be faxed or mailed to a list of recipients. On the contrary, only a few keystrokes would be necessary to communicate these documents to one person or to a hundred people. The process of distributing corporate publications—from telephone directories to technical manuals—would be simplified, as well as more time- and cost-efficient. The same goes for those in the business of publishing books, magazines, and newspapers. Imagine, then, creating, viewing, printing, and communicating entirely in electronic form.

And why not? If, today, I can buy one television to watch all the channels and one phone to talk to anyone, why shouldn't the computer I buy be able to communicate effectively with all other computers?

Shouldn't we, as an industry, fulfill the promise of network computing and implement the cross-platform standards that will make all our lives easier? If we make this vision a reality, we will enter a future in which we can ask a simple question and get a simple answer.

Expanding the Reach of
LAN-Based Electronic Mail

by Brett Warthen
President, InFinite Technologies

Author Bio

Brett Warthen is president of Infinite Technologies in Owings
Mills, Maryland, a software development company specializing in electronic
mail and add-on utilities for electronic mail systems.

Brett is a volunteer sysop on the Novell NetWire family of forums on
CompuServe and an active participant on several e-mail-based discussion
lists.

You can reach Brett via e-mail at the following addresses:

MHS:	Brett @ Infinite (via CSERVE or NHUB)
CompuServe:	>MHS:Brett@Infinite (or 76704,63)
Internet:	Brett@Infinite.mhs.CompuServe.com
FAX:	+1-410-363-3779

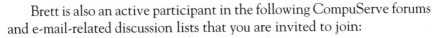

Brett is also an active participant in the following CompuServe forums and e-mail-related discussion lists that you are invited to join:

CompuServe:	PCVENF Section 13 (Infinite Technologies forum)
	NOVC Section 5 (Novell MHS/E-Mail forum)
MHS:	Library @ Infinite (via CSERVE or NHUB) (include a subject line of INDEX for more info, or SUBSCRIBE to participate)
	Library @ Novell (include a subject line of GUIDE for more info, or SUBSCRIBE to participate)

Executive Summary

The LAN-based electronic mail (e-mail) environment can be a confusing array of terminology and standards. This paper explores standards and proposed standards in the LAN-based e-mail arena from such vendors as Novell, Lotus, and Microsoft.

While Lotus and Microsoft struggle to open up and better define their environments, Novell's MHS (Message Handling Service) has emerged as the *de facto* standard for communication between LAN-based e-mail systems. This paper examines MHS and a number of the third-party products and services that enhance MHS, providing connectivity between different e-mail systems and platforms and expanding the reach of electronic mail today.

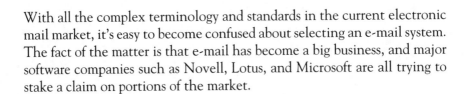

With all the complex terminology and standards in the current electronic mail market, it's easy to become confused about selecting an e-mail system. The fact of the matter is that e-mail has become a big business, and major software companies such as Novell, Lotus, and Microsoft are all trying to stake a claim on portions of the market.

As IBM once proved when it dominated the mainframe computer market, the marketing technique of FUD (fear, uncertainty, and doubt) can be incredibly effective when the target market has a limited understanding of an environment. In this paper, we'll try to clear up the FUD, by explaining the terminology and discussing many solutions available today.

LAN-Based Messaging: Defining the Players

LAN-based e-mail is divided into at least three major camps:

- Novell
- Lotus
- Microsoft

Novell is unique in that it is not providing an e-mail front-end as part of the solution. Instead, Novell is concentrating on back-end e-mail transport engines that are supported by a growing number of front-end e-mail vendors.

When discussing LAN e-mail, we often use terms such as *front-end* and *back-end*. The front-end, or user agent, is the application that enables you to compose, read, and reply to messages. The back-end, or mail transport engine, is the application that provides mail delivery services and transport services between systems. Essentially, the user agent submits messages to the transport engine with requests for delivery, and the transport engine delivers any incoming messages to the user agent.

Novell's mail transport strategy is two-tiered. The basic product, NetWare MHS (short for Message Handling Service), is a DOS-based messaging store and forward engine, originally developed by Action Technologies as a transport service for their Coordinator electronic mail product.

MHS and its Standard Message Format (SMF) API specification are currently supported with more than 150 commercially available products. Through the SMF interface, numerous e-mail applications can easily exchange mail, including Infinite Technologies' ExpressIT!, NoteWork

Corporation's The NoteWork, Da Vinci Systems' eMail, BeyondMail from Beyond, Inc., and more.

NetWare Global Messaging (NGM) is an NLM-based (NetWare Loadable Module/sever-based) messaging store and forward engine that Novell is in the process of introducing. NGM will be backward-compatible with MHS 1.5, and Novell plans to offer add-on connectivity modules for other environments including SMTP, X.400, and SNADS. However, there are third-party gateways that currently provide connectivity to these environments available for MHS today, so if you require this additional connectivity now, it may be prudent to explore the current market alternatives.

Lotus and Microsoft are both essentially user agent vendors, selling electronic mail products, also based on technologies acquired from other companies.

However, Lotus cc:Mail and Microsoft Mail both provide their own message transport services together with the user agent portion. These transport services typically lack the range of third-party support that exists for the Novell MHS environment. To a large extent, these environments are less open for third-party enhancements.

Ironically, if you want to connect a Lotus cc:Mail e-mail system to a Microsoft Mail e-mail system, Novell's MHS is the most convenient common ground, because both products provide gateways that connect with Novell's MHS.

Similarly, WordPerfect Office (WPO) from WordPerfect Corporation uses its own proprietary transport mechanism. A growing number of WPO users are using the WPO-to-MHS gateway option and MHS as a transport mechanism between sites, because it is more widely supported.

No discussion of LAN-based message transports would be complete without mentioning two better known messaging protocols: SMTP and X.400.

SMTP (Simple Mail Transport Protocol) is a messaging transport protocol defined for the exchange of e-mail between UNIX hosts. A very large international e-mail backbone, known as "the internet," provides worldwide e-mail connectivity through SMTP. The internet is used and sponsored primarily by the government and educational institutions. Gateways that connect LAN-based messaging systems to the internet through SMTP (direct link) or UUCP (dial-up/async) are excellent options for connecting with the outside world.

X.400 is the official OSI standard for e-mail exchange between computer systems. In the 1980s, many people expected X.400 to become the standard messaging transport protocol for e-mail exchange between systems. Instead, the complexity and cost of X.400 has left X.400 better suited for e-mail exchange between disparate systems.

At this time, Novell's MHS product has become the *de facto* standard for messaging between local area network and PC platforms. This is evidenced by the fact that the other vendors often have to gateway to MHS to provide connectivity to other LAN-based systems.

Access outside of the LAN environment is most often accomplished through third-party MHS gateways, although vendors such as Microsoft, Lotus, and WordPerfect do provide their own suite of gateways specific to their products.

LAN-Based Messaging: The Battleground

The current battleground in the LAN-based messaging environment is over the APIs (Application Program Interfaces) used for communications between e-mail front-ends and their back-end engines.

Novell's NetWare MHS and NetWare Global Messaging define an interface called the Standard Message Format (SMF), which is how an application interfaces to the Novell Messaging Engines.

Novell publishes a "NetWare SMF Solutions Guide" that lists third-party products supporting SMF. Instructions on acquiring this guide are included at the close of this paper.

The SMF specification is often criticized by developers because it provides only a directory- and file-based interface for message submission and receipt. In other words, message files are created following the SMF format, in specific directories.

Three versions of the SMF interface are currently in existence:

- SMF-64 (MHS 1.1 native interface, circa 1988) is limited to eight-character user and workgroup names, one file attachment per message, and one recipient per message.

- SMF-70 (MHS 1.5 native interface, circa 1991) supports up to 64 file attachments per message and up to 64 recipients in a single transmission instance of a message.

- SMF-71 (NetWare Global Messaging and MHS 2.0, circa 1992) breaks the eight-character user and workgroup name limitations and lifts the limitation of 64 recipients in a single message. (Note: At the time of this writing, MHS 2.0 is not yet shipping, and MHS 1.5 is still the current version of the DOS-based engine.)

Lotus and Microsoft have announced competing procedural APIs for access to their message transport services. Procedural APIs define function calls (DLLs in the Windows and OS/2 environments, linkable libraries in the DOS environment) that applications can call from higher level languages for messaging-related functions.

Both the Lotus and the Microsoft specifications are intended to allow front-ends to access various message transport engines. This would have the largest effect on nonmessaging applications that could include messaging as another function within the application.

The Lotus specification, called VIM (Vendor Independent Messaging, also sometimes jokingly known as Vendors Ignoring Microsoft), was endorsed by Novell, Borland, and Apple, with limited endorsement from IBM. VIM grew out of the OMI (Open Messaging Interface) introduced, but never delivered, by Lotus in 1991. VIM libraries are planned for the DOS, Windows, and OS/2 environments.

The Microsoft specification, called MAPI (Messaging Applications Programming Interface), is a Windows-centric API that will be included with future versions of the Windows product. The idea is to provide messaging services to Windows applications, independent of the messaging transport service installed.

At this stage, both VIM and MAPI are specifications waiting for libraries to enable application developers to begin sending messages through these APIs. Novell has also pledged that both the VIM and MAPI specifications will be supported by Novell messaging engines.

Mail-enabled applications are an extremely exciting idea, and with the macro language flexibility of popular Windows applications such as WordPerfect for Windows, Ami Pro, Microsoft Word for Windows, Microsoft Excel, and more, why should we have to wait for VIM or MAPI?

Indeed, creating a message in the SMF format may be difficult from within a Windows macro, but several of the vendors of MHS/SMF-based e-mail front-ends provide messaging services that can be called through macros in Windows applications. So if you're in one of these applications, you can easily invoke a macro through a menu option or button bar to send the current document or the selected text.

Da Vinci Systems' eMail for Windows defines a set of DDE (Dynamic Data Exchange) functions that other applications can invoke to send messages through MHS.

Finansa's WinMail and Infinite Technologies' ExpressIT! for Windows include DLLs (Dynamic Link Libraries) that can be called by any application or macro language for sending a message through MHS, without the limitations of an active DDE link. The Infinite DLL is also available as a separate product, SendIT! for Windows.

In the DOS environment, free utilities such as SendIT! from Infinite Technologies make it easy to submit messages in the SMF format.

The Novell MHS Environment

As was mentioned earlier, Novell's NetWare MHS has become the *de facto* standard for LAN-based messaging. Contrary to a common misconception, MHS supports both Novell and other DOS-compatible networks.

MHS provides e-mail transport services between LANs and remote systems over asynchronous dial-up links, over bridged LANs (internetwork connections in MHS terminology), and through public hub services such as Novell's NHUB service and the CompuServe/MHS hub option.

Novell NHUB is a public hub service provided free by Novell. MHS hubs can connect to each other through NHUB, using NHUB as an intermediary hop. MHS hubs must dial the NHUB phone number in San Jose, California, to send or receive mail through this service. Presently, between 750 and 1,000 MHS hubs are registered for this service.

The CompuServe/MHS hub is a surcharged public hub service provided by CompuServe, Inc. Thanks to CompuServe's extensive data network, CompuServe provides local phone numbers for dial-up access in most areas of the United States, as well as a growing number of international access points. Additionally, the CompuServe/MHS hub service provides access to CompuServe Mail accounts, internet addresses, AT&T Mail, and AT&T Easylink, as well as FAX services.

The MHS product also defines a gateway interface to allow third-party gateway products to provide delivery services to other environments. When MHS receives a message that is addressed to an installed gateway process, MHS will load the defined gateway process to perform e-mail delivery.

Third-party gateway products exist to provide connectivity to the following environments (to name but a few):

- SMTP, UUCP, Internet
- X.400
- SNADS, PROFS, Office Vision, AS/400
- VAXMail, DEC All-in-One
- Wang Office
- MCI Mail
- AT&T Mail
- FidoNet

SMTP gateway services are provided by Computer Mail Services' S-Bridge product, and a shareware product named XGATE (download

XGATE.ZIP from PCVENF Library 13 on CompuServe, or use the keyword XGATE with Library @ Infinite).

UGATE is a popular shareware gateway that connects MHS to a UNIX host using UUCP over dial-up or dedicated asynchronous lines (download UGATE.ZIP from PCVENF Library 13 on CompuServe, or use the keyword UGATE with Library @ Infinite). Using UGATE to dial into the UUNET service is an inexpensive way to gain connectivity with the internet. NoteWork Corporation also connects the MHS and UUCP environments with The NoteWork MHS/UUCP Gateway.

Additionally, the CompuServe/MHS hub service provides internet connectivity services.

X.400 gateway services are provided by Retix, Touch Communications, and Frontier Technologies Corporation. With NetWare Global Messaging, Novell will also soon be providing an optional X.400 connectivity module.

IBM Mainframe connectivity is available from Novell with its Messaging Connect product, as well as gateway services from SoftSwitch. Blue Rainbow Software also provides a gateway between MHS and Office Vision/400 on an IBM AS/400 midrange computer.

Connectivity to DEC VAX-based e-mail systems is available through products from Joiner Associates and Xitel.

Lightspeed Mail Gateway from MacSoft provides e-mail exchange between MHS and Wang Office.

For MCIMail connectivity, M-Bridge from Computer Mail Services is available.

NoteWork Corporation offers an MHS to AT&T Mail gateway, A-GATE for MHS, and similar connectivity is offered by the CompuServe/MHS hub service.

For connecting FidoNet-based bulletin boards with MHS, there is a shareware product named FidoGate (download FIDOGT.ZIP from PCVENF Library 13 on CompuServe, or use the keyword FIDOGATE with Library @ Infinite).

Thanks to Novell's relatively open specifications for defining gateway processes, there are also quite a few third-party products implemented as MHS gateways that provide nontraditional extensions to e-mail capabilities, including:

- Message forwarding

- Alpha numeric paging

- Remote file retrieval

- Discussion Lists/List Servers

- Voice mail

- Print Job transmission between sites

- FAX gateways

Message forwarding (ForwardIT! from Infinite Technologies, Da Vinci Assistant from Da Vinci Systems) allows messages sent to one address to be forwarded or copied to another address without requiring user intervention, which is useful for traveling users or users who must temporarily receive their e-mail at another location.

An alpha numeric paging gateway (PageIT! from Infinite Technologies) provides the capability for messages to be sent through electronic mail to alpha numeric (full text) pagers. Salesmen and service technicians can easily receive their e-mail while out of the office and can receive additional information on phone calls and service calls.

Remote file retrieval utilities (MHS Librarian from Infinite Technologies and a shareware product named Clerk) enable users to request files and other data through e-mail requests, providing bulletin-board-type capabilities on top of store and forward e-mail systems.

Discussion Lists (MHS Librarian from Infinite Technologies) is another name for the type of service provided by the popular List Servers on the internet. Essentially, users are allowed to subscribe to a list, generally by an e-mail request for subscription, and any messages sent to the list address are automatically rebroadcast to the list of subscribers. In the MHS world, popular discussion lists include LIBRARY @ NOVELL (send a request with GUIDE for more information) and LIBRARY @ INFINITE (send a request with INDEX for more information, or SUBSCRIBE to subscribe). Both of these lists are available through the CSERVE and NHUB public hubs (LIBRARY @ NOVELL requires that your host be defined to NHUB).

The LIBRARY @ NOVELL service is a customized application built using the rules and message-filtering capabilities of BeyondMail in conjunction with the Distributor product from WorkFrame, Inc.

VoxLink provides several innovative products linking e-mail systems with voice mail systems. E-mail messages can be converted to voice mail messages, and voice mail messages can even be sent through e-mail and played over a PC speaker.

Print Job transmission between sites is provided by a unique application called MhsQ! by Infinite Technologies. Essentially, e-mail jobs sent to a NetWare print queue on one system can be automatically compressed and transmitted through MHS to another site where they are printed. Admittedly a unique application, MhsQ! illustrates some of the open-ended possibilities for extending MHS with gateway processes.

FAX gateways are provided by quite a few vendors. At a minimum, these products provide the capability for users to submit out-bound FAX requests through MHS e-mail. More advanced systems also support the ability to route in-bound FAXes to MHS mailboxes for viewing. Two of the most popular products in this market are the Optus FacSys and Castelle FaxPress.

MHS gateway possibilities don't stop with these. For more information on developing your own custom MHS gateways, Novell publishes the "NetWare SMF Programmer's Reference." Additionally, a utility called RunIT! that ships with the Infinite Technologies' MHS Scheduler product also enables you to easily create your own batch files that run as MHS gateways, allowing tape backups or other automated tasks to run on the MHS server.

What to Choose?

By this stage, it should be apparent that I am a strong believer in the Novell Messaging environment and the complementary third-party products and utilities developed for this environment.

It is no secret that my company has made a significant investment in producing products for this environment. However, we chose this environment because of its openness, its widespread third-party support, and the overall flexibility of the MHS environment.

First and foremost, I am an e-mail user requiring wide area connectivity to allow my business to communicate with distributors, resellers, end users, and other industry contacts. I chose the MHS platform for my business, because thanks to third-party gateway support, it was the only solution that could adequately fit these needs.

How to Contact Vendors Mentioned in This Paper

Beyond Incorporated (BeyondMail)—617-621-0095; FAX: 617-621-0096

Blue Rainbow Software (MHS to AS/400 gateways)—206-357-8971; FAX: 206-357-9047

Castelle (FaxPress FAX gateway)—408-496-0474; FAX: 408-496-0502

CompuServe (CompuServe MHS Mail Hub)—614-457-MAIL; FAX: 614-457-8149

Computer Mail Services (S-Bridge/MHS to SMTP, M-Bridge/MHS to MCIMail, V-Bridge/MHS to Banyan Vines Mail)—313-352-6700; FAX: 313-352-8387

Da Vinci Systems (Da Vinci eMail, Da Vinci Assistant)—919-881-4320; FAX: 919-787-3550; MHS: InfoRqst @ DaVinci

Finansa Limited (WinMail)—+44-582-662268 (U.K.); FAX: +44-582-662461; MHS: Sales @ Finansa

Frontier Technologies Corporation (MHS to X.400 gateway)—414-241-4555; FAX: 414-241-7084

Infinite Technologies (ExpressIT!, ForwardIT!, PageIT!, MHS Librarian, MhsQ!, MHS Scheduler, SendIT!)—410-363-1097; FAX: 410-363-3779; MHS: Sales @ Infinite

Joiner Associates (MHS to DEC VAX gateways)—608-238-4454; FAX: 608-238-8986

MacSoft (Lightspeed Mail Gateway/MHS to Wang Office)—805-324-4291; FAX: 805-324-1437

NoteWork Corporation (The NoteWork, A-GATE for MHS, The NoteWork MHS/UUCP Gateway)—617-734-4317; FAX: 617-734-4160

Novell (MHS, NetWare Global Messaging, NHUB, Messaging Connect)—408-473-8989; FAX: 408-428-9668 (Attn: Messaging Products Marketing); MHS: Message @ NovellPM

Optus (FacSys FAX gateway)—908-271-9568; FAX: 908-271-0698

Retix (MHS to X.400 gateway)—213-399-2200; FAX: 213-458-2685

Touch Communications (MHS to X.400 gateway)—408-374-2500; FAX: 408-374-1680

WorkFrame, Inc. (Distributor, EmailWorks MHS Utility Agents)—617-491-4678.

VoxLink Corporation (e-mail to voice mail connections)—615-297-4271; FAX: 615-665-2812

Xitel (MHS to DEC VAX gateways)—215-647-2866; FAX: 215-993-9127

52

Protecting Your Network from Virus Infection

by Danie Watson
Marketing Director, Ontrack Computer Systems

Author Bio

Danie Watson is the marketing director at Ontrack Computer Systems, of Eden Prairie, Minnesota. Active in anti-virus research since 1990, Ontrack is affiliated with an international network of anti-virus researchers and is a distributor of Dr. Solomon's Anti-Virus Toolkit. Ontrack is a member of the National Computer Security Association (NCSA) of Washington, DC; the Computer Anti-Virus Research Organization (CARO) of Hamburg, Germany; and the North American affiliate of the European Institute of Anti-Virus Research (EICAR) of London, England. Ontrack has the only internationally accredited anti-virus research facility in the Upper Midwest. Ontrack Data Recovery, a subsidiary of Ontrack Computer Systems, is recognized worldwide as the leader in data recovery service technology.

Executive Summary

Like it or not, computer viruses are on the rise, more than doubling in number each year. Virus writers have begun to network, banding together as an underground community, and they are developing more destructive viruses daily. The battle lines are being drawn between the virus writers and the anti-virus researchers, and your computers are the battleground.

Because networks are designed to share files, they provide an ideal breeding ground for the spread of viruses, and they are challenging to keep clean. It is important to educate yourself about viruses, understand your risks, develop prevention procedures, and be prepared to contain an infection on your network, should one occur.

The number of computer viruses in circulation has increased almost tenfold each year for the past three years. They are increasing not only in number, but also in the severity of damage they can inflict. Although the problem has received a lot of media attention, and although more than half of all companies have been infected, few network managers (and fewer users) are trained in virus protection.

Understanding viruses and how they can attack your network is step one. Learning to keep your network clean is step two. Being prepared for an outbreak is step three.

How Viruses Threaten Networks

A virus is a program designed to copy itself without any action (or knowledge) by the user. For example, a virus might attach itself to the FORMAT command and be run unwittingly every time you format a diskette, or to COMMAND.COM, or to any other executable file. The virus code runs before the original program and then passes control to the real program. The virus code then copies the virus to another file on another disk and replicates itself. Some viruses use other methods of replication that are even more subtle.

Trojans are the "payload" that accompany viruses. They are programs that deliberately set out to cause unknown effects on your computer, and they *replicate with* viruses as they copy themselves. The main problem with a virus is usually the side effects produced by the Trojan. These vary widely. Some produce a significant slowdown of a system, or simulate hardware problems, or display silly messages on the screen. Others, however, have a more destructive mission, such as low-level formatting cylinder zero on your hard disk, which can render the disk inaccessible.

The Network Breeding Ground

Like any computer program, a virus is written for a specific operating system, and as of this writing there were no known viruses able to defeat network security and attach to network operating system files. Networks do need to be secured from DOS-based viruses, however, because they can damage valuable network data, slow data access, and enable the rapid spread of a virus. Networks were invented to permit the sharing of files, and viruses can capitalize on this. After a virus is introduced onto a network, it will have the same access rights as the user. If the user can alter executable files on the network, so can the virus. When the file server has become infected, networks become dynamite breeding grounds for viruses.

The Changing LANscape of Virus Technology

Several recent developments in virus technology point to an alarming trend: virus writers are working overtime to design viruses that can evade detection by anti-virus scanners. And unfortunately, they are improving their ability to share technology by banding together as an underground community.

Like other programs, viruses have their moments of technological breakthroughs. Polymorphic viruses, which became more widespread in 1991, contain a double whammy that makes them technically the most infectious viruses. First, they are self-encrypting and self-garbling. Second, they alter their own virus signature each time they copy. If you had a hundred copies of the virus, no two would look alike.

For example, Tequila is a widespread polymorphic virus, written by two men age 18 and 20 in Switzerland. One of them worked for a shareware vendor; he deliberately introduced the virus onto the distribution diskettes, rapidly spreading the virus worldwide.

Most anti-virus scanners will detect only one, or several, occurrences of such a virus, but unless your scanner detects and cleans *all* occurrences, the virus will still be in your system. Alarmingly, an engine for this type of virus has been shared by virus writers, and polymorphic viruses are apt to become much more prevalent.

Your server could also be threatened by boot sector viruses, such as Ogre and Michelangelo, if you boot your server from a floppy diskette. Boot sector viruses are not able to spread across the network but can cause severe damage to your valuable file server data.

Stealth viruses were first detected by researchers in 1987, when the Brain virus was uncovered. Since then, they have become altogether too common. As the name implies, stealth viruses aim to avoid detection, and because they generally avoid flashy tricks, the casual user is unlikely to notice them. Undetected, they are able to spread very quickly.

Viruses that are designed to avoid detection by anti-virus software are known as advanced stealth viruses. Number of the Beast (so called because of the "666" in its code) is an advanced stealth virus that manipulates the system file tables in DOS. It is exactly 512 bytes long, and it conceals itself in memory. If there is any attempt to read the first 512 bytes of an infected file while the virus is in memory, it retrieves the original 512 bytes that it has placed after the end of the file, and presents those instead. Some anti-virus software can then be fooled into thinking that the file is unchanged from the original.

These are just a few of the techniques used by virus writers in their battle with anti-virus software developers. In 1991, there were even several viruses introduced that have been dubbed "anti-anti-virus viruses," because they attack specific anti-virus programs to disable them. The cat-and-mouse game continues.

Computer users have used electronic bulletin board systems (BBSs) for years to share useful information. Now, virus writers are using them as well.

Condemned by the anti-virus community, these underground "virus exchange" BBSs are used by virus authors as a forum to share virus source code, provide one another with technical support, and alert the community to developments in anti-virus technology. They even produce their own newsletter. Access is restricted to virus authors by a tiered system that requires an upload of a new virus to continue access. These have become appalling virus-generating systems.

Practicing Safe Network Computing

Some networks are known to be more vulnerable to virus infection than others. Putting security measures in place to prevent infections can be time-consuming and can reduce the network's efficiency. You must assess your risk and choose security measures that balance your need for security with your need for performance. After all, if viruses are a nuisance that interfere with efficient network use, and virus protection procedures are a nuisance that interfere with efficient network use, what's the point?

The point is that the biggest nuisance of all is virus cleanup, and coping with lost or damaged data. The old adage applies: an ounce of virus prevention is worth a pound of virus cure.

Measuring Your Risk

In the virus game of three-card monte, you must keep your eye on the floppy. The more diskettes you have, and the more freely they are traded about, the higher your risk. Here is a list of questions to consider:

- Do you allow public access to your network (such as in an educational institution)?

- Are there a large number of unrestricted nodes, and lots of diskettes at your site?

- Is your file server in an unlocked, unrestricted area?

- Do you allow outside vendors, customers, or computer service personnel to place diskettes in your computers without scanning them for viruses?

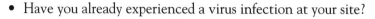

- Have you already experienced a virus infection at your site?

If you answered yes to any of these questions, experts would place you in a high-risk category and would suggest that you adopt strong virus-protection procedures.

Developing a Protection Strategy

The recommended protection strategies tend to be easy to understand but harder to implement. Remember, users rarely spread viruses intentionally. Don't tell users that if they bring in a virus they'll be punished (unless you are sure their actions were malicious). If you do, you will be the last one to know if an infection occurs, when you need to be the first.

Here are some protection "do's and don'ts":

- Back up, back up, back up. The best defense you have is to maintain frequent, *virus-free* backups.

- Check all incoming diskettes for viruses. *All* of them. Set up an isolated machine for this purpose, and notify everyone of its location and use.

- Use write-protect tabs. Instead of throwing away those little tabs that come in the diskette box, use them. They can prevent the virus from copying to your diskettes.

- Get your software from reputable sources, and do not pirate software. Remember, even shrink-wrapped software direct from the manufacturer can carry viruses.

- Buy a good anti-virus software package, learn to use it effectively, and keep it up-to-date. (I recommend Dr. Solomon's Anti-Virus Toolkit.)

- Use the security provided with your network operating system. Restrict access to executable files, limiting access to search and execute. This will enable users to search for and run the files they need without being able to copy or write to them. (Not only will you prevent the spread of viruses, you also will curtail software piracy.)

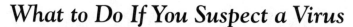

What to Do If You Suspect a Virus

The biggest danger when facing a virus infection is panic. Some viruses take full advantage of the tendency to panic, such as launching a destructive Trojan when the user hits Ctrl-Alt-Del. Although viruses and Trojans are very real concerns, the most frequent computer problems are still human error and hardware failure, which can both be rescued by maintaining a decent backup system. It is far more important to keep a cool head and a good backup than it is to worry about all the Trojans and viruses in the world.

The most important symptom of a virus is that it alters executable code. This might be .COM, .EXE, .SYS, .OVL, or .OVR files, or the boot sector or partition record of the disk. If any executable files are changed, it is quite likely that you have a virus, unless you can find another explanation for an executable change, such as an upgrade or reinstallation that patches the original program files. Naturally, you are keeping precise records on the sizes of your executable files and comparing them daily, right? Of course not.

This brings us back to the original problem—how do you know if you've got a virus? The classic virus symptom is when you have the same problem on several computers. Several problems on one computer could be hardware, or software, or both, but the same problem on several computers means the same software bug in the application program, the same network problem, the same electricity problem, or a virus.

Identify the Virus and Its Source

The easiest way to be certain whether you have a virus—and if so, which one—is to use reliable anti-virus software to scan your system. If you do have a virus, it is important to positively identify it and to learn more about its potential effect on your system. This will keep your panic level to a minimum, assist you in an orderly and effective clean-up, and help you identify the source of the virus so that you can prevent future infections.

Indeed you may not be able to identify the source of the virus, but it is important that you try. The network log may provide some clues. If you have an infected file, look in the network log for its owner, and then check the owner's drive and diskettes. If these are also infected, the owner may know something about their origin. They may have been taken home for work over the weekend, sent by a magazine as a bonus for subscribing, or recently downloaded from a BBS. Knowing the source is very helpful in preventing reinfection.

Organize a Cleanup

Do not start deleting and reformatting. What if your backup is no good? And what if you format over your record of the source of the virus? *Do* seek expert advice. You may have to set aside your pride, but virus technology is changing daily; what you knew to be true about viruses yesterday may not be true today.

It will become necessary to inform decision makers within your organization of the infection. When informed, they may want to act immediately. Again, consider your course of action carefully, and do not panic. If the virus was introduced from—or passed along to—someone outside your organization, it is generally responsible to inform your outside contacts of the need to cooperatively address the problem. Discussing virus infections was once considered taboo, but *not* discussing them has often proved to be more damaging to a firm's reputation.

You will need the willing cooperation of users, who will need to turn over all their diskettes and backups for scanning and cleaning. Make it clear you are not looking for a scapegoat, just viruses. Not even one diskette should be overlooked in this process, considering that it was probably one lone diskette that caused the problem in the first place. Then you will need to set aside time for the cleanup. Often, this is done on a weekend, because it is time-consuming and generally requires that the network be downed for this purpose. Use reliable anti-virus software to examine every diskette and hard disk in the building, plus other data storage media, to check for viruses (if you have one, you may have more). To do that, you must go around to the user areas and check the media there, or you will need to organize all the diskettes into a central checking location. In this case you will need to ensure that all diskettes are returned to their rightful owners by asking users to clearly label all media with their name and location.

As a measure of the scope of the project you face, assume an average of 100 floppies per computer (they hide in desk drawers, file drawers, briefcases, and so on). You would be wise to encourage users to clean their home computers and diskettes as well, because these are a common source of reinfection. An organization with 200 computers will probably require a cleanup team of 20 people, whereas a company with 20 computers will require a team of 6. Cleanup usually requires several days.

Preventing Reinfection

After all media have been scanned, and all infected media cleaned with anti-virus software, you must review the prevention procedures discussed earlier in this paper. If you have an infection and you fail to clean up in an orderly fashion, including implementing a future virus protection plan, experts say your chances of reinfection are 90 percent within 30 days.

If you became infected because you had no prevention measures in place, you should implement them now. If you did have security in place, take comfort in knowing that your situation is not uncommon. Think of it as fire-prevention measures—they don't ensure you will never have a fire, but they reduce your chances of outbreak and give you safe guidelines to follow if you do.

Putting Viruses in Perspective

Computer viruses are a problem—and a growing one. In 1987 there were only a handful of viruses. A year later there were about 50; the following year, 200. By the end of 1991, the number of viruses had exploded to more than 1,000. All indications are that this rapid growth trend will continue. Infection rates in large corporations have been documented at 65 percent (DataQuest, November 1991), more than double what they were two years before.

But it's the word *problem* that is the key. Virus infection is just another computer problem that, if caught early, is no more of a nuisance than an unreliable hard drive. The more preventive measures you can take against viruses getting into your system the better, but users are only human. Suspect diskettes are bound to slip through the net at some time. So remember the wise words of William Shakespeare: "Readiness is all."

Index

Symbols

4M Token Ring Network
  (TRN/4), 191
8mm tape drives, 368
16M Token Ring Network
  (TRN/16), 191

A

A-GATE for MHS (NoteWork
  Corporation), 469
accessing
  network
    databases, 357
    node address restrictions,
      319-320
    printer nodes, 319

adapters
  bus master, 55
  credit card LAN, 142
  drivers, 55-56
  external LAN, 139
    cost, 140
    installation and
      configuration, 140
    speed, 141
  nonbus master, 55
  performance, 53-54
  RAM, 57
  reliablility, 59
Adobe Systems Incorporated, 451
advanced stealth viruses, 474
algorithms in data location,
  300-302
Alpha Software Corporation, 353
Altair (Motorola), 397

anthemizing, 156
APIs (Application Program
  Interfaces), 327-329
    MAPI (Messaging Applica-
      tions Programming Inter-
      face), 462-463
    need for, 349-350
    procedural, 462
    SMF (Standard Message
      Format), 461-462
    VIM (Vendor Independent
      Messaging), 462
application isolation, 123
Application Programming
  Interfaces, *see* APIs
applications
    high-level network
      administration, 210-213
    in knowledge-based systems,
      92-93
    mid level network
      administration, 211-212
    wiring closet management, 212
Apriori (Answer Computer
  Corp.), 89, 94
Archive Planning Profile, 371
archives, 366
    restore capability verification,
      370
ARCnet
    alternatives to, 194-204
      16Mbps Token Ring
        Network, 196
      ARCNETPLUS, 197-200
      EtherNet, 194-195
      partial system changes,
        196-197

cost investment, 190
hardware support, 203-204
integration, 190
Internet Protocol (IP), 202
performance improvements,
  191-192
standards, 200-204
staying power of, 190
success of, 193-194
ARCNETPLUS, 192-194
    as alternative to ARCnet,
      197-200
    hardware support, 203-204
    purchasing decisions, 205-206
    systems compatibility, 199
    wiring, 199
ARCserve backup application, 47
ARLAN (Telesystems), 398
Artisoft, Inc., 1-6
Artisoft Sounding Board, 6
ArtiSound recorder software, 6
Asynchronous Transfer Mode
  (ATM), 407
AT&T, 339
ATM (Asynchronous Transfer
  Mode), 407
audits, 369
    software licensing, 323-328
augmentation, distributed
  bindery, 299-302
AUTOEXEC.BAT software
  delivery systems, 325
automated backup/restore
  systems, 370-372
Automated Design, Windows
  Workstation, 289

B

backups, 47-48, 366
    integrated applications, 371
    problems, 369-372
    restore capability verification, 370
    software licenses, 324-325
Backup Planning Profile, 371
backup/restore systems
    automated, 370
    manual, 370-372
    NetWare namespace, 370
    nodes, 366
    problems, 369-372
Banyan servers, 368-369
BBSs (bulletin board services), viruses, 474-475
Beach, Gary J., 7-9
Berglund, Elizabeth G., 15-16
Bernoulli Optical Systems Company, 216
Bernoulli removable disk storage drive, 215-221
Beyond Incorporated (BeyondMail), 468
BeyondMail (Beyond Incorporated), 468
Bickmann, Lee, 28
bindery
    distributed, augmentation, 299-302
    serverless, 300-302
Blue Rainbow Software, 465-468
Bond, Elaine R., 27-28
boot sector viruses, 474

Borland (InterBase Server), 224, 229
Boston Computer Exchange, 359
bus master adapters, 55
Bushnell, Nolan, 37
business user databases, 356

C

C2-level security, 128
cable analyzers, 209
Carbon Copy Plus (Microcom), 333
case-based reasoning systems, 90
Castelle (FaxPress FAX gateway), 467-468
CBR Express (Inference Corp.), 89
cc:Mail (Lotus), 460
CCITT, X.500 Recommendation, 300-302
central server theory, 298-302
    decay of, 299-302
central servers, 299-302
Certified NetWare Engineer (CNE), 21
chaotic systems, 82
Cheyenne Software, 45-46
Chumbley, Jeff, 53
client-network demands, 302
client-server model, evolution, 302
CMIP (Common Management Information Protocol), 417
CNE (Certified NetWare Engineer), 21

CNOS (Corporate NOS), 156
CO/Session (Triton Technologies Inc.), 333
Common Management Information Protocol (CMIP), 417
communications technology, 378
   deregulation, 379
   framework, 382-387
   globalism, 379
   industry characteristics, 381-382
   privatization, 379
   standards, 380
   trends, 379-381
compliance options, software licenses, 322-325
CompuServe/MHS hub, 464, 468
Computer Mail Services (M-Bridge), 465-468
computer-telephone integration COMPUTERWORLD (CTI), 39-41
computing platforms, 340
confidential information protection, network databases, 357
CONFIG.SYS, software delivery systems, 325
connectivity, integrated, 97-104
Control network management level, 245-246
converging network technologies, 38-39
copyright law, 317
Corporate Networks, 179
Corporate NOS (CNOS), 156
Corrigan, Patrick H., 61
costs, data management, 371

credit card LAN adapters, 142
crises, storage management, 372-373
cross-platform standards, 452-456
CTI (computer-telephone integration), 39-41
customer contact, through help desks, 87-88
customization capabilities, DOS, 339

D

Da Vinci Assistant, 468
Da Vinci eMail, 463, 468
Da Vinci Systems, 468
data
   corruption safeguards, 357
   entry (network databases), 356-357
   integrity, databases, 356
   location
      algorithms, 300-302
      distributed file system, 300-302
      DNW, 301-302
   management costs, 371
   mirrored, 368
   protection
      archives, 366
      backups, 366
      LANs, 366-375
      off-site vaulting, 366
      restores, 366
   rates, increasing, 57-58
   transfer, DOS, 339
Data General Avion, 339

database management systems, 354
database/librarian, 370
databases, 354
 business users, 356
 data integrity, 356
 ease-of-learning, 355
 information handling, 356
 interactive, and OLCP (online complex processing), 230
 networking, 354
 relational, 125
 see also network databases
Datapoint Corporation, 191
DCA/Microsoft Communications Server, 130
DCE (Distributed Computing Environment), 129
de facto standards
 ARCnet, 200
 MHS (Message Handling Service), 458-467
 open systems, 255-259
 see also standards
DEC VAXstation, 339-340
decision-support software, 353
dedicated duty servers, 299-302
 types
Dell, Michael S., 67-68
desktop computing
 and network management, 432
 Intel strategies, 434-439
 hardware, 344-346
Desktop Management Task Force (DMTF), 437-438
DESQview/X DOS PC, 339-340

Digital Equipment, 339
discussion lists, 466-467
distributed bindery, augmentation, 299-302
distributed computing, 342-351
 APIs, need for, 349-350
 bottoms-up requirements, 343-344
 DOS, 338-340
 hardware, 344-346
 open systems, 347-349
 tops-down requirements, 344
Distributed Computing Environment (DCE), 129
distributed file system
 data location, 300-302
 DNW, 300-302
 file
 availability, 300-302
 duplication, 300-302
 location, 301
 selection, 300-302
 transmission, 301
 file pointer index location, 301-302
 goals, 301-302
 prerequisites, 302
 protocols, 302
Distributed NetWare (DNW), 299-302
distribution
 network load, 298-302
 nodes, 320
DMTF (Desktop Management Task Force), 437-438

DNW (Distributed NetWare), 299-302
  data location, 301-302
  domains, 300-302
  file access, 301-302
  file location, goals, 301-302
  file management responsiveness, 301-302
  file server to network mutation, 300-302
  function of file server, 299-302
  future of
    distributed file system, 300-302
    file scattering, 300-302
    network entity, 300-302
    serverless bindery, 300-302
    serverless file services, 300-302
  network login, 300-302
  serverless
    bindery, 300-302
    file services, 300-302
  user groupings, 299-302
docking stations
  advantages, 137-138
  disadvantages, 138-139
documentation uncoupling, software licensing, 323, 327-329
domains, 130
  DNW (Distributed NetWare), 300-302
DOS
  customization capabilities, 339
  data transfer, 339
  distributed computing, 338-340

enhancement software, 339
market share, 446
memory management, 339
multiplatform computing, 338-340
multitasking, 339
open systems computing, 338-340
windowing, 339
X programs, 340
X Window System
  DESQview/X, 339
  X Server, 339
downsizing with Enterprise Servers, 74
downtime, 391-394

E

e-mail, 303
  and LANs, 305
  and workgroup computing, 306
  APIs (Application Program Interfaces), 461-463
  customer challenges, 304
  customizable systems, 311-312
  growth of, 305
  LAN-based messaging infrastructure (Microsoft), 308-309
  Lotus cc:Mail, 460
  messaging infrastructure, 307-308
  MHS (Message Handling Service), 458-467
  Microsoft Mail, 460

open systems, 311-312
SMTP (Simple Mail Transport
  Protocol), 460-461
vendor support, 312-313
workgroup applications,
  310-311
East West Education
  Development Foundation, 360
Edwards, James, 73
electronic mail, *see* e-mail
electronic post offices, 162-163
  future of, 165-166
  history of, 164-165
Emerald Systems Corporation,
  365
Enhanced Parallel Port (EPP),
  141
enhancement software, DOS, 339
Enterprise Servers
  forces creating
    customer demand, 74
    market drivers, 75
    product vacuum, 76
  openness, 78
  power of, 76-77
  reliability, 77
  scalability, 77
environmental concerns, software
  licensing, 323-325
EPP (Enhanced Parallel Port),
  141
Erwin, Jeff, 79
EtherNet LANs, 4
  as alternative to ARCnet,
    194-195
  cost investment, 190

integration, 190
staying power of, 190
Expert Advisor (Software
  Artistry), 89
Expert Sniffer (Network General
  Corp.), 212
expert systems, 80-84
  imporving help desks, 86-87
  RBES, 91
ExpressIT! (Infinite Technologies), 463, 469
external LAN adapters, 139
  cost, 140
  installation and configuration,
    140
  local printer support, 142
  portability, 141-142
  speed, 141

F

FacSys FAX gateway (Optus),
  467-469
fault tolerance, 123
fax, 265-269
  computers and, 267-268
  gateways, 467
  LAN, 50-51, 268-269
    routing methods, 268
FaxPress FAX gateway (Castelle),
  467-468
FDDI, 58
FidoGate shareware gateway, 465
file servers
  function of in DNW, 299-302
  future function of, 299-302
  serverless, 300-302

file-grooming applications, 371
file-migration applications, 371
files
   access
      DNW, 301-302
      network databases, 357-358
      transparent, 374-375
   aging profiles, 375
   availability, distributed file
     system, 300-302
   duplication, distributed file
     system, 300-302
   location, goals, 301-302
   transfers, 369
   management, 373
   restores, 368
   scattering of data, 300-302
   selection, distributed file
     system, 300-302
   shared, 298
   split reads, 300-302
Finansa Limited (WinMail), 463,
  468
Fortune 500, 322
ForwardIT! (Infinite Technologies), 469
Foster, Gail M., 85
frames, size, 57
FreePort (Windata), 398
Frontier Technologies Corporation, 468
Fryer, Bruce, 97

G

Garrett, Kelly, 106
Gates, Bill, 117-118

Gates, Dirk I., 135
Gianforte, Greg, 145
Gill, Bob, 153
Glagow, Steve, 161
global data networks
  evolution of, 62-64
  problems with, 64-66
global updating (network databases), 358
Go Corporation (Hobbit), 400
graphical user interface (GUI),
  93
groupware, 10, 271-284
  challenges in, 281-284
  Lotus Notes, 273-274, 279-280
  reasons for growth, 274-277
  standards, 282-283
GUI (graphical user interface),
  93

H

hardware, desktop computing,
  344-346
Hayes, Dennis, 167-168
Hayes LANstep, 172, 176
HEL, Inc., 241-242
help desks
  effectiveness, increasing, 86-87
  functions
    customer contact, 87-88
    problem control, 88
    service provision, 88
Henderson, Tom, 179
Hewlett Packard, 339
high-level protocol management,
  208-213

high-speed connections
  need for, 302
  power requirements, 302
Hobbit (Go Corporation), 400
Hollingsworth, Robert, 189
Host Resources MIB Working
  Group, 437-438
HP 9000 Series, 339
Hutchinson, Scott, 207-208

I

IBM, 339
  4M Token Ring Network
    (TRN/4), 191
  16M Token Ring Network
    (TRN/16), 191
  InfoMan, 94
  OS/2 2.0, 346
  RS/6000, 339, 339-340
IEEE (Institute of Electrical and
  Electronics Engineers), open
  systems, defining, 252
implementation management,
  software licensing, 326
Infinite Technologies, 457-458,
  469
InfoMan (IBM), 94
Inforcorp, 395-396
Information at Your Fingertips,
  118
information environments, 41
information handling, databases,
  356
Information Technology (IT), 8
Information Technology Summit
  (ITS), 35

infrared LANs, 398
Institute of Electrical and Electronics Engineers, *see*, IEEE
integrated connectivity, 97-98,
  102-104
integration
  backup applications, 371
  file-grooming applications, 371
  storage media, 374-375
  telephone technologies, 39-41
Integrity Software, 297
Intel Corp.
  LANProtect, 435
  LANSight Support, 435
  network management, 431-440
    demand for, 432-433
    end systems, 433
    sixth area of network
      management, 433
    strategies, 434-439
  Single Agent Technology
    (SAT), 436-437
  SNMP Services, 435
intelligent hubs, 404-408
  routing, 406-407
  RubSystem, 407
intelligent text retrieval systems
  (ITRs), 90
interactive databases, OLCP
  (online complex processing),
  230
InterBase Server (Borland), 224,
  229
interfaces
  GUI, 93
  in knowledge-based systems,
    93

metering software, 324-325
peer-to-peer, 111
International Data Corporation
   (IDC), workgroup computing,
   10
international graphic standards, X
   Window System, 338
Internet
   open systems standard,
      257-258
   Request for Comments (RFC)
      series, 258
Internet Activities Board (IAB),
   257-258
Internet Engineering Task Force
   (IETF), 257
Internet Protocol (IP), 202
Internet Research Task Force
   (IRTF), 257
interoperability
   and multivendor computing,
      31-32
   of LANs, 6
   of open systems, 253-254
Iomega Corporation, 215-216
Iomega TAPE 250 drive, 215-216
IP (Internet Protocol), 202
IT (Information Technology), 8
ITRs (intelligent text retrieval
   systems), 90
ITS (Information Technology
   Summit), 35

J

JetFax, Inc., 265-269
Joiner Associates, 465, 469

Joseph, Michael, 215-216

K

Kahn, Philippe, 223
Kalpana, Inc., 407-408
knowledge-based systems
   evaluating
      applications, 92-93
      integration with other
         programs, 94-95
      maintenance, 93
      user interfaces, 93
      vendor experience, 95
   uses, 89-92

L

LAN IOS (Local Area Network
   Integrated Office System), 10
LAN Manager for Windows NT,
   130-131
LAN NW386 3.1x
   disadvantages, 301-302
   location of files, 301-302
   transmission of files, 301-302
language simplification, software
   licensing, 323-327
LANProtect (Intel), 435
LANs (local area networks), 63,
   320, 365-369
   ARCnet, *see* ARCnet
   ARCNETPLUS, *see*
      ARCNETPLUS
   client/server relationship,
      298-302
   data protection, 366-375

downtime, cost of, 391-392
environmental considerations, 204
EtherNet, *see* EtherNet
hardware, 344-346
implementation,101-102
interoperability, 6
LANtastic (Artisoft, Inc.), 1-2
licensing agreements, 318-319
login script, 301-302
management, 431
    demand for, 432-433
    end systems, 433
    Intel strategies, 434-439
    sixth area of network
      management, 433
Novell, *see* Novell
partial system changes, 196-197
partnering, 16-18
    selection requirements, 20
    with NSIs, 19
    with SIs, 19
    with VARs, 20
peer-to-peer, 2-6
performance, improving, 191
physical considerations, 204
portable computers on, 136
    credit card LAN adapters, 142
    docking stations, 137-139
    external LAN adapters, 139-142
    PDAs, 143
security, 346-347
software, 146-147
    delivery systems, 325

licensing, software packs, 323-325
support, 148-150
technology, 173-174
tetherless, 143
user needs, 170-173
vendors, 147-148
wireless, 396-401
    future of, 400-401
    infrared, 398
    radio based, 397-398
    standards, 398-399
LANSight Support (Intel), 435
LANtastic (Artisoft, Inc.) LAN, 1-2, 6
Lee, King, 231
LIBRARY @ NOVELL discussion list, 466-467
licensing, *see* software licensing
Licensing Service Application Programming Interface (LSAPI), 328
Lightspeed Mail Gateway (MacSoft), 465
Local Area Network Integrated Office System (LAN IOS), 10
local area networks, *see* LANs
local procedure calls, 123
location
    file pointer index, 301-302
    of files, LAN NW386 3.1x, 301-302
login script, 301-302
Lotus Development Corporation, 271-272
    cc:Mail, 460
    VIM (Vendor Independent Messaging), 462

Lotus Notes, 273-274, 279-280
low-level protocol management,
  208-210
LSAPI (Licensing Service
  Applications Programming
  Interface), 328
Lubert, Howard, 241-242
Lytton, Nina, 249-250

M

M-Bridge (Computer Mail
  Services), 465
Mach system, 122
Macintosh, market share, 446
MacSoft (Lightspeed Mail
  Gateway), 465, 469
MAILbus (DIgital), 164
Mailman, Josh, 265
maintenance of networks, 68-72
Managed network management
  level, 247-248
management software, 326
Management Decisions Systems,
  Inc. (MDS), 353
managing networks, 24, 410-412
  Control level, 245-246
  desktop computing, 432
  features, 419-420
  goals, 414-416
  high-level protocol, 208-213
  Intel strategy, 434-439
  LANs, 431-440
  Managed level, 247-248
  mid level protocol, 211-212
  Monitor level, 246-247
  NOS (Network Operating

  System), 231-240
  OSI standard, 417
  Rudimentary level, 243-245
  sensitive data, 219
  Single Agent Technology
    (Intel), 436-437
  SNMP (Simple Network
    Management Protocol),
    412-414
  standards, 214, 417
  unified environment, 436
Manzi, Jim, 271-272
MAPI (Messaging Applications
  Programming Interface),
  311-312, 462-463
Marks, Howard, 285
Massachusetts Software Council,
  353
McCann, John T., 297
MCS (Microsoft Consulting
  Services), 312
MDS (Management Decisions
  Systems, Inc.), 353
memory
  management, DOS, 339
  protection, 123
Message Handling Service
  (MHS), 458-469
Messaging Applications Program-
  ming Interface (MAPI),
  311-312, 462-463
Messaging Connect (Novell),
  465, 469
messaging services, 162-163
  future of, 165-166
  history of, 164-165
metering software, 321-327

interfaces, 324-325
NOS integration, 327
MHS Librarian (Infinite Technologies), 466, 469
MHS (Message Handling Service), 458-469
MHS Scheduler (Infinite Technologies), 469
MhsQ! (Infinite Technologies), 467-469
micro-kernels, 126
Microcom (Carbon Copy Plus), 333
Microcomputer Managers Association (MMA), 315-318, 327-329
Microsoft Corporation, 303
  electronic messaging strategy, 306-308
    customizable systems, 311-312
    LAN-based infrastructure, 308-309
    open systems, 311-312
    vendor support, 312-313
    workgroup applications, 310-311
  MAPI (Messaging Applications Programming Interface), 311-312, 462-463
Microsoft Consulting Services (MCS), 312
Microsoft Mail, 460
Microsoft Mail for AppleTalk Networks, 308-309
Microsoft Mail for PC Networks, 308-309

Microsoft Product Support Services (PSS), 312
Microsoft Windows, 340, 365
  as dominant operating system environment, 445-450
  market niche, 448
  technology advancements, 447-448
  version 3.1
    applications, adding, 288-289
    DOS prompt, removing, 296
    FastDisk, enabling, 294
    File Manager icons, removing, 296
    .INI files, 295
    installing applications, 295-296
    integrating into NetWare LANs, 286-296
    persistent connections, 294
    restricting Program Manager customization, 289-291
    screen savers, enabling, 292
    SETUP program, automating, 287
    swap files, creating, 293
    user's shell, updating, 288
Microsoft Windows NT operating system, 118
  application availability, 121
  application isolation, 123
  benefits, 131
  built-in networking, 128-131
  capacity, 125
  development of, 122
  ease of use, 120

fault tolerance, 123
hardware support, 125
high-end implementation,
  119-120
Information at Your Fingertips,
  118
local procedure calls, 123
mainstream releases, 119
memory protection, 123
micro-kernels, 126
MS-DOS compatability, 121
performance, 122
portability, 125
productivity, 120
responsiveness, 123
scalability, 125
security, 127-128
symmetric multiprocessing,
  127
Microsoft WOSA, 328
mirrored data, 368
MIS (Management Information
  System), 108, 340, 355-356
MIT, 339
MMA (Microcomputer Managers
  Association), 315-318, 327-329
Monitor network management
  level, 246-247
Motorola
  Altair, 397
  wireless LANs, 400
Mulholland, James, 331
multimedia, 404-405
multiplatform computing,
  338-340
multiprocessing, symmetric, 127
multitasking, 339-340

DOS, 339
multiuser databases, *see* network
  databases
multivendor computing, 28
  education, 32
  information exchange, 32
  interoperability and, 31-32
  software licensing, 33
  trends, 30
Myers, Therese E., 337

N

namespace
  backup/data management
    functions, 370
  systems integration, 370
NCE (NETWERC Certified
  Engineer), 21
NCR (WaveLAN), 398
neural networks, 89
NetFRAME Systems Inc.,
  441-443
NetWare, 368
  file management, responsive-
    ness, 301-302
  future
    improvements, 299-302
    revisions, 299-302
  growth, 298
  namespace
    backup/data management
      functions, 370
    systems integration, 370
  Windows 3.1, integrating,
    286-296
    applications, adding,
      288-289

DOS prompt, removing, 296
FastDisk, enabling, 294
File Manager icons,
removing, 296
.INI files, 295
installing applications,
295-296
persistent connections, 294
restricting Program Manager
customization, 289-291
screen savers, enabling, 292
SETUP program, auto-
mating, 287
swap files, creating, 293
user's shell, updating, 288
NetWare Global Messaging
(NGM), 460, 469
NetWare Name Service (NNS),
299-302
NETWERC Certified Engineer
(NCE), 21
network analysis systems,
hazards of, 81-84
Network Application Installer
(NAI), 296
NETWORK COMPUTING
magazine, 421-422
network databases
accessing, 357
confidential information
protection, 357
data corruption safeguards, 357
data entry, 356-357
file access, 357-358
global updating, 358
record locking, 358
Network General Corporation,
389-390

Expert Sniffer, 212
network nodes, 322-325
Network Operating System, *see*
NOS
Network System Integrators
(NSIs), 19
Networked Database, 354
networks
accessing, node address
restrictions, 319-320
adapter packet drivers, 203
analysis systems, 80-84
global data
evolution, 62-64
problems, 64-66
history, 99-100
installation problems, 101
LANs, *see* LANs
load distribution, 298-302
login (DNW), 300-302
management, 24, 410-412
Control level, 245-246
desktop computing, 432
features, 419-420
goals, 414-416
high-level protocol, 208-213
Intel strategy, 434-439
LANs, 431-440
low-level protocol, 208-210
Managed level, 247-248
mid-level protocol, 211-212
Monitor level, 246-247
NOS (Network Operating
System), 231-240
OSI standard, 417
Rudimentary level, 243-245
sensitive data, 219

Single Agent Technology
(Intel), 436-437
SNMP (Simple Network
Management Protocol),
412-414
standards, 214-417
unified environment, 436
neural, 89-91
nodes, accessing, 319
partners, 17-26
planetary, 175-176
protocol, 54
rate of return, increasing,
390-394
downtime, 393-394
network management, 393
systems design, 393
training, 392-393
relational databases, 356
remote maintenance and
support, 68-72
software
licensing, 316-317, 322-326
pricing, 322-325
splitting applications, 338-340
technologies, converging,
38-39
telephone, 38
Windows dominance of,
445-450
Networks Are Our Lives, Inc.,
285
networkwide
general file services
establishment of, 299-302
need for, 299-302
login
advantages, 301-302

DNW, 301
neural networks, 89-91
NEWIPX (Windows Resource
Kit) program, 288
NGM (NetWare Global Messaging), 460
NHUB (Novell), 464, 469
NNS (NetWare Name Service),
299-302
nodes, 340
accessing
networks, 319
printers, 319
backups, 366-368
distribution, 320
network, 322-325
per network, 372
nonbus master adapters, 55
NOS (Network Operating
System), 154, 321
CNOS, 156
future of, 158
management tools, 231-240
goals, 236-239
metering software, integration,
327
role of, 154-155
software licensing, metering,
324-325
Notes, *see* Lotus Notes
NoteWork Corporation, 465, 469
Novell Corp., 374
Messaging Connect, 465, 469
MHS (Message Handling
Service), 458-469
NetWare Global Messaging,
469

NHUB, 464, 469
servers, 368-369
NSIs (Network System Integrators), 19
NT file system (NTFS), 123

O

Object Linking and Embedding (OLE) protocol, 448
OCTuS, 37-38
off-site
archives, 369
vaulting, 366
Olbert, Art, 341
OLCP (online complex processing), 224, 228-229
OLE (Object Linking and Embedding) protocol, 448
OLTP (online transaction processing), 224-228
online complex processing (OLCP), 224, 228-229
online transaction processing (OLTP), 224-226
disadvantages, 226-228
Ontrack Computer Systems, 471
Open Software Foundation (OSF), 348-349
open systems, 250-251, 347-349
benefits, 253-255
realizing, 263-264
DOS, 338-340
electronic messaging strategies, 311-312
IEEE P1003.0 definition, 252
NOS management tools, 231-240

standards, 255-260
vendors, 260-262
Open Systems Advisors, Inc. (OSA), 249-250
Open Systems Interconnect (OSI) model, 201-202
operating systems
Microsoft Windows NT, 118
application availability, 121
benefits, 131
built-in networking, 128-131
capacity, 125
development of, 122
ease of use, 120
fault tolerance, 123
high-end implementation, 119-120
Information at Your Fingertips, 118
local procedure calls, 123
mainstream releases, 119
memory protection, 123
performance, 122
portability, 125
productivity, 120
responsiveness, 123
scalability, 125
security, 127-128
symmetric multiprocessing, 127
OS/2, 426-427
selecting, 422-427
System 7, 423
UNIX, 424, 425
Optus (FacSys FAX gateway), 467-469

Oracle database server, 368
OS/2 operating system, 426-427
    market share, 446
    Release 2.0, 346
OSF (Open Software Founda-
    tion), 348-349
OSI (Open Systems Intercon-
    nect) model, 201-202
    network management stan-
        dard, 417
OURS, 28
    Information Technology
        Summit (ITS), 35
    members, 29
    origins, 33-34

P

packet burst NCP protocol, 56
Packet Driver standards, 203
PageIT! (Infinite Technologies),
    466, 469
partnering, 16-18
    selection requirements, 20
        archiving, 24
        cost, 23
        disaster recovery, 24
        equipment knowledge, 21
        industry commitment, 23
        inheritance plans, 24
        outside help, 23
        rapport level, 22
        reference checks, 21
        resources, 22
        stability, 20
        support, 21
        vendor medallions, 21

virus protection, 24
working relationships, 21
    with NSIs, 19
    with retailers, 20
    with SIs, 18-19
    with VADs, 20
    with VARs, 18-20
Pastman, Stuart, 105
PC/LAN Centric Development,
    110-113
    challenges, 113-114
    solutions, 115
pcAnywhere (Symantec), 333
PCMCIA, 142
PCs (personal computers)
    impact of, 108-109
    recycling, 360-363
PDAs (Personal Digital Assis-
    tants), 143, 350
peer-to-peer
    interfaces, 111
    LANs, 2-6
PENs, 350
performance adapter, 53-54
persistent connections
    (Windows 3.1), 294
personal computers, *see* PCs
Personal Digital Assistants
    (PDAs), 143, 350
planetary networks, 175-176
PNMS (Peregrine Systems), 94
polymorphic viruses, 473-474
portability, 340
portable computers, 136
    credit card LAN adapters, 142
    docking stations, 137-139
    external LAN adapters,
        139-142

PDAs (Personal Digital Assistants), 143
post offices, electronic, 162-163
  future of, 165-166
  history of, 164-165
pricing network software, 322-325
printers, accessing nodes, 319
procedural APIs, 462
protocols
  analyzers, 209-212
  network, 54
  packet burst NCP, 56
  SMTP (Simple Mail Transport Protocol), 460-461

Q-R

Quarterdeck Office Systems, Inc., 337

Rabins, Richard, 353
radio-based wireless LANs, 397-398
RAID (Redundant Array of Inexpensive Disks), 300-302
RAM adaptors, 57
Randall, Alex, 359
RBES (rule-based expert systems), 91
RDBMS (relational database management system), 224-225
  OLCP (online complex processing), 228-229
  OLTP (online transaction processing), 225-226
record locking (network databases), 358

recycling PCs, 360-363
Redundant Array of Inexpensive Disks (RAID), 300-302
relational databases, 125
  networking, 356
reliability adapters, 59
remote node environment, 333-334
remote procedure call (RPC), 129
removable disk storage, 216
  advantages, 220
  multiuser PCs, 219-220
  satellite users of, 217-218
  sensitive data management, 219
responsiveness
  DNW file management, 301-302
  NetWare file managements, 301-302
restore capability verification
  archive systems, 370
  backup systems, 370
restores, 366
  automated, 371
  duration of, 370
  single file, 369
retailers, partnering with, 20
Retix, 469
Rogers, Lawrence D., Dr., 365
Rohal, John P., 377-378
routers, and intelligent hubs, 406-407
RPC (remote procedure call), 129
RubSystem intelligent hub, 407
Rudimentary network management level, 243-245

rule-based expert systems
  (RBES), 91
RunIT! (Infinite Technologies),
  467

S

Saal, Harry J., 389-390
Saber Menu System for Windows
  (Saber Software), 289
Saber Software Corporation,
  207-208
    Saber Menu System for
      Windows, 289
Sandifer, Chip, 409
SAP (Service Advertising
  Protocol), 299-302
SAT (Single Agent Technology),
  436-437
Schatt, Stan, 395-396
Schmidt, Ron, 403
Schoof, C. John (Artisoft, Inc.),
  1-6
security
    LAN, 346, 347
    Microsoft Windows NT
      operating system, 127-128
    server-based software applica-
      tions, 48-50
SendIT! (Infinite Technologies),
  463, 469
server-based software, 46
    backup, 47-48
    management, 50-51
    security, 48-50
servers
    Banyan, 368-371

characteristics, 371
DCA/Microsoft Commu-
  nications, 130
fax, 50-51
Novell, 368-371
Oracle database, 368
storage, 374
Service Advertising Protocol
  (SAP), 299-302
shared
    data access, 354
    files, 298
shrink wrap law, 317
SI (systems integrator), 18-19
Silicon Graphics Indigo, 339
Simple Mail Transport Protocol
  (SMTP), 460-461
Simple Management Protocol
  (SMP), 417
Simple Network Management
  Protocol (SNMP), 412-414
Single Agent Technology (SAT),
  436-437
SIs (system integrators), 19
SITELOCK (Brightwork Devel-
  opment), 297
SMF (Standard Message Format),
  459-462
SMP (Simple Management
  Protocol), 417
SMS (Storage Management
  Services), 374
SMTP (Simple Mail Transport
  Protocol), 460-461
SNMP (Simple Network Man-
  agement Protocol), 412-414

SNMP Services (Intel), 435
software
    ArtiSound, 6
    decision-support, 353
    delivery systems, 325-328
    lending, 320
    management, 326
    metering, 321, 327
    portability, 340
    pricing, 322-325
    remote control, 333-335
    restricted access methods, 320
    server-based, 46
        backup, 47-48
        management, 50-51
        security, 48-50
    unauthorized access safeguards,
    327
software licensing, 33, 316-317
    agreements
        concurrent use, 325-326
        consistency, 323-325
        file server, 325-326
        issues, 317
        site licenses, 325-326
    audits, 328
    backup copies, 324-325
    compliance options, 322-325
    documentation uncoupling,
    323, 327-329
    education, 328
    environmental concerns,
    323-325
    implementation management,
    326
    language simplification,
    323-327

metering software, 324
    interfaces, 324-325
methodologies, 328
    concurrent use, 318-325
    per machine, 318-325
    per server, 318-325
    per user, 318-325
    site/entity license, 318-325
MMA survey findings, 317-329
network user, 323
preferences, 325
prices, 323-325
single user, 323
software delivery systems, 325
software packs, 323-325
standardization, 326-328
support, 322
truth in licensing, 323,
    327-329
upgrades, 322, 327
verification problems, 324-325
Software Publishers Association
    (SPA), 321, 328
Sony, 339
(SPA) Software Publishers
    Association, 321, 328
split reads, 300-302
splitting applications, 338-340
spread spectrum technology,
    397-398
Springer Technologies, Inc., 216
Standard Message Format (SMF),
    459-462
standards
    ARCnet, 200-204
    CMIP (Common Management
    Information Protocol), 417

communications technology, 380

cross-platform, 452-456

groupware, 282-283

network management, 214, 417

open systems, 255-260

Packet Driver, 203

SMP (Simple Management Protocol), 417

SNMP (Simple Network Management Protocol), 412-414

software licensing, 326-328

wireless LANs, 398-399

stations, docking

  advantages, 137-138

  disadvantages, 138-139

stealth viruses, 474

storage management

  crises, 372-373

  multiple sites, 372-373

  solutions, 373-375

  user needs, 374-375

storage media, integration, 374-375

storage server, 374

Strom, David, 421-422

Sun SPARCstation, 339-340

superservers, 442-443

support, network, 68-72

Symantec (pcAnywhere), 333

symmetric multiprocessing, 127

SynOptics Communications, 403-408

System 7, 423

systems

  case-based reasoning, 90

  chaotic, 82

  expert, 80-84

    improving help desks, 86-87

    RBES, 91

  ITRs, 90

  knowledge-based

    evaluating, 92-95

    uses, 89-92

  Mach, 122

  management, 347

  network analysis, 80-84

  NOS, 154

    CNOS, 156

    future, 158

    role of, 154-155

  X.400-compliant messaging, 165

systems integration, NetWare namespace, 370

systems integrator (SI), 18

T

tape

  drives, 8mm, 368

  mounts, 368

  rotation, 368

TCNS, 58

technologies

  expert sytems, 80-84

  LAN, 173-174

  network, converging, 38-39

  telephone

    integrating, 39-41

    network support and maintenance, 68

Technology Securities Research, 377-378
telecomputing, 332-336
    remote control environment, 332-333
    remote node environment, 333-334
telephone networks, 38
telephone technologies
    integrating, 39-41
    network support and maintenance, 68
Telesystems (ARLAN), 398
tetherless LANS, 143
Thomas, Chris, 429-430
tiered password systems, 357
Token Ring Network (TRN)
Torresi, Enzo, 441
Touch Communications, 469
transparent file access, 374-375
Triton Technologies, 331
TRN (Token Ring Network), as alternative to ARCNET, 196
TRN/4 (4M Token Ring Network), 191
TRN/16 (16M Token Ring Network), 191
Trojan programs, 473

U

UGATE shareware gateway, 465
unauthorized access safeguards, 327
UNIX operating system, 424-425
    Data General Avion, 339
    HP 9000 Series, 339
    IBM RS/6000, 339
    market share, 446
    Silicon Graphics Indigo, 339
    Sun SPARCstation, 339
upgrading software, licensing, 327
user groupings, DNW, 299-302
user needs, storage management, 374-375

V

VADs (value added dealers), 20
VARs (value added resellers), 18-20
Vendor Independent Messaging (VIM), 462
vendors
    e-mail, 312-313
    open systems, 260-262
verification problems, software licensing, 324-325
VIM (Vendor Independent Messaging), 462
viruses
    advanced stealth, 474
    and bulletin board services, 474-475
    boot sector, 474
    cleanup, 478-479
    identifying source, 477-478
    polymorphic, 473-474
    protecting against, 24, 472-479
    reinfection, preventing, 479
    server-based antivirus software, 48-50
    stealth, 474
    symptoms, 477

Trojan programs, 473
VisiSoft, 409
VMS (DEC VAXstation), 339
VoxLink Corporation, 469

W

Walkenhort, Sherri H., 445
WANs (Wide Area Networks), 63
Warnock, John E., 451
Warthen, Brett, 457-458
Watson, Danie, 471
WaveLAN (NCR), 398
Wide Area Networks (WANs), 63
WIN.INI, software delivery systems, 325
Windata (FreePort), 398
windowing, 339-340
    DOS, 339
Windows, *see* Microsoft Windows
Windows Open Systems Architecture (WOSA), 129, 448
Windows operating system, *see* Microsoft Windows NT operating system
Windows Resource Kit, 287
    NEWIPX program, 288
Windows Workstation (Automated Design), 289
WinMail (Finansa Limited), 463, 468
wireless LANs, 396-401
    future of, 400-401
    infrared, 398
    radio based, 397-398
    standards, 398-399

wiring
    ARCNETPLUS, 199
    closet management software, 212
WordPerfect Office (WPO), 460
WorkFrame, Inc., 469
workgroup computing, 8-9
    and e-mail, 306
    features for successful, 10-11
    pioneers in, 12
    productivity and, 12-13
WOSA (Windows Open Systems Architecture), 129, 448
WPO (WordPerfect Office), 460

X

X Clients, 339
X Consortium, 339
X programs, DOS, 340
X Server, X Window System, 339
X Toolkits, 339
X Window System, 338-340
    international graphic standards, 338
    X Client, 339
    X Server, 339
X workstations, 340
X.400 OSI standard, 165, 461, 465
X.500 Recommendation, 300-302
X/Open Portability Guide (XPG), 251, 258-259
XGATE shareware gateway, 465
Xitel, 465, 469
Xpress Librarian (Emerald Systems), 370-371
XTree Company, 231-240

Y-Z

Z-NOTE notebook computers,
 103
Z-SERVER towers, 103
Z-STATION desktops, 103